ENCORE TRICOLORE 2
nouvelle édition

ARCHBISHOP ILSLEY SCHOOL
021-706 4200

TEACHER'S BOOK

Sylvia Honnor and Heather Mascie-Taylor

ICT Consultant: Terry Atkinson

Text © Sylvia Honnor and Heather Mascie-Taylor 2001

The right of Sylvia Honnor and Heather Mascie-Taylor to be identified as authors of this work has been asserted by them in accordance with the Copyright, Designs and Patents Act 1988.

All rights reserved. No part of this publication may be reproduced or transmitted in any form or by any means, electronic or mechanical, including photocopy, recording or any information storage and retrieval system, without permission in writing from the publisher or under licence from the Copyright Licensing Agency Limited, of 90 Tottenham Court Road, London W1T 4LP.

Any person who commits any unauthorised act in relation to this publication may be liable to criminal prosecution and civil claims for damages.

Published in 2001 by:
Nelson Thornes Ltd
Delta Place
27 Bath Road
CHELTENHAM
GL53 7TH
United Kingdom

01 02 03 04 05 / 10 9 8 7 6 5 4 3 2 1

A catalogue record for this book is available from the British Library

ISBN 0 17 440325 9

Page make-up by TechSet

Printed and bound in Great Britain by Antony Rowe

Acknowledgements

The authors and publisher would like to thank the following people for their contribution to this book:
Terry Atkinson for writing the ICT sections
Terry Murray for writing the assessment notes.

CONTENTS

Encore Tricolore 2
nouvelle édition

Section 1
Introduction to the course

Introduction — 4

Components — 4
1. Students' Book — 4
2. Teacher's Book — 4
3. CDs — 5
   List of recorded items — 5
4. Flashcards — 6
   List of flashcards — 6
5. Copymasters — 7
   List of copymasters — 7

Planning the course — 8
1. Covering the National Curriculum — 8
2. Covering the QCA Scheme of Work — 10
3. Building on the National Literacy Strategy — 10
4. Covering the Scottish Guidelines — 10
5. Covering the Curriculum in Northern Ireland — 11
6. Encore Tricolore 2 nouvelle édition: Teaching Plan — 12

Developing skills — 14
1. Developing listening skills — 14
2. Developing speaking skills — 14
3. Developing reading skills — 14
4. Developing writing skills — 14
5. Developing understanding and application of grammar — 15
6. Developing language-learning skills — 15

Differentiation — 16
1. Support and extension material — 16
2. Au choix — 16
3. Copymasters — 16
4. Differentiation by task — 16
5. Differentiation by outcome — 16
6. Selective use of items — 16

Developing cultural awareness — 16

Assessment — 16
1. Épreuves (informal assessment) — 16
2. Contrôle (formal assessment) — 16

Using Information and Communication Technology (ICT) — 17
1. Introduction — 17
2. ICT and the National Curriculum — 18
3. Key ICT uses — 18
4. Points to note — 21
5. Classroom organisation — 22
6. How to enter accents — 22
7. Useful websites for teachers and students — 23
8. CALL software (Computer-Aided Language Learning) — 24
9. Books relating to ICT — 24

Section 2
Activities for language learning

Games — 25
1. Number games — 25
2. General vocabulary games — 25
3. Flashcard games — 26
4. Mini-flashcard games — 26
5. Games for practising verbs — 27
6. Spelling games — 28
7. Extra practice activities — 28
8. The Universal Board Game — 28

Songs — 29
Using the songs in Encore Tricolore 2 — 29

Section 3
Teacher's notes

Unité 1	En ville	30
Unité 2	On fait des projets	48
Unité 3	Au collège	70
Unité 4	En famille	92
Unité 5	Bon appétit!	112
Unité 6	En voyage	134
Unité 7	Ça va?	154
Unité 8	Rendez-vous!	174

Contrôle — 190

Encore Tricolore 2
nouvelle édition

SECTION 1

Introduction

Encore Tricolore nouvelle édition builds on the proven strengths and approach of **Tricolore** and **Encore Tricolore** and incorporates new features to bring it into line with current teaching requirements.

The course features:
- a systematic and comprehensive approach to grammar progression, with clear explanations and extensive practice
- interesting topics, set in authentic contexts, from France and other French-speaking countries
- user-friendly vocabulary and grammar reference sections to encourage independent learning
- differentiation which is integral to the course and fully referenced and explained in the Teacher's Book
- the development of study skills, with systematic training in strategies for listening and reading

Key features of the new edition are:
- *Écoute et parle* – systematic teaching of the interrelationship of sounds and writing
- assessment materials, both informal and formal, as an integral part of the course
- *Presse-Jeunesse* – magazine-style reading sections in the Students' Book
- Student CDs for independent listening and speaking practice
- an English–French glossary in addition to the French–English glossary

Components

Encore Tricolore 2 nouvelle édition is planned to give a wealth of teaching material in as compact and easily usable a form as possible. The components are:

- **Students' Book**
- **Teacher's Book**
- **Copymasters**
- **5 CDs**
- **100 Flashcards** (on CD-ROM)

These five components are planned to cover one complete year's work. They are fully integrated and cross-referenced and designed to be motivating, thorough, practical and easy to use.

1 Students' Book

The Students' Book is the main teaching tool of the course and contains the essential core material, reference sections and a full range of items for consolidation, extension and revision. There are also sections for reading for pleasure and systematic practice in linking sounds and writing. It comprises:

- **8 units**

These contain all the core material, with a full range of practice tasks and with regular grammar explanations in the *Dossier-langue* boxes.

At the beginning of each unit students can see what they will learn and the end of unit summaries (*Sommaires*) provide comprehensive reference lists. Together these provide a complete learning framework for the unit. These summaries are also provided on copymasters for completion and retention by the students.

- **Au choix**

This section contains further practice material. It includes separate pages of **support** and **extension** tasks for each unit, and also pages of **general** tasks. For more details, see the notes on differentiation (TB 16).

- **Presse-Jeunesse**

These magazine-style sections appear after *Unités* 2–7 inclusive and provide material for reading for pleasure. They can be used when they appear in the Students' Book or at any time later and are intended for students to work on alone. Although they use mainly the vocabulary and structures introduced by that time in the core units, they also contain a small amount of additional language.

No tasks are included in the *Presse-Jeunesse* sections in the Students' Book, but they are accompanied by optional copymasters with comprehension and practice activities.

- **À l'ordinateur**

For easy reference, these two pages (148–149) list vocabulary and expressions linked with computers, the Internet, sending e-mails etc.

- **Vocabulaire par thèmes**

The *Vocabulaire par thèmes* section has been added to this stage and students should be encouraged to consult it regularly. It lists the main topic vocabulary taught in **Encore Tricolore 1**. Much of this vocabulary is revised in the *Rappel* copymaster activities (see TB 7). Topic vocabulary taught in **Encore Tricolore 2** is listed in the *Sommaire* for each unit.

- **Tips for language learning**

This is a completely new reference section which includes the following:
- Tips for learning vocabulary and verbs
- Tips for understanding French
- Skimming and scanning
- Reading for detail
- Using a dictionary or glossary
- Understanding and pronouncing words in French

Teachers could draw the attention of students to these tips early in the year and they can then refer to this section as needed.

- **Grammaire**

A reference section covering the main grammar points and irregular verbs taught in **Encore Tricolore 1 and 2 nouvelle édition**.

- **Glossaires**

Two glossaries are provided at the end of the Students' Book, French–English and English–French.

2 Teacher's Book

This book has three sections:

Section 1: general information, ICT activities
Section 2: games, songs
Section 3: detailed teaching notes and solutions for all items in the Students' Book and in the Copymasters and a full transcript of all recorded items; notes on informal assessment (*Épreuves*) and formal assessment (*Contrôle*)

Section 1
- a detailed teaching plan of **Encore Tricolore 2 nouvelle édition** which can form the basis for a Scheme of Work
- suggestions for:
  - developing language skills
  - developing language-learning skills
  - linking sounds and writing
  - developing understanding and application of grammar
  - assessing progress
  - differentiation
  - developing cultural awareness
- advice on using ICT:
  - key ICT uses
  - classroom organisation
  - hardware, copyright, the Internet
  - useful websites, software, books
- complete lists of:
  - flashcards
  - copymasters
  - recordings
- notes about:
  - the National Curriculum (with details of levels and coverage of the 'Knowledge, skills and understanding' section)
  - the QCA Scheme of Work for Key Stage 3
  - the National Literacy Strategy
  - the Scottish Guidelines
  - the Curriculum in Northern Ireland

Section 2
This gives details of a wide range of games and practice activities for use in pairs, groups or as a class. It also includes notes on songs.

Section 3
This section gives unit by unit suggestions for teaching with the materials.

Each unit begins with a clear plan, setting out the language and functions of the unit and the links with the National Curriculum. It lists exactly which materials will be needed.

The teaching suggestions which follow are divided into a logical sequence of Areas. These include solutions for each task, transcripts of recorded items and suggestions for follow-up work.

The unit notes also include solutions for copymasters which can be used with that unit, e.g. *Écoute et parle* (interrelationship between sounds and writing), *Tu comprends?* (listening comprehension practice), *Épreuves* (informal assessment), *Contrôle* (formal assessment), *Rappel* (vocabulary revision) and *Presse-Jeunesse* (reading practice).

Activity labels (such as reading, speaking, extension, support) are supplied for every task, indicating which skills etc. are involved.

The following symbols are also used:

SB 56	Students' Book page number
1	Task number
1	*Au choix* task number
1	*Écoute et parle* task number
CM 2/4	Copymaster number (unit/number)
CM 115	Copymaster page number
FC 18–26	Flashcard number(s)
TB 30	Teacher's Book page number
🎧 1/18	Recorded item (CD number/track)
🎧 SCD 1/4	(Student CD number/track)
🎧	Transcript
	Pairwork activity
	ICT activity

3 CDs
There are five CDs, all containing a wide variety of lively material, recorded by French native speakers and at a speed and level which the students can understand.

List of CDs
Class CD 1
  Tracks 1–14: *Unité 1*
  Tracks 15–31: *Unité 2*

Class CD 2
  Tracks 1–18: *Unité 3*
  Tracks 19–36: *Unité 4*

Class CD 3
  Tracks 1–21: *Unité 5*
  Tracks 22–39: *Unité 6*

Class CD 4
  Tracks 1–16: *Unité 7*
  Tracks 17–31: *Unité 8*
  Tracks 32–36: *Contrôle*

Student CD 1 (for independent study)
  Tracks 1–48: *Écoute et parle*

Student CD 2
  Tracks 1–29: *Tu comprends?*

🎧 List of recorded items

Class CD 1

Unité 1
SB 6 (1)	On fait des courses
SB 8 (2)	Le marchand de glaces
SB 9 (4)	Une conversation
SB 10 (2)	À l'épicerie
SB 11 (4)	C'est combien?
SB 12 (1)	On achète des provisions
SB 13 (4)	Une fête
SB 14 (1)	Quel magasin!
SB 15 (5)	Les cartes postales
SB 16 (1)	Le shopping
CM 1/13	Épreuve: Écouter

Unité 2
SB 18 (4)	C'est qui?
SB 20 (1)	Des vacances en Europe
SB 21 (4)	Projets de vacances
SB 21 (7)	On visite le pays
SB 22 (2)	Ils voyagent comment?
SB 23 (6)	Une soirée internationale
SB 24 (1)	Pendant les vacances
SB 24 (2)	Maintenant ou plus tard?
SB 25 (4)	La fête de Daniel
SB 26 (1)	Où habitent-ils?
CM 2/7	Au val de Loire
SB 28 (2)	Claire
SB 123 (4)	Ce n'est pas possible
CM 2/14	Épreuve: Écouter

🎧 List of recorded items (continued)

Class CD 2
Unité 3
SB 34–35 (1)	Notre collège
SB 127 (1)	On va à quelle école?
SB 35 (4)	Des clubs et des activités
SB 36 (2)	Dans la cour
SB 127 (2)	On parle de la journée scolaire
SB 37 (5)	C'est quel jour?
SB 38 (1)	Pour aller au collège
SB 39 (6)	Le matin, chez Charlotte
SB 39 (7)	Le soir, chez Michel
SB 42 (1)	Une journée pas idéale
SB 42 (3)	Tu aimes quelles matières?
SB 44 (1)	Après les cours
SB 46 (1)	Le collège Jules Verne
SB 46	Chantez! Les matières
CM 3/15	Épreuve: Écouter

Unité 4
SB 50 (1)	Bienvenue en France
SB 51 (3)	Daniel et la famille Martin
SB 51 (6)	La famille de Daniel
SB 52 (1)	Julie et la famille Lebois
SB 53 (6)	Présent ou passé?
SB 54 (1)	Un coup de téléphone
SB 55 (4)	Quand exactement?
SB 56 (1)	Aux magasins
SB 57 (6)	On achète des souvenirs
SB 58 (3)	Activités au choix
SB 59 (5)	Une journée difficile
SB 60 (2)	Perdu et retrouvé
SB 131 (5)	À Giverny
SB 62 (2)	Bon retour
CM 4/13	Épreuve: Écouter

Class CD 3
Unité 5
SB 66–67 (1)	Les cafés en France
SB 67 (2)	Qu'est-ce qu'on prend?
SB 68 (1)	On va au café?
SB 68 (3)	On vend des glaces
SB 69	Chantez! Que désirez-vous?
SB 71 (3)	Dans la rue
SB 71 (5)	Le sandwich surprise
SB 72 (1)	Les sandwichs de M. Corot
SB 73 (4)	Au bureau de M. Corot
SB 74 (1)	Un désastre pour Emmanuel
SB 75 (3)	Oui ou non?
SB 77 (2)	Le menu pour ce soir
SB 77 (3)	Qu'est-ce qu'on va manger?
CM 5/8 (1)	Voici le menu
SB 78 (3)	Mme Dubois
SB 78 (4)	M. Lemaître
SB 78 (5)	Vous avez choisi?
CM 5/13	Épreuve: Écouter

Unité 6
SB 82 (1)	On part bientôt
SB 82 (3)	Pour aller au collège
SB 83 (5)	À la gare
SB 84 (1)	Au bureau des renseignements
SB 84 (4)	Qu'est-ce qu'on cherche?
SB 85 (5)	Au guichet
SB 85 (7)	Dans le train
SB 87 (4)	La vie est facile avec un robot!
SB 88 (1)	Martin et Émilie
SB 90 (3)	Une journée en famille
SB 90 (5)	Un coup de téléphone
SB 91 (7)	Une sortie
SB 139 (5)	Une interview avec Jean-Luc
SB 92	Chantez! Paris-Genève
CM 6/14	Épreuve: Écouter

Class CD 4
Unité 7
SB 96 (1)	Je n'ai rien à me mettre
SB 97 (2)	Mes vêtements favoris
SB 98 (2)	Qui parle?
SB 143 (2)	Vous allez me reconnaître?
SB 101 (3)	C'est quelle valise?
TB (Area 4)	Chantez! Alouette
CM 7/6 (1)	Moi, j'ai mal
SB 105 (7)	C'est quelle image?
SB 106 (1)	Ça ne va pas!
SB 106 (2)	Tout le monde est malade
SB 107 (4)	Chez le médecin
CM 7/8 (1)	Au téléphone
CM 7/13	Épreuve: Écouter

Unité 8
SB 147 (1)	Quelle heure est-il?
SB 110 (1)	Qu'est-ce qu'on va faire?
SB 111 (3)	Trois conversations
CM 8/2	Qu'est-ce qu'on fait?
SB 112 (2)	Qui dit cela?
SB 113 (3)	Vous sortez souvent?
SB 114 (1)	Es-tu libre ce soir?
SB 115 (5)	Rendez-vous
SB 147 (4)	On parle des loisirs
CM 8/5 (1)	Samedi dernier
SB 119	Chantez! Sabine, ce n'est pas grave…
CM 8/10	Épreuve: Écouter

Contrôle
CM 139	Contrôle: Écouter

Student CD 1
CM 1/9	Écoute et parle
CM 2/10	Écoute et parle
CM 3/11	Écoute et parle
CM 4/9	Écoute et parle
CM 5/9	Écoute et parle
CM 6/10	Écoute et parle
CM 7/9	Écoute et parle
CM 8/6	Écoute et parle

Student CD 2
CM 1/10	Tu comprends?
CM 2/11	Tu comprends?
CM 3/12	Tu comprends?
CM 4/10	Tu comprends?
CM 5/10	Tu comprends?
CM 6/11	Tu comprends?
CM 7/10	Tu comprends?
CM 8/7	Tu comprends?

4 Flashcards

There are 100 colour flashcards, including many photographs. In this edition the flashcards are on CD-ROM. This allows the teacher to view and print images individually and in groups, as needed. Full details accompany the CD-ROM.

The flashcards provide:
- the main visual aid for presenting vocabulary
- a stimulus for oral work
- the key element in many oral games and activities.

See below for a full list of flashcards and TB 26 for ideas for flashcard games.

List of flashcards

Shops
1. baker's
2. confectioner's
3. butcher's
4. delicatessen
5. book shop
6. tobacconist's

Food and stamps
7. pain au chocolat
8. box of chocolates
9. ice cream (strawberry and vanilla)
10. packet of crisps
11. mushrooms
12. portion of tomato salad
13. quiche
14. continental sausage
15. prawns
16. litre carton of milk
17. packet of sweets
18. sugar
19. butter
20. jar of jam
21. French postage stamps

Transport
22. bus
23. plane
24. boat
25. motorbike
26. metro train
27. TGV train
28. car
29. coach
30. bike
31. walker in boots

Leisure
32. fishing
33. taking photos
34. sailing
35. at a theme park
36. playing tennis
37. ice-skating
38. going to town

School rooms
39. library
40. computer room
41. science lab
42. outdoor school yard
43. gym
44. canteen

Reflexive verbs
45 boy waking up
46 girl getting up
47 boy getting washed
48 girl getting dressed
49 bus stopping
50 boy going to bed
51 boy and girl resting
52 boys and girls hurrying
53 boys swimming
54 girls who are bored

Verbs
55 boy and girl eating pizza
56 boy using mobile phone in street
57 girl playing guitar
58 girl buying CD in music shop
59 boy and girl surfing the net
60 boy and girl gardening

Souvenirs
61 key ring
62 comic book
63 T-shirt
64 poster
65 flag

Snacks and drinks
66 *croque-monsieur*
67 ham sandwich
68 pizza
69 *crêpe*
70 mint-flavoured drink
71 freshly squeezed lemon juice

Max à Paris
72 American male tourist leaving hotel
73 Tourist arriving at Eiffel tower in bus
74 Tourist climbing up stairs to 2nd stage
75 Tourist entering lift, reading book
76 Lift arriving at 3rd stage
77 Tourist, holding book, looking at view from 3rd stage
78 Book falling from top of Eiffel tower
79 Tourist going down in lift
80 Tourist getting out of lift and finding book

Expressions with avoir
81 hot
82 cold
83 hungry
84 thirsty
85 temperature
86 bad head and foot

Clothing
87 trainers
88 shoes
89 sweat shirt
90 shirt
91 jacket
92 trousers
93 jeans
94 swimming costume + trunks
95 sunglasses

Entertainment
96 firework display
97 funfair
98 beach
99 ice rink
100 football match

5 Copymasters

There are 150 copymasters, containing a wide variety of material and giving practice in all four skills and training in language-learning strategies.

- **Expendable material**

Some of the copymaster worksheets are intended to be expendable, e.g. those containing crosswords, word searches or grids for completion by the student. Others, including several sheets of mini-flashcards, can be cut up and used for pair or group activities. The *Sommaire* and grammar practice sheets can be stuck into the student's exercise book or file for future reference.

- **Assessment**

The students' sheets for assessment tests, *Épreuves* (informal) and *Contrôle* (formal) are provided on copymasters.

- **Écoute et parle**

These copymasters provide material for the teaching and practice of the interrelationship between sounds and writing, which is a major requirement of the new curriculum. They provide practice of pronunciation and speaking and include gapped conversations and role-playing for language-lab type practice.

- **Tu comprends?**

Self-instructional listening tasks, with accompanying CD, provide useful material for homework or for students working independently in class.

- **Rappel**

There is a *Rappel* copymaster for each unit, containing mainly vocabulary games and revision tasks. Taken together, they cover all the main vocabulary topics of ***Encore Tricolore 1***, as listed in the *Vocabulaire par thèmes*, and also give consolidatory practice for some of the new topics of ***Encore Tricolore 2***.

Each sheet has about four tasks and the topics covered are not necessarily linked with the units in which they feature, though some lead into the unit which follows. For example, the *Rappel* for *Unité 1* gives revision of core question and answers about oneself, one's family and pets, some general vocabulary of things in a bedroom and a lead-in to *Unité 2*, with revision of names of places in a town and directions.

The copymasters can be used at any time, for homework or a cover lesson, and could be filed for quick revision later on.

- **Sommaire**

The *Sommaire* for each unit is also given in an incomplete form on copymaster for completion and retention by students.

List of copymasters

Unité 1
CM 1/1   *On mange et on boit* [revision]
CM 1/2   *Les verbes en -er* [grammar]
CM 1/3   *Les verbes en -re* [grammar]
CM 1/4   *Les quantités* [mini-flashcards]
CM 1/5   *Les verbes en -ir* [grammar]
CM 1/6   *ne … pas, ne … plus* [grammar]
CM 1/7   *Les verbes sont utiles* [grammar]
CM 1/8   *C'est utile, le dictionnaire!* [dictionary skills]
CM 1/9   *Écoute et parle* [independent listening]
CM 1/10 *Tu comprends?* [independent listening]
CM 1/11 *Sommaire* [consolidation, reference]
CM 1/12 *Rappel* [revision]
CM 1/13–1/16 *Épreuve*

Unité 2
CM 2/1   *L'Europe* [map]
CM 2/2   *Les transports* [mini-flashcards]
CM 2/3   *Des mots croisés (voir et venir)* [grammar]
CM 2/4   *Des activités* [mini-flashcards]
CM 2/5   *Projets de vacances* [grammar]
CM 2/6   *La France* [map]
CM 2/7   *Au val de Loire* [listening]
CM 2/8   *Des mots croisés (aller et pouvoir)* [grammar]
CM 2/9   *C'est utile, le dictionnaire!* [dictionary skills]
CM 2/10 *Écoute et parle* [independent listening]
CM 2/11 *Tu comprends?* [independent listening]
CM 2/12 *Sommaire* [consolidation, reference]
CM 2/13 *Rappel* [revision]
CM 2/14–2/17 *Épreuve*

List of copymasters (continued)

Unité 3
CM 3/1   *La page des jeux* [vocabulary practice]
CM 3/2   *Deux mots croisés* [grammar]
CM 3/3   *L'interview d'un boulanger* [reading]
CM 3/4   Reflexive verbs [mini-flashcards, grammar]
CM 3/5   *La famille Guille* [grammar]
CM 3/6   *La routine du matin* [grammar]
CM 3/7   *J'aime lire* [reading]
CM 3/8   *vouloir* and *pouvoir* [grammar]
CM 3/9   *devoir* [grammar]
CM 3/10   *C'est utile, le dictionnaire!* [dictionary skills]
CM 3/11   *Écoute et parle* [independent listening]
CM 3/12   *Tu comprends?* [independent listening]
CM 3/13   *Sommaire* [consolidation, reference]
CM 3/14   *Rappel* [revision]
CM 3/15–3/18   *Épreuve*

Unité 4
CM 4/1   *La famille et les amis* [vocabulary practice]
CM 4/2   *Chez une famille* [writing, vocabulary practice]
CM 4/3   *Une lettre* [reading, presentation]
CM 4/4   *Des activités* [mini-flashcards]
CM 4/5   *Des souvenirs et des cadeaux* [mini-flashcards]
CM 4/6   *Ce, cet, cette, ces* [grammar]
CM 4/7   *Des verbes au passé composé* [grammar]
CM 4/8   *Des mots croisés* [grammar]
CM 4/9   *Écoute et parle* [independent listening]
CM 4/10   *Tu comprends?* [independent listening]
CM 4/11   *Sommaire* [consolidation, reference]
CM 4/12   *Rappel* [revision]
CM 4/13–4/16   *Épreuve*

Unité 5
CM 5/1   *Au café* [mini-flashcards]
CM 5/2   *On prend quelque chose?* [role play]
CM 5/3   *Un repas en famille* [grammar]
CM 5/4   *Des mots croisés* [grammar]
CM 5/5   *Présent ou passé?* [grammar]
CM 5/6   *Voici le menu* [mini-flashcards]
CM 5/7   *Comprends-tu le menu?* [dictionary skills]
CM 5/8   *Au restaurant* [listening]
CM 5/9   *Écoute et parle* [independent listening]
CM 5/10   *Tu comprends?* [independent listening]
CM 5/11   *Sommaire* [consolidation, reference]
CM 5/12   *Rappel* [revision]
CM 5/13–5/16   *Épreuve*

Unité 6
CM 6/1   *partir et sortir* [grammar]
CM 6/2   *À la gare* [reading]
CM 6/3   *On prend le train* [mini-flashcards]
CM 6/4   *Max à Paris (1)* [mini-flashcards, grammar]
CM 6/5   *Max à Paris (2)* [mini-flashcards, grammar]
CM 6/6   *À la montagne* [grammar]
CM 6/7   *aller et sortir* [grammar]
CM 6/8   *Dans le passé* [grammar]
CM 6/9   *Cartes postales des vacances* [writing]
CM 6/10   *Écoute et parle* [independent listening]
CM 6/11   *Tu comprends?* [independent listening]
CM 6/12   *Sommaire* [consolidation, reference]
CM 6/13   *Rappel* [revision]
CM 6/14–6/17   *Épreuve*

Unité 7
CM 7/1   *Encore des vêtements* [mini-flashcards]
CM 7/2   *mettre* [grammar]
CM 7/3   *C'est utile, le dictionnaire!* [dictionary skills]
CM 7/4   *Faites des descriptions* [grammar]
CM 7/5   *Les clowns* [writing, vocabulary practice]
CM 7/6   *Ça ne va pas* [listening]
CM 7/7   *Avoir – un verbe utile* [grammar]
CM 7/8   *On est malade* [listening]
CM 7/9   *Écoute et parle* [independent listening]
CM 7/10   *Tu comprends?* [independent listening]
CM 7/11   *Sommaire* [consolidation, reference]
CM 7/12   *Rappel* [revision]
CM 7/13–7/16   *Épreuve*

Unité 8
CM 8/1   *Le calendrier et l'heure* [revision]
CM 8/2   *Qu'est-ce qu'on fait?* [listening, writing]
CM 8/3   *On s'amuse* [speaking (pairwork)]
CM 8/4   *Tu aimes lire?* [reading]
CM 8/5   *Qu'est-ce qu'on a fait?* [grammar, listening]
CM 8/6   *Écoute et parle* [independent listening]
CM 8/7   *Tu comprends?* [independent listening]
CM 8/8   *Sommaire* [consolidation, reference]
CM 8/9   *Rappel* [revision]
CM 8/10–8/13   *Épreuve*

CM 133–138   *Presse-Jeunesse 1–6*
CM 139–145   *Contrôle*
CM 146   *Contrôle:* Record sheet
CM 147–155   Music for songs

Planning the course

■ Covering the National Curriculum

Encore Tricolore 2 nouvelle édition covers attainment levels 1–6 of the National Curriculum.

Developing knowledge, skills and understanding

1 **Acquiring knowledge and understanding of the target language** *Pupils should be taught:*	***Encore Tricolore 2 nouvelle édition***
a *the principles and interrelationship of sounds and writing in the target language*	*Écoute et parle* Understanding and pronouncing words in French (SB 154)
b *the grammar of the target language and how to apply it*	A major feature of the course. Grammar is explained in *Dossier-langue* sections of the Students' Book and presented and practised extensively.
c *how to express themselves using a range of vocabulary and structures.*	A major feature of the course.

2 Developing language skills *Pupils should be taught:*	***Encore Tricolore 2 nouvelle édition***
a how to listen carefully for gist and detail	A major feature of the course with regular practice tasks for class and individual work.
b correct pronunciation and intonation	*Écoute et parle*. See also SB 154.
c how to ask and answer questions	Taught and practised throughout the course, with numerous pairwork activities. *Questions et réponses* is a series of tasks which practises matching correct answers to questions. Includes some topic-specific sections, e.g. *Unité 4* 'Understand and answer questions when staying with a French family'. From *Unité 5* onwards, includes questions and answers in the perfect tense.
d how to initiate and develop conversations	Many activities practise this, e.g. *Inventez des conversations*.
e how to vary the target language to suit context, audience and purpose	Practised through substitution tables, but mainly covered in later stages of **Encore Tricolore**.
f how to adapt language they already know for different contexts	Covered mainly in later stages of **Encore Tricolore**.
g strategies for dealing with the unpredictable [for example, unfamiliar language, unexpected responses]	*Tips for understanding French* (SB 153)
h techniques for skimming and for scanning written texts for information, including those from ICT-based sources	*Skimming and scanning, Reading for detail* (SB 153)
i how to summarise and report the main points of spoken or written texts, using notes where appropriate	*Complète le résumé* tasks in Students' Book. Tasks on copymaster, linked with *Presse-Jeunesse* pages.
j how to redraft their writing to improve its accuracy and presentation, including the use of ICT.	Suggestions in the Teacher's Book for using ICT for preparing letters, messages, brochures etc.
3 Developing language-learning skills *Pupils should be taught:*	
a techniques for memorising words, phrases and short extracts	Grouping words into topics (*Sommaires*), colour-coding genders, identifying word endings of nouns to indicate gender, memory games, routine practice of useful phrases and expressions with flashcards. See *Tips for learning vocabulary and verbs* (SB 152).
b how to use context and other clues to interpret meaning [for example, by identifying the grammatical function of unfamiliar words or similarities with words they know]	*Presse-Jeunesse* sections in the Students' Book and related copymasters. See *Tips for understanding French* (SB 153).
c to use their knowledge of English or another language when learning the target language	Regular items in *Écoute et parle* sections focus on comparisons with English. See also *Tips for understanding French* (SB 153).
d how to use dictionaries and other reference materials appropriately and effectively	Tasks such as *C'est utile, le dictionnaire* provide practice in using the glossary or dictionaries. Reference material for grammar and vocabulary provided in the Students' Book. See also *Using a dictionary or glossary* (SB 153).
e how to develop their independence in learning and using the target language.	Many tasks are self-instructional, e.g. in *Rappel*, *Écoute et parle* and *Presse-Jeunesse* sections. *Tu comprends?* is a series of listening tasks with a student CD for independent use. *Vocabulaire de classe* sections provide support for using target language in class.
4 Developing cultural awareness *Pupils should be taught about different countries and cultures by:*	
a working with authentic materials in the target language, including some from ICT-based sources [for example, handwritten texts, newspapers, magazines, books, video, satellite television, texts from the Internet]	Authentic printed materials used in the Students' Book, where appropriate. Suggestions for Internet sites given in the Teacher's Book. *Presse-Jeunesse* sections include slightly adapted articles from French magazines for young people.
b communicating with native speakers [for example, in person, by correspondence]	Suggestions in Teacher's Book for forming class links and video-conferencing. *Unité 4* is based on an exchange visit and other activities are linked to communicating with French correspondents.
c considering their own culture and comparing it with the cultures of the countries and communities where the target language is spoken	Most of *Unité 4* is based on an exchange visit and all units contain some material involving comparisons of this kind.
d considering the experiences and perspectives of people in these countries and communities.	Recordings, letters, articles etc. from people from different French-speaking countries and communities.

Covering the National Curriculum

5 Breadth of study *During Key Stages 3 and 4, pupils should be taught the knowledge, skills and understanding through:*	*Encore Tricolore 2 nouvelle édition*
a communicating in the target language in pairs and groups, and with their teacher	A major feature of the course, with detailed suggestions in the Teacher's Book and Students' Book.
b using everyday classroom events as an opportunity for spontaneous speech	Suggestions in the Teacher's Book. *Vocabulaire de classe* sections in *Écoute et parle* provide support for this.
c expressing and discussing personal feelings and opinions	Expressing preferences and giving opinions and reasons are included in most units.
d producing and responding to different types of spoken and written language, including texts produced using ICT	A major feature of the course, with detailed suggestions in the Teacher's Book and Students' Book.
e using a range of resources, including ICT, for accessing and communicating information	Suggestions in the Teacher's Book and Students' Book for useful resources, including Internet sites.
f using the target language creatively and imaginatively	*À toi!* sections in the Students' Book encourage students to personalise and vary language learnt.
g listening, reading or viewing for personal interest and enjoyment, as well as for information	Recorded stories, songs, *Presse-Jeunesse* sections etc.
h using the target language for real purposes [for example, by sending and receiving messages by telephone, letter, fax or e-mail]	Tasks in the Students' Book for writing letters, messages and e-mails in most units.
i working in a variety of contexts, including everyday activities, personal and social life, the world around us, the world of work and the international world.	*Encore Tricolore 2* covers the following contexts: • everyday activities • the international world • personal and social life • the world around us. Other contexts are covered in later stages.

2 Covering the QCA Scheme of Work

Encore Tricolore nouvelle édition has taken into account the QCA Scheme of Work for Key Stage 3, with its emphasis on clear progression in language learning. *Encore Tricolore 1–3* covers all the language content and contexts for learning, although sometimes the order is slightly different. Classroom instructions, pronunciation and spelling rules are taught mainly in the *Écoute et parle* section. As recommended by QCA, students are introduced to grammatical rules and terminology at an early stage so that they are equipped with the knowledge to construct their own sentences and become independent language learners.

3 Building on the National Literacy Strategy

Encore Tricolore nouvelle édition builds on the knowledge about language that students will bring with them from their primary school, based on their work using the National Literacy Strategy, in the following ways:

- identifying points of grammar to understand how the French language works
- using appropriate grammatical terminology in the *Dossier-langue* and *Grammaire* sections
- familiarising students with spelling and pronunciation patterns to encourage greater accuracy
- making comparisons between English and French to increase general awareness of language.

4 Covering the Scottish Guidelines

The table below is based on the Modern Languages Guidelines (5–14) consultation draft, published by the Scottish Consultative Council on the Curriculum, 1999. It indicates how *Encore Tricolore 2 nouvelle édition* covers the strands for each skill.

A key feature of these guidelines is knowing about language, and this is also a central aim of *Encore Tricolore nouvelle édition*. The course emphasises learning how to use grammar and structures in a flexible way and how to recognise the spelling patterns and unique features of the language. Grammar is first presented in use, then explained in a *Dossier-langue* section, then practised through a variety of different activities and games. Students are also encouraged to identify similarities and differences between English and French.

Modern Language Guidelines (draft)	*Encore Tricolore 2 nouvelle édition*
Listening Knowing about language	Identifying sounds, intonation, recognising linguistic patterns (subject + verb etc.).
Listening for information and instructions	Use of the target language for class activities, general listening activities for gist and detail. Listening strategies suggested throughout Teacher's Book.
Listening and reacting to others	Pairwork, group and class activities.
Listening for enjoyment	Songs, *Des phrases ridicules*.

Modern Language Guidelines (draft)	*Encore Tricolore 2 nouvelle édition*
Speaking *Knowing about language*	Structured practice through *Inventez des conversations* and other speaking activities. Appropriate pronunciation and intonation.
Speaking to convey information	Personal conversations, role-play activities, information gap tasks, colour-coded conversations – expanding and adapting basic dialogues.
Speaking and interacting with others	Pair, group and class activities, games etc.
Speaking about experiences, feelings and opinions	In most units students express opinions and preferences, say how they feel and give reasons.
Reading *Knowing about language*	Use reading strategies to help access unfamiliar language, use grammatical and contextual clues, skim and scan texts, practice in using a dictionary. See SB 152–153 and CM 1/8, 2/9, 3/10, 7/3.
Reading for information and instructions	Read rubrics, signs, labels, captions, simple postcards, e-mail messages, letters, route directions etc.
Reading aloud	Understanding and pronouncing words in French (SB 154 and *Écoute et parle* copymasters). Read parts in scripted conversations.
Reading for enjoyment	Stories, poems, short articles (*Presse-Jeunesse* sections).
Writing *Knowing about language*	Noticing similarities and differences between English and French. Awareness of language patterns, e.g. regular -er verbs, adjectival agreement etc. Using a dictionary to check genders, irregular plurals etc.
Writing to exchange information and ideas	Write short messages, e-mails and letters. Use a word processor to amend and present written information.
Writing to establish and maintain personal contact	Exchange simple letters and e-mails with pen-friend etc.
Writing imaginatively	*À toi!* sections – expressing personal opinions and production of language. Invent simple word puzzles. Play *Le jeu des conséquences*.

5 Covering the Curriculum in Northern Ireland

At the time of writing, the Northern Ireland Curriculum was under review. The following table indicates how **Encore Tricolore nouvelle édition** covers the Contexts for Learning and Associated Topics for Key Stage 3 in current use (April 2001).

Context 1: Everyday Activities **Topics**	*Encore Tricolore 2 nouvelle édition*
a Home and school life	Unité 3, Unité 4
b Food and drink	Unité 1, Unité 5
c Shopping	Unité 1
d Eating out	Unité 5
Context 2: Personal Life and Social Relationships **Topics**	
a Self, family and friends	Unité 4, Unité 8
b Health	Unité 7
c Holidays and Leisure	Unité 2, Unité 6, Unité 8
d Celebrations and special occasions	Unité 5, Unité 8
Context 3: The World Around Us **Topics**	
a House and home	Unité 4
b Town and countryside	Unité 2
c Getting around	Unité 2, Unité 6
d Weather	Unité 2

Teaching Plan

6 Encore Tricolore 2 nouvelle édition: Teaching Plan

Unité 1	En ville
When	Autumn Term
Topics	• shops and what they sell • quantities, money, number and prices • shopping for food
Grammar	• revision of partitive • revision of -er, -re and -ir verbs • expressions of quantity followed by de, d' • ne … pas de, ne … plus de
ICT	• phrase generation • buying food for a picnic from an Internet shopping site • spreadsheet shopping list activity
Écoute et parle: Interrelationship between sounds and writing	• the French alphabet • pronunciation of c • the endings -ial, -iel
National Curriculum Levels	Some students levels 3–4+ Most students levels 2–4 All students levels 2–3
Rappel	• self, family, pets • things in a bedroom • places in a town, directions

Unité 2	On fait des projets
When	Autumn Term
Topics	• countries, capital cities, nationalities • means of transport • expressions of future time • describing towns, villages, location, facilities • reading and writing postcards • revision of leisure activities and weather
Grammar	• prepositions with towns/countries • voir, venir (present tense) • aller + infinitive • pouvoir + infinitive
ICT	• setting up e-mail correspondents • creating illustrated sentences • finding out about French towns from Internet • designing a poster/leaflet about local facilities • sending a virtual postcard
Écoute et parle: Interrelationship between sounds and writing	• numbers • pronunciation of ch and qu • the ending -in
Reading for pleasure	Presse-Jeunesse 1 (SB 32–33, CM 133)
National Curriculum Levels	Some students levels 4–5 Most students levels 3–4 All students levels 2–3
Rappel	• numbers • school vocabulary • computer vocabulary

Unité 3	Au collège
When	Autumn Term
Topics	• school life in France, school day, school subjects • daily routine, travel to school • opinion of subjects and using Internet at school
Grammar	• using dire, lire and écrire • using prendre, apprendre and comprendre • using reflexive verbs • using vouloir
ICT	• making a labelled plan of classroom or school • laying out a school timetable • writing a short description • organising a survey
Écoute et parle: Interrelationship between sounds and writing	• the French alphabet • pronunciation of h and i • the ending -ie
Reading for pleasure	Presse-Jeunesse 2 (SB 48–49, CM 134)
National Curriculum Levels	Some students levels 3–5 Most students levels 3–4 All students levels 2–3
Rappel	• days of the week, months • weather • time

Unité 4	En famille
When	Spring Term
Topics	• revision of clothing and family vocabulary • introducing people, staying with a family • talking about souvenirs and presents • saying goodbye and thanking people for their hospitality
Grammar	• revision of present tense of avoir • contrasting past and present tenses • perfect tense with avoir, regular -er, -re, -ir verbs • using ce, cet, cette, ces
ICT	• using speech bubbles (call-outs) • opening an electronic phrase book • sentence reconstruction
Écoute et parle: Interrelationship between sounds and writing	• numbers • pronunciation of g • the endings -ieux, -yeux
Reading for pleasure	Presse-Jeunesse 3 (SB 64–65, CM 135)
National Curriculum Levels	Some students levels 3–5+ Most students levels 3–5 All students levels 2–4
Rappel	• household tasks • sport, music, other leisure activities

Teaching Plan

Section 1 — Introduction to the course

Unité 5	Bon appétit!
When	Spring Term
Topics	• buying drinks, snacks, ice-creams • describing food and recent meals, expressing likes and dislikes • discussing the menu, ordering meals in a restaurant
Grammar	• using *boire* (present tense) • using *pour* + infinitive (optional) • revision of perfect tense with regular verbs • using irregular past participles • questions in the perfect tense • the perfect tense in the negative
ICT	• text reconstruction • finding French restaurant menus on the web • making an illustrated menu
Écoute et parle: Interrelationship between sounds and writing	• the letter *r* • the endings *-u*, *-ue*
Reading for pleasure	*Presse-Jeunesse 4* (SB 80–81, CM 136)
National Curriculum Levels	Some students levels 4–5+ Most students levels 4–5 All students levels 3–4
Rappel	• colours • festivals and greetings • expressions of time (past, present, future)

Unité 6	En voyage
When	Spring/Summer Term
Topics	• revision of time, 24-hour clock, numbers 0–1000 • travel by train, air, coach and boat • station signs, buying a train ticket, understanding travel information • describing a recent day out
Grammar	• using *partir* (present tense) • revison of *être* (present tense) • *il faut* + infinitive • perfect tense with *être* • using the perfect tense with *avoir* and *être*
ICT	• making signs using clip art, autoshapes etc. • planning a journey by train from the SNCF website • text reconstruction • using clip art to illustrate a story and use a spell checker
Écoute et parle: Interrelationship between sounds and writing	• numbers • pronunciation of *u* and *ou* • the ending *-ment*
Reading for pleasure	*Presse-Jeunesse 5* (SB 94–95, CM 137)
National Curriculum Levels	Some students levels 4–5+ Most students levels 4–5 All students levels 3–4
Rappel	• meals, food, drink • food shops

Unité 7	Ça va?
When	Summer Term
Topics	• discussing clothes, colours and what to wear • describing appearance (mainly facial) • talking about parts of the body • saying how you feel and describing what hurts • health; at the doctor's
Grammar	• using *mettre* (present, perfect) • agreement of adjectives • using direct object pronouns • *avoir mal* + parts of the body; other expressions with *avoir* • using the imperative • using *dormir* (optional)
ICT	• phrase generation • visual presentation of some adjectives using word art, clip art plus text, font sizes etc. • text reconstruction • creating a labelled picture using a drawing programme • finding a French website devoted to animals
Écoute et parle: Interrelationship between sounds and writing	• nasal vowels: *-am*, *-an*, *-em*, *-en*; *-on* • the ending *-ure*
Reading for pleasure	*Presse-Jeunesse 6* (SB 109, CM 138)
National Curriculum Levels	Some students levels 4–5+ Most students levels 4–5 All students levels 3–4
Rappel	• members of the family • rooms in a house • school subjects

Unité 8	Rendez-vous!
When	Summer Term
Topics	• revision of dates, festivals, time • finding out what's on • giving, accepting, refusing invitations • arranging to meet • discussing leisure activities; buying tickets • making comparisons
Grammar	• using *sortir* (present, perfect) • revision of other common verbs • using *si*, *quand*, *mais* • revision and practice of perfect tense • *c'était* as a lexical item
ICT	• making a virtual trip to a theme park • developing a matching exercise using authoring software • making playing cards using clip art • designing a party invitation • organising a survey on going out • exchanging e-mails
Écoute et parle: Interrelationship between sounds and writing	• nasal vowels: *-im*, *-in*, *-ain*; *-um*, *-un* • the endings *-eau*, *-aux*
National Curriculum Levels	Some students levels 5–6 Most students levels 4–5 All students levels 3–4
Rappel	• clothes • adjectives • towns and countries

Developing skills

1. Developing listening skills

Training in careful listening for detail and for gist is a key feature of the course.

There are no 'paused' recordings as it is left to the teacher's discretion to decide the number of times the tape is played, when there should be pauses, and the speed of building up from simple to more demanding tasks. The only exception to this is in the *Contrôle*, which simulates examination-type conditions. The recordings for the speaking tasks which appear on the *Écoute et parle* copymasters also have pauses so students can give their answers, before they hear the correct reply.

The full text of all recorded items appears in Section 3 of the Teacher's Book.

Recorded listening material can be broadly grouped as follows:

- **Intensive listening**

Students know what to listen for and have to select specific information from the recorded text and listen in sufficient detail to respond, e.g. by matching a description to a picture or answering simple *Vrai ou faux?* questions.

Often there is an additional task, at a higher level (often in *Au choix* extension), in which students listen for an opinion or for additional details.

Most of the listening practice in **Encore Tricolore 2** is intensive.

- **Listening for gist**

In this type of listening, students listen to find out what happened at the end of a story or to discover the mood of the speakers. In items of this kind the teacher should make it clear that students should not worry if they can't understand every word but should just listen for the main points as they probably will do when they hear real French people talking.

- **Interrelationship between sounds and writing**

Student CD 1 is devoted to intensive practice linked with different sounds, French and English pronunciation, linking sounds with spelling patterns etc. These sections appear on copymasters at the end of each unit and are entitled *Écoute et parle*.

- **Independent listening**

At the end of each unit there is a section called *Tu comprends?* which includes three or four recorded tasks (Student CD 2) and a copymaster. The tasks, intended for listening practice by students working alone, are based on the language content of the unit.

2. Developing speaking skills

The National Curriculum states that students should learn how to express themselves using a range of vocabulary and structures.

Particular emphasis is placed on the following:
- correct pronunciation and intonation
- how to ask and answer questions
- how to initiate and develop conversations
- how to vary the target language to suit context, audience and purpose.

These are addressed fully in the course, both by on-going training in listening and speaking, in every unit, and also with more targeted training linked with the above points.

Examples of this are:

a individual pronunciation practice, using the *Écoute et parle* copymasters and Student CD 1

b asking and answering questions in the present tense (*Unités 1–4*) and in the perfect tense (*Unités 5–8*)

c pairwork and role-play practice based in the Students' Book and on copymasters

d 'colour-coded conversations', called *Inventez des conversations*, which appear regularly throughout the Students' Book. Students practise a basic conversation, then vary and adapt it by substituting other words and expressions from the colour-coded sections.

Consolidation

At the end of each *Écoute et parle* section there is a recorded conversation to provide extra practice of the language in the unit. See also hints on pronunciation in *Understanding and pronouncing words in French* (SB 154).

3. Developing reading skills

There is a wide range of reading material in **Encore Tricolore 2**, including practice in intensive reading to discover specific information and reading for gist, e.g. to find out a story line.

Reading strategies and tips are listed and explained in *Tips for language learning* (SB 152–154).

- **Presse-Jeunesse**

These magazine sections appear after *Unités 2–7* in the Students' Book and can just be used alone as reading for pleasure. However, for more practice of comprehension and reading skills, they should be used with the accompanying copymasters. Students' attention can be drawn to reading strategies, as listed in the National Curriculum requirements, e.g.

- techniques for skimming and for scanning written texts for information, including those from ICT-based sources
- how to use context and other clues to interpret meaning, for example, by identifying the grammatical function of unfamiliar words or similarities with words (see SB 153)
- using ICT.

- **ICT and reading skills**

In many units of the Students' Book, there are suggestions for using ICT programmes such as *Fun with Texts* to allow students to work on a reading passage at their own pace, involving such activities as unjumbling text, sequencing and cloze procedure activities (see TB 18–24).

- **Using dictionaries and other reference material**

Practice in using dictionaries and the Students' Book French–English and English–French glossaries 'appropriately and effectively' is given regularly through items such as *C'est utile, le dictionnaire* and through activities on copymaster. See also *Using a dictionary or glossary* (SB 153).

4. Developing writing skills

Training in writing is in line with National Curriculum requirements and plenty of practice activities are provided, e.g.

- **Copywriting**

There is still some copywriting, e.g in labelling tasks on copymasters, in word games and matching, sorting and gap-filling tasks.

Students also use computers to make labels or posters for the classroom.

- **Learning new words**

Students soon begin to practise writing familiar words, then phrases from memory, mainly through a wide range of games and word activities.

The *Sommaire* sections at the end of each unit encourage students to learn lists of vocabulary on a regular basis. For extra practice, there are incomplete versions of the *Sommaire* for each unit on copymaster. Students can complete the missing English words from memory or by reference to the Students' Book. It is hoped that this extra activity will help to consolidate the core language. The completed sheets could be filed for reference.

ICT activities such as *Fun with Texts* also train students to learn spelling patterns.

- **Adapting a model by substituting text/ adapting known language to new contexts**

There are a lot of Students' Book activities based on writing sentences using substitution tables. They begin with simple sentence work, but more creative and open-ended writing is gradually introduced, especially through the *À toi!* items in which students adapt the language they have learnt to make personal statements, state likes and dislikes and express opinions.

Sometimes option boxes in the Students' Book can be used in cut and paste activities on a computer.

- **Developing independence in learning and using the target language**

Students are encouraged to use dictionaries and other reference materials appropriately and are trained through such activities as *C'est utile, le dictionnaire* to use dictionaries and the *Glossaires* at the back of the book.

The vocabulary in the *Sommaires* is listed alphabetically within topics to make it easy for students to refer to.

Students are also trained to refer to the *Dossier-langue* explanations and to the grammar section at the back of the book. In addition, they are encouraged to make their own ICT verb tables and 'electronic phrase book' (see TB 19).

- **Using the Target Language creatively and imaginatively/Producing different types of written language**

These skills are built up gradually through many easy tasks on copymasters or through Students' Book items such as writing simple e-mails. This builds up to more open-ended tasks such as *À toi!* In these items, students adapt the language they have learnt to make personal statements, state likes and dislikes and express opinions.

- **Re-drafting writing to improve its accuracy**

Students are encouraged to use word-processing software and to consult reference materials to check and improve their work.

5 Developing understanding and application of grammar

Grammar is a central feature of **Encore Tricolore**. Throughout the course, new grammatical structures are introduced through oral/aural and sometimes reading activities. Students are encouraged to work out rules for themselves before referring to the English explanation, in the *Dossier-langue* sections. This is immediately followed by practice activities and games, to help students to absorb the grammatical patterns and use them.

There is a grammar reference section, including verb tables, at the back of the Students' Book and students are encouraged to make up their own computer-generated verb tables.

- **Grammar in Action**

Grammar in Action is a series of workbooks designed to accompany each stage of **Encore Tricolore**. The books provide extensive practice in French grammar and reinforce and extend students' grammar skills. The existing edition of *Grammar in Action 2* is designed to accompany **Encore Tricolore 2** (original edition) and includes page references to the Students' Book.

Grammar in Action 2 can continue to be used both independently and with **Encore Tricolore 2 nouvelle édition**.

6 Developing language-learning skills

The National Curriculum emphasises training in language-learning skills stating that pupils should be taught:

- **techniques for memorising words, phrases and short extracts**

In **Encore Tricolore 2 nouvelle édition**, students are given regular hints for memorising, e.g. learning nouns with their gender.

Useful tips are given where relevant, e.g. *Tips for learning vocabulary and verbs* (SB 152).

The *Sommaire* section at the end of each unit brings vocabulary together for easy reference. This gives a sense of progress and emphasises the importance of regular learning as an essential language-learning skill. The *Sommaire* sections are also repeated on copymasters in the form of completion tasks which can be filed and retained for reference.

- **to use their knowledge of English or another language when learning the target language**

Grammar is explained in English, and the *Dossier-langue* sections and a range of notes in the Teacher's Book all use knowledge of English to help in learning the target language.

There are references to some regular spelling patterns in English and French on the *Écoute et parle* copymasters.

- **to look out for clues**

Through training in reading strategies (see SB 153), students are taught to use clues to discover meaning, such as similarities to English (cognates), as well as context and grammatical function.

Differentiation

1 Support and extension material

Encore Tricolore 2 nouvelle édition contains material for most of the ability range. All the core teaching items are in the main Students' Book text, but tasks for support and extension are linked to many of these activities and are set out in *Au choix*.

2 Au choix

This section of the Students' Book provides teachers and students with **extension** (harder items) and **support** (more practice at the same or an easier level). There are also other items, classed as **general**, which could be used by any or all students. Students can work on most of these tasks independently.

3 Copymasters

Some of these are for consolidation and several have an incline of difficulty, to allow even the less able students to try harder items if they wish.

4 Differentiation by task

This can be done using *Au choix*. Some students can work on an extension task while others do a support task. Usually this range of options is indicated in the teacher's notes.

5 Differentiation by outcome

Some tasks, especially the open-ended ones such as *À toi!*, can be carried out at various levels according to the level of ability of the student. For example, to offer more support for the less able, the item could be treated as a class activity and the text built up on the board to be copied down. In other cases, gap-filling tasks can be made easier by giving students options to choose from, which can be written on the board and copied.

6 Selective use of items

The teaching of each new area of language follows a sequence of steps: presentation, discovery and explanation of new language, practice of new vocabulary and structures, leading to full communicative use.

The initial presentation, through oral/aural work, the explanation of new structures and some practice is appropriate for all.

After this, there is room for selection, for example, by using some of the materials for differentiation, listed above, or choosing from the suggestions for practice tasks, games and ICT activities, listed in Section 2 and in the notes for the individual units. This selection will be influenced by the time available and the abilities and needs of students.

Carousel group work

It can be useful sometimes to organise a lesson on a 'Carousel' system. This involves groups doing a series of activities in sequence. Some of these can be harder than others and, depending on the plan for moving round, some activities can be made more demanding than others for differentiation purposes. Also, fairly straightforward tasks (even exercises) can alternate with something more light-hearted. It is best to have at least one more activity in progress than there are groups, so that no-one is waiting around until the next activity is available.

For this type of group work, group leaders will be needed. They can be chosen by their group or the teacher. Some time will need to be spent training the group leaders and helping them to prepare materials, but people who have done this have found it very rewarding in terms of progress and enjoyment, and the activities set up can often be re-used or adapted for other groups or occasions.

Developing cultural awareness

In **Encore Tricolore nouvelle édition** students are introduced to a variety of countries in which French is spoken and throughout the course, the emphasis is on authenticity of language and of background information. In **Encore Tricolore 2 nouvelle édition**, the focus is mainly on France and French family life, but some items relate to the wider francophone community such as Québec and Sénégal The illustrations include a varied selection of recent photos of life in France, mainly featuring young people.

Students are encouraged to look up background information on the Internet and also gradually build up direct contacts with French-speaking individuals or school classes.

Assessment

Assessment is an integral part of **Encore Tricolore 2 nouvelle édition** and is of two types:

1 Épreuves (informal assessment)

These informal tests are on copymasters and appear after each of the eight units. The teacher's notes, solutions and mark allocations appear at the end of each unit in Section 3 of this book.

The skills tested are listening, speaking, reading and writing combined with grammar, with between two and four tasks per skill, at different levels (starting with easy tasks, but with a built-in incline of difficulty).

Students will find them useful to check their own progress and pinpoint areas that need further revision before they carry out the more formal assessment (*Contrôle*).

The *Épreuves* relate specifically to the unit just completed. The listening material relating to these informal tests is at the end of each unit.

These tests can be used for continuous assessment or more informally in class, for homework or for a cover lesson as extra practice and consolidation.

2 Contrôle (formal assessment)

Encore Tricolore 2 nouvelle édition includes one formal assessment test (*Contrôle*). The students' sheets can be found in one section at the end of the Copymasters, the mark scheme is in the Teacher's Book and the recordings for the listening assessment are on CD 4.

This *Contrôle* includes tasks in all four language skills covering *Unités 1–7*. Extra material from the *Unité 8*

Épreuve could be added if this unit has been taught, or items tesing *Unités 6–7* could be omitted if schools find this fits in better with their examination timing.

The *Contrôle* has been designed to provide:

- a means of checking how much of the language and structures taught in preceding units has been assimilated by students
- evidence to help determine the National Curriculum Levels attained by students in each of the four language skills (Attainment Targets)
- a way of recording progress made by students – a Record sheet for students (CM 146) is provided for this purpose
- a pointer towards lack of progress in any language skill (enabling the teacher to take the necessary steps for support)
- an introduction, at a basic level, to the type of target-language testing used in external exams, giving students a head start in developing the examination techniques they are going to need at a later date.

The *Contrôle* provides a series of tasks at various levels, with an incline of difficulty within each paper. Levels covered are 2–6.

The mark schemes for the *Contrôle* (TB 200–206) provide the teacher with:

- instructions for administering the tasks, where necessary
- solutions for all tasks that are not open-ended
- a points system, adding up to 100 points for each test, for easy conversion to percentages
- information for converting the points scored to National Curriculum levels
- transcripts for the recorded material.

The mark scheme, and the tasks themselves, are closely linked to the approach set out by the QCA Exemplification Materials and Optional Tests and Tasks for Key Stage 3.

The following points should be borne in mind in relation to the various sets of papers:

Listening
- The papers for listening are designed to be expendable.
- Each item is recorded twice, without any sound effects or interruptions and is clearly spoken by a native French speaker. It must be remembered that playing the material a third time, except where specified, could affect a student's performance and cause an artificially high score to be obtained.

Speaking
- These sheets are designed to be re-used and there is no need for students to write on them.
- The teacher is best placed to decide when to give out the tasks prior to the assessment and whether to allow students to record their own work (see individual mark schemes for more detailed information).

Reading
- As with the listening, these papers are designed to be expendable.
- The use of dictionaries should not be permitted.

Writing
- These sheets are designed to be re-used.
- The use of dictionaries should not be permitted.
- Because many of these tasks are open-ended, the marking is quite complicated, but full details are provided in the individual mark schemes.

Finally, it is important to remember that the assessment tasks of the *Contrôle* should not be used in isolation to determine the National Curriculum levels attained by students. They are designed to supplement rather than replace knowledge accumulated by the teacher from everyday assessment of student performance as they work through the various activities.

Using Information and Communication Technology (ICT)

1 Introduction

ICT has been fully integrated into **Encore Tricolore 2**.

Each unit contain specific suggestions for incorporating ICT into the learning process. Some of the activities suggested are ones in which ICT is used as a tool to support the learning of French. Examples include:

- text manipulation activities such as gap-filling
- use of web exercises to practise vocabulary
- use of word processing in phrase and vocabulary building.

There are genuinely communicative activities based on the use of ICT as a communications medium, for example:

- World Wide Web activities in which students can learn about aspects of life and culture in French-speaking countries from authentic materials
- communicating with other learners and native speakers via e-mail
- live interaction with a correspondent via a video conference link.

Thus, **Encore Tricolore 2** will enable ICT to add value to the process of learning French. Whenever ICT is advocated, care has been taken to design activities which genuinely add something to the learning process that could not be achieved without the technology – it's not just ICT for the sake of it!

2 ICT and the National Curriculum

The integrated approach to ICT is fully in line with the National Curriculum for Modern Foreign Languages in England and Wales and with similar requirements elsewhere. Through this integrated approach students will benefit to the full from frequent opportunities to use technology, as prescribed by the National Curriculum. The table below sets out some of the key skills, as listed in the Programme of Study, that can be developed through using ICT:

Acquiring knowledge of language • the grammar of the target language and how to apply it	• using CD-ROMs to study language patterns • using text manipulation to encourage thinking about language patterns
Developing language skills • listening skills • adapt language for use in different contexts • skimming and scanning written texts for information	• using multi-media software for listening practice • using word processing to redraft and improve writing and to adapt language for different contexts • reading web pages on the Internet
Developing language-learning skills • how to use dictionaries and other reference materials appropriately and effectively	• using electronic dictionaries and glossaries and electronic encyclopaedia
Developing cultural awareness • working with authentic materials in the target language, including some from ICT-based sources • communicating with native speakers [in person or by correspondence]	• sending and receiving e-mail • reading web pages on the Internet, reading e-mails
Learning activities • using language for real purposes	• sending and receiving e-mail

There is also a requirement in all subjects to develop ICT skills. In the next table, these requirements are listed in column one with suggested MFL activities in column two:

\multicolumn{3}{l	}{*Pupils should be given opportunities to apply and develop their ICT capability through the use of ICT tools to support their learning in all subjects. Pupils should be given opportunities to support their work by being taught to:*}
a	find things out from a variety of sources, selecting and synthesising the information to meet their needs and developing an ability to question its accuracy, bias and plausibility	• read web pages on the Internet • use electronic dictionaries and glossaries and electronic encyclopaedia
b	develop their ideas using ICT tools to amend and refine their work and enhance its quality and accuracy	• use word processing including spell-checking and thesaurus
c	exchange and share information, both directly and through electronic media	• send and receive e-mail • take part in video conferences
d	review, modify and evaluate their work, reflecting critically on its quality, as it progresses.	• build and develop a self-description file • build vocabulary and/or grammar reference files

3 Key ICT uses

E-mail
E-mail provides the opportunity to communicate with native speakers. There are many tasks that can be used with e-mail. For beginners, the basic tasks that could be covered include:

- reading an e-mail in French from a correspondent in the link school
- replying to an e-mail
- writing an e-mail message and sending it to a correspondent
- sending an e-mail greetings card (advice on this is given in the notes on *Unité 6*).

With growing confidence, e-mail can be used with attachments. This allows a file to be sent along with an e-mail. The file might be a database file, a word file, a digital photograph or any other file which is attached to the e-mail and sent with it. Students could then exchange all sorts of electronic resources with French-speaking students around the world. The classroom survey in electronic form gains in purpose if it is to be sent to a partner and if the partner will also be sending one from France or Belgium or wherever.

Databases and spreadsheets
These programs can be used for simple activities such as:

- collating information about pets, members of the class or other topics which can then be displayed in graphs, updated and edited; the material can also be used as a basis for oral work
- working with figures to add up prices or convert currencies.

Word processing
There are many uses for word processing in languages lessons including:

- developing electronic phrase books (see TB 19)
- building up a file in which students write a self-description

- creative writing – framework poems (poems made out of a list of words supplied by the teacher), captions for interesting images, simple narratives, unusual menus
- descriptive writing – postcards, letters, shopping lists, menus.

There is a range of word-processing programs. Which one is best for your students depends mainly upon what they are used to using in school. For example, if they usually use *Claris/Apple Works* for word processing, databases and spreadsheets, it makes sense to use the same program in French. Otherwise, they will have to unlearn what they already know in order to learn how to use a new program. In most schools there will be a preferred option and that is the one for you to use since your learners will be comfortable with it. That said, there are a number of questions that you may want to put to your ICT manager to check how suitable the programs are for French.

- Is it possible to input/display French characters and accents?
- Is there a spell-checking option for word processing in French?
- Is a French language version of the program available? (Although readily available in French-speaking countries these are not common in the UK and can be an expensive option, but one that ensures that menus and commands on screen are in the target language.)
- Is there a good range of clip art for pupils and teachers to incorporate into their work?
- Is there a French thesaurus option?

Using tables is an easy option with most word-processing programs and provides a wealth of possibilities in language learning. Here are three examples:

- **Verb tables**

Students can use a template to lay out verb paradigms and keep a record of all the verbs they meet on disk and print this out from time to time for ease of reference. Here is the basic template:

Tense	Perfect with avoir		
Infinitive			
j'ai		I have	
tu as		you (sing.) have	
il/elle/on a		he/she/one has	
nous avons		we have	
vous avez		you (pl./polite) have	
ils/elles ont		they have	

Here is a completed example for *jouer* in the perfect tense:

Tense	Perfect with avoir		
Infinitive	jouer	to play	
j'ai	joué	I have	played
tu as	joué	you (sing.) have	played
il/elle/on a	joué	he/she/one has	played
nous avons	joué	we have	played
vous avez	joué	you (pl./polite) have	played
ils/elles ont	joué	they have	played

For regular verbs, it is a simple matter to use FIND and REPLACE (found on the EDIT menu) to substitute the participles in French/English, e.g. travaillé/worked.

- **Electronic phrase book**

Students can create an electronic vocabulary/phrase book using tables to lay out the columns. This is best done using a word-processing package such as *Microsoft® Word* or *Word Perfect* – choose whichever program is the school's preferred option.

Set up the file by using a table with two columns of equal width. The phrase book can be organised according to the following principles:

- sections on each topic or unit (i.e. cumulatively rather than alphabetically), French to English only
- other non-topic specific vocabulary, e.g. conjunctions, prepositions etc.
- classroom vocabulary, including that for use in ICT lessons, also listed in the order that the new phrases and words are met
- a combined section made up of all the words from the first three sections. This section can be sorted into alphabetical order using the SORT function (in *Word* this is found in the Table menu). Include both French–English and English–French sections.

The electronic phrase book can be saved on the school network, depending on disk space available, but students should also take copies on their own floppy disks.

A printed copy is also very useful.

A starter phrase book could be produced by the teacher based on the first few units.

This phrase book can then be used by students when working on the computer. For example, when writing self-descriptions or e-mails, students can copy and paste phrases from the phrase book to their sentences. The phrase book can be added to when undertaking reading exercises with *Fun with Texts* or websites by copying and pasting words. Phrase book use and maintenance should be encouraged whenever students use the computers.

Periodically, teachers could check the phrase books. Later, students can use spell-checking software in French to check their own phrase books.

- **Phrase generator**

Any word processor can be used in phrase generation work. It is best to use the standard school program as the students should be familiar with this. A table is very helpful in setting up the phrase generator. On most programs there will be a simple menu command to INSERT A TABLE through which you specify the number of rows and the number and width of columns – this should be planned on paper in advance. The final table may then look like this (example from *Unité 7*):

	ami	est	assez	grand
Mon/Ma	amie			grande
	sœur			petit
	frère	n'est pas	très	petite
	mère			mince
	père			de taille moyenne

The students can use copy and paste to create the phrases. Some may have good ICT skills and can use the mouse to drag and drop.

Spell checking is available for most word-processing packages, although until recently it was usually offered as an expensive option. Since *Microsoft® Office 2000* now includes foreign language spell checking, many schools will be able to have access to this facility. However, you will need to ensure that it is installed and so may need to check with the ICT co-ordinator. Once installed, you can set the language to French for a given document and then use spell checking normally. Along with the spell check there will also be other tools such as grammar checking (dubious value) and thesaurus – the latter is an excellent tool for students to extend their vocabulary, although perhaps more useful with more advanced students.

Word processing provides a wide range of fonts, some of which enhance learning, for example the French handwriting fonts PlumbaL and CrayonL.

These can be used in many different ways, e.g. see the activity on menus in Unité 5. It is a simple matter to install these fonts on a PC, although you will need the assistance of the ICT co-ordinator to install them on the network. If you are using your home computer or a departmental one you can download the fonts from the following website: http://home.worldnet.fr/~Elogedu/

Once downloaded, the fonts must be installed on your computer. They will then be available in all programs that use fonts.

Text manipulation

Good language practice can be provided with text manipulation software, e.g. *Fun with Texts*. Students can work on ready-made texts which are commercially available or teachers can develop texts themselves, thereby ensuring that the level and the language are relevant to the class. Text manipulation can help develop grammatical awareness, comprehension and spelling. If the text used is a model text, e.g. a letter, work on it gives excellent practice prior to proceeding to writing an original or personalised version of the model.

The best known and most widely available program is *Fun With Texts*, but there are other such programs commercially available. There are also free programs that can be downloaded from the Internet and some schools have developed their own software. Most programs allow the teacher to set up a text by typing it in. There are then a number of activities that students can do with that text such as a cloze exercise where students have to fill in the missing word or a line re-ordering where students have to put the jumbled lines of the text back into the right sequence. All of these tasks are variations of pencil and paper exercises but they do have certain added elements such as instant feedback on whether something is right or wrong, a scoring facility and a help facility. The software is easy to use and can be adapted to almost any content, so you could develop text manipulation exercises for all units. Some ready-made texts have been devised and can be purchased from software suppliers or downloaded from the Internet. Some websites offer on-line learning materials developed by languages teachers. Many of these have been developed using the *Hot Potatoes* software which is available free of charge from the University of Victoria, Canada: http://web.uvic.ca/hrd/halfbaked.

You can download the program from their website and then develop your own activities or you can direct your pupils to sites made by other languages teachers – the *Hot Potatoes* site has a list of these. Some pilot *Hot Potatoes* exercises linked to the units of **Encore Tricolore 2** can be accessed via this website:
http://www.atkinsonconsulting.co.uk.

Word processing software can also be used to develop text manipulation activities such as sentence re-ordering or cloze. The word processor will not correct the students' work automatically but may be preferable in that it allows for more open-ended or creative activities such as the phrase-generation activity which is described earlier in these notes.

There are various software packages that allow you to create simple interactive matching exercises. Any of the *Trouve les paires* exercises could be used as language content. Use software such as *Hot Potatoes (JMatch)* or *The Authoring Suite (Matchmaster)* from Wida Software.

Desktop publishing

Many schools have publishing software that allows the user to lay out text and images. If your students have been taught how to use this software in their ICT lessons they will be able to make things in French such as:

- a tourist brochure
- an invitation to a party
- posters
- menus
- signs

If you have installed the French handwriting fonts noted above, you can achieve an authentic French look.

CD-ROMs and multi-media

CD-ROMs can be very useful at the practice stage to enable students to work intensively at their own pace and level. Suitable practice is provided by a variety of language learning programs. These programs offer a variety of exercises such as matching, multiple choice, true or false and games which provide simple vocabulary practice of the basic topics.

The CD-ROM is really just a mass storage device. It is particularly useful for multi-media software which involves vast amounts of data. This type of software is very useful in modern languages because it makes it possible to include sound in the program as well as images, animation and video.

Each CD-ROM program will have its own strengths and they often cater to a very specific purpose, e.g. *The French Grammar Studio*. There are descriptions of CD-ROMs on Camsoft's website as well as ordering information: http://www.camsoftpartners.co.uk.

CD-ROMs for reference

There are a number of CD-ROMs available that can provide useful resources for pupils to look up information. The advantage of such programs is that the information obtained is in a format that allows the student to re-use it within their own work – a benefit but also a potential liability!

Some programs to consider:
- *Microsoft® Encarta* (French) – an encyclopaedia on a CD-ROM;
- electronic dictionaries on CD-ROM, bilingual or monolingual;
- CD-ROMs on towns and regions – usually available from tourist offices in France;
- CD-ROMs on specific topics – the human body, world atlas, sports.

Authentic CD-ROMs can be purchased in France or via the Internet. Many titles aimed at children and young people could be of use. Clip art could also be useful and can be bought on CD-ROM.

Working with graphics and images

Images can be used in many different ways, both by students and teachers. Images may be ready made in the form of clip art or symbol fonts or can be drawn on the computer using a paint package or the built-in drawing facilities of word processing or desktop publishing. The Internet is an excellent source of images – for famous people, for objects and for places in France and other French-speaking countries.

Ideas for students to use images include:
- adding images to students' written work;
- making a poster for classroom display;
- making an electronic poster for a simple oral presentation using data projector or electronic whiteboard.

Ideas for teaching with images include:
- flashcards, e.g. Simpsons, Mr Men, tourist attractions;
- overhead transparencies – symbol fonts such as Wingdings give useful images which can help to emphasise meaning in role-plays, e.g.

[symbol font examples]

- using fonts: there are millions of fonts available, many as freeware which can be found and downloaded on the Internet – try typing *picture fonts* into a search engine. In this way, it is possible to find fonts on animals and weather. Programs such as *Corel Draw* have many fonts included, e.g. furniture and building;
- worksheets with images to provide guidance and hints on what students are expected to write or say;
- activities where students add labels to pictures and vice-versa;
- writing a simple phrase or sentence to describe an image;
- making sets of cards for word games.

Combining text and images on screen is a very useful activity in language learning. Desktop publishing programs, e.g. *Microsoft® Publisher* are specifically designed for combining text and images. Presentation programs such as *Microsoft® PowerPoint* can also be used very effectively for combining text and graphics with some facility for animation. Word processing is another possibility but positioning text and graphics is quite tricky so the easy way around this is to use a table as in the suggested activity on holidays in *Unité 2* (TB 53). Whichever approach you adopt, there are endless possible activities for students to do, e.g.

- use speech bubbles with characters to make a comic strip;
- use captions with pictures to create a picture story;
- write a poem with an illustration.

Presentation
The computer makes a very powerful presentation tool that can be used to present new vocabulary, grammar points, dialogues and simple picture stories. It can also be used by students to support simple oral presentations.

The basic equipment needed for this includes a computer (laptop or desktop machine) and a projection device: the computer can be linked to a data projector if the school has one. It is also possible to connect a computer to an overhead projector, but this requires additional hardware. Alternatively, computers can be connected up to television sets – this requires a large screen television and a television adaptor.

Finally, some classrooms are being equipped with electronic whiteboards that produce a large screen display and are also interactive.

Some schools have networks that allow all screens to display what is on one of the work stations – this is an excellent facility for 'show and tell' at the end of an ICT session. Students could present posters, survey charts, web search findings etc. and give an oral commentary in the target language.

Any software can be used to give presentations or demonstrations but there is also specialist presentation software such as *Microsoft® PowerPoint* which allows you to develop very effective slide shows.

Internet/World Wide Web
If students have access to the World Wide Web via the Internet they may like to consult relevant web pages to support their learning about aspects of French life and culture. They will not understand all of the information given but will be able to work out the gist of sections particularly where they are interested in the topic and where lively presentation and good use of graphics aid comprehension and boost motivation.

There are many possible ways to use the Internet:
- to look for information;
- to read for pleasure;
- to do practice activities available via the Internet;
- to produce a web page for the class;
- to check the meaning or common usage of words and phrases;
- to find sites which support the production of teaching materials, e.g. wordsearches, crosswords (one example is http://puzzlemaker.school.discovery.com/).

Video conferencing
If video conferencing facilities are available in schools it is possible for students to watch and listen to a video correspondent via a video conferencing link and to speak themselves to the correspondent. This can be a demanding activity as it calls for maturity. For beginners, it may be best if they speak in their mother tongue. The main learning benefit will come from listening to their correspondents speaking French to them. This can be highly motivating but calls for extensive preparation by the teachers in each country.

Writing
The computer is a very useful tool for writing and as pupils develop their language capacity they will be able to benefit from more written work. Some pupils may want to do much of their writing on computer and this should be encouraged, where access is possible, since it will enable them to do better work. In fact, the computer can enhance writing considerably. It might be possible to use writing frames to do this – these are templates that work with word processing. One commercially available package for writing frames that could be used is *French Frames for Writing – Creative and Imaginative Writing (Age 11–14)* by Julie Adams (Publisher: Folens ISBN 1841638773).

It should be noted that there is much more benefit in using a computer to draft and redraft work than there is in writing by hand and then transcribing to computer, which is an activity that is often seen by Ofsted inspectors and one which they are very critical of.

4 Points to note

Guidance on hardware
If you are able to specify hardware for use by students learning French, here are some points to consider:
- Is there a fast CD-ROM drive to allow rapid access to sound and pictures?
- Is there a DVD-ROM drive to allow access to new software sold in that medium?
- What monitor size is available? (A large 17" screen is good for pair work.)

- Computer sound: is there a playback and record facility?
- Are there headphones with a splitter to allow two sets of headphones to be used with one computer?
- Is there an easy-to-use microphone?
- Video conferencing: is there a record facility so that pupils can see a replay of the exchange? (Note that this facility is often claimed but can be very hard to get to work!)
- Network: can the network run a CD-ROM?
- Data projector: does the school have a portable data projector that you can use in your own classroom for wide screen display of a computer screen? (It could be useful for presentations and demonstrations by teacher and students.)
- Electronic whiteboard: this also provides a large screen for class viewing, but with the added advantage that you can operate the computer from the screen with a pointer that works like a mouse.
- A lower cost alternative to projectors and whiteboards is a large-screen TV connected via an adaptor to the computer – this will be useful if space is limited and the classroom already has a large-screen TV.

Copyright issues

The issue of copyright in dealing with electronic materials should be regarded in the same way as for any other published materials. However, there are some particular points that should be kept in mind:

- legally obtained clip-art images can be used for making teaching and learning materials
- web pages are often copyright free but it is important to consider the source of the web page – does the web page developer own the copyright for the material on the page? Some images on the Web may be copyrighted but many are not. However, the images may have been placed on the Web without the copyright holder's permission. In the circumstances, it is hard to give clear advice. For those who wish to make absolutely certain of this issue, there is usually a contact e-mail address on web pages which could be used to seek permission. Having said all of this, much on the Web is freely copiable and this is often stated. It will sometimes be a question of judgement. If the image is to be used solely in your own school for educational purposes then it is unlikely to infringe copyright. This area is a difficult one and teachers must follow their own judgement or be advised by head teachers or ICT managers.

Finding sites on the Internet

There are many search engines on the Internet so it is best to choose one that students are familiar with. There are French versions of the common ones such as Yahoo (www.yahoo.fr) and Altavista (www.altavista.fr). One of the fastest search engines is Google (www.google.com) and this has an extra advantage in that it has language options that allow it to work entirely in French.

5 Classroom organisation

There are three main ways in which ICT can be an integral part of your French lessons:

1 Access to a computer room, with about 15 computers, i.e. roughly one computer between two pupils

The computers will probably be linked to the school network and possibly also to the Internet. It is often useful to ask students to work together in pairs and some of the best learning occurs as a result of collaboration and discussion. Sometimes you will want your students to work individually, e.g. when writing a self-description. In that case, it may be possible for half the class to work on computer and the other half to do related work.

2 A small number of computers available in the modern languages area which may or may not be linked to the school network/Internet

This facility is useful to provide:

- differentiated work for individuals and small groups, e.g. vocabulary building using a CD-ROM for students who have missed work or fallen behind
- an ICT activity as part of a carousel of other activities that students work through in groups
- part of a jigsaw of activities in which students collect information from different sources (print, listening, ICT) and then collate this in groups

It is very useful to have someone to provide support for students if they are using the computers outside the teaching room. This could be provided by a sixth former, a Foreign Language Assistant (FLA) or a student teacher. It is important that students have had an introduction to the program that they are to use and some hands-on experience. Alternatively, distribute computer literate students across the groups so that there is always at least one person in each group who can provide help if anyone gets stuck.

3 A single computer in the ML classroom, usually not linked to network or Internet

This can be very useful if there is some facility for projection or large screen display. The teacher can use the computer for presentations or demonstrations. Students can use the computer to support them in giving a simple oral presentation. Even with one computer, it is possible for students to work in pairs on an activity at the computer and for each pair to have completed the activity over the course of two or three lessons.

6 How to enter accents

Students will need to know how to enter accents in the various programs that they use – word processing, e-mail, text manipulation, desktop publishing, presentation, web pages etc. Some of these programs have a simple method for entering accents, e.g. *Microsoft® Word*. This is fine if that is the only program used but the method will not work for other programs. The way around this is to make sure that students understand the ALT code method as well as any program-specific shortcuts. This is because the ALT code method works on most programs. The Toolbar method, described below, is also effective if your school computers are equipped with it. Ultimately, students will need to know a range of methods since they are likely to use different computers at school, at home and in libraries.

1 The 'ALT Key' Method

On most computers found in UK schools – PC, Macintosh and Acorn – foreign characters can be generated in any application by combining the ALT key with other keystrokes, e.g.

- on the Mac, ALT + e then e generates é.
- on the PC, ALT + 130 or ALT + 0233 generate é.

The ALT codes for the PC for French are shown in the table (on page 24) which has been designed to be photocopied for pupils to refer to when using the computers.

2 The 'Toolbar' Method
Add letters by clicking the required character on the toolbar with the mouse. One toolbar program is Patrick Smears' *FrKeys* for the PC. Acorn computers come with *!Chars*, which performs a similar function.

3 Microsoft® Word Method
In *Microsoft® Word*, pressing CTRL+ apostrophe then e generates é. Grave accents can be generated by pressing CTRL and the key to the left of the number 1, then release both keys and type the vowel to be accented. Circumflex accents are generated by pressing CTRL + shift 6, then release all three keys and type in the vowel. The cedilla is generated by pressing CTRL + comma and then release both keys before typing c. A complete list of this method is available under the Help section (international characters) – this list might be printed out for students if this method is favoured. However, this method only works with *Microsoft® Word*.

7 Useful websites for teachers and students

French search engines (*Des moteurs de recherche*)
   http://fr.altavista.com
   www.google.com/intl/fr/
   www.lycos.fr
   www.voila.fr
   www.yahoo.fr

Many of the French search engines have useful junior sections, e.g.
   http://fr.dir.yahoo.com/Societe/Groupes_et_communautes/Enfants/
   http://espace.junior.voila.fr/
   www.lycos.fr/dir/Loisirs/Jeux_et_concours/Pour_enfants/

General information about France
French government information, statistics etc.
   www.diplomatie.gouv.fr/
The following site gives the words of many songs plus biographical details of famous singers.
   www.paroles.net/

French press
- **National newspapers**

Le monde
   www.lemonde.fr
Libération
   www.liberation.fr
Le Figaro
   www.lefigaro.fr

- **Regional newspapers**

Ouest-France
   www.france-ouest.tm.fr
Les dernières nouvelles d'Alsace
   www.dna.fr/dna/
Le progrès
   www.leprogres.fr/
La voix du nord
   www.lavoixdunord.fr/
Sud-ouest
   www.sudouest.com/
La dépêche
   www.afp.com/depeche/accueildm.html
Le Parisien
   www.manchette.com/parisien/

- **Magazines and weeklies**

Télérama
   www.telerama.fr

L'équipe
   www.madmedia.fr/manchette-sports/index1.html
Paris Match
   www.parismatch.com
Le Point
   www.lepoint.fr
Le Nouvel Observateur
   http://quotidien.nouvelobs.com/

French TV and radio
TF1   www.tf1.fr
France 2   www.france2.fr/
France 3   www.france3.fr/
Canal plus www.canalplus.fr/
La cinquième www.lacinquieme.fr/
Arte   www.arte.fr/
Ina   www.ina.fr/
M6   www.m6.fr/
TV5   www.tv5.org
Radio France (France Inter, France Culture etc.)
              www.radio-france.fr
RTL   www.rtl.fr
Europe 1   www.europe1.fr

General interest sites for children
Premiers pas sur Internet – general interest site, with discussions and contributions from children from French-speaking countries.
   www.momes.net
   www.apreslecole.fr

Okapi (French teenage magazine)
   www.okapi.bayardpresse.fr

General information about France
   www.zipzapfrance.com/index2.html

Language teaching
Association for Language Learning (ALL)
   www.languagelearn.co.uk
Centre for Information on Language Teaching (CILT)
   www.cilt.org.uk
Centre International d'Études Pédagogiques, Sèvres, France
   www.ciep.fr
Lingu@net (This site provides useful links to other websites for languages.)
   www.linguanet.org.uk

Exchanges
Central Bureau for International Education and Training
   www.centralbureau.org.uk
   www.wotw.org.uk

ICT organisations
British Education Communications and Technology Agency (BECTA)
   www.becta.org.uk
Modern Foreign Languages and Information Technology Project (MFLIT)
   www.vtc.ngfl.gov.uk/resource/cits/mfl
The Microelectronics in Education Unit in Wales (MEU)
   www.meucymru.co.uk
Scottish Council for Educational Technology (SCET)
   www.scet.com

Education in England
Department for Education and Employment
   www.dfee.gov.uk
National Curriculum
   www.nc.uk.net
Qualifications and Curriculum Authority (QCA)
   www.qca.org.uk

Section 1 Introduction to the course

23

Education in Wales
Currciulum and Assessment Authority for Wales
www.accac.org.uk

Education in Scotland
Scottish Qualifications Authority
www.sqa.org.uk

Scottish virtual teacher's centre
www.svtc.org.uk

Learning and Teaching Scotland
www.ltscotland.com

Education in Northern Ireland
Northern Ireland Council for the Curriculum, Examinations and Assessment
www.ccea.org.uk

Virtual greetings cards
There is a category of virtual greeting card sites on Yahoo:
www.yahoo.fr/Commerce_et_economie/Societes/Cadeaux/Cartes_de_voeux/

Virtual postcards can be sent to penfriends or even to someone else in the school. Websites for virtual postcards can be found with a simple search on Yahoo France. Just type *cartes virtuelles* in the search box and click on *Recherche*.

Other websites are listed at the beginning of each unit in Section 3.

8 CALL software (Computer-Aided Language Learning)

Many ICT materials are available for helping language learners, some as CD-ROMs, some as disks, others in both formats. Sometimes site licences are included in the price and sometimes they are extra. It is important to check that the desired item is available in a form that is compatible with the system in your school.

Fun with Texts
This is the most well known of the text manipulation packages. It can be obtained from:

Camsoft Ltd., 10 Wheatfield Close, Maidenhead, Berkshire, SL6 3PS (Tel: 01608 825206)

You can also find out more about *Fun with Texts* and other Camsoft materials at their website:

http://www.camsoftpartners.co.uk

There are many more packages available offering cloze and text manipulation exercises, e.g. *Gapkit* (also from Camsoft, this package allows cloze with multi-media).

Over 200 cloze packages on the Web are listed on the following site along with software reviews and a list of sites with downloadable demos:

http://www.linguasy.com

CD-ROMs
Each CD-ROM program will have its own strengths and they often cater to a very specific purpose. There are a number of programs that are specifically designed for beginners and which offer a good range of listening and reading practice activities in the topics of **Encore Tricolore 2**. Some of the more common ones are:

All in one Language Fun

Triple Play Plus French

The BBC's *French Experience* double CD

CD-ROM reviews can be found at the BECTA website.
http://www.becta.org.uk/information/cd-roms/index.html

On-line materials
Some websites offer on-line learning materials developed by languages teachers. Many of these have been developed using the *Hot Potatoes* software which is available free of charge from the University of Victoria, Canada:

http://web.uvic.ca/hrd/halfbaked

You can download the program from their website and then develop your own activities or you can direct your pupils to sites made by other languages teachers – the *Hot Potatoes* site has a list of these.

Some pilot *Hot Potatoes* exercises linked to the topics of **Encore Tricolore 2** can be accessed via this website:

www.atkinsonconsulting.co.uk

9 Books relating to ICT

Atkinson, T (1992): *Hands off – it's my go!* London, CILT/NCET

Atkinson, T (1998): *WWW: The Internet*, London, CILT (InfoTech 3)

Buckland, D (2000): *Putting achievement first. Managing and leading ICT in the MFL department*, London, CILT (InfoTech 5)

Hewer, S (1997): *Text manipulation*, London, CILT (InfoTech 2)

NCET (1997): *Accent on IT – practical training and support for KS3*, Coventry, NCET (Video pack).

Slater, P & Varney-Burch, S: *Multimedia in language learning*, London, CILT (InfoTech 6)

Townsend, K (1997): *E-mail*, London, CILT (InfoTech 1)

How to type French accents using ALT codes

- make sure the NUMBER LOCK light is on – if not, press NUM LOCK key on the number pad to switch it on
- press and keep held down the ALT key
- type in using the number pad the ALT code for the relevant accented letter – either code number should work

133 à (0224)	140 î (0238)	182 Â (0194)	216 Ï (0207)
131 â (0226)	139 ï (0239)	128 Ç (0199)	Œ (0140)
135 ç (0231)	œ (0156)	212 È (0200)	226 Ô (0212)
130 é (0233)	147 ô (0244)	144 É (0201)	235 Ù (0217)
138 è (0232)	151 ù (0249)	210 Ê (0202)	234 Û (0219)
136 ê (0234)	150 û (0251)	211 Ë (0203)	174 « (0171)
137 ë (0235)	183 À (0192)	215 Î (0206)	175 » (0187)

SECTION 2

Games

Encore Tricolore 2
nouvelle édition

Many of the games described here are applicable for a wide range of language practice. A game which is particularly appropriate for a specific area is mentioned in the relevant unit notes.

In many games the teacher is the caller at the beginning, but students can soon be encouraged to take over this role.

1 Number games

- **Chef d'orchestre**

For this the class is divided into two teams (*en avant* and *en arrière*). The 'conductor' says any number and points to one of the teams who must call out the next or the previous number depending on which team is indicated.

- **Comptez comme ça!**

The caller starts by saying *Comptez comme ça!* and begins to count in a particular way, either forwards or backwards or alternate numbers or later in multiples of 2, 3 etc. Students join in as soon as they can with the right sequence and are out if they count a wrong number. The caller changes the sequence at intervals by saying *Maintenant, comptez comme ça!* and beginning again.

A group version of this can be played in which only the group the caller points at counts in the sequence which s/he begins.

- **Dice games**

Ordinary dice can be used for number games or special ones made using higher numbers or with words on, such as the six persons of the verb paradigm etc.

The simplest form of dice games is for a player to throw the dice, marked with a selection of numbers, and then say aloud the number or word that they throw. One group can throw for another and students unable to say the right words are out.

- **Loto (Bingo)**

Students can make a class set of Bingo cards, as illustrated below, and play with buttons as counters. Similarly, they can play a simpler version by just writing any four numbers on a scrap of paper and crossing them off as they are said by the caller. This game is useful when the numbers are learnt as words, as the winner must show her/his paper to the teacher and will be eliminated if the words are incorrectly spelt.

Below is a series of 36 cards, all bearing a different group of numbers, which is included for teachers' convenience, so that each child can be given a different group to make. Further cards including numbers 20–40 and 40–60 could be prepared.

This type of Bingo is also an excellent standby for practice of almost any set of vocabulary, days of the week, months, colours, parts of a verb etc. For example, when learning the date, students write four days or months in words on a piece of paper and cross them off as the caller says them, saying *Loto!* when all four have been said.

- **Le dix magique**

This is a pontoon-type game. The French for pontoon is *vingt et un*, but this version uses a total of ten so is called *Le dix magique*.

Students make a simple set of cards with numbers 1–10. They place the cards upside down and turn them over one at a time, saying the number, until they get exactly 10. If they get 11 or more they are 'bust' (*fichu!*) and they must start again. The best of five turns is the winner.

2 General vocabulary games

These can be used for practising numbers and areas of vocabulary, e.g. food, pets etc.

- **Effacez!**

Numbers, pictures or words are written on the board in random order. When the caller names an item on the board, a student must rush out and rub the item off.

This can be played by the teacher just pointing at the next student, who has five seconds only to locate and erase the right item. It can also be played in groups or in teams. In the latter case it is advisable to write two sets of items, one set on each half of the board, and to provide two board rubbers. If the teacher wants the items left on for further practice they could be ringed in coloured chalk or pen instead of being rubbed off.

This is an excellent game for matching the written word to vocabulary previously met only aurally.

- **Les deux échelles (a dice game)**

Two or more six-rung ladders can be drawn on the board with a number (or word, part of verb etc.) on each rung. Each team or group throws the dice and reads out the number or word and, if it is the next on the ladder, it is crossed off and the team moves up to the next rung. No number or word must be crossed off until that rung is reached and the first team to reach the top of the ladder wins.

See also **Dice games** and **Loto** (TB 25).

- **Qu'est-ce qu'il y a dans la boîte?**

This game can be played with any selection of objects linked with a recent vocabulary topic, e.g. classroom objects, pictures of animals, clothes etc.

First show the class the things to be used and practise the vocabulary. The objects are then taken out of sight and placed one at a time in a box for the class to guess which one is there each time.

- **Vrai ou faux? (True and false chairs)**

This is a useful game for mixed or lower ability classes as it does not involve all the class in speaking or writing. Each team has two chairs labelled *vrai* and *faux*. The teacher (or a student) makes any statement and a member of each team comes out and sits on the true chair if s/he thinks the statement is true and on the false one if not. Sitting on the right chair wins a point for that team. (If the teams are too level, points can be given for the first child to sit on the right chair each time.)

1	9	1	12	3	10	8	15	7	12	5	11	5	12	7	10	14	19
11	16	10	17	12	19	16	17	18	19	14	16	14	17	19	20	16	17

16	14	6	15	3	11	6	12	2	11	4	12	4	10	4	13	8	11
6	17	17	18	13	20	17	18	13	16	14	19	15	17	15	20	18	19

8	10	2	10	5	14	2	8	9	11	3	12	3	9	2	9	9	12
14	15	12	15	16	19	17	19	19	20	14	15	6	18	11	20	17	18

7	16	9	14	5	13	9	13	7	9	1	7	6	12	4	11	1	8
17	18	15	16	15	18	18	19	13	16	18	20	13	15	13	18	10	15

- **Touché-coulé (Battleships)**

This well-known game (best played in pairs) can be adapted to practise various bits of language. In its simplest form students are given the area of vocabulary to be practised, e.g. a verb paradigm, numbers, days of the week etc. or a set of flashcards is put up as a reminder. Each person writes down on paper any three of the alternatives. Each player in turn guesses one item that the other person has written and if guessed correctly, the player must cross it out. The first one to eliminate their partner's items has won.

More complicated versions, nearer to the original, involve writing the items in a particular place on squared paper or a plan so that one player says to their opponent, e.g. *A3, tu as …!*)

- **Je pense à quelque chose**

The basic guessing game, in which someone thinks of a word (within a given range) and the others have to guess it by asking *C'est un/une …?*

- **Jeu de mémoire (Kim's game)**

Everyone looks at a set of objects, words or information for a set time (say, 2 minutes). Then one or more of these is removed or the whole lot are covered up, and the class has to remember as many objects, facts or words as possible.

3 Flashcard games

For guessing games involving flashcards the class should always be shown all the cards to be used first and the French for these should be practised or checked before the game begins.

- **Qu'est-ce que c'est? (Guess the back of the flashcard)**

It is better to limit the cards to a single topic, so that there are not too many to choose from.

The pile of flashcards is shuffled and the caller holds up a card with the picture facing her/him and says *Qu'est-ce que c'est?* Other students ask *C'est un/une (+ noun)?* and the person who guesses correctly comes out and acts as caller.

- **Ce n'est pas … (Guess what the card isn't)**

This is played with the whole class, as a group game or in pairs. One player holds up a card, face away, and the other person(s) guess what it is not, e.g.

– *Ce n'est pas un chien.*
– *Vrai.*
– *Ce n'est pas une souris.*
– *Vrai.*
– *Ce n'est pas un lapin.*
– *Faux – c'est un lapin.*

This is a good morale booster as the answer is more often right than wrong!

- **Des questions**

The teacher picks up one of a group of flashcards and asks a question about it. S/he gives the card to the student who answers correctly. When all the cards are given out, the students with them come to the front and ask a question about their card to someone else in the class who then receives the card if s/he answers correctly. This goes on until all the class have had a turn.

- **Où vas-tu?**

To practise the verb *aller*, all the flashcards referring to places should be put up around the room. The teacher or a student tells someone, e.g. *Va à la gare!* The student gets up and goes to the relevant place and on the way is asked *Où vas-tu?* If s/he answers correctly s/he continues and the teacher asks someone else *Où va-t-il/elle?* If s/he replies incorrectly s/he sits down and someone else is told to go somewhere. If s/he replies correctly and arrives at the destination s/he has a point.

- **Morpion (Flashcards noughts and crosses)**

This game can be played with a variety of vocabulary. The example given practises places in a town.

Stick nine 'places in a town' flashcards to the board, face outwards if you want the activity to be easy and face inwards if you want it to be difficult (in which case you will have to memorize the positions of the cards yourself!). Students play this in two teams, with each team asking the way to a place (*pour aller au …*) in turn. The card representing the place they asked the way to is then removed and replaced with X or 0. The object of the game is to get three in a row.

- **Trois questions (Mind reading)**

This is good for practising verbs + nouns.

Tell students that you are going to read their minds. Put up a number of flashcards and tell a student to think hard about one of them (get the thinker to tell her/his neighbour or write down which s/he has chosen, as a safeguard). Then ask three questions and if you have read her/his mind by then you get a point, if not the class gets a point.

Examples:
1 être (+ room)
 Teacher: *Tu es dans la salle à manger?*
 Student: *Non, je ne suis pas dans la salle à manger.*
 Teacher: *Tu es dans le salon?*
 Student: *Non, je ne suis pas dans le salon.*
 Teacher: *Tu es dans la cuisine?*
 Student: *Oui, je suis dans la cuisine.*
 or *Non, je ne suis pas dans la cuisine.*
 or *Non, je suis (+ correct place)*

2 avoir (+ pets)
 Teacher: *Tu as un lapin.*
 Student: *Oui, j'ai un lapin.*
 or *Non, je n'ai pas de lapin* etc.

3 aller (+ place)
 Teacher: *Tu vas à l'église.*
 Student: *Oui, je vais à l'église.*
 or *Non, je ne vais pas à l'église* etc.

This game can be adapted for use with a wide range of structures and can be played teacher v class, group v group, team v team, girls v boys etc.

4 Mini-flashcard games

The flashcard games which follow can be played in pairs or small groups, with the sets of mini-flashcards made from the worksheets.

- **Pelmanism (group or pair game)**

Use double sets of word cards, mini-flashcards or picture cards + matching word cards. In turn, students turn over a pair of cards to see if they match. They say the word on or represented by the cards, then turn them face downwards again in the same place – unless they form a pair, in which case they pick them up and keep them.

- **Le jeu des sept familles (Happy Families or Fish!)**

Using four sets of mini flashcards for each group, or a set of home-made cards, this game can be played as normal, using *As-tu…?/Oui, j'ai/Non, je n'ai pas …*

- **Loto de vocabulaire (Flashcard Bingo)**

Students could make their own sets of *Loto* cards with four divisions and either draw or cut out and stick on pictures of four of the things depicted on the flashcards. Each group of students could make sets of cards dealing with a different vocabulary area and then change them round for vocabulary revision games. The example below uses vegetables and fruit.

potato	carrot	carrot	cabbage	cabbage	cauliflower
cabbage	cauliflower	cauliflower	chips	chips	peas
cauliflower	chips	chips	peas	peas	beans
peas	beans	beans	lettuce	lettuce	apple
beans	lettuce	lettuce	apple	apple	pear
apple	pear	pear	orange	orange	peach
pear	orange	orange	peach	peach	banana
peach	banana	banana	strawberry	strawberry	grapes

Players need four counters or buttons each.

The caller should shuffle the pile of relevant flashcards and turn them up one at a time saying *Voilà des pommes de terre* etc.

The winner (who must shout *Loto!*) is the player whose card is first full and who can also say the four things shown on it in French. If the first to finish cannot say the words in French s/he is out and the caller continues until the next card is full.

Suitable vocabulary areas for this are *en ville, les magasins, à la maison, au collège, les transports, les vêtements, les parties du corps, les boissons, on mange ça, les villes et les pays, à la gare*.

The statements to be made by the caller can be extended to practise relevant structures, e.g. *J'aime les pommes de terre. Il y a des carottes.*

- **Oui ou non?**
The leader has a pile of flashcards in front of her/him. S/he picks one up at a time and shows it to the group, making a statement about it in French followed by *Oui ou non?*

If the statement is true, everyone says *Oui* and repeats it; if it is not, they say *Non*. Anyone speaking in the wrong place or failing to repeat a true statement is out. The winner becomes the new leader.

This type of game can be adapted to almost any topic, with or without flashcards. Students can make statements about classroom objects, pictures etc. and follow the statement with *(Répondez) oui ou non(?)*

The game could also be played with individuals. The group leader shows a card to one person at a time and makes a statement about it. The student replies *Oui* and repeats the statement, or *Non*.

- **'Carousel' version**
Each group could have sets of flashcards, each on a different subject. Then groups could rotate after five minutes or so to practise different sets of vocabulary.

- **Games with 2 sets of cards**
  Bataille! (Snap)
Flashcard snap in which they say the name of each card as they put it down. The first player to call *Bataille* wins the pile of cards.

  Contre la montre
This is a race against time in which each student sorts their cards into fruit and vegetables, masculine and feminine, good and bad weather, inside or outside, as appropriate.

Mots et images
One player says the name of an object from their hand. The other player selects the appropriate card from their own hand and puts it on the table. Then this player says a name and the first player puts the appropriate card on the table, and so on.

5 Games for practising verbs

These are in addition to those already mentioned.

- **Verb dice**
Make a big cardboard dice, but instead of numbers write on it *je, tu, il/elle/on, nous, vous, ils/elles*. Students throw the dice in turn and must say (or write on the board) the correct part of whatever verb they are practising. Each group could make its own cube dice or use a six-sided pencil. The verbs could also be used in sentences, e.g. *Je suis à l'épicerie.*

- **Loto des verbes**
Students write down three or four persons of a verb on their paper and play as before. Alternatively, about ten infinitives should be put on the board and everyone writes down the same person of four of them (this enables one person + relevant ending to be practised at a time). This game and the one above (**Verb dice**), could also be used to practise the perfect tense.

- **Le jeu des mimes (Miming)**
Students take turns to mime an action. The teacher or group leader says *Qu'est-ce qu'il/elle fait?* Students guess the action by asking *Tu regardes la télévision? Tu écoutes la radio?* etc. The actor answers *Oui, je regarde la télévision* or *Non, je ne regarde pas la télévision*, as appropriate.

- **Le jeu des mimes (Group version)**
Students could work in groups of four or five, a representative of each group doing a mime in turn, and the members of the other groups writing down a guess for each mime. When enough mimes have been done (say, two or three per group), the groups can then be asked to guess in turn and to score a point for each correct guess. The points are totalled to find the winning group. This game can also be played using the perfect tense, e.g. *Qu'est-ce qu'il a fait? Qui a dansé?*

- **Les verbes en cercle (Circle paradigm practice)**
A number of subjects (nouns and pronouns) are written on the board, in random order, in the form of a circle, e.g.

Christophe
Je   Magali et Olivier
Nous   Tu
On   Ils
Vous

The teacher calls out a sentence, e.g. *Je joue au tennis*, and then points to any of the subjects in the circle and asks someone to modify the sentence accordingly. The person chosen then continues clockwise round the circle until stopped by the teacher. This practice drill should move quickly, with frequent changes of speaker, sentence and points on the circle. Different nouns and pronouns should be used whenever this is played.

This game can also be played using the perfect tense.

- **Les verbes en désordre (Scrambled verbs)**
Write the pronouns and the six (or nine) parts of the verb in random order on each side of the board. One from each team comes out and rings *je* and the part which goes with it. Then, when this is done correctly, the next marker comes out and rings *tu* and the verb in a different colour, and so on until one team has correctly unscrambled the verb.

This game can also be played using the perfect tense.

6 Spelling games

- **Dix secondes**
Words linked with a particular topic are written on the board. A member of each team in turn has to see how many of the words s/he can spell correctly in, say, ten seconds. (The speller stands facing away from the board.) The words are crossed out or ticked when spelt so the choice gets smaller.

- **Spelling consequences**
Students in groups spell words one letter at a time, in turn. Each group has to say a new letter and must be 'on the way' to making a French word that makes sense, preferably from a given vocabulary area, e.g. *En ville* or *Les fruits et les légumes*.

If anyone thinks they know the word, they put their hand up, the spelling stops and they guess. If correct, their group gets a point and takes over, starting a new word. If wrong, the speller says which word they were spelling and the speller's group start a new word, gaining one point. If anyone suspects that a group has added a letter when they had not got a word in mind, they can challenge. If they were right, they gain a point and take over with a new word. If wrong, the speller's group gets a point and starts a new word.

7 Extra practice activities (vocabulary and verbs)

- **Numbered lists for pair work**
There are several versions of this activity:

a Each student writes a numbered list of the words to be learnt, with the French words on one side of the paper and the English on the back. They then test each other, one looking at the French side of the sheet and the other at the English. If one doesn't know the answer, the other tells her/him the number.

b Students try to catch each other out by saying a number the other one doesn't know. This can also be played by two pairs competing against each other.

c **Les mots contre la montre**
The game is played as above, but against the clock – use a stopwatch if possible. Each partner in turn has to identify ten items from numbers given by the other partner, in as short a time as possible.

One of the advantages of these games is that the very fact of making the cards or lists themselves is helping students to learn the vocabulary.

- **Making wordsearches to set to each other**
Limit each one to, say, ten words to be chosen from a given topic. Clues to be given in the opposite language to the words in the square.

- **Group brainstorming**
After revision of topic or homework learning of vocabulary, give groups 5/10 minutes to write down as many words as they can connected with the topic, e.g. *Les vacances, Dans la maison, La famille*.

Then check by letting each group in turn read out an answer. Groups score 1 point for any expression which others also have but 5 points for any correct answer which no-one else has. (Teacher can check winning group's answers for correct spelling etc.)

- **Memory masters**
Some students find it useful to make their own 'memory masters' on which they write important new grammatical rules, lists of topic vocabulary or verb paradigms. These are pieces of card small enough to go in the pocket and the idea is that they should be brought out and learnt and referred to at odd moments. Teachers could have a regular Friday check to see if the week's 'memory master' has been learnt or pupils could quiz each other on them at regular intervals.

If the cards are made with the English on one side and the French on the other, the language can be practised with the following pair game:

Partner A holds up a card so that s/he can see one side and Partner B can see the other. Points are awarded for the first one to say correctly what is on the other side of the card. The sides are changed round periodically and double points are awarded for the answers from the French side.

A similar sort of personal record of vocabulary etc. can be made on a computer – see **Electronic phrase book** in the ICT section, TB 19.

8 The Universal Board Game

This game is very useful for practising almost any vocabulary item, structure, phrase or model question/answer combination. It is very undemanding in terms of teacher time, easy to organize and play and very adaptable.

The game basically comprises an A4 sheet on which is drawn a path of approximately 100 squares, numbered in sequence from 1–100. This can take whatever form you like, from very artistic 'snake patterns' to simply dividing the sheet into squares to make a grid pattern, numbered in sequence like this:

100	99	98	97	96	95	94	93	92	91
81	82	83	84	85	86	87	88	89	90
80	79	78	77	76	75	74	73	72	71
61	62	63	64	65	66	67	68	69	70
60	59	58	57	56	55	54	53	52	51
41	42	43	44	45	46	47	48	49	50
40	39	38	37	36	35	34	33	32	31
21	22	23	24	25	26	27	28	29	30
20	19	18	17	16	15	14	13	12	11
1	2	3	4	5	6	7	8	9	10

Make two sets of cards with questions on. These can vary widely, but some suggestions are below. These sets of cards can also be used for other games, e.g. Happy Families, Snap! or Pelmanism. Also they can be built up into a store of revision packs – different groups work with different topic packs and then exchange topics with another group, e.g. clothes, sport, food, school, leisure activities etc.

Students then throw a dice and move:

- if they land on an even-numbered square, they turn over a card from one pile;
- if they land on an odd-numbered square they pick up a card from the other pile.

One pile can contain words in French to be said in English. The other can contain either words in English or picture stimuli which have to be said in French.

The cards are in the piles face downwards. When students have used a card, it goes on the bottom of its pile.

If they answer the questions correctly, students get another throw (up to a maximum of three!), and if they answer them wrongly or not at all they go back two squares.

The winner is the first to 100 or the one who has got furthest in the time available.

- **Variations**
  a Some subjects are suitable for using in a 'split format' – i.e. either pile can form the question and the other automatically gives the answer (e.g. English/French: chips/*les frites* – if you pick up the English you give the French and vice-versa – **but** make sure the piles are kept level and 'synchronised'!
  b Other question/answer combinations are not reversible, e.g.
  Question: *Il y a combien de jours dans une semaine?*
  Answer: *Il y en a sept.*
  In this case the answer must appear on the reverse of the card and will be visible to the other contestants (when it is held up) but not to the person answering the question.
  If the cards do not contain the answers either on the reverse or on the other pile, it will be necessary somehow to make the answers available to the players, e.g. by providing a sheet with the answers on for each group of players.

- **Easy ideas for cards**
  1   Numbers
  Figures and words, e.g.
  2/*deux*, 85/*quatre-vingt-cinq*
  Simple sums in figures, to be read out in French, e.g.
  5 + 17 = 22,
  or in words: *cinq et dix-sept font vingt-deux*

  2   Vocabulary
  French/English (as above)
  French/picture
  Missing word, e.g.
  La souris … petite./est

3   Simple grammar
Adjectives, e.g. *une fleur/(blanc/blanche)*
or *une fleur* (white)/*blanche*
Verbs, e.g.
nous (manger)/mangeons
or *nous* (eat)/*mangeons*
or *À midi nous … le déjeuner./mangeons*
Masculine/feminine, e.g.
homme/femme, beau/belle.

- **A bit harder**
  4   Questions and answers
  Things students sometimes muddle, e.g.
  Qui?/Who?
  Qui est-ce qui?/Who?
  Qu'est-ce qui?/What?
  Qu'est-ce que?/What?
  or in sentences, e.g.
  *Qu'est-ce que tu aimes comme fruit?/
  J'aime les pommes* etc.
  *Est-ce que tu aimes les pommes?/
  Oui, j'aime les pommes.*

  5   Negatives
  J'aime les pommes/Je n'aime pas les pommes.
  There are endless possibilities!

Songs

Using the songs in *Encore Tricolore 2*

There are five songs on the CDs, especially written and performed for **Encore Tricolore 2**. The words of the songs can be found in the Students' Book (except for *Alouette*, which is only on copymaster). The musical scores, comprising melodies, guitar chords and words, are on CM 147–155.

Les matières (Unité 3) SB 46, CM 147–148
Que désirez vous? (Unité 5) SB 69, CM 149–150
Paris-Genève (Unité 6) SB 92, CM 151–152
Alouette (Unité 7) TB (Area 4), CM 153
Sabine, ce n'est pas grave … (Unité 8) SB 119, CM 154–155

There are two recorded versions of each song, one version including the words and the other an instrument-only version.

The vocal version of each song can be:
- listened to by the students simply for enjoyment
- used as the stimulus material for various types of listening comprehension tasks or games
- used as a device to teach the song to students – they may be able to sing along with this version on CD, or sing along with the teacher (who may choose to play the accompaniment or not) independently of the CD.

The instrument-only version of each song may be used in class as a means of encouraging students to perform the song unaided by vocal support from the CD or the teacher, and thus this version lends itself to independent preparation and performance by small groups.

Students preparing the songs in this way may be encouraged to perform them in extra- or cross-curricular contexts, for example departmental parents' evenings, school assemblies or as projects in conjunction with performing arts departments within the school.

The instrumental backing of the songs has been designed to be accessible and relatively simple in terms of musical structure and progression; thus, students with some musical training (in conjunction with music teachers or musically-able language teachers) might be expected to be able to produce full instrumental and vocal interpretations of these songs, by study of the CD and melody/guitar chords score, in any of the extra- or cross-curricular contexts described above. Have fun!

Encore Tricolore 2
nouvelle édition

unité 1   En ville

Areas	Topics	Grammar
1	Talking about French shops and what they sell Revision of food	Revision of partitive
2		Revision of -er verbs *acheter, préférer, compléter*
3		Using the verb *vendre* (to sell) and other -re verbs
4	Saying how much you want to buy	Expressions of quantity followed by *de, d'*
5	Talking about money, number and prices	
6	Shopping for food	
7		Using the verb *choisir* (to choose) and other -ir verbs
8	Saying there isn't any/any more	Negative followed by *de* (*ne ... pas de* and *ne ... plus de*)
9	Further activities and consolidation	Revision of all regular verbs

National Curriculum Information

Some students   levels 3–4+
Most students   levels 2–4
All students   levels 2–3

Revision

Rappel (CM 1/12) includes revision of the following:
- self, family, pets
- things in a bedroom
- places in a town, directions

Sounds and writing
- the French alphabet
- pronunciation of c
- the endings *-ial, -iel*

See *Écoute et parle* (CM 1/9 and TB 44).

ICT opportunities
- phrase generation
- buying food for a picnic from an Internet shopping site
- spreadsheet shopping list activity

Assessment
- Informal assessment is in *Épreuves* at the end of this unit (TB 46, CM 1/13–1/16)
- Formal assessment (*Unités 1–7*) is in the *Contrôle* (TB 190, CM 139–145).

Students' Book

Unité 1 SB 6–17
Au choix SB 120–121

Flashcards

1–21   shops, food and stamps

CDs

1/1–14
Student CD 1/1–6, 2/1–3

Additional

Grammar in Action 1, pp 8–11, 21, 25, 27–29
Grammar in Action 2, pp 19

Copymasters

CM 1/1	*On mange et on boit* [revision]	
CM 1/2	*Les verbes en -er* [grammar]	
CM 1/3	*Les verbes en -re* [grammar]	
CM 1/4	*Les quantités* [mini-flashcards]	
CM 1/5	*Les verbes en -ir* [grammar]	
CM 1/6	*ne ... pas, ne ... plus* [grammar]	
CM 1/7	*Les verbes sont utiles* [grammar]	
CM 1/8	*C'est utile, le dictionnaire!* [dictionary skills]	
CM 1/9	*Écoute et parle* [independent listening]	
CM 1/10	*Tu comprends?* [independent listening]	
CM 1/11	*Sommaire* [consolidation, reference]	
CM 1/12	*Rappel* [revision]	
CM 1/13	*Épreuve: Écouter*	
CM 1/14	*Épreuve: Parler*	
CM 1/15	*Épreuve: Lire*	
CM 1/16	*Épreuve: Écrire et grammaire*	

Language content

French shops (Areas 1 and 3)

la boucherie
la boulangerie
la charcuterie
la crémerie
l'épicerie (f)
la librairie
le marchand de glaces
le marchand de légumes/de fruits
la parfumerie
la pâtisserie
la pharmacie
la poissonnerie
le (bureau de) tabac

Shopping (Areas 1 and 6)

Je voudrais
Avez-vous …?
C'est combien?
Vous désirez?
C'est tout?
Et avec ça?
Je regrette, mais je n'ai pas de …
Je suis désolé, mais il n'y a plus de …

Discussing where to go shopping (Areas 1–3)

Où est-ce qu'on peut acheter des timbres?
On peut acheter des timbres au tabac.

Things to buy (Areas 1 and 6)

une baguette
un biscuit
des bonbons (m)
des chips (m)
un concombre
des champignons (m)
une glace
un journal
un magazine
une quiche
un pain au chocolat
du saucisson
un timbre

Expressions of quantity (Area 4)

une boîte de
une bouteille de
100 grammes de
250 grammes de
un kilo de
un demi-kilo de
une livre de
un litre de
un morceau de
un paquet de
une portion de
une tranche de

Money, number and prices (Area 5)

l'argent (m)
un billet
un cent
un euro
la monnaie
une pièce
un porte-monnaie

Saying there isn't any more (Area 8)

Il n'y a pas de fruits.
Il n'y a plus de légumes.

-er verbs (Area 2)

acheter   préférer

-re verbs (Area 3)

vendre   descendre
attendre   répondre

-ir verbs (Area 7)

choisir   pâlir
finir   rougir
remplir   grossir
réussir   maigrir

Useful websites

Some French supermarkets and chain stores

Auchan – www.auchan.fr
Carrefour – www.carrefour.fr
E.Leclerc – www.leclerc-cannes.com/
Monoprix – www.monoprix.fr

Other stores

www.fnac.fr – the *FNAC* bookshops and multimedia stores sell books, DVDs, videos, cassettes, CDs etc. You can search for titles of French books here and find out the prices.

www.amazon.fr – Amazon online bookshop in France

En ville unité 1

Section 3

**Area 1
Talking about French shops and what they sell
Revision of food and of the partitive article**
SB 6–7, **1**–**3**
Au choix SB 120, **1**–**2**
Au choix SB 121, **1**
CM1/1
FC 1–6
CD 1/1
Grammar in Action 1, page 21

FC 1–6, SB 6

SPEAKING
READING
WRITING

Presentation

a Using flashcards, revise items of food that were taught in **Encore Tricolore 1**, perhaps following this oral revision by using CM1/1.

Perhaps play some vocabulary games or have a Spelling Bee to give further practice of vocabulary from **Encore Tricolore 1**, and gradually introduce other food and drink items which occur on SB 6.

b Grammar in Action 1, page 21, sets out the forms of the partitive article and revises common food. This would be ideal for revision at this stage and could be done as an oral or written activity. Alternatively, it could be used as consolidation at the end of this area.

c Using flashcards, revise *le magasin, le marché* and *le supermarché* from **Encore Tricolore 1** and teach the names of the new shops which appear here, i.e. *la boulangerie-pâtisserie, la boucherie, la charcuterie, l'épicerie, la librairie* and *le tabac*.

Give further background information where relevant, e.g.

- although *la boulangerie* and *la pâtisserie* are traditionally different shops, it is increasingly common to see both as parts of a single business
- explain the differences between *la boucherie* and *la charcuterie* (much more like our delicatessen)
- stamps can now be bought in many other places besides *le tabac*, although the traditional *carotte* is still a good thing to look for if you want to buy any. Self-adhesive stamps are also becoming more popular.

To help with comprehension of the text and with oral practice, teach *vendre* and *on peut acheter*, although both will be taught more fully and for active use later in the unit.

Give plenty of oral practice, bringing together the shops and the items for sale, e.g.

Voici la boulangerie-pâtisserie. Ici, on vend du pain et des gâteaux etc.

Où est-ce qu'on peut acheter …? Qu'est-ce qu'on peut acheter à la boucherie? etc.

CM 1/1 WRITING
On mange et on boit

This copymaster provides revision of food and drink and of the partitive article.

Solution:

1 Mots croisés en images

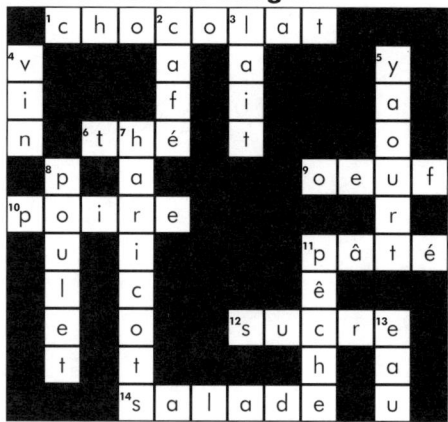

	¹c	h	²c	o	³l	a	t		
⁴v			a		a			⁵y	
i			f		i			a	
n		⁶t	⁷h	é		t			o
⁸p		a						⁹o	e	u	f
¹⁰p	o	i	r	e				r	
u		i				¹¹p	â	t	é
l		c				ê			
e		o		¹²s	u	c	r	¹³e	
t		t				h		a	
	¹⁴s	a	l	a	d	e		u	

2 Ça, c'est ridicule
1 rouge, **2** fruit, **3** légume, **4** boisson, **5** légume, **6** chaude, **7** froide

3 Des phrases
1 du, **2** de la, **3** de l', **4** du, **5** des/des, **6** du, **7** de la/du

SB 6–7, 1/1 LISTENING
READING
WRITING
1 On fait des courses SPEAKING

Use the pictures of shops on SB 6 for further practice of the names of shops. Ask students to look at the text and at the food items in the box below and make a few guesses at where these words will go. They can then listen to the recording and note down the words to fill the gaps.

After correcting this, students could eventually read aloud in pairs the conversations with shopkeepers.

Solution: **1h** *des glaces*, **2e** *des pains au chocolat*, **3c** *de la viande*, **4f** *du pâté*, **5d** *de la confiture*, **6a** *des chips*, **7b** *des journaux*, **8g** *des timbres*

On fait des courses

A Voici la boulangerie-pâtisserie. Mme Gênet travaille à la boulangerie-pâtisserie. Elle vend des gâteaux, des tartes, des chocolats et aussi des glaces.
  – Est-ce que vous vendez des croissants ici?
  – Bien sûr. Je vends des croissants et des pains au chocolat et naturellement, je vends toutes sortes de pain.

B Voici la boucherie.
  – Bonjour, Monsieur. Vous vendez du jambon?
  – Ah non. Je vends de la viande, par exemple du steak ou du poulet, mais je n'ai pas de jambon.
  – Alors, où est-ce qu'on peut acheter du jambon?
  – Pour le jambon, allez à la charcuterie, ou peut-être à l'épicerie.

C Voici la charcuterie. À la charcuterie, on peut acheter du jambon, du saucisson et du pâté. Si vous préférez, il y a aussi des plats préparés, par exemple des quiches et des portions de salade.

D Voici une épicerie.
– Ici, on peut acheter beaucoup de choses. Regarde, il y a du sucre, de l'eau minérale, de la confiture, du beurre et des chips.

E – Voici une librairie.
– Regarde, ici on vend des livres, des journaux et des magazines. Tu cherches un magazine informatique?
– Non, je préfère un magazine sur la musique ou la mode – je trouve ça plus intéressant!

F Voici un tabac.
– Ah bon, on vend des timbres au tabac. Si nous achetons des timbres ici, nous pouvons envoyer nos cartes postales à nos amis.

SB 7   **READING**

2 Aux magasins

Students prepare this individually, matching up the two parts of the sentence. This task could be corrected orally, with students reading out complete sentences, for added practice.

This item supplies the expressions *à la boulangerie, au marché* etc. which can be referred to while working on the next task.

Solution: 1d, 2a, 3f, 4b, 5g, 6e, 7c, 8h

SB 7   **WRITING**

3 Ici, j'achète …

Start with some revision of the partitive article, if needed. Students read each sentence to see what is sold and then supply the name of the shop, referring to the previous two items, if necessary. They then complete the sentence with the correct partitive article, referring to the revision box (*Pour t'aider*).

Solution:
1 À l'épicerie, j'achète du beurre et de l'eau minérale.
2 À la boulangerie, j'achète des baguettes.
3 À la charcuterie, j'achète du jambon et de la salade de tomates.
4 Au marché, j'achète des carottes et des oranges.
5 À la boucherie, j'achète de la viande et du poulet.
6 Au tabac, j'achète des timbres.
7 À la librairie, j'achète des magazines.
8 À la charcuterie, j'achète du pâté.

Differentiation

For further practice, use the *Au choix* support and extension tasks as follows.

AU CHOIX SB 120   **SUPPORT**
                                                              WRITING

1 C'est quel magasin?

Students identify which shop sells the illustrated goods and write the shop names.

Solution: 1 à la boulangerie, 2 à la charcuterie,
3 à la boucherie, 4 à la librairie,
5 à la boulangerie, 6 à l'épicerie,
7 à la pâtisserie, 8 à la pâtisserie

AU CHOIX SB 120   **SUPPORT**
                                                              WRITING

2 Les magasins

This is a straightforward vocabulary practice task in which students complete the names of shops by adding the missing vowels.

Solution: 1 le tabac, 2 la librairie, 3 la boucherie,
4 la pâtisserie, 5 l'épicerie,
6 la boulangerie, 7 la charcuterie,
8 le marché

AU CHOIX SB 121   **EXTENSION**
                                                              WRITING

1 Tu fais des courses

This task is for consolidation of shop names and the partitive. It is similar to *Ici, j'achète …* (SB 7), but harder.

Students complete the lists with the correct part of the partitive article and express their answer as a complete sentence, saying which shops they go to.

Solution:

*Mardi, je vais à l'épicerie et à la boulangerie. J'achète du beurre et des baguettes.
Mercredi, je vais à la charcuterie et à l'épicerie. J'achète du jambon, de la limonade et des carottes.
Jeudi, je vais à la boucherie et au tabac. J'achète de la viande et des timbres.
Vendredi, je vais à la charcuterie et à la librairie. J'achète de la salade de tomates et des magazines.
Samedi, je vais à la boucherie et à l'épicerie. J'achète du poulet, des fraises et de l'eau minérale gazeuse.
Dimanche, je vais à la boulangerie-pâtisserie. J'achète des croissants et de la glace à la vanille.*

GRAMMAR IN ACTION 1, PAGE 21   **GRAMMAR**

Using *du, de la, de l', des*

This sets out the forms of the partitive article and revises common food. For further consolidation, this could be done as an oral or written activity.

**Area 2
Revision of -er verbs
SB 7, 4-5
CM 1/2
Grammar in Action 1, pages 8–11, 25**

Revision of -er verbs   **PRESENTATION**

Begin by revising -er verbs orally, perhaps using some of the games suggested in Section 2 (TB 25–29), and then refer students to the *Dossier-langue* (SB 7).

En ville unité 1

CM 1/2
Les verbes en -er
WRITING

This gives graded practice of -er verbs and could be used here, or later, perhaps for homework, for consolidation.

Solution:
1 **Qu'est-ce qu'on fait?**
   1c, 2a, 3b, 4e, 5f, 6g, 7d
2 **Le verbe travailler (*to work*)**
   je travaille   nous travaillons
   tu travailles   vous travaillez
   il travaille   ils travaillent
   elle travaille elles travaillent
3 **Au club des jeunes**
   A 1 adore, 2 passe, 3 joue, 4 jouons, 5 gagnons,
      6 adore, 7 préfère, 8 aime, 9 travaillons,
      10 espérons, 11 habite, 12 passe, 13 regarde,
      14 essayons, 15 inventons
   B 1 regarde – Christophe
      2 aime – Lisa
      3 inventent – Christophe et Marc
      4 travaille – Tiffaine
      5 joue – Kévin
      6 passe – Marc
      7 jouent – les copains de Kévin
      8 aiment, préfèrent – Lisa et Tiffaine

SB 7
Dossier-langue
-er verbs
GRAMMAR

When students have read through the *Dossier-langue*, check that they know the regular endings and have understood the accent changes in *acheter* and *préférer*.

SB 7
4 J'aime ça!
GRAMMAR PRACTICE

Students find the pairs, which involves matching subject and verb.

Solution: 1b, 2a, 3g, 4d, 5c, 6f, 7e

WRITING
SPEAKING

Follow-up

A phrase generation activity based on *acheter* could be used if students have access to computers, e.g.

Moi, j'	achète	des bonbons.
		des chips.
Ma sœur		du chocolat.
Mon frère		des vêtements.
		des CDs.
Mes copains et		des magazines.
moi, nous	achetons	des cadeaux.
		des livres.
Mes amis	achètent	des jeux électroniques.

Des jeux
Qu'est-ce que j'achète?
GRAMMAR PRACTICE
SPEAKING

To practise the verb *acheter* (+ food) orally, play a guessing game as a class or group activity. A student chooses a shop and says, e.g.
Je suis à la charcuterie. Qu'est-ce que j'achète?
The others guess, e.g. *Tu achètes du pâté?* and the person who guesses correctly chooses the next shop.

En ville, j'achète …

This is a simple cumulative game which can be played in groups.
Student A says *Moi, j'achète* (+ purchase), *et toi*, (+name), *qu'est-ce que tu achètes?*
Student B repeats *Moi, j'achète* (+ purchase) and adds on something else.
If used after Area 4, the game can be made harder in several ways, e.g. by asking students to include expressions of quantity (*deux melons, un demi-kilo de pommes* etc.) or by giving extra marks if the things bought follow an alphabetical sequence (*J'achète une baguette et des chocolats* etc.).

Further oral work
SPEAKING

Give more practice of -er verbs, *acheter* and *préférer* with questions such as *Qu'est-ce que tu préfères manger à la récré/pour ton goûter? Et tes amis, qu'est-ce qu'ils préfèrent?* etc.

SB 7,
SPEAKING
WRITING

5 À toi!

This task brings together the new verb forms and some of the vocabulary of the first two areas.

À discuter
The list of questions is used first for a speaking task, in which students take turns to ask each other questions. The teacher could also go round the class, asking different students one or two of the questions at random.

À écrire
Students choose three questions and write them out with their own replies.

It is suggested that each student uses these as the basis of their own electronic phrase book, adding to it each time a similar activity occurs and learning some sample questions and answers by heart (see TB 19).

GRAMMAR IN ACTION 1, PAGES 8–11, 25
GRAMMAR PRACTICE

For more practice of -er verbs, students could work from Grammar in Action 1, pages 8–11 or do CM 1/2 (see above).
For further practice of *acheter*, *préférer* and *compléter*, they could use Grammar in Action 1, page 25.

Area 3
Using the verb *vendre* and other *-re* verbs
SB 8–9, 1–5
Grammar in Action 1, page 29
CM 1/3
CD 1/2–3

SB 8 READING
SPEAKING/WRITING

1 Qu'est-ce qu'on vend?

Students can do this multiple choice task orally or in writing. The answers could be corrected orally, with students reading the correct sentences aloud.

Solution: 1a, 2b, 3b, 4b, 5a, 6c, 7a, 8a

SB 8 GRAMMAR

Dossier-langue
vendre (to sell)

This *Dossier-langue* is designed for class question and answer work. Students look for all the parts of the verb *vendre* in the preceding text and, from their answers, the teacher can build up the paradigm on the board and use it to compare the endings with *-er* verbs.

SB 8, 🎧 1/2 LISTENING
WRITING
SPEAKING

2 Le marchand de glaces

Students listen and complete the interview with varying amounts of help.

Ask students to note which endings are sounded, as they listen to the recording. Check the spellings of the verbs before students use the script to read the interview aloud in groups of three.

Solution: **1** *(vous) vendez*, **2** *(je) vends*, **3** *(nous) vendons*, **4** *(vous) vendez*, **5** *(je) vends*, **6** *(on) vend*, **7** *(tu) vends*, **8** *(je ne) vends (pas)*, **9** *(je) vends*, **10** *(je) vends*

🎧 **Le marchand de glaces**

M. Delarue est marchand de glaces. Il vend des glaces, des boissons, des bonbons etc. dans le parc. Pendant les vacances, son fils, Simon, travaille avec lui et ils vendent beaucoup de choses.
– Est-ce que vous vendez des glaces ici, toute l'année?
– Je vends des glaces surtout en été, mais le reste de l'année, nous vendons beaucoup d'autres choses, comme par exemple des hot-dogs et des frites.
– Qu'est-ce que vous vendez surtout aux enfants?
– Alors aux enfants, je vends surtout des glaces et des bonbons.
– Et aux adultes?
– Aux adultes, on vend des hot-dogs, des frites, des glaces aussi, quand il fait chaud.
– Et toi, Simon, tu vends des hot-dogs et des frites aussi?
– Moi, non. Je ne vends pas de plats chauds. Je vends surtout des boissons froides. Quelquefois, je vends aussi de la barbe à papa, mais je déteste ça, car à la fin, je suis couvert de sucre!

SB 8, SPEAKING

3 Où est-ce qu'on vend ça?

In this pairwork activity, students use a dice or a number cue and ask each other questions about which shop sells the listed products.

SB 9, GRAMMAR

Dossier-langue
More regular *-re* verbs

The explanation could be followed with a game, such as writing the stem on the board, then adding the endings according to the instructions given by members of the class (e.g. 1st person singular, or *je*?).

This could be followed by a game of *Effacez!* with the endings being rubbed off in the same way.

More able students could be asked to make up sentences, each including part of one of these verbs. Students should add the verbs to their own electronic word lists

SB 9, 🎧 1/3 GRAMMAR PRACTICE
LISTENING

4 Une conversation

Students complete the conversation with the correct parts of *-re* verbs. They then listen to the recording as a check, paying particular attention to which endings are pronounced.

After this, they could read the conversation aloud in pairs and some could perhaps be recorded.

Solution: **1** *(Sandrine) répond*, **2** *(Tu) descends*, **3** *(Vous) descendez*, **4** *(Nous) descendons*, **5** *(j')attends*, **6** *(Tu) attends*

🎧 **Une conversation**

Samedi après-midi, le téléphone sonne et Sandrine répond.
– Allô, oui!
– Salut, Sandrine, c'est Isabelle. Tu descends en ville?
– Oui, oui, avec ma sœur. Nous prenons l'autobus à trois heures.
– Ah bon. Vous descendez où en ville?
– Nous descendons place du marché. Et toi, tu prends le bus aussi?
– Non, je vais en ville avec ma mère, alors j'attends devant la boulangerie, ça va?
– Oui, ça va. Tu attends devant la boulangerie vers trois heures.
– D'accord. À tout à l'heure.

unité 1 En ville

Section 3

35

SB 9 READING / GRAMMAR PRACTICE

5 Une surprise pour Mangetout

Students supply the correct form of regular -re verbs to complete this story.

Questions can be asked about the completed text or students could make up *vrai ou faux?* statements to set to others.

More able students could try telling the story, using the pictures as a framework (an OHT could be used for class storytelling with this item), or the story could be used with *Fun with Texts*.

Solution: 1 *descend*, 2 *attend*, 3 *répond*, 4 *attend*, 5 *descendent*, 6 *répondent*, 7 *descend*, 8 *attendent*, 9 *attendez*, 10 *attendons*

GRAMMAR IN ACTION 1, PAGE 29   GRAMMAR PRACTICE
Using *vendre* and other -re verbs

This provides excellent further practice of -re verbs and could be used in class or for homework.

CM 1/3   WRITING
Les verbes en -re

This copymaster gives graded practice of *vendre* and other -re verbs and would be suitable for homework.

The first task is just a completion task to practise the paradigm. The second task provides practice of *vendre* only and the crossword includes other regular -re verbs (*attendre, descendre, répondre*).

Solution:

1 Des verbes utiles

je	vends	descends
tu	vends	descends
il/elle/on	vend	descend
nous	vendons	descendons
vous	vendez	descendez
ils/elles	vendent	descendent

2 C'est à vendre?
1 *vends*, 2 *vends*, 3 *vend*, 4 *vends*, 5 *vends*, 6 *vendent*, 7 *vend*, 8 *vendez*, 9 *vendons*

3 Mots croisés

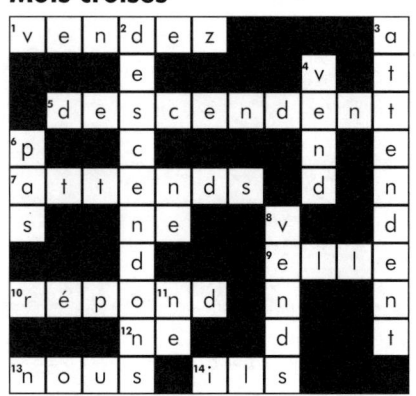

Area 4
Saying how much you want to buy
Expressions of quantity

SB 10, **1**–**3**
Au choix SB 120, **3**, SB 121, **2**
CM 1/4
CD 1/4
Grammar in Action 1, page 27

PRESENTATION
Expressions of quantity, weights etc.

Begin by revising the numbers already known and teach higher numbers, using games and activities suggested in Section 2 (TB 25–29).

For practice, dictate some weights for the class to write down in numbers then to put in order, from the lightest to the heaviest, e.g.
un kilo – cent grammes – deux cent cinquante grammes – cent cinquante grammes – deux kilos – un demi-kilo – cinq cents grammes

SB 10   SPEAKING / WRITING
1 Aujourd'hui, j'achète …

Using actual objects, quick sketches, or some of the twelve mini-flashcards on CM 1/4, teach *une portion de, une tranche de* and *un petit/grand morceau de*, before asking the class to do this puzzle.

The answers can be jotted down initially in the form of number + letter, e.g. 1D, but should then be given in full, either orally or in writing.

Solution: 1D, 2A, 3C, 4J, 5B, 6F, 7E, 8I, 9H, 10G

SB 10   GRAMMAR
Dossier-langue
Expressions of quantity

After reading through this brief explanation, students could make their own list of expressions of quantity and enter it into their electronic phrase book (TB 19).

They could also use the list as the basis for wordsearches which they can set to each other.

CM 1/4   SPEAKING / LISTENING / WRITING
Les quantités

This copymaster, which consists of twelve mini-flashcards, could be used in a variety of ways to teach and practise this vocabulary, including making the sheet into an OHT.

The pictures each have a caption for completion, so the sheet can be used for a written task.

Solution: 1d, 2j, 3a, 4f, 5i, 6b, 7g, 8e, 9k, 10c, 11l, 12h

SB 10, 🎧 **1/4**   **LISTENING**

2 À l'épicerie

Students listen to the recording and note the quantity. The answers can be given orally or written down, depending on the ability of the class.

Solution:

1 6 tranches de jambon
2 1 kilo de pêches
3 2 portions de salade de tomates
4 1 livre de carottes
5 3 paquets de biscuits
6 1 grand morceau de fromage
7 2 boîtes de tomates
8 1 litre d'eau minérale

🎧   À l'épicerie

1 Bonjour, Monsieur. Six tranches de jambon, s'il vous plaît.
2 Bonjour, Madame. Je voudrais un kilo de pêches, s'il vous plaît.
3 Bonjour, Madame. Je voudrais deux portions de salade de tomates.
4 Bonjour, Monsieur. Donnez-moi une livre de carottes, s'il vous plaît.
5 Je voudrais trois paquets de biscuits, s'il vous plaît.
6 – Bonjour, Monsieur. Un grand morceau de fromage, s'il vous plaît.
   – Comme ça, Madame?
   – Oui, ça va bien, merci.
7 Bonjour, Madame. Deux boîtes de tomates, s'il vous plaît.
8 Bonjour, Madame. Je voudrais un litre d'eau minérale, s'il vous plaît.

SB 10,   **SPEAKING**
                                                 WRITING

3 C'est pour un pique-nique

a S'il vous plaît
Students work in pairs and take turns to order the items allocated to them.

b Le jeu des listes
Each student makes a short shopping list of four of the items illustrated. They then ask questions in turn to see who is the first to guess the whole of their partner's list.

Differentiation

For further practice, use the *Au choix* support and extension tasks as follows.

Au choix SB 120   **SUPPORT**
                                             SPEAKING
3 Des listes à faire   **WRITING**

This is a simple completion task which could be done as an oral or writing task.

Solution:

1a *250 grammes de fromage
une boîte de thon
un kilo de pêches*
    *un demi-kilo de haricots verts
100 grammes de thé
un pot de confiture
un paquet de chips
un litre de lait
une bouteille de vin rouge*

1b Le magasin = l'épicerie

2a *200 grammes de pâté
6 tranches de jambon
une portion de salade de tomates
deux portions de quiche
un grand morceau de camembert*

2b Le magasin = la charcuterie

Au choix SB 121   **EXTENSION**
                                                WRITING
2 Invente des listes

These lists could be drawn up individually or by students working in pairs. There are no 'correct' answers, so the lists will have to be checked individually.

The lists could be used for further practice later for shopping dialogues.

GRAMMAR IN ACTION 1, PAGE 27 GRAMMAR PRACTICE

Expressions of quantity

This provides further practice of expressions of quantity, if required.

> **Area 5**
> **Talking about money, number and prices**
> SB 11, **4**–**5**
> CD 1/5

                                       PRESENTATION

Numbers and prices

First play some number games for revision (see TB 25). Dictate some numbers to be written in figures, concentrating especially on the higher numbers and use these for a game of *Effacez!*

Talk briefly about the euro, its use in France and elsewhere. Encourage students to look up on the Internet the current French prices of some common food items, magazines etc. Dictate some prices in euros for them to jot down.

SB 11, 🎧 **1/5**   **LISTENING**
4 C'est combien?

Students should listen to the dialogues first to find out how to ask the price of something. This can be written on the board for future reference. They then listen to find out the price of each item. The first answers are multiple choice, but for the last two, students supply the price.

This task would be suitable for work on individual listening equipment or in a multi-media lab.

Solution: **1a, 2b, 3c, 4 €2,60, 5 €5,30**

En ville unité 1

Section 3

🎧 **C'est combien?**

1 – Bonjour, Daniel. Tu désires?
  – Je voudrais du poisson pour mon chat, s'il vous plaît.
  – Voilà. C'est tout?
  – Oui. C'est combien, s'il vous plaît?
  – C'est un euro quatre-vingts.
  – Voilà, Monsieur.
  – Merci. Au revoir, Daniel.

2 – Bonjour, Madame Dublanc.
  – Bonjour, Monsieur. Je voudrais une bouteille de vin rouge et un litre de lait, s'il vous plaît.
  – Voilà, Madame.
  – Merci. C'est combien?
  – Ça fait dix euros cinquante en tout.
  – Merci. Au revoir, Monsieur.

3 – Bonjour, Monsieur.
  – Bonjour, Madame Laval.
  – Une boîte de chocolats, s'il vous plaît, et un paquet de biscuits.
  – Voilà. C'est tout?
  – Oui. C'est combien?
  – Voyons … ça fait quatre euros quarante-cinq en tout.
  – Voilà. Au revoir, Monsieur
  – Au revoir, Madame Laval

4 – Bonjour, Claudine. Qu'est-ce que tu veux?
  – Je voudrais un grand paquet de chips et une bouteille de limonade, s'il vous plaît.
  – Voilà. C'est tout?
  – Oui. C'est combien?
  – Bon, le paquet de chips, un euro … et la limonade, un euro soixante. Ça fait deux euros soixante en tout.
  – Voilà. Au revoir, Madame.
  – Au revoir, Claudine.

5 – Bonjour, Monsieur.
  – Bonjour, Madame. Un pot de confiture, s'il vous plaît.
  – Quelle sorte de confiture?
  – Fraise. Et une petite boîte de thon. C'est combien?
  – Voyons, ça fait cinq euros trente en tout.
  – Voilà. Au revoir, Madame.
  – Au revoir, Monsieur.

SB 11,   **LISTENING**
                                                        SPEAKING

5 Au supermarché

a Students work in pairs. One gives the price in euros of one of the items shown, their partner has to correctly identify the item at that price.

b Students take turns to ask each other the price of something.

                                                        READING
                                                        WRITING

Follow-up
Au cybermarché – on achète un pique-nique

Students are given a budget and a choice of shopping sites on the Internet in which to spend it (this could be restricted to food and drink for picnic). With this information, they could produce a shopping list. This activity can work well with limited Internet access as pupils can work in groups. Items and prices can be copied from the web page and pasted into a spreadsheet to produce the list, using the sum function to keep track of spending.

Various French supermarket chains have an Internet shopping facility that tells you the price of most items. For example, Leclerc in Cannes had the following list of fruits and prices at the time of writing:

Citron	1 kg	€1,75
Ananas	pièce	€1,95
Avocat	pièce	€0,75
Pommes golden	2 kg	€2,28
Fraise	500 g	€2,28
Kiwi	barquette	€1,52
Kiwi	pièce	€0,30
Oranges	2 kg	€1,36
Citron non traité	500 g	€1,06
Pomelos rose	pièce	€0,60
Pommes	barquette	€1,67
Oranges	3 kg	€3,03

Other *rayons* available include:

Petit déjeuner	*Bébé*
Pâtes, Féculents, Soupes	*Vins, Champagnes*
Conserves	*Apéritifs, Alcools*
Assaisonnement	*Eaux, Sodas, Bières*
Biscuits, Desserts	*Beauté, Soins, Hygiène*
Gourmandises	*Droguerie*

To find the websites, go to Yahoo France and look under *Commerce* and then *Société* and then *Distributeurs/Revendeurs*. Comparison of prices with UK retailers could also be undertaken – Tesco have a web site with a facility for price comparison among UK retailers.

Alternatively, if Internet access is not available in the lesson, either pupils or the teacher can print out some lists of prices from web sites and students can work from these.

**Area 6
Shopping for food**
SB 12, **1**–**2**
CD 1/6
FC 7–21

FC 7–21   **PRESENTATION**

Shopping

First revise all the main items of food and drink met so far, and the expressions of quantity and money taught earlier in the unit, using flashcards and games.

Give a selection of flashcards for the grocer's to a student, and say:

Tu es l'épicier … Bonjour, Monsieur/Madame, je voudrais du sucre, s'il vous plaît … Merci.

Perhaps use a chain game in which a student asks to buy something, then chooses someone else who repeats what they have said and adds on something else, e.g.

Teacher: *Je voudrais une bouteille de limonade.* (Student A)…

Student A: *Je voudrais une bouteille de limonade et une boîte de thon … etc.*

38

SB 12, 🎧 1/6, 💻   **LISTENING**
                                           READING

1   On achète des provisions

Students listen to the dialogues to find out what each customer buys, noting down the correct letter from the item illustrated.

Then ask students to listen for the following expressions and write these on the board:
Je voudrais…, C'est tout? C'est combien? and *Avez-vous …?*

These should be practised by working on the conversations, which increase in length and complexity.

If computers are available, students could key in their dialogue as part of a programme such as *Fun with Texts* and then use cloze tests, word order games etc. to help them learn. They can also set similar problems to each other.

Solution: 1e, 2h, 3d a, 4 c b f g

🎧   **On achète des provisions**

1 – Bonjour, Madame. Un paquet de chips, s'il vous plaît.
 – Voilà.
 – Merci, Madame.

2 – Bonjour, Madame.
 – Bonjour, Mademoiselle.
 – Je voudrais une boîte de saumon, s'il vous plaît.
 – Voilà.
 – C'est combien?
 – Un euro soixante-dix. Merci. Au revoir.
 – Au revoir, Madame.

3 – Bonjour, Madame.
 – Bonjour, Monsieur. Vous désirez?
 – Avez-vous des haricots verts?
 – Oui. Voilà.
 – Alors, je voudrais un kilo de haricots verts, s'il vous plaît, et un chou-fleur.
 – Voilà. C'est tout?
 – Oui. C'est combien?
 – Deux euros, s'il vous plaît.
 – Au revoir, Madame.
 – Au revoir, Monsieur, et merci.

4 – Bonjour, Madame.
 – Bonjour, Monsieur. Vous désirez?
 – Avez-vous des kiwis?
 – Oui, Monsieur, j'ai des kiwis.
 – Alors, donnez-moi un demi-kilo de kiwis, s'il vous plaît, et un pot d'olives.
 – Oui, et avec ça?
 – Deux cents grammes de saucisson sec et une bouteille de coca.
 – Voilà, c'est tout?
 – Oui, c'est tout.
 – Alors, ça fait trois euros cinquante, s'il vous plaît.
 – Voilà, Madame.
 – Merci, Monsieur. Au revoir.
 – Au revoir, Madame.

SB 12, 👥 🎧 1/6   **SPEAKING**
                                      LISTENING

2   Inventez des conversations

The dialogues in the Students' Book are the same as those used in the previous item and could be played again as a model for students' own dialogues.

The dialogues are graded, with each successive one expanding the language used. When students have practised the standard dialogues, they should work in pairs, incorporating the various colour-coded options.

💻   **CONSOLIDATION**
                                   SPEAKING
Follow-up   **LISTENING**
Shopping lists

A spreadsheet shopping list activity could be used for consolidation here. Students prepare a shopping list for a typical family. Items of food and drink to be purchased are listed in column one. Prices in euros are given in column two. The equivalent price in other currencies (sterling, Swiss francs etc.) can be shown in successive columns, calculated automatically by the exchange rates which can be entered in another section of the sheet, allowing for exchange fluctuations to be recalculated automatically.

The class could all work on the same activity or different groups could use different family sizes or different shops. Price comparisons between the different shops could then be considered.

Sources of prices could be local supermarkets and/or use of the Internet.

This provides a great deal of aural and oral work done either in front of the computer or using print-outs.

Area 7
Using the verb *choisir* (to choose) and other *-ir* verbs
SB 13, **3**–**5**
CM 1/5
CD 1/7
Grammar in Action 2, page 19

SB 13   **READING**

3   On choisit bien

Students match captions with the correct picture. This item presents all the parts of the verb *choisir*.

Solution: 1c, 2a, 3e, 4b, 5f, 6d

SB 13   **GRAMMAR**

Dossier-langue
Regular *-ir* verbs

When students have found the different parts of *choisir*, say the parts aloud, asking the class to repeat them and to notice which endings are sounded. Write the first part of the paradigm of one of the other *-ir* verbs on the board and ask students to come out and add other parts to it.

More able students could try to make up a sentence containing part of one of the other verbs listed and some humorous examples could be given, e.g. *Quand Richard regarde ses devoirs de français, il pâlit.*

SB 13, 🎧 1/7   READING / LISTENING / SPEAKING

4 Une fête

Students read and complete the conversation with the correct parts of *-ir* verbs.

The spelling of their answers will need to be checked and they can then listen to the recording as a guide to pronunciation. After this they could use the text as a playscript, read it aloud in groups of five and perhaps record it.

Solution: **1** *finissent,* **2** *choisit,* **3** *finissent,* **4** *choisis,* **5** *choisissez,* **6** *choisis,* **7** *choisis,* **8** *finissent*

🎧 **Une fête**

– Christophe, Karine, Simon et Nathalie habitent dans un petit village au bord de la mer, mais assez loin de la ville. Il n'y a pas grand-chose à faire dans le village. Les quatre amis décident d'organiser une fête.
– Zut alors! C'est bientôt les grandes vacances, les cours finissent samedi matin, mais il n'y a rien à faire dans notre village. Si on organisait une fête?
– Bonne idée – mais qu'est-ce qu'on peut faire?
– Si on habite en ville, c'est très facile! On choisit un restaurant et tout le monde dîne ensemble.
– Oui, mais les transports en commun finissent vers huit heures et après ça, c'est impossible de rentrer au village.
– Alors, qu'est-ce qu'on peut faire? Simon, tu as de bonnes idées, tu choisis quelque chose, toi!
– Hop-là! J'ai une idée. On va organiser un grand pique-nique sur la plage, mais à minuit!
– Fantastique! Nathalie et Karine, vous choisissez la nourriture. Simon, tu choisis les boissons et …
– Et toi, Christophe, qu'est-ce que tu vas faire?
– Euh … ben, moi, je choisis les invités.
– Ils finissent par organiser un superbe pique-nique. La fête est réussie et tout le monde est content!

SB 13   READING/WRITING

5 Des questions

Students reply to the questions, all of which contain part of an *-ir* verb.

Solution: (other versions are possible)
1 *Les cours finissent samedi matin.*
2 *Les transports en commun finissent vers huit heures.*
3 *Simon.*
4 *Nathalie et Karine.*
5 *Simon.*
6 *Il choisit les invités.*

GRAMMAR IN ACTION 2, PAGE 19 GRAMMAR PRACTICE

Using regular *-ir* verbs (*finir, choisir* etc.)

The activities on this page provide further practice of *-ir* verbs.

CM 1/5   GRAMMAR / WRITING

Les verbes en -ir

This worksheet gives further easy practice of regular *-ir* verbs.

Solution:

1 finir (*to finish*)
   je finis   nous finissons
   tu finis   vous finissez
   il/elle finit   ils/elles finissent

2 Les cadeaux de Noël
Students supply the correct part of *choisir* and follow the lines to see which present everyone chooses.
   1 *André choisit un vélo.*
   2 *Magali choisit des CD.*
   3 *Les jumeaux choisissent un ordinateur.*
   4 *Je choisis un jean.*
   5 *Daniel choisit un baladeur.*
   6 *… tu choisis …*
   7 *… un chien.*

3 Complète les bulles
   1 *remplissez,* **2** *Abolissez,* **3** *obéit,* **4** *finissons,* **5** *réussissent,* **6** *Choisis!*

**Area 8
Saying there isn't any/any more**
SB 14–15, **1**–**5**
Au choix SB 121, **3**
CM 1/6
CD 1/8–9
FC 7–21
Grammar in Action 1, page 28

FC 7–21   PRESENTATION

Je regrette

Start with some oral work, setting some items out as a shop or using flashcards and magazine pictures. Put just a few items out and get students to come out and ask for things, answering: *Je suis désolé/Je regrette, mais je n'ai pas de …*

Students can soon take over the teacher's role in this, and usually enjoy playing this part (with appropriate Gallic shrugs).

SB 14, 🎧 1/8   LISTENING

1 Quel magasin!

This exercise includes examples of *ne … pas* followed by *de*. First teach *porte-monnaie* and any other words likely to present difficulties, perhaps adding a short 'Find the French' activity.

Play the conversation before students do the *Vrai ou faux?* activity, which presents the written form of *pas de*.

Encourage the class to work out that *de* or *d'* are used instead of the full partitive after *pas*.

Explain that M. Léon owns the *épicerie* but runs the shop in a rather peculiar way.

Solution: 1 *vrai*, 2 *vrai*, 3 *vrai*, 4 *faux*, 5 *faux*, 6 *vrai*, 7 *vrai*, 8 *vrai*

🎧 Quel magasin!

– Bonjour, Marie.
– Bonjour, Monsieur.
– Qu'est-ce que tu désires? Tu as ta liste?
– Oui, Monsieur. Je voudrais un kilo de carottes, s'il vous plaît.
– Je suis désolé, je n'ai pas de carottes! Il n'y a pas de légumes le mercredi.
– Alors, donnez-moi cinq cents grammes de bananes.
– Ah non! Je regrette, nous n'avons pas de bananes. Il n'y a pas de fruits aujourd'hui.
– Eh bien, je voudrais du lait. Un litre de lait, s'il vous plaît.
– Du lait? Ah non, Marie, il n'y a pas de lait. Il y a du lait seulement le dimanche.
– Oh, alors, donnez-moi deux bouteilles de vin rouge, Monsieur.
– Désolé, il n'y a pas de vin rouge. J'ai seulement du vin blanc.
– Quel magasin! Vous n'avez pas de fruits, il n'y a pas de légumes, on n'a pas de lait et il n'y a pas de vin rouge. Avez-vous des biscuits, Monsieur?
– Mais bien sûr. Nous avons un grand choix de biscuits.
– Bien, deux paquets de biscuits, s'il vous plaît, comme ça, et une tablette de chocolat.
– Voici les biscuits, mais je regrette, je n'ai pas de chocolat.
– Vous n'avez pas de chocolat! Ah non! Eh bien, les biscuits, c'est combien?
– Deux euros, s'il te plaît.
– Mais … où est mon porte-monnaie? Zut alors! Vous, vous n'avez pas de provisions et moi, je n'ai pas d'argent!
– Bof, là, là, là, là.

SB 14   GRAMMAR

Dossier-langue
Pas de (d')

When students have read this short explanation, ask a few questions to practise *ne … pas de/d'*, e.g.
Il y a du vin dans ce placard?
Tu as des pommes de terre dans ton cartable?

AU CHOIX SB 121   EXTENSION
READING
WRITING

3 Je n'ai pas de lait

This task is in two parts, the first one easier than the second. All students could do part **a**, which involves matching captions to pictures.

Solution: 1c, 2f, 3h, 4a, 5d, 6g, 7b, 8e

In part **b**, students read through the picture strip, then complete the summary to practise *de* + noun after the negative. This part could be done by all, or just by the more able students.

Solution: 1 *pas de lait*, 2 *supermarché*, 3 *pas de pêches*, 4 *pas de magazines*, 5 *pas de pain au chocolat*, 6 *pas de lait*

SB 14   SPEAKING
WRITING

2 Le jeu des sept différences

This gives productive practice of *ne … pas de* and can be done as an oral or written activity.

Solution: *Dans le deuxième chariot, il n'y a pas de thé, de sucre, de chips, de pommes, de petits pois, de bonbons, de limonade.*
(Dans le premier chariot, il n'y a pas de confiture, de fromage, de gâteau, de carottes, de poires, de pêches, de coca.)

SB 14, SB 120, 🗣   SPEAKING

3 Au marché

In these two similar information-gap tasks, one student asks for items on a shopping list and the partner acts as the shopkeeper/stall holder and sells the items if available (most are not!).

The first student has to note down the items which were available.

The students then change roles so that each plays the shopkeeper and practises saying *Je n'ai pas de …* or *Il n'y a pas de …*

🗣   SPEAKING

Follow-up
Désolé!

For further practice, students can play this game in pairs, each partner choosing a shop and writing down three or four things that are sold there. Lists of possible shops and contents could be built up on the board from suggestions by students before the activity begins and used for reference.

Each in turn asks to buy something from the other one's shop. The reply is either *Voici …* or *Désolé(e), je n'ai pas de …*

Each partner crosses off the things that have been sold, and the first one to empty the other's shop of goods has won.

GRAMMAR IN ACTION 1, PAGE 28 GRAMMAR PRACTICE

Saying there isn't any – *pas de*

This page should also be useful for further practice of *ne … pas de*.

ne … plus de   PRESENTATION

Demonstrate the meaning of *ne …plus de* with classroom objects, e.g.
Voici un livre, un crayon, un stylo etc. Je donne le livre à Richard. Maintenant, je n'ai plus de livre.
Voilà, Anne, je te donne le crayon. Maintenant, je n'ai plus de crayons etc.

SB 15   **READING**

4   Dani fait des courses

Students have to match texts to eight of the pictures. Several of the texts include examples of *ne ... plus* and can be used to make clear the meaning and use of this construction.

Solution: **1** (no text), **2D, 3E, 4A, 5H, 6C, 7F, 8B, 9G, 10** (no text)

Dossier-langue   **GRAMMAR**
Some, no more

Go through this explanation and summary with the class to check that it has been understood.

Follow-up   **SPEAKING**

For further practice of *ne ... plus de/d'* the teacher could act the following sequence with an able student or students.

The students could act as customers and ask for various items from the teacher's shop (which has run out of everything except French books), e.g.

Teacher: *Voici mon magasin.*
Student: *Je voudrais un kilo de pommes.*
Teacher: *Désolé(e), je n'ai plus de pommes.*
Student: *Ça ne fait rien. Avez-vous des poires?*
Teacher: *Ah, je regrette, je n'ai plus de poires.*
Student: *Ça ne fait rien. Alors des oranges. Avez-vous des oranges?*
Teacher: *Non, je n'ai plus d'oranges.*
Student: *Qu'est-ce que vous avez comme fruits?*
Teacher: *Je n'ai plus de fruits ... mais j'ai beaucoup de livres. Voulez-vous un livre? Ce livre est très intéressant!*

SB 15, 🎧 **1/9**   **LISTENING**
                                               WRITING
5   Les cartes postales   **SPEAKING**

This item brings together all the forms of the partitive article, including examples of *ne... pas de* and *ne ... plus de*. Refer students to the *Dossier-langue* on SB 7 and SB 15.

Students listen to the recorded version, before completing the script with the correct form of the partitive article.

Later, students could use this as a playscript, or the item could form the basis of an activity using *Fun with Texts* or *Copywrite*.

Solution: **1** *des*, **2** *des*, **3** *de*, **4** *de*, **5** *des*, **6** *de*, **7** *de*, **8** *du*, **9** *des*, **10** *de*, **11** *de*, **12** *de*, **13** *d'*, **14** *de l'*, **15** *d'*, **16** *de*, **17** *des*, **18** *des*, **19** *de*, **20** *des*

🎧   **Les cartes postales**

L'épicier est assis sur une chaise et il dort. Un client entre dans l'épicerie.

– Bonjour, Monsieur. Je voudrais des cartes postales, s'il vous plaît.
– Comment? Des cartes postales? Je regrette, Monsieur, mais je ne vends pas de cartes postales. C'est une épicerie ici.
– Alors, donnez-moi un kilo de pommes ... et des cartes postales!
– Je regrette, Monsieur, mais je n'ai plus de pommes. Et je n'ai pas de cartes postales non plus!
– Bon, ça ne fait rien. Donnez-moi du pain ... et des cartes postales!
– Je n'ai pas de pain! Je n'ai pas de cartes postales!
– Bon, bon, ça va! Vous n'avez pas de pain. Vous n'avez pas d'eau minérale non plus, sans doute?
– Si, j'ai de l'eau minérale. Une bouteille d'eau minérale. Voilà. C'est tout?
– Oui, c'est tout.
– Vous êtes sûr?
– Oui, je suis sûr.
– Vous ne voulez pas de cartes postales?
– Des cartes postales? Non. Pourquoi? Vous vendez aussi des cartes postales?
– Non, je ne vends pas de cartes postales!
– Il est fou, cet épicier!
– Bon, au revoir, Monsieur.
– Oui, c'est ça, c'est ça ... au revoir!

Le client sort. L'épicier va s'asseoir sur sa chaise. Soudain, un autre client entre dans l'épicerie.

– Pardon, Monsieur. Vous avez des cartes postales?

Follow-up   **WRITING**
Vrai ou faux?

Students could make up some *vrai ou faux?* statements based on task 5, write them down and set them to each other. Alternatively, the following could be set by the teacher, either as a listening task, or, if they are written on the board, as a reading activity.

1 Le client veut acheter des cartes postales.
2 Il n'y a plus de pommes à l'épicerie.
3 À l'épicerie, ils n'ont plus de pain.
4 Il n'y a plus d'eau minérale.
5 Le client achète une bouteille de limonade.
6 On ne vend pas de cartes postales à l'épicerie.

CM 1/6,   **READING**
                                           SPEAKING

ne ... pas, ne ... plus

This copymaster could be used here for further practice of *ne ... pas de/plus de*.

1 Beaucoup ou pas du tout?

The first item is a reading task in which students choose the right caption for the pictures.

Solution: **1a, 2b, 3c, 4c, 5b**

The other two tasks are for speaking practice in pairs, first of all a conversation with suggested substitutions, which can be done as a dice dialogue, and finallly a follow-up to this, in the form of a dice game, to be played in pairs.

Area 9
Further activities and consolidation

SB 16, **1**–**3**
SB 17
Au choix SB 121, **4**
CM 1/7–1/16
CD 1/10–14
Student CD 1/1–6, 2/1–3

SB 16, 🎧 1/10   **READING**
                                                         LISTENING
1   **Le shopping**   **WRITING**

Students first go through the questions and answers with the teacher, make a guess at what the answers will be and complete the gapped replies.

There could also be some oral work, based on these questions, in which students reply for themselves and their families.

They then listen to the recording, check their guesses against the actual answers and correct the sentences. Draw the attention of the students to the change from the spoken 1st person verbs to the written 3rd persons and also to the change from the use of the 2nd person in asking questions and the 1st person in giving answers.

Solution: **a** *deux,* **b** *(des) croissants,* **c** *(des) pains au chocolat,* **d** *au marché,* **e** *(les) chips,* **f** *(des) fruits,* **g** *des chips,* **h** *du chocolat*

🎧   **Le shopping**

1 – Pardon, Madame. Combien de pain achetez-vous par jour?
    – J'achète deux baguettes par jour, mais le dimanche, mes enfants vont à la boulangerie et ils choisissent toujours des croissants ou des pains au chocolat.
2 – Excusez-moi, Madame. Est-ce que vous préférez acheter les fruits et les légumes à l'épicerie ou est-ce que vous descendez au marché?
    – Alors, si possible, je descends au marché. Je préfère acheter les fruits et les légumes là-bas – ils sont plus frais!
3 – Qu'est-ce que tu choisis normalement, pour la récré?
    – J'adore les chips ou quelquefois, je mange des fruits.
4 – Madame, est-ce que vos enfants mangent beaucoup de bonbons? Oui ou non?
    – Non, non. En général, ils préfèrent des chips ou du chocolat.

SB 16, 💻   **GRAMMAR**

Dossier-langue
The three groups of regular verbs

This *Dossier-langue* table sets out clearly all three types of regular verbs, including those with slight variations, e.g. *acheter, préférer.* The table could be added to the students' electronic verb table (see TB 19) and should be useful as a reference point.

The three kinds of regular verbs could then be practised orally, using some of the verb games suggested in Section 2 (TB 27).

Check whether the class can spot examples of each kind of verb in the questions and answers above.

CM 1/7   **LISTENING**
                                              READING

Les verbes sont utiles

This copymaster gives further practice of all three kinds of regular verbs. It could be done now as consolidation or later for revision.

Tasks 1–3 give 'straight' grammar practice, but task 4 is a reading task. For extra practice, students could be asked to find the infinitives of the ten verbs used to fill the gaps.

Solution:

1 Verbena, le serpent français
A   *-er*   *-re*   *-ir*
       manger   *vendre*   *choisir*
       aimer   *rendre*   *finir*
       parler   *descendre*
       acheter
B   *infinitif*

2 Trois sortes de verbes

	chanter	choisir	répondre
je	chante	choisis	réponds
tu	chantes	choisis	réponds
il/elle	chante	choisit	répond
nous	chantons	choisissons	répondons
vous	chantez	choisissez	répondez
ils/elles	chantent	choisissent	répondent

3 Comment dit-on cela?
1 *je travaille,* **2** *il demande,* **3** *il réussit,* **4** *nous comptons,* **5** *elles attendent,* **6** *je préfère,* **7** *elle explique,* **8** *nous finissons,* **9** *elle choisit,* **10** *ils achètent*

4 Dans l'Arctique
1 *dure,* **2** *continuent,* **3** *rend,* **4** *mange,* **5** *attendent,* **6** *finit,* **7** *brille,* **8** *choisissent,* **9** *commence,* **10** *dansent*

SB 16   **WRITING**
                                      GRAMMAR

2   **Aimes-tu faire les courses?**

Students complete these short letters with the correct verb forms. This item could form the basis of some class discussion, for or against shopping.

Solution: **1** *je déteste,* **2** *je descends,* **3** *je trouve,* **4** *Nous choisissons,* **5** *porte,* **6** *passent,* **7** *j'attends,* **8** *j'adore,* **9** *nous préférons,* **10** *on vend,* **11** *Nous achetons*

Au choix SB 121   **EXTENSION**
                                     GRAMMAR

4   **Chasse à l'intrus**

This gives further practice with all three types of regular verbs.

Solution: **1c, 2a, 3d, 4c, 5d**

En ville unité 1

SB 16 🔊, 💻   SPEAKING / WRITING

3 À toi!

This task brings together much of the language about shopping.

It is used first as a speaking task in which students choose questions which they ask each other in turns.

For the second part of the task, students choose questions and write them out with their own replies. It is suggested that each student adds these to their own electronic phrase book and learns some sample questions and answers by heart.

Section 3

CM 1/8   DICTIONARY SKILLS
C'est utile, le dictionnaire!

This is the first of four worksheets which focus on dictionary skills (see also CM 2/9, 3/10, 7/3). This series provides guidance and practice in the effective use of a bilingual dictionary. Each self-contained worksheet covers a specific aspect of dictionary use.

For use at any appropriate point in *Unité 1*, or later, this introductory sheet starts with a brief explanation of how a dictionary is organised and is followed by two short tasks, practising alphabetical order.

Solution:

1 Dans l'ordre alphabétique

	français	anglais	catégorie
1	un camion	lorry	un véhicule
2	le Canada	Canada	un pays
3	un canard	duck	un oiseau
4	une cerise	cherry	un fruit
5	un champignon	mushroom	un légume
6	une chemise	shirt	un vêtement
7	un cheval	horse	un animal

2 Sur cette page
On peut trouver ces mots sur la page: **b** cheval, **c** cheveu, **d** chien

CM 1/9, 🎧 SCD 1/1–6   INDEPENDENT LISTENING / SOUNDS AND WRITING
Écoute et parle

This copymaster provides pronunciation and speaking practice.

1 À la française

🎧 À la française

1 accent
2 chips
3 conversation
4 fruit
5 journal
6 organise
7 pièce
8 pot

2 Et après?

Solution: **1** b, **2** e, **3** i, **4** m, **5** q, **6** u, **7** x, **8** z

🎧 Et après?

1 a, **2** d, **3** h, **4** l, **5** p, **6** t, **7** w, **8** y

3 Des phrases ridicules

🎧 Des phrases ridicules

Cent cinquante citrons descendent du ciel.
Le curé compte les cartes dans un coin de la cathédrale.

4 Les terminaisons: -ial et -iel

Solution: **1**d, **2**f, **3**e, **4**c, **5**a, **6**b

🎧 Les terminaisons: -ial et -iel

1 officiel
2 spécial
3 partiel
4 glacial
5 essentiel
6 commercial

5 Vocabulaire de classe

Solution: **1** faux, **2** pas, **3** cahier, **4** bonne, **5** est, **6** Qui, **7** le

🎧 Vocabulaire de classe

1 C'est vrai ou faux?
2 Ce n'est pas difficile.
3 Je ne trouve pas mon cahier.
4 Choisis la bonne bulle.
5 Quelle est la réponse correcte?
6 Qui commence?
7 Regardez le tableau.

6 Des conversations

🎧 Des conversations

1 Les fruits et les légumes
– Qu'est-ce que tu préfères comme fruit?
(pause)
– Je préfère les bananes et les fraises.
– Est-ce qu'il y a un fruit que tu n'aimes pas?
(pause)
– Oui, je n'aime pas les abricots et je déteste les kiwis.
– Et les légumes, tu les aimes?
(pause)
– J'aime beaucoup les carottes et les petits pois, mais je n'aime pas les choux-fleurs.

2 On fait des courses
– Où vas-tu d'abord?
(pause)
– Je vais à la boulangerie. Je vais acheter une baguette et des pains au chocolat.
– D'accord. Alors moi, je vais à l'épicerie. Qu'est-ce que j'achète pour le pique-nique?
(pause)
– Deux cent cinquante grammes de fromage, deux paquets de chips et du coca.
– Et après, où est-ce que tu m'attends?
(pause)
– Je vais t'attendre devant le cinéma.

3 Au tabac
– Bonjour, Mademoiselle. Vous désirez?
(pause)

– Ces trois cartes postales, s'il vous plaît.
– Voilà. C'est tout?
(pause)
– Je voudrais trois timbres pour l'Angleterre, s'il vous plaît.
– Désolé, Mademoiselle, mais je n'en ai plus.
(pause)
– Alors, où est-ce qu'on vend les timbres?
– Allez à la poste. Ce n'est pas loin.

CM 1/10, SCD 2/1–3 INDEPENDENT LISTENING

Tu comprends?

Students could do any or all of the three items on this worksheet, now or later as revision.

1 Ou vont-ils?

Solution: Luc   Sandrine   Les deux
1b, 2c, 3d,   4f, 5a, 6e,   7g

Ou vont-ils?

1 – Où vas-tu d'abord, Luc?
– Je vais à la boulangerie-pâtisserie. Je vais acheter du pain pour Maman et une glace pour moi!

2 – O.K. Moi, je vais d'abord à la boucherie. Je vais acheter le poulet pour dimanche.

3 – Voilà Sandrine. Maintenant, je vais à l'épicerie. Et toi, où vas-tu?

4 – Je vais à la charcuterie. Je vais acheter de la salade de tomates et du pâté.

5 – Bon. Maintenant, je vais à la librairie pour mon magazine informatique. Où vas-tu, Sandrine?

6 – Je vais au marché. Je vais acheter des légumes et des fruits. Et après ça, moi, je voudrais une limonade ou un coca.

7 – Excellent. Moi aussi. On va au café, tous les deux.

2 Qu'est-ce qu'on fait?

Solution: 1b, 2b, 3c, 4b, 5a, 6b

Qu'est-ce qu'on fait?

1 – On va en ville? Tu as des courses à faire?
– Non. Je préfère rester à la maison et regarder la télé.
– D'accord, moi aussi. Je suis très fatigué.

2 – Un kilo de pêches, s'il vous plaît, et des fraises. J'adore les fraises!

3 – Quelle heure est-il? Ce bus est toujours en retard!
– Il est déjà cinq heures. Quand est-ce que le bus va arriver?

4 – Qu'est-ce que tu prends Caroline, une pomme ou une banane?
– Une banane, s'il te plaît.
– Tu n'aimes pas les pommes?
– Si, si, j'aime les pommes, mais je préfère les bananes.

5 – Bonjour, Madame. Vous avez des croissants? Alors donnez-moi quatre croissants, s'il vous plaît.

6 – Alors qu'est-ce qu'on fait – des sandwichs au jambon ou au fromage?
– Au fromage. Tout le monde aime ça.
– Bon. Et choisissons des gâteaux – on prend des pains au chocolat ou des tartes aux pommes?
– Oh, des pains au chocolat – ils sont délicieux ici!

3 On va acheter ça

Solution: The following should be ticked:
1, **3**, **5**, **7**, **8**, **10**

On va acheter ça

– Il faut aller aux magasins aujourd'hui. Il ne reste plus beaucoup à manger.
– D'accord. Alors, qu'est-ce qu'il faut acheter?
– Voyons. Est-ce qu'il y a du pain? Non, il n'y a plus de pain. Alors, on va acheter du pain.
– Est-ce qu'il y a de la confiture?
– Oui, il y a de la confiture de fraises. Mais il n'y a plus de beurre.
– Alors du pain et du beurre. Et des tomates? J'adore les tomates.
– Oui, oui, il y en a beaucoup, mais il n'y a plus de pommes. Alors, mets des pommes sur ta liste.
– D'accord, des pommes, et quoi encore? Du jambon?
– Non, il y a quatre tranches de jambon dans le frigo. Mais il n'y a plus de fromage. Achète du fromage, s'il te plaît.
– Bon … du fromage. Et du café? Est-ce qu'il y a du café?
– Oui, il y a du café, mais il n'y a plus de lait, alors achète du lait.
– Du lait … et puis des chips? J'aime bien les chips.
– Oui, on n'a plus de chips. Alors un gros paquet de chips. Et puis un paquet de biscuits – des biscuits au chocolat.
– C'est tout?
– Oui, je pense que c'est tout.

SB 17, CM 1/11

Sommaire

A summary of the main structures and vocabulary of this unit. Students fill in gaps on the copymaster. They should check their answers against the Students' Book page.

unité 1 En ville

Section 3

45

CM 1/12
Rappel 1
REVISION

This copymaster can be used at any point in the course for revision and consolidation. It provides revision of core question and answers about oneself, one's family and pets, some general vocabulary of things in a bedroom and a lead-in to *Unité 2*, with some names of places in a town and directions. The reading and writing tasks are self-instructional and can be used by students working individually for homework or during cover lessons.

Solution:

1 Questions et réponses
A **1** *Comment,* **2** *as,* **3** *Où,* **4** *ville,* **5** *as/regardes,* **6** *frères,* **7** *Quel,* **8** *que*
a *à,* **b** *m',* **c** *ai,* **d** *j'ai,* **e** *c'est/nous sommes,* **f** *ville,* **g** *enfant,* **h** *ans*
B **1b, 2h, 3a, 4f, 5c, 6g, 7e, 8d**

2 Dans la chambre
(any ten) *une télévision, un T-shirt, un téléphone portable, un tableau, une table, un taille-crayon, un tapis, un trombone, des tennis, des timbres, une tortue, une trompette, une trousse*

3 Mots croisés (les animaux)

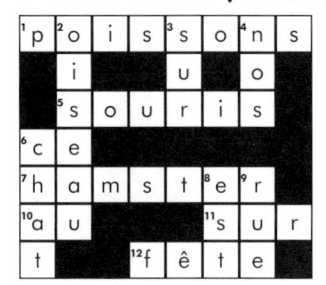

	¹p	²o	i	s	³s	o	⁴n	s
		i			u		o	
	⁵s	o	u	r	i	s		
	⁶c	e						
⁷h	a	m	s	t	⁸e	r		
¹⁰a	u			¹¹s	u	r		
t			¹²f	ê	t	e		

Épreuve – Unité 1

These worksheets can be used for an informal test of listening, speaking, reading and writing or for extra practice, as required. For general notes on administering the *Épreuves*, see TB 16.

CM 1/13, 🎧 1/11–14
LISTENING
Épreuve: Écouter

A Marie fait les courses (NC 2)
Solution: **1a, 2d, 3e, 4c, 5g, 6f, 7b**

(mark /6: 4+ shows understanding of a range of familiar statements)

🎧 Marie fait les courses

1 Je vais à la boulangerie. Je vais acheter une baguette.
2 Je vais acheter un kilo de bananes.
3 Maintenant, je voudrais une glace.
4 Je vais acheter des chips pour mon frère.
5 Et je vais acheter un journal pour mon père.
6 Je vais au tabac. Je vais acheter un timbre.
7 Maintenant, je veux des bonbons pour ma sœur.

B Les quantités (NC 3)
Solution: **1a, 2c, 3d, 4g, 5b, 6e, 7f**

(mark /6: 4+ shows understanding of short dialogues, spoken at near normal speed without any interference)

🎧 Les quantités

1 – Et pour vous, Mademoiselle?
  – Deux paquets de chips, s'il vous plaît.
2 – Qu'est-ce que vous voulez?
  – Je voudrais deux cents grammes de fromage, s'il vous plaît.
3 – Et avec ça?
  – Donnez-moi une boîte de jambon, s'il vous plaît.
4 – Bonjour, Mademoiselle.
  – Bonjour. Avez-vous deux kilos de pommes de terre, s'il vous plaît?
5 – Qu'est-ce que vous voulez, Mademoiselle?
  – Une tranche de quiche, s'il vous plaît.
6 – De l'eau minérale?
  – Non, une bouteille de vin, s'il vous plaît.
7 – C'est tout?
  – Alors … Un pot de confiture, s'il vous plaît.

C Ça coûte combien? (NC 3)
Solution: **1b, 2c, 3a, 4a, 5b, 6a, 7c**

(mark /6: 4+ shows understanding of short messages spoken at near normal speed without interference)

🎧 Ça coûte combien?

1 Une douzaine d'œufs? Ça coûte 1 euro 20.
2 Alors … Une bouteille de vin et un litre de lait coûtent 2 euros 30.
3 La boîte de chocolats, c'est … 3 euros 60.
4 Une barquette de fraises coûte 2 euros 80.
5 Un pot de confiture coûte 1 euro 10.
6 Le poisson est cher. C'est 5 euros 90.
7 Un melon, c'est 50 cents la pièce.

D Marie est dans quel magasin? (NC 4)
Solution: **1a, 2e, 3d, 4c, 5b, 6f, 7h, 8g**

(mark /7: 5+ shows ability to identify and note main points and some detail)

🎧 Marie est dans quel magasin?

1 Vous voulez des concombres et des champignons? Il n'y en a plus.
2 Du pain? Non. Mais nous avons des gâteaux délicieux!

En ville unité 1 — Section 3

46

3 Que voulez-vous? Les livres sont ici et les journaux sont là-bas.
4 La poissonnerie est là-bas. Mais notre viande est bonne et pas très chère, Mademoiselle.
5 Bonnes? Les baguettes ici sont toujours bonnes, Mademoiselle!
6 Les pêches ici sont formidables!
7 Du parfum? Ah non, pas ici. J'ai des timbres, si vous voulez, mais en face, ils vendent du parfum.
8 De la viande? … Non. Des fruits? … Non. Ici, je vends du poisson.

CM 1/14   SPEAKING
Épreuve: Parler

Students should be given the sheet up to a week before the assessment to give them time to choose whether to do 1 or 2 and to give them time to prepare and practise both conversations – the structured one (A) and the open-ended one (B) – with their partners. For Task B pupils should be made aware that 12 marks are available for the responses suggested by the visuals but that another mark is available for giving extra information about likes and dislikes.

Mark scheme

Section A: mark /12: 3 marks per response
- 1 mark for a response that is clear and conveys all of the information requested, in the form of a complete phrase or sentence, though not necessarily an accurate one. The questions and answers may seem a little disjointed, like separate items rather than parts of a coherent conversation.
- 2 marks for a response that is clear and conveys all of the information requested in the form of a complete phrase or sentence, though not necessarily an accurate one. The language must flow reasonably smoothly and be recognisable as part of a coherent conversation.
- 3 marks for a clear and complete response that flows smoothly as part of a clear and coherent conversation. The language must be in complete sentences or phrases that are reasonably accurate and consistent as far as grammar, pronunciation and intonation are concerned.

Section B: mark /13: 3 marks per response, as above, +1 bonus mark for adding one or two items of extra information about personal preferences (i.e. using knowledge of language to adapt and substitute single words and phrases).

Summary:
Marks	7–13	14–18	19–25
NC Level	2	3	4

CM 1/15   READING
Épreuve: Lire

A   Au supermarché (NC 1)
Solution: 1f, 2g, 3d, 4e, 5c, 6b, 7a

(mark /6: 4+ shows understanding of single words)

B   M. Mally indique le magasin (NC 2)
Solution: 1e, 2c, 3g, 4b, 5d, 6a, 7f

(mark /6: 4+ shows understanding of short texts, identifying main points)

C   C'est bon? (NC 3)
Solution: 1c, 2a, 3b, 4a, 5a, 6c, 7b

(mark /6: 4+ shows understanding of short texts including likes, dislikes and feelings)

D   L'anniversaire de Paul (NC 4)
Solution: 1b, 2a, 3c, 4b, 5c, 6b, 7a, 8c

(mark /7: 5+ shows understanding of short stories and ability to note main points and some detail)

CM 1/16   WRITING
Épreuve: Écrire et grammaire

A   Au club des jeunes (NC 1)
Solution: 1 *trouve*, 2 *entend*, 3 *finissent*, 4 *remplit*, 5 *vendent*, 6 *choisissez*, 7 *parle*, 8 *préfères*, 9 *achetez*

(mark /8: 5+ shows ability to select appropriate words to complete sentences and copy them correctly)

B   Une liste (NC 1)

(mark /8: 1 mark for each blank. Allow minor spelling errors. Do not allow repeats or use of the example. 6+ shows ability to write single words correctly.)

C   Samedi matin (NC 4)

This is an open-ended task.

Mark scheme
- 1 mark for each shopping activity comprehensively mentioned (up to a maximum of 5). No credit for using the example.

Subtotal: 5
- 4 marks for very accurate spelling throughout (ignore minor errors)
- 3 marks for generally accurate spelling throughout
- 2 marks for fairly accurate spelling throughout
- 1 marks for occasional successful spelling
- 0 marks little or nothing of merit

Subtotal: 4
(mark /9: 6+ shows ability to write individual paragraphs of about three or four sentences, drawing largely on memorised language)

unité 1 En ville

Section 3

Encore Tricolore 2
nouvelle édition

unité 2 On fait des projets

Areas	Topics	Grammar
1	Countries, capital cities, nationalities (mainly Europe)	
2	Prepositions with towns and countries	Revision of *aller* *voir* (present tense)
3	Means of transport	*venir* (present tense)
4	Revision of leisure activities Expressions of future time	*aller* + infinitive
5	Describing towns and villages, location and facilities	
6		*pouvoir* + infinitive
7	Reading and writing postcards Revision of weather	
8	Further activities and consolidation	

National Curriculum Information

Some students	levels 4–5
Most students	levels 3–4
All students	levels 2–3

Revision

Rappel (CM 2/13) includes revision of the following:
- numbers
- school vocabulary
- computer vocabulary

Sounds and writing

- numbers
- pronunciation of *ch* and *qu*
- the ending *-in*

See *Écoute et parle* (CM 2/10, TB 64).

ICT opportunities

- setting up e-mail correspondents
- creating illustrated sentences showing where different characters are going on holiday
- finding out more information about French towns, from the Internet
- designing a poster or a short leaflet about local facilities
- sending a virtual postcard

Reading strategies

Presse-Jeunesse 1 (SB 32–33, CM 133)

Assessment

- Informal assessment is in *Épreuves* at the end of this unit (TB 67, CM 2/14–2/17)
- Formal assessment (*Unités 1–7*) is in the *Contrôle* (TB 190, CM 139–145).

Students' Book

Unité 2 SB 18–31
Au choix SB 122–125

Flashcards

22–31 transport
32–38 leisure

CDs

1/15–31
Student CD 1/7–12, 2/4–6

Additional

Grammar in Action 2, pp 5–7, 11

Copymasters

CM 2/1	*L'Europe* [map]	
CM 2/2	*Les transports* [mini-flashcards]	
CM 2/3	*Des mots croisés (voir et venir)* [grammar]	
CM 2/4	*Des activités* [mini-flashcards]	
CM 2/5	*Projets de vacances* [grammar]	
CM 2/6	*La France* [map]	
CM 2/7	*Au val de Loire* [listening]	
CM 2/8	*Des mots croisés (aller et pouvoir)* [grammar]	
CM 2/9	*C'est utile, le dictionnaire!* [dictionary skills]	
CM 2/10	*Écoute et parle* [independent listening]	
CM 2/11	*Tu comprends?* [independent listening]	
CM 2/12	*Sommaire* [consolidation, reference]	
CM 2/13	*Rappel* [revision]	
CM 2/14	*Épreuve: Écouter*	
CM 2/15	*Épreuve: Parler*	
CM 2/16	*Épreuve: Lire*	
CM 2/17	*Épreuve: Écrire et grammaire*	
CM 133	*Presse-Jeunesse 1* [reading]	

Language content

Countries (Area 1)

l'Allemagne (f)
l'Autriche (f)
la Belgique
l'Espagne (f)
la France
la Grèce
l'Irlande (f)
l'Irlande du Nord (f)
l'Italie (f)
la Suisse
l'Angleterre (f)
l'Écosse (f)
le Danemark
le Portugal
le Royaume-Uni
le pays de Galles
les Pays-Bas (m pl)
le Canada
le Sénégal
le Maroc
les États-Unis (m pl)

Transport (Area 3)

(en) avion (m)
(en) bateau (m)
(en) bus (m)
(en) car (m)
(à) cheval (m)
(en) métro (m)
(à) mobylette (f)
(à/en) moto (f)
(à) pied (m)
(en) taxi (m)
(en) train (m)
(à) vélo (m)
(en) voiture (f)

Expressions of time (Area 4)

demain
ce soir
lundi (mardi etc.) prochain
la semaine prochaine

Describing locations (Area 5)

C'est …
une grande ville
une ville moyenne
une petite ville
un village
dans le nord
dans le sud
dans l'est
dans l'ouest
au centre
à la campagne
à la montagne
sur la côte
près de …

Talking about what you can do (Area 6)

Qu'est-ce qu'on peut faire ici/dans la ville/dans la région?
On peut visiter le château.
Est-ce qu'on peut faire du ski?
Non, on ne peut pas faire ça.
Est-ce que je peux jouer sur l'ordinateur?

Useful websites

National tourist offices

Belgium – www.go-belgium.net
Switzerland – www.swisstourisminfo.com
Quebec, Canada – www.bonjourquebec.com/
Morocco – www.tourisme-marocain.com/
Senegal – www.primature.sn/tour/

Towns and cities in France

Many local tourist offices can be found by typing the name of the town in the following address: www.mairie-town.fr (e.g. www.mairie-rouen.fr)

Tourist sights

www.tour-eiffel.fr – this site has a lot of interesting information about the Eiffel Tower including statistics, history, practical information and even an online quiz.

www.rio.gouv.qc.ca – the official website of the Montreal Olympic park with information about the history of the park and the Olympic tower.
www.liberty.netliberte.org – this website has information in French about the creation of the Statue of Liberty, its history, statistics etc.

Penfriends

www.momes.net – from the home page, the *Correspondants* menu gives access to messages from children who want to find penfriends. You can respond to the ads directly from the page.
www.franceworld.com – this website offers school children and students the possibility to contact students from all over the world according to interests. Once you have registered, you can have access to the database of 15,000 users of 70 nationalities.

**Area 1
Countries, capital cities,
nationalities (mainly Europe)**
SB 18–19, **1**–**4**
SB 20, **1**–**3**
CM 2/1
CD 1/15–16

PRESENTATION

Countries in Europe

If possible, use a map of Europe to present the names of these European countries: *la France, la Suisse, l'Italie, l'Espagne, la Belgique, l'Allemagne, l'Espagne, le Royaume-Uni, l'Irlande (du Nord), l'Écosse, l'Angleterre, le pays de Galles*

The outline map on CM 2/1 could be used to make an OHT. Other European countries are taught later in the area and a map of Europe is given on SB 20.

SB 18–19   **READING**

On surfe sur le Net
... pour trouver un(e) correspondant(e)

The details of correspondants are closely based on the sort of items which appear on the *Momes* website (see TB 49).

Talk through the item briefly, perhaps reading aloud some of the entries to give the pronunciation of key words, such as *francophones, Genève, Bruxelles, Royaume-Uni*.

Students could then work on the item, perhaps in pairs, to find out the main points, looking up any key words which could be written on the board and used for *Effacez!* or other word games (see TB 25). This could be followed by some simple oral questions from the teacher.

SB 18   **READING**

1   5-4-3-2-1

This task highlights some of the main vocabulary of the text.

Solution:

Any 5 of: *l'Espagne, la Suisse, la France, l'Italie, la Belgique, l'Allemagne, le Royaume-Uni, l'Irlande, le Canada*
Any 4 of: *l'italien, le français, l'allemand, l'anglais, l'espagnol*
Any 3 of: *Rome, Bruxelles, Berlin, Madrid*
Any 2 of: *le ski, l'équitation, le football, le hockey, le basket*
Any 1 of: *la trompette, le piano, la guitare*

SB 18   **READING**

2   Vrai ou faux?

When checking the answers orally, give the correct answers for the false statements. Students may not be able to do this for all answers as they have not practised all the language, e.g. adjectives of nationality.

Solution: **1** *vrai,* **2** *faux (Il est français.),* **3** *faux (Elle habite dans un village près de Genève.),* **4** *vrai,* **5** *faux (Il est italien.),* **6** *vrai,* **7** *faux (Elles sont belges.),* **8** *vrai,* **9** *faux (Il habite en Allemagne.),* **10** *vrai,* **11** *faux (Elle est espagnole.),* **12** *vrai*

SB 18,   **SPEAKING**

3   Oui ou non?

Students work in pairs, each choosing one person from those on SB 19 and replying with *oui, non* or *je ne sais pas*, according to their details.

SB 18, 🎧 **1/15**   **LISTENING**
                                                      READING

4   C'est qui?

Students listen to the recording in order to identify the penfriends from the details given. As this is a demanding task, use the pause button after each item so students can read through the text to find the answers. It would work best with individual listening equipment.

Solution: **1** *Laura,* **2** *Nicole,* **3** *Stefan,* **4** *Émilie,* **5** *Mathieu,* **6** *Cassandra,* **7** *Roberto*

🎧   **C'est qui?**

Sept personnes ont trouvé un correspondant sur Internet.
1 Ma correspondante est belge. Elle habite à Bruxelles et elle parle français et anglais. Elle aime la musique et la danse. Elle a une amie qui s'appelle Nicole.
2 Moi aussi, j'ai une correspondante qui habite en Belgique. C'est l'amie de Laura. Comme moi, elle adore surfer sur le Net. On s'écrit des e-mails très souvent. C'est amusant.
3 Mon correspondant est allemand. Comme moi, il est très sportif. Son sport préféré est le basket. Il aime aussi la musique. Il habite à Berlin en Allemagne.
4 Ma correspondante habite dans un village en Suisse. Elle adore les animaux, surtout les chevaux. En hiver, elle fait du ski aussi.
5 Mon correspondant habite à Honfleur. Il s'intéresse à l'informatique et il aime les jeux électroniques. Il a 13 ans.
6 Ma correspondante est espagnole. Elle habite à Madrid. Elle parle espagnol, anglais et français. Elle aime lire, écouter de la musique et aller au cinéma. On va discuter des films et des livres qu'on a aimés.
7 Mon correspondant habite à Rome en Italie. Il adore la musique. Il parle italien et il apprend le français au collège.

E-mail correspondents

If teachers wish to follow up the idea of the class having e-mail correspondents, or if the school has access to video-conferencing facilities, see TB 21 for suggestions.

SB 20 — **PRESENTATION / READING**

L'Europe

The map and flags provide a reference for the European countries covered in this unit.

If available, use a larger map of Europe to present the names of the European countries shown, or make an OHT from CM 2/1. Then ask students to give names of countries and build up a list on the board. These are the names of countries included on the map:

le Royaume-Uni	la Grèce
l'Écosse	la Suisse
le pays de Galles	l'Autriche
l'Angleterre	l'Allemagne
l'Irlande (du Nord)	le Luxembourg
la France	la Belgique
l'Espagne	les Pays-Bas
le Portugal	le Danemark
l'Italie	

Some oral work could be based on this, e.g.

C'est quel pays? C'est dans le nord de l'Europe et son nom commence par la lettre D. (le Danemark)
C'est au sud de la France. Sa capitale est Madrid. (l'Espagne)
Le drapeau de ce pays est tricolore, mais c'est vert, blanc et orange. (l'Irlande)
C'est un pays dans le sud de l'Europe. Athènes est la capitale du pays. (la Grèce)
Quels pays se trouvent entre l'Allemagne et l'Italie? (l'Autriche, la Suisse) etc.

SB 20, 🎧 **1/16** — **LISTENING**

1 Des vacances en Europe

This listening task gives the pronunciation of some of the European countries and cities. Students should listen to each item and note down the country mentioned, using the car identification letters (as given on the map, SB 20) or the name of the country in full. Able students could give one or more detail about the country given in the publicity.

Solution:
1. DK (le Danemark); les jardins de Tivoli
2. G (la Grèce); des temples anciens/ruines célèbres/le Parthénon
3. A (l'Autriche); les lacs/les montagnes/la musique
4. B (la Belgique); les chocolats
5. I (l'Italie); le Colisée/ruines romaines/les spaghettis/les pizzas
6. D (l'Allemagne); les châteaux/les forêts/Berlin
7. E (l'Espagne); la guitare/le soleil/le flamenco
8. IRL (l'Irlande); la côte ouest/Dublin
9. CH (la Suisse); la montagne/le ski/les jolis paysages
10. P (le Portugal); les sports nautiques

🎧 **Des vacances en Europe**

Voilà des idées pour passer vos vacances en Europe.

1. Visitez Copenhague, au Danemark. C'est une belle ville où vous pouvez visiter les jardins de Tivoli. Le Danemark, c'est fantastique!
2. Vous aimez les monuments anciens? Alors, allez en Grèce. En Grèce, vous pouvez voir des temples anciens et des ruines célèbres, comme le Parthénon à Athènes.
3. Les lacs, les montagnes, la musique. Venez découvrir le pays de Mozart. Passez vos vacances en Autriche. Il y a beaucoup de choses à faire.
4. Vous aimez les chocolats? Les chocolats belges sont délicieux et très célèbres. La Belgique est un petit pays au cœur de l'Europe. Venez en Belgique. Mmm, c'est bon, le chocolat belge!
5. L'histoire des Romains, ça vous intéresse? Vous voulez voir le Colisée et d'autres ruines romaines? Vous aimez les spaghettis et les pizzas? N'hésitez pas, visitez l'Italie cet été.
6. Vous aimez les châteaux et les forêts? Vous aimez les grandes villes, comme Berlin? Visitez l'Allemagne – c'est un grand pays très varié.
7. La guitare, le soleil, le flamenco – venez en Espagne. Vous êtes sûr de passer de bonnes vacances.
8. Cet été, passez vos vacances sur l'île verte. Venez en Irlande. Découvrez la magnifique côte ouest ou visitez Dublin, la belle capitale.
9. Vous aimez la montagne, le ski, les jolis paysages? Visitez la Suisse. Venez découvrir la montagne cet été.
10. Vous aimez les sports nautiques, comme la planche à voile et le surf? Passez vos vacances au Portugal. Sur la côte atlantique du Portugal, vous pouvez faire beaucoup de sports nautiques.

SB 20 — **READING**

2 C'est quel pays?

Students have to locate major cities and capitals in the correct country.

Solution: 1 *les Pays-Bas*, 2 *l'Espagne*, 3 *le Danemark*, 4 *la Grèce*, 5 *la Suisse*, 6 *l'Allemagne*, 7 *l'Autriche*, 8 *le Portugal*

SB 20, — **SPEAKING**

3 L'ABC des villes et des pays

Students work in pairs to give the name of a town or a country beginning with each letter of the alphabet using mainly those introduced in the unit.

There could be a competition to see which pair can get the furthest.

Suggestions:
A l'Allemagne, l'Autriche, Athènes
B Bruxelles, la Belgique
C Copenhague
D le Danemark
E l'Espagne
F la France
G la Grèce
H Le Havre, Honfleur
I l'Irlande, l'Italie

CM 2/1 — **PRESENTATION / WRITING**

L'Europe

The outline map of Europe can be completed by students and filed for reference.

unité 2 On fait des projets   Section 3

On fait des projets unité 2

**Area 2
Prepositions with towns and countries
Revision of *aller
voir* (present tense)**
SB 21, **4**-**7**
Au choix SB 122, **1**
Au choix SB 123, **1**
Au choix SB 124, **1**-**2**
CD 1/17–18
Grammar in Action 2, page 6

Section 3

SB 21, 🎧 1/17 LISTENING

4 Projets de vacances

a Students listen to the dialogues in order to complete the matching task.
b When they have found out the holiday destinations, they should look at the pictures and perhaps try to remember or guess the answers, before listening to the recording again to check their answers. When checking the destinations, encourage students to read out the complete sentence to practise the use of prepositions with towns and countries.

Solution:

1f	La famille Legrand va en Suisse.	(**E**)
2c	Le collège Jules Verne va à Athènes.	(**A**)
3d	M. et Mme Rousseau vont au Sénégal.	(**C**)
4b	Nicolas et Sophie vont au Canada.	(**D**)
5a	La famille Leblanc va à Londres.	(**B**)
6e	Hélène va aux États-Unis.	(**F**)

🎧 **Projets de vacances**

1 – Ah, bonjour, Mme Legrand. Vous allez en vacances cet été?
– Oui, nous partons en famille en juillet. Nous allons rendre visite à mon frère en Suisse. Il a une maison à la montagne et nous allons faire des promenades à la montagne.

2 – Et vous, Luc et Cécile?
– Nous allons en voyage scolaire avec le collège Jules Verne.
– Et où allez-vous?
– Nous allons à Athènes en Grèce. Nous allons visiter des monuments anciens.

3 – Vous partez en vacances, M. et Mme Rousseau?
– Oui, cet été, nous allons au Sénégal en Afrique. Nous espérons voir des animaux sauvages dans un parc national. Ça va être très intéressant.

4 – Nicolas et Sophie, vous partez en vacances?
– Oui, nous allons faire du camping au Canada, alors j'espère qu'il va faire beau.

5 – M Leblanc, qu'est-ce que vous faites pendant les vacances avec votre famille?
– Nous allons chez des amis à Londres. Ça va être bien parce qu'il y a beaucoup de choses à faire. Moi, je veux surtout faire la grande roue et voir Londres d'en haut.

6 – Hélène, qu'est-ce que tu vas faire pendant les vacances?
– Moi, je vais rendre visite à ma tante qui habite aux États-Unis. Nous allons prendre l'avion à New York et passer quelques jours dans la ville. Ça va être super.

SB 21 GRAMMAR

Dossier-langue
Saying to, at or in a town or country

Students read through the explanation and find other examples in the unit so far. Check that students have worked out that most European countries end in -e and are therefore feminine.

SB 21 READING
SPEAKING

5 Où vont-ils en vacances?

This maze puzzle provides practice of prepositions with known towns and countries and some new ones. Present and practise these first:
– Montréal, c'est une grande ville dans quel pays?
– C'est au Canada.
– Et Dakar, c'est la capitale de quel pays en Afrique?
– C'est la capitale du Sénégal.
– Marrakech est une ville importante en Afrique du nord. C'est dans quel pays?
– C'est au Maroc.

Solution:

1 M. et Mme Duhamel vont à Montréal au Canada.
2 Suzanne Lambert va à Athènes en Grèce.
3 Vincent Lacan va à Londres en Angleterre.
4 Luc Martin va à Rome en Italie.
5 Sébastien Bonnard va à Dakar au Sénégal.
6 M. et Mme Denise vont à Marrakech au Maroc.

SB 21, SPEAKING

6 Devine la destination

Students choose a secret destination, then work in pairs to discover what the other person has chosen.

Differentiation

For further practice, use the *Au choix* support and extension tasks as follows. See TB 16 for notes on differentiation.

AU CHOIX SB 122 SUPPORT
WRITING

1 C'est quel pays?

This provides practice in writing the correct country in a sentence with prepositions. Students could refer to the map (SB 20) for help, if required, or the task could be prepared orally first.

Solution: **1** au pays de Galles, **2** en Écosse, **3** en Irlande, **4** en Angleterre, **5** en Allemagne, **6** en France, **7** en Suisse, **8** en Espagne

Au choix SB 124   **GENERAL WRITING**

1   On va à l'étranger

This provides practice in using the correct part of *aller* and the correct prepositions with towns and countries.

GRAMMAR IN ACTION 2, PAGE 6   **GRAMMAR PRACTICE**

Using prepositions – travelling around

This provides further practice of the prepositions *près de*, *de* (from), *à* with towns, *en*, *au*, *aux* with countries.

Au choix SB 123   **EXTENSION WRITING**

1   Quelle est la destination?

Students write a sentence to describe where each group is going and then make up their own destination for themselves.

Solution:
1 *Notre collège va à Rome, en Italie.*
2 *Notre famille va à Athènes, en Grèce.*
3 *Mes amis vont à Paris, en France.*
4 *Mon frère va à Berlin, en Allemagne.*
5 *Nous allons à Cardiff, au pays de Galles.*
6 *Ma correspondante va à Londres, en Angleterre.*

SB 21, 1/18   **LISTENING**

7   On visite le pays

This task presents different parts of the verb *voir*.
a Students should first listen to the recording to find the missing words

Solution: 1 *marché*, 2 *tour*, 3 *Paris*, 4 *enfants*, 5 *île*

b Then they should work out which country the tourists are in.

Solution: 1 *au Maroc*, 2 *au Canada*, 3 *en France*, 4 *en Angleterre*, 5 *aux États-Unis*

On visite le pays

1 – Vous voyez, devant vous, la médina – c'est un marché où on trouve de tout.
 – On voit des marchés comme ça dans beaucoup de pays arabes.
2 – Tu vois cette tour là-bas? Qu'est-ce que c'est?
 – C'est la Tour Olympique à Montréal.
3 – Est-ce qu'on voit la Tour Eiffel d'ici?
 – Oui, d'ici, nous voyons tout Paris.
4 – D'ici, vous voyez bien la grande roue.
 – Ah oui! Est-ce que les enfants voient ça? Regardez, Henri et Lucie, ça, c'est la grande roue d'où on voit tout Londres.
5 – Vous voyez la Statue de la Liberté?
 – Sur l'île? Oui, je la vois.

SB 21   **GRAMMAR**

Dossier-langue
voir (to see)

Students should look for the missing parts of *voir* in the previous item and copy out the verb. They should then add it to their electronic verb list.

Au choix SB 124   **GENERAL READING**

2   Des phrases

Students choose the correct part of *voir* to complete the sentences.

Solution: 1 *vois*, 2 *vois*, 3 *voyez*, 4 *vois*, 5 *voient*, 6 *voient*, 7 *voit*, 8 *voit*

CONSOLIDATION WRITING

Holiday destinations

Use clip art maps for this activity. Most school networks have extensive clip art libraries. If you have access to *Microsoft® Word* at home or at school you should be able to use on-line clip art which has many different maps available. These could be downloaded by you before the lesson to save students wasting time surfing.

The task is for students to create illustrated sentences showing where different characters are going on holiday. The characters can be real or imaginary. Real characters could be pop, sports or media personalities and images of these can be found on the web. Alternatively, you might have images of the class via a digital camera or, better still, of their penfriends from earlier activities. If you have a scanner, photographs could be scanned in.

If you use the word processor for this, tables work best to help layout. With a three column layout you can have:

(Insert here a picture of a person, e.g. the footballer Thierry Henry.)	**Thierry Henry va au Sénégal.**	(Insert here a map of the destination, in this case to show in which part of Africa Sénégal is situated.)

As an introductory exercise, you could prepare a table yourself with either blanks or jumbled pictures/phrases to be sorted.

If you use a publishing program such as *Microsoft® Publisher* or a presentation program such as *Microsoft® PowerPoint*, text and graphics can be positioned on the screen without the need for a table.

unité 2 On fait des projets   Section 3

On fait des projets — unité 2

> **Area 3**
> **Means of transport**
> *venir* (present tense)
> SB 22–23, **1**–**9**
> Au choix SB 122, **2**–**3**
> CD 1/19–21
> CM 2/2–2/3
> Grammar in Action 2, page 11
> FC 22–31

Section 3

FC 22–31 (FC 23 ET1) — PRESENTATION

Means of transport

Using the flashcards, teach and practise the different means of transport through various games, e.g. *Loto*, Guess the back of the flashcard, or saying how you **won't** be travelling (i.e. what the flashcard is **not** showing). See TB 26–27. FC 23 from *Encore Tricolore 1* can be used for *à cheval*.

CM 2/2 — PRESENTATION

Les transports

This contains mini-flashcards showing means of transport, which could be completed by students, stuck on card and used to practise this vocabulary. See Flashcard games (TB 26).

It could also be used to make an OHT for oral practice.

Solution: 1e, 2a, 3c, 4d, 5h, 6b, 7f, 8g, 9j, 10i, 11l, 12k

SB 22 — PRESENTATION

1 Les transports

This presents different means of transport (including taxi, coach and metro) + prepositions and provides the picture cues for task 2 *Ils voyagent comment?*

Play a simple oral game where the teacher or a student reads out one of the captions and the class have to say the letter by the correct picture. Then ask students to close their books and see how many means of transport they can remember. These could be written on the board as they are mentioned and used for a game of *Effacez!*

SB 22, 🎧 1/19 — LISTENING

2 Ils voyagent comment?

Students listen to the conversations to find out how each person is travelling. They should write down the letter of the appropriate means of transport, as illustrated in task 1 *Les transports*. Able students could also write down the destination.

Solution: 1b, 2h, 3j, 4a, 5d, 6c, 7k, 8l, 9e, 10i

🎧 Ils voyagent comment?

1 – Tu vas en Angleterre au mois de juillet, n'est-ce pas? Tu prends l'avion?
 – Oui, je vais à Londres en avion.
2 – Nous allons visiter le musée cet après-midi. Tu viens?
 – Oui, je veux bien, mais vous y allez comment?
 – Nous y allons en voiture.
3 – Tu vas au stade à vélo?
 – Oui, je prends mon vélo.
4 – Allons en ville en bus. Voici le bus numéro 7 qui arrive.
 – Oui, d'accord.
5 – Alors, Jean-Pierre, tu vas au match de rugby à pied?
 – Non. Je vais au match en moto, avec Claude.
6 – On va à l'île de Ré cet après-midi?
 – Oui, je veux bien. C'est à quelle heure le bateau?
 – Oh, il y a un bateau toutes les vingt minutes.
7 – Comment vas-tu au collège, Chantal?
 – Normalement, je prends ma mobylette.
8 – Et toi, Jacques. Comment vas-tu au collège?
 – Oh, moi, j'y vais à pied d'habitude.
9 – Alors, on va à la Tour Eiffel cet après-midi?
 – Oui, et on prend le métro – c'est tout près.
10 – On fait une excursion au château de Versailles dimanche?
 – Oui, bonne idée, mais nous n'avons pas de voiture.
 – Ça ne fait rien. Il y a un car qui va directement au château de notre hôtel.
 – Très bien. Nous y allons en car.

Jeux — PRACTICE

1 C'est bon ou c'est ridicule?
Make some sensible and silly statements, to which students have to respond *c'est bon* (for a sensible statement) or *c'est ridicule* (for a silly statement), e.g.

Je vais à Chicago à pied. (C'est ridicule!)
Nous allons en France en avion. (C'est bon!)

2 On voyage comment?
The class could play a sentence completion game in two teams, the first starting a sentence and the second having, say, ten seconds to finish it with a means of transport that makes sense, e.g.

Team A: *Nous allons à Madrid …*
Team B: *… en avion.*

SB 22 — WRITING

3 Les voyages

This task involves writing some of the new vocabulary. Students complete each sentence with an appropriate form of transport.

Au CHOIX SB 122 — SUPPORT / READING

2 On va où?

This provides further practice of the present tense of *aller*.

Solution: 1c, 2d, 3e, 4a, 5f, 6b

SB 22 — WRITING

4 On y va comment?

In this puzzle, students have to write a sentence using the correct part of *aller* (referring to *Les verbes*, SB 160, if necessary), the destination and the means of transport.

Solution:
1 *Lucie va au cinéma en bus.*
2 *Marc va à la piscine à pied.*
3 *Ils vont à la Tour Eiffel en métro.*
4 *Tu vas à la maison en taxi?*
5 *Nous allons à Bruxelles en car.*
6 *On va au stade en bus.*
7 *Les garçons vont à Édimbourg en train.*
8 *Mon père va au Danemark en avion.*

SB 23 — WRITING

5 Bon voyage!

Students write out a complete description of the journey undertaken. As a further optional activity, they could work individually or as a group to make up the details of a similar journey using a variety of means of transport.

Solution: 1 *en voiture*, 2 *en train*, 3 *en bus*, 4 *en taxi*, 5 *en bateau*, 6 *à pied*, 7 *en train*, 8 *en métro*, 9 *en car*, 10 *à vélo*

SB 23, 🎧 1/20 — LISTENING

6 Une soirée internationale

This task presents different parts of the verb *venir*. Students listen to the conversations and decide whether the sentences in their books are true or false. Able students could correct the false statements.

Solution: 1 *vrai*, 2 *faux (Il vient de Genève/de la Suisse.)*, 3 *vrai*, 4 *faux (Ils viennent en voiture.)*, 5 *vrai*, 6 *faux (Ils viennent d'Édimbourg.)*, 7 *vrai*, 8 *vrai*

🎧 **Une soirée internationale**

1 – Salut, Christine. Tu es française?
– Non, je suis canadienne. Je viens de Montréal, au Canada.
2 – Tu connais le garçon là-bas?
– Oui, c'est Sébastien
– Est-ce qu'il vient du Canada aussi?
– Non, il est suisse. Il vient de Genève.
3 – Et toi, Karim, d'où viens-tu?
– Moi, je viens du Maroc.
4 – Est-ce que Cécile vient ce soir?
– Oui, elle vient, mais plus tard, avec son frère.
– Comment viennent-ils?
– Ils viennent en voiture.
5 – Vous venez souvent en France, Alex et Daniel?
– Oui, assez souvent. Nous venons chaque été pour voir nos grands-parents.
6 – Et vous venez d'où en Écosse?
– Nous venons d'Édimbourg
7 – Et vous, Jabu et Pirane, d'où venez-vous?
– Nous venons du Sénégal, en Afrique.
8 – Et vous venez souvent en France?
– Non, nous ne venons pas souvent en France.

SB 23 — GRAMMAR

Dossier-langue
venir (to come)

This gives the complete paradigm of *venir* and mentions *revenir* and *devenir*.

SB 23 — READING

7 Des phrases complètes

Students pair up the subject with the correct part of *venir*.

Solution: 1f, 2c, 3h, 4a, 5d, 6g, 7e, 8b

SB 23, SB 124 — SPEAKING

8 D'où viennent-ils?

This information gap task gives practice in using the 3rd person of *venir* with *de* + feminine countries.

Au CHOIX SB 122 — SUPPORT / READING

3 Des questions et des réponses

Some students could do this item rather than the next open-ended task.

Solution: 1g, 2b, 3e, 4a, 5d, 6f, 7c

SB 23 — SPEAKING

9 À toi!

Students practise asking each other questions about transport and then write out their own answers to four of the questions. If you prefer, students could write answers to all the questions.

CM 2/3 — READING / WRITING

Des mots croisés (voir et venir)

This copymaster provides crosswords to practise the verbs *voir* and *venir*.

Solution:

1 voir

¹v	o	y	e	z		
o						
y		²v	o	³i	s	
o		o		l		
⁴n	o	u	s		⁵v	
s		s			o	
			⁶j		i	
⁷v	o	i	e	n	t	

unité 2 On fait des projets

Section 3

55

On fait des projets unité 2

2 venir

	¹v	i	e	n	²n	e	n	³t
	e				l			u
	n				l			
⁴o	n		⁵v	i	e	n	s	
	s		i					
		⁶j	e				⁷i	
	⁸v	e	n	e	z		l	
			t				s	

GRAMMAR IN ACTION 2, PAGE 11   GRAMMAR PRACTICE
Using the verb *venir*

This provides further practice of the present tense of *venir*, *revenir* and *devenir*.

Area 4
Revision of leisure activities
Expressions of future time
aller + infinitive
SB 24–25, **1**–**8**
Au choix SB 122, **4**
Au choix SB 124, **3**–**4**
CD 1/21–23
CM 2/4–2/5
Grammar in Action 2, page 7
FC 32–38

FC 32–38   PRESENTATION
Qu'est-ce qu'on va faire?

Use flashcards to teach and practise the following: *On va* + *aller à la pêche, visiter un château, prendre des photos, faire du camping, visiter des monuments, jouer au tennis, visiter un parc d'attractions, faire de la voile.*

Use the transport flashcards for the following
FC 30   bike – *faire du vélo*
FC 29   coach – *faire des excursions en car*
FC 31   walking – *faire des promenades*
If available, use the flashcards from **Encore Tricolore 1** as well.

CM 2/4   PRACTICE
Des activités

The mini-flashcards can be used for further practice in pairs or, if an OHT is made, as a class activity (see TB 26–27 for further details).

Solution: 1c, 2k, 3a, 4b, 5i, 6d, 7h, 8e, 9l, 10j, 11f, 12g

SB 24, 🎧 1/21   LISTENING
                       READING
1 Pendant les vacances

a Students listen to the recording and find the correct symbol.

Solution: 1g, 2h, 3f, 4e, 5d, 6b, 7c, 8a

56

b Students then find the correct caption for each symbol.

Solution: a7, b3, c8, d5, e2, f6, g1, h4

level 3.

🎧 **Pendant les vacances**

1 – Qu'est-ce que tu vas faire la semaine prochaine?
– Je vais passer une semaine à Londres. J'ai un nouvel appareil, alors je vais prendre beaucoup de photos.

2 – Est-ce que ta sœur va à Londres aussi?
– Non, elle va rendre visite à sa correspondante à Berlin, en Allemagne.

3 – Où allez-vous cet été?
– Nous allons au pays de Galles.
– Au pays de Galles? Vous allez visiter des châteaux?
– Ah oui, nous allons visiter beaucoup de châteaux – ça va être très intéressant.

4 – Est-ce que tu vas faire du vélo en août?
– Oui, je vais faire du vélo aux Pays-Bas avec un groupe de jeunes. J'espère que ça ne va pas être trop fatigant.

5 – Qu'est-ce que tu vas faire pendant les vacances?
– Je vais rester à la maison. Je vais retrouver mes amis et nous allons jouer au football au parc.

6 – Qu'est-ce que ton frère va faire pendant les vacances?
– Il va jouer au golf. Il aime beaucoup ça.

7 – Et Sophie et Nicole, qu'est-ce qu'elles vont faire cet été?
– Elles vont passer cinq jours à Paris.
– Alors elles vont monter à la Tour Eiffel?
– Ah oui, ça c'est certain!

8 – Thomas et Luc, qu'est-ce qu'ils vont faire en juillet?
– Ils vont aller à la pêche en Écosse.

SB 24   GRAMMAR
Dossier-langue
The infinitive of the verb

As both *aller* and *pouvoir* + the infinitive are taught in this unit, it is worth spending some time explaining the infinitive form and how to find it from different parts of a regular verb (see *Au choix* SB 124).

AU CHOIX SB 124   GENERAL
Dossier-langue
The infinitive

This gives an explanation of how to find the infinitive from different parts of the verb. Students need to do this when looking up the meaning of French verbs in a dictionary.

Au choix SB 124 — GENERAL

3 Trouve l'infinitif

This gives practice in working out the infinitive for regular and irregular verbs. It could be done orally, if time is short.

Solution:

a		b		c		d	
1	jouer	1	choisir	1	vendre	1	voir
2	écouter	2	finir	2	répondre	2	être
3	chanter	3	réussir	3	rendre	3	aller
4	regarder	4	remplir	4	attendre	4	avoir
5	demander	5	choisir	5	entendre	5	venir
6	visiter	6	rougir	6	vendre	6	faire

SB 24 — GRAMMAR

Dossier-langue
aller + the infinitive

This explains the structure *aller* + the infinitive of the verb.

SB 24, 🎧 1/22 — LISTENING

2 Maintenant ou plus tard?

This task provides further practice in recognising *aller* + infinitive and distinguishing this from verbs in the present tense. Teach *prochain/prochaine*, then play the recording or read out the following sentences and ask students to note what is happening **now** (*maintenant* – **M**) or what is going to happen **later** (*plus tard* – **T**).

Solution: 1M, 2T, 3T, 4M, 5M, 6T, 7M, 8T, 9T, 10M

🎧 **Maintenant ou plus tard?**   *level 2*

1. Je regarde la télé.
2. Je vais regarder un film à la télé ce soir.
3. Je vais arriver chez toi à huit heures.
4. Lucie arrive chez son ami.
5. Je fais les courses.
6. Je vais faire les courses vendredi prochain.
7. On joue sur l'ordinateur.
8. Tu vas jouer au tennis la semaine prochaine?
9. On va manger au restaurant dimanche prochain.
10. Pierre mange à la maison.

Au choix SB 122 — SUPPORT

4 Demain

This gives practice in distinguishing between the use of *aller* + infinitive and the present tense.

Solution: Demain: 2, 4, 7, 8, 9, 11

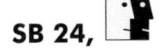

SB 24, — SPEAKING / WRITING

3 Le jeu des voyages

This item can be used in various ways for speaking and writing practice:
- as a pairwork task, using a dice or random numbers to select the options;
- as a game of consequences, with each student writing down a different option on a piece of paper and then passing it on;
- as a written task with individual students writing out the details of the journey selecting from the options given. Imaginative students could invent more fictional journeys on this model.

SB 25, 🎧 1/23 — LISTENING / READING

4 La fête de Daniel

Students listen to the recording first without looking at the text. Check that students understand the general gist, e.g.
Sophie, est-ce qu'elle aime sortir le samedi soir?
Elle téléphone à ses amis. Est-ce qu'ils sont libres samedi soir?
Où vont-ils? Ils vont à la fête de Daniel?
Et Sophie, est-ce qu'elle a une invitation à la fête de Daniel?
Mais à la fin, est-ce qu'elle va aller chez Daniel aussi?

Next students could listen again, following the text, and note Sophie's alternative suggestions for Saturday evening.

Help students to notice how these future plans are presented in French and see how many examples of *aller* + infinitive they can find.

If wished, students could act or read aloud the story, or perhaps record it as a radio play in groups.

🎧 **La fête de Daniel**

Demain, c'est samedi. Sophie aime sortir le samedi soir. Elle téléphone à ses amis.
– Allô?
– Bonjour, Nicole. Qu'est-ce que tu vas faire demain soir?
– Demain soir? Je vais aller chez Daniel.
…
– Allô?
– Salut, Charlotte. Il y a un bon film au cinéma Rex demain. Tu viens?
– Ah non, Sophie, je regrette, mais …
– Mais qu'est-ce que tu vas faire alors?
– Je vais aller chez Daniel. C'est son anniversaire, il va organiser une fête.
…
– Allô!
– Bonjour, Jean-Claude. Qu'est-ce que tu vas faire demain? On va écouter de la musique chez moi. Tu viens?
– Mais demain soir à huit heures, je vais …
– Ah non, toi aussi, tu vas aller chez Daniel demain? Ça alors …
– Mais écoute Sophie, je …
…
– Qu'est-ce que je vais faire? … Oui, c'est ça. Je vais téléphoner à Daniel. Mais je ne vais pas parler de sa fête.
…
– Allô!
– Bonjour, Daniel! Ici Sophie. Demain soir, on va aller à la discothèque avec des amis. Tu viens avec nous?

57

On fait des projets unité 2

– Mais Sophie, attends! Demain soir, je vais donner une fête chez moi. Tu ne viens pas?
– Comment? Quelle fête?
– Pour mon anniversaire. Tu n'as pas ton invitation?
– Mon invitation? … Ah non!
– Ça ne fait rien. Mais tu vas venir, n'est-ce pas? C'est à huit heures.
– Bon, d'accord, je vais venir chez toi. Au revoir, Daniel … et à demain!

SB 25   READING
5   C'est faux!

Students read and correct the false statements.

Solution:
1 Sophie aime *sortir* samedi soir.
2 Elle *téléphone* à Nicole.
3 Samedi soir, Charlotte va aller chez *Daniel*.
4 Daniel va organiser *une fête*.
5 Jean-Claude va aller *chez Daniel*.
6 Beaucoup de personnes vont à la fête de *Daniel*.
7 Finalement, Sophie téléphone à *Daniel*.
8 Sophie va aussi aller à la fête *samedi* soir.

FC 32–38, CM 2/4   SPEAKING
Expressions of future time

Using the flashcards of leisure activities or an OHT of CM 2/4, make statements about when you are going to do things, e.g.

Demain, je vais jouer au tennis.
Lundi prochain, je vais aller à la pêche.
La semaine prochaine, je vais faire de l'équitation.

Then ask students questions, prompting a reply with a flashcard, e.g.

Qu'est-ce que tu vas faire demain/mercredi prochain/samedi après-midi/la semaine prochaine?

SB 25   WRITING
6   C'est quand?

Students write out the expressions of time in order and with the English.

Solution:
ce soir – this evening
demain – tomorrow
mercredi matin – Wednesday morning
jeudi prochain – next Thursday
vendredi après-midi – Friday afternoon
samedi soir – Saturday evening
dimanche prochain – next Sunday
la semaine prochaine – next week

SB 25   SPEAKING/WRITING
7   Des projets

This provides open-ended practice in talking or writing about future plans.

SB 25,   SPEAKING
8   Oui ou non?

Students note down any activity mentioned on SB 25 or SB 24 and then work in pairs to guess the activities listed by each person.

Au choix SB 124   GENERAL SPEAKING/WRITING
4   Hélène Renard

This extends the topic of transport to include distance and weather conditions. Revise main weather conditions first and work through part of the task orally. Students should then be able to complete the task individually or working in pairs.

Solution:
1 Elle va aller à Lille en voiture.
2 Elle va aller à Toulouse en train.
3 Elle va aller à Genève en avion.
4 Elle va aller à Amsterdam en train.
5 Elle va aller à Paris (centre-ville) en bus.
6 Elle va aller à Lyon en voiture.
7 Elle va aller à Bruxelles en voiture.
8 Elle va aller à Bordeaux en train.

CM 2/5   GRAMMAR PRACTICE
Projets de vacances

This provides further practice of *aller* + the infinitive.

Solution:
1 aller
Je vais, Tu vas, Il/Elle va, Nous allons, Vous allez, Ils/Elles vont

2 Qu'est-ce qu'on va faire?
  1 *Nous allons faire du camping en Italie.*
  2 *Je vais faire de la voile en Allemagne.*
  3 *Il va faire de l'équitation au Maroc.*
  4 *Ils vont faire un stage de musique en Suisse.*
  5 *Tu vas jouer au golf en Espagne?*
  6 *Elles vont chanter avec une chorale au Canada.*

3 On pense aux vacances
1 *vas*, 2 *allez*, 3 *vais*, 4 *vont*, 5 *allons*, 6 *va*, 7 *va*, 8 *allez*, 9 *vais*, 10 *vas*

4 Du plus tôt au plus tard
d, a, g, f, b, c, e

Grammar in Action 2, page 7   GRAMMAR PRACTICE
Using *aller* + infinitive

This provides further practice of *aller* + the infinitive and expressions of future time.

Area 5
Describing towns and villages, location and facilities
SB 26, **1**–**3**
CD 1/24
CM 2/6

SB 26, CM 2/6 — PRESENTATION
Voici la France

Talk briefly about the map (SB 26), or use an OHT of the map on CM 2/6, asking questions about towns and locations (using *nord, sud, est, ouest, centre* etc.). Give plenty of oral practice of the names of towns, perhaps asking students to spell some of them.

SB 26, 🎧 1/24 — LISTENING
1 Où habitent-ils?

Students could first guess where each person lives. To give them some clues, read out the following:
Émilie habite dans une grande ville, dans le sud de la France.
Mathieu habite au bord de la mer, dans une petite ville, dans le nord de la France.
Dominique habite une ville moyenne près des Alpes.
Lucie habite au centre de la France.
Pierre habite une grande ville dans l'ouest de la France.

To narrow their choice, you could also mention that the five people live in a different one of the five places listed in task 2. Students then listen to check their answers.

Solution: 1 *Toulouse,* 2 *Honfleur,* 3 *Annecy,* 4 *Savigny,* 5 *Nantes*

🎧 **Où habitent-ils?**

1 Salut! Je m'appelle Émilie et j'habite à Toulouse. C'est une grande ville dans le sud de la France. À Toulouse, on peut visiter la cité de l'espace – c'est un grand musée avec des expositions, des jeux interactifs, un planétarium etc. C'est très intéressant.

2 Bonjour. Moi, je m'appelle Mathieu. J'habite à Honfleur. C'est une petite ville dans le nord de la France. C'est sur la côte. En été, beaucoup de touristes visitent la ville. C'est très joli. On peut visiter le port et la ville et on peut aller à la plage.

3 Salut! Moi, c'est Dominique. J'habite à Annecy. C'est une ville moyenne dans l'est de la France. Annecy est à la montagne et en hiver, on peut faire du ski dans la région. Il y a aussi un grand lac où on peut faire des sports nautiques.

4 Alors moi, je m'appelle Lucie et j'habite à Savigny. C'est un petit village près de Montluçon au centre de la France. C'est à la campagne, alors il n'y a pas grand'chose à faire. Mais on peut faire des promenades et on peut faire de l'équitation.

5 Salut! Moi, je m'appelle Pierre et j'habite à Nantes. C'est une grande ville dans l'ouest de la France. À Nantes, on peut visiter le château – c'est assez intéressant.

SB 26 — READING
2 Des villes et des villages

Students have to find two sentences to describe each place. They may need to listen to the recording again to check their answers. The sentences provide useful vocabulary for describing the students' own towns.

Solution:
1 *Nantes* **b**, **g** (**i** also applies)
2 *Savigny* **c**, **f**
3 *Toulouse* **a**, **j**
4 *Annecy* **e**, **h**
5 *Honfleur* **d**, **i**

Tourist information

If time is available, students could find out more information about these or other French towns, from the Internet (see TB 49) or local tourist offices. Information and photos obtained could be used to build up a class display with information around a central outline map.

SB 26 — WRITING
3 À toi!

Students should now be able to write a brief description of the location of their own town or village.

Area 6
pouvoir + infinitive
SB 26, **4**
SB 27, **5**–**6**
SB 28, **1**–**3**
Au choix SB 122, **5**
Au choix SB 123, **2**–**5**
CD 1/25–27
CM 2/7–2/8
Grammar in Action 2, page 5
FC 32–38

FC 32–38 — SPEAKING
Qu'est-ce qu'on peut faire dans ta ville?

Introduce the idea of describing local leisure facilities using *on peut* and *on ne peut pas* with appropriate activities, using the flashcards as required, e.g.
Qu'est-ce qu'on peut faire ici/dans la région?

A chain question game could be played, e.g.

Student A: *Est-ce qu'on peut faire de l'équitation?*
Student B: *Oui/Non/Je ne sais pas. Est-ce qu'on peut faire de la voile/jouer au golf/visiter des monuments?* (etc.)

unité 2 On fait des projets   Section 3

59

SB 26, **SPEAKING**

4 Qu'est-ce qu'on peut faire ici?

Students could take it in turns to say a sentence about the availablity or absence of leisure facilities, using *on peut* and *on ne peut pas*. The class could have a competition to see which pair can make up the most sentences.

WRITING

Follow-up

Perhaps working in pairs or groups, students could design a poster or a short leaflet about local facilities for French visitors to the area. For extra support, a suitable description could be built up on the board with suggestions from the class and then copied out.

Students could look at some websites of French towns (see TB 49) and their own town or area website (if available) to find ideas. They could prepare material in French using word processing or desktop publishing.

CM 2/7, 1/25 **LISTENING**

Au val de Loire

When students have listened to the recording for the first time, ask a few questions, e.g.
Les Lambert organisent quelle sorte de vacances?
Ils font du camping? Ils vont à l'hôtel?
Comment vont-ils voyager?
Ils vont visiter un autre pays/une autre région?
Ils vont visiter quelle région de France?

Teach *ils peuvent*, e.g.
Est-ce que les touristes peuvent faire beaucoup de choses à Montrichard?
Oui, ils peuvent jouer au tennis/golf, faire du camping, aller à la pêche etc.

Then students can listen again in order to complete the activities on the copymaster.

Solution:

1 Au val de Loire

Distractions:	Chambord	Chaumont	St-Aignan	Montrichard
visiter des caves				✓
aller à la pêche		✓	✓	✓
faire des promenades dans la forêt	✓			
jouer au tennis				✓
aller à la piscine			✓	✓
faire du camping		✓	✓	✓
jouer au golf				✓
louer des vélos				✓
visiter un château	✓	✓	✓	✓
faire de l'équitation	✓			
faire de la voile			✓	✓

2 Un résumé
1 vont, 2 vont, 3 regardent, 4 peut,
5 aller, 6 peuvent, 7 peuvent, 8 château

3 Des activités sportives
A, C, E, H, I

Au val de Loire

La famille Lambert va partir en vacances dans le val de Loire. Ils vont prendre leur voiture et ils vont faire du camping. Christophe et Suzanne regardent les brochures de la région.
– Moi, je voudrais aller à Chambord. À Chambord, on peut visiter le château, on peut faire de l'équitation et on peut faire des promenades dans la forêt.
– Et est-ce qu'on peut faire du camping?
– Ah non. Il n'y a pas de terrain de camping.
– Alors, nous ne pouvons pas aller à Chambord.
– Tiens, à Chaumont, il y a un terrain de camping deux étoiles.
– Et qu'est-ce qu'on peut faire là-bas?
– On peut aller à la pêche et on peut visiter le château.
– C'est tout? Qu'est-ce qu'il y a encore?
– On peut faire du camping à Saint-Aignan. Oh, c'est bien! On peut visiter le château, on peut aller à la pêche et on peut faire de la voile. Moi, j'aimerais bien faire de la voile.
– Est-ce qu'il y a une piscine?
– Oui, il y a une piscine en plein air.
– Est-ce qu'on peut jouer au tennis?
– Ah, non. On ne peut pas jouer au tennis.
– Papa ne va pas être content, s'il ne peut pas jouer au tennis.
– Ça y est, nous pouvons aller à Montrichard. On peut tout faire là-bas. Il y a un terrain de camping, deux piscines. Écoute … 'Les touristes peuvent jouer au golf ou jouer au tennis. Ils peuvent aller à la pêche, louer des vélos ou faire de la voile. À part les activités sportives, les touristes peuvent visiter des caves vinicoles et déguster le vin de la région'.
– Et nous pouvons visiter le château de Chenonceaux. Ce n'est pas loin. C'est très bien, allons à Montrichard.

CM 2/7 **SPEAKING EXTENSION**

Practice of *pouvoir*

With able students, use the completed copymaster to practise *pouvoir* orally, e.g.
Qu'est-ce que les touristes peuvent faire à Chambord?

Then students can work in pairs or small groups, one in each group acting as a travel agent and the others asking what they can do in the different towns, practising:
Est-ce qu'on peut …?
Oui/Non, on (ne) peut (pas) faire ça.
Qu'est-ce que nous pouvons faire à …?

SB 27 **PRESENTATION**

5 C'est quelle bulle?

Students read the captions (which use different parts of *pouvoir*) and match them to the cartoons.

Solution: 1c, 2e, 3d, 4b, 5f, 6a

SB 27   **GRAMMAR**

Dossier-langue
pouvoir (to be able, can)

This explains the use of *pouvoir*. Mention that *pouvoir* is one of the most common verbs in use.

SB 27   **READING**
                                                            WRITING

6   Des questions et des réponses

This task provides practice in using different forms of *pouvoir* (present tense).

Solution:

a **1** *peut*, **2** *peux*, **3** *pouvons*, **4** *peuvent*, **5** *peux*, **6** *peut*
b **a** *pouvez*, **b** *peut*, **c** *peux*, **d** *peux*, **e** *peuvent*, **f** *peut*
c **1f, 2d, 3a, 4e, 5c, 6b**

SB 28   **PRACTICE**

1   Le guide, c'est toi!

Go through the symbols in the leaflet first to check that they are understood, e.g.
À Saint-Martin, qu'est-ce qu'on peut faire?
Et à Sancerre? Et à Amboise?

Students then work on this task in pairs; one person asking the question, the other checking the details before giving the reply. They could change roles after question 4. Alternatively, students could do this individually as a written or oral task.

Solution:

1 *Oui, vous pouvez faire du camping à Saint-Martin.*
2 *Oui, on peut aller à la pêche à Sancerre.*
3 *Oui, on peut louer un vélo à Amboise.*
4 *Oui, vous pouvez aller à la pêche à Vouvray.*
5 *Non, ce n'est pas possible.*
6 *Oui, on peut jouer au tennis à Amboise.*
7 *Non, ce n'est pas possible.*
8 *Oui, vous pouvez faire de la voile à Sancerre.*

SB 28, 🎧 1/26   **LISTENING**

2   Claire

This illustrates the use of *pouvoir* + the infinitive for asking permission to do something. Check that students understand the symbols. Then play the recording so students can note down the numbers by the things Claire asks permission to do.

Then re-use the phrases and encourage students to produce the words Claire used with the help of the table.

Solution: **10, 7, 6, 8**

🎧   **Claire**

– Pardon Madame, est-ce que je peux téléphoner à mes parents, s'il vous plaît?
– Bien sûr, Claire, mais ... tout va bien?
– Oh, oui oui, mais aujourd'hui, c'est l'anniversaire de mon père.
– Ah bon, vas-y alors! Puis qu'est-ce que tu vas faire ce soir, Claire?
– Est-ce que je peux sortir ce soir, Madame?
– Oui oui, mais qu'est-ce que tu vas faire?
– Je vais aller au cinéma avec des copains. On passe un bon film.
– Oui, c'est bien. Est-ce que tu veux manger quelque chose maintenant?
– Non merci, Madame. Je ne veux pas manger. Mais est-ce que je peux avoir quelque chose à boire?
– Oui, oui. Il y a de la limonade et du jus de fruit dans le frigidaire.
– Et demain soir, Madame, est-ce que nous pouvons aller au match de football?
– Oui, d'accord. Tu vas y aller avec Jean-Pierre et ses copains, n'est-ce pas?
– Oui Madame, c'est un grand match et j'adore le football.

SB 28   **SPEAKING**
                                                            WRITING

3   Ben est chez son correspondant

Basing their answers on the previous item, students decide what Ben says when asking permission to do the activities represented by the symbols. This can be prepared in writing or just done orally.

Solution:

Est-ce que je peux ...
1 *sortir ce soir?*
2 *téléphoner à mes parents?*
3 *regarder un film à la télé?*
4 *lire le journal?*
5 *aller au match de football?*
6 *jouer sur l'ordinateur?*
7 *écouter un CD?*
8 *écouter la radio?*

S'il te plaît   **SPEAKING**

As an extra activity, a game on the lines of 'Simon says' could be played. One student from each team in turn asks permission to do something, adding or omitting *s'il te plaît* at the end, e.g.
Est-ce que je peux regarder la télé?
If *s'il te plaît* is omitted, the person being asked says *Non, tu ne peux pas.*
If *s'il te plaît* is included, the person asked replies *Oui, tu peux faire ça.*

GRAMMAR IN ACTION 2, PAGE 5   **GRAMMAR PRACTICE**

Using the verb *pouvoir*

This provides further practice of *pouvoir*.

Differentiation

AU CHOIX SB 122,   **SUPPORT**
                                                            SPEAKING

5   Qu'est-ce qu'on peut faire?

This pairwork task combines weather expressions with *pouvoir* + activities.

unité 2 On fait des projets   Section 3

On fait des projets — unité 2

Section 3

Au choix SB 123
EXTENSION / SPEAKING / WRITING

2 C'est permis?

In this task students give or withold permission depending on whether the activity is an indoor or outdoor one. It could be done as a written or as a speaking task, with one student reading the question and the other replying.

Solution:
1 *Non, tu ne peux pas jouer dans le jardin.*
2 *Oui, tu peux regarder la télévision.*
3 *Non, tu ne peux pas jouer au football.*
4 *Non, tu ne peux pas faire une promenade.*
5 *Oui, tu peux écouter un CD.*
6 *Non, tu ne peux pas faire du vélo.*
7 *Oui, tu peux jouer sur l'ordinateur.*
8 *Non, tu ne peux pas aller au parc.*

Au choix SB 123,
EXTENSION / SPEAKING / WRITING

3 Qu'est-ce que nous pouvons faire ce week-end?

In this pairwork task, each student lists some possible leisure activities then works with a partner to guess the activities the other person has listed.

Au choix SB 123, 1/27
EXTENSION / LISTENING

4 Ce n'est pas possible

Students should listen to the conversations and choose the right excuse from those printed in the book.

Solution: 1b, 2a, 3f, 4d, 5e, 6c

🎧 Ce n'est pas possible

1 – Annette, est-ce que tu viens au parc cet après-midi? On va faire du roller.
 – Ah, c'est dommage. Cet après-midi, je ne peux pas. Je vais rendre visite à ma tante.

2 – Est-ce que Philippe peut venir à Paris avec nous, dimanche?
 – Je ne sais pas. Un moment, s'il vous plaît … Ah, non, je suis désolée. Dimanche, il va jouer un match de hockey.

3 – Nous allons faire une promenade à la campagne demain. Tu viens avec nous, Cécile?
 – Demain? Ah, non, ce n'est pas possible. Demain, je vais faire de l'équitation avec mon père.

4 – Lundi prochain, nous allons voir le nouveau film de James Bond. Est-ce que vous pouvez venir avec nous?
 – Désolés, lundi prochain, nous allons au théâtre avec le collège.

5 – Vendredi, nous allons faire un pique-nique à la plage. Est-ce que Claude et Camille peuvent venir aussi?
 – Ah, non, je regrette, mais vendredi, nous allons rentrer à la maison.

6 – Est-ce que tes parents viennent au collège ce soir?
 – Non, je suis désolé. Ils ne peuvent pas venir, parce qu'ils travaillent tard à l'hôpital ce soir.

Au choix SB 123
EXTENSION

5 Désolé

This gives practice in combining *pouvoir* + infinitive and *aller* + infinitive, e.g.

Désolé, je ne peux pas sortir, parce que je vais faire mes devoirs.

CM 2/8
CONSOLIDATION/SUPPORT

Des mots croisés (aller et pouvoir)

For consolidation or support, students could work on these two crosswords, which provide practice of the present tense of *aller* and *pouvoir*, respectively.

Solution:

1 Des mots croisés (aller)

	¹a	l	l	o	²n	s
	l				o	
	l		³i		u	
⁴e	l	l	e	s		
	z				⁵v	
				⁶v		o
			⁷v	a		n
⁸v	a	i	s			t

2 Des mots croisés (pouvoir)

¹p	²o	u	v	o	³n	s
⁴o	n				o	
u		⁵p	e	u	x	
v		⁶i		s		
⁷e	l	l	e	s		⁸p
z					⁹j	e
		¹⁰t				u
¹¹p	e	u	v	e	n	t

Area 7
Reading and writing postcards
Revision of weather
SB 29, 4
SB 30, 1
(FC 27–33 ET1)

Area 8
Further activities and consolidation
SB 30, 2, SB 31, SB 32–33
Au choix SB 125, 5
CM 2/9–2/17, 133
CD 1/28–31
Student CD 1/7–12, 2/4–6

unité 2 On fait des projets

Section 3

(ET1 FC 27–33) REVISION
Weather

Revise weather expressions using the ***Encore Tricolore 1*** flashcards (27–33), if available.

SB 29 READING SPEAKING/WRITING
4 Le jeu des cartes postales

Ask some simple questions about the pictures first, e.g.

A Ça, c'est une photo d'une sculpture en glace – c'est un cheval. À Québec, on fait des sculptures en glace pour le carnaval d'hiver.
B Ça, c'est une photo de la mer des Caraïbes. On voit des palmiers. Ils sont jolis, non?
C Voilà un camping, mais il ne fait pas beau. Il pleut et il y a de la boue partout. (Explain *boue* = mud) etc.

a Students should then read through the texts and match them up with the pictures.

Solution: 1D, 2C, 3E, 4F, 5B, 6A

b Students choose to answer two (or all) questions from each group about the content of the postcards.

SB 30 WRITING
1 Des cartes postales

Students should then be able to write a short postcard based on the guidelines given which bring together many of the themes of the unit.

Virtual postcards

Many sites on the Internet offer virtual postcards and there are a number of French ones which offer a choice of messages, images from France and also the chance to write your own message. To find a site, try searching for *cartes virtuelles* on a French search engine, e.g. **www.yahoo.fr** or **www.lokace.fr**.
There are generic sites which offer a range of designs and greetings and also highly specialised ones such as football clubs, tourist attractions etc.
Students might send the virtual card to their exchange partner or to friends in the class or school.

SB 30 READING
2 Les vacances idéales

Students complete the sentences with the correct part of *pouvoir*, then choose the three sentences which best represent their own ideal holiday.

Solution: 1 on peut, 2 nous pouvons, 3 les jeunes peuvent, 4 on peut, 5 les visiteurs peuvent, 6 vous pouvez, 7 nous pouvons, 8 on peut

Au choix SB 125 GENERAL READING
5 La boîte aux lettres

This is a fairly demanding item. Students read through the different opinions and decide which means of transport is favoured by each writer.

The answers can be checked orally, e.g.

Sophie écrit: Nous prenons toujours la voiture. C'est plus pratique et c'est moins cher … etc.

Alors, Sophie préfère la voiture.

Et Jean-Luc? Il préfère le métro et le bus.

Magali, qu'est-ce qu'elle préfère comme moyen de transport pour un long voyage? Elle préfère le train.

Mais Jean-Paul préfère le car. Pourquoi? Parce que c'est moins cher.

Et Anne-Marie, qu'est-ce qu'elle aime comme moyen de transport? Elle aime prendre son vélo.

Then students should give their own preferred means of transport, if possible, giving one advantage and one disadvantage.

CM 2/9 DICTIONARY SKILLS
C'est utile, le dictionnaire!

The dictionary skills worksheets (1/8, 2/9, 3/10 and 7/3) can be used at any appropriate point in the course and are not specifically linked with any units, although they have been listed with certain units where it would seem appropriate to use them.

This worksheet provides practice in using both the French-English and English-French sections to find translations of nouns and the French-English section to check genders and irregular plural forms of nouns. As before, all the words are listed in the *Glossaire* in the Students' Book so students do not need access to a separate dictionary in order to do the tasks.

On fait des projets — unité 2

Section 3

Solution:

1 Qu'est-ce que c'est en anglais?

français	anglais
1 une main	hand
2 un doigt	finger
3 un hérisson	hedgehog
4 une jambe	leg
5 un genou	knee
6 un bras	arm

2 C'est quoi en français?

anglais	français
1 an apricot	un abricot
2 a peach	une pêche
3 a cherry	une cerise
4 a mushroom	un champignon
5 a pineapple	un ananas
6 a raspberry	une framboise

3 C'est masculin ou féminin?

français	m/f	anglais
1 a oiseau	m	bird
b cadeau	m	present, gift
c eau	f	water
d manteau	m	coat
2 a journée	f	day
b année	f	year
c mosquée	f	mosque
d lycée	m	senior school

4 Singulier et pluriel

singulier	pluriel	anglais
chapeau	chapeaux	hat
tableau	tableaux	picture
animal	animaux	animal
cheval	chevaux	horse
journal	journaux	newspaper
œil	yeux	eye
grand-père	grands-pères	grandfather
petit-enfant	petits-enfants	grandchildren

CM 2/10, SCD 1/7–12 INDEPENDENT LISTENING

Écoute et parle

This copymaster provides pronunciation and speaking practice.

1 À la française

À la française

1 centre
2 bus
3 hockey
4 impatience
5 monument
6 question
7 région
8 village

2 Et après?

Solution: 3 – 5 – 10 – 13 – 18 – 22 – 54 – 86

Et après?

2 – 4 – 9 – 12 – 17 – 21 – 53 – 85

3 Des phrases ridicules

Des phrases ridicules

Le chien cherche les champignons au chocolat sous la chaise.
Je quitte le Québec sur le quai quatre-vingt-quinze.

4 Les terminaisons: -in

Solution: 1d, 2a, 3c, 4e, 5b, 6f

Les terminaisons: -in

1 destin
2 cousin
3 dessin
4 enfin
5 dauphin
6 lapin

5 Vocabulaire de classe

Solution: 1 devoirs, 2 six/6, vingt-sept/27, 3 quarante et un/41, 4 lundi, 5 parler, 6 question, 7 livre

Vocabulaire de classe

1 Voici vos devoirs.
2 Faites l'exercice six à la page vingt-sept.
3 Apprenez le vocabulaire à la page quarante et un.
4 C'est pour un contrôle lundi prochain.
5 Pouvez-vous parler plus lentement, s'il vous plaît?
6 Pouvez-vous répéter la question, s'il vous plaît?
7 Est-ce que je peux avoir un livre, s'il vous plaît?

6 Des conversations

Des conversations

1 Une fête internationale
– D'où vient Stefan?
(pause)
– Il vient de Berlin en Allemagne.
– Et Maria et Mercedes, d'où viennent-elles?
(pause)
– Elles viennent de Madrid, en Espagne.
– Comment viens-tu à la fête ce soir?
(pause)
– Je viens en voiture.

2 Demain
– Qu'est-ce qu'on peut faire demain?
(pause)
– On peut jouer au tennis ou aller à la piscine.
– Je veux bien jouer au tennis.
(pause)
– D'accord, on va aller au parc à dix heures.
– Et demain soir?
(pause)
– Demain soir, on peut aller au cinéma.
– Oui, bonne idée.

3 Des projets

– Quand vas-tu partir?
(pause)
– Je vais partir samedi prochain.
– Où vas-tu aller?
(pause)
– Je vais aller à Dieppe.
– C'est où, exactement?
(pause)
– C'est une petite ville dans le nord de la France.
– Comment vas-tu voyager?
(pause)
– Je vais prendre le train.

CM 2/11, 🎧 SCD 2/4–6 INDEPENDENT LISTENING

Tu comprends?

1️⃣ Où sont-ils?

Students listen to the recording and complete the table.

Solution:

les pays les personnes	All.	Éc.	Esp.	Ét-Un	Irl.	Mar.	pdeG	Suisse
1 André et Lucie			✓					
2 Jean-Pierre		✓						
3 Alice	✓							
4 les Simon							✓	
5 Luc								✓
6 Magali						✓		
7 Daniel				✓				
8 Sophie et Claire					✓			

🎧 Où sont-ils?

1 – Où sont André et Lucie?
– Ils sont chez leur oncle à Barcelone en Espagne.
– Ils sont en Espagne?
– Oui.

2 – Et Jean-Pierre, où est-il?
– Il est chez son correspondant à Édimbourg en Écosse.
– Ah, il est en Écosse.

3 – Alice est chez sa correspondante aussi?
– Oui, elle est à Hambourg en Allemagne.
– Hambourg, c'est dans le nord de l'Allemagne, non?
– Oui, c'est dans le nord.

4 – Et les Simon sont en vacances aussi?
– Oui, ils sont au pays de Galles. Ils font un circuit à vélo.
– Ils vont souvent au pays de Galles, non?
– Oui, ils ont des amis là-bas.

5 – Est-ce que Luc est en Suisse?
– Oui, il est à Genève, chez ses grands-parents.

6 – Et Magali, où est-elle?
– Elle est au Maroc.
– Ah oui, c'est vrai. Elle passe trois semaines au Maroc, je crois.

7 – Et Daniel, il passe ses vacances aux États-Unis, je suppose?
– Oui, il est chez son père à New York.

8 – Sophie et Claire font du camping, non?
– Oui, elles font du camping en Irlande.
– En Irlande – ça doit être bien.

2️⃣ Quand vont-ils rentrer?

Students listen to the recording and find the pairs.

Solution: 1d, 2b, 3e, 4c, 5f, 6h, 7g, 8a

🎧 Quand vont-ils rentrer?

1 – André et Lucie vont rentrer quand d'Espagne?
– Ils vont rentrer jeudi prochain.
– Jeudi prochain, ah bon.

2 – Et Jean-Pierre, quand va-t-il rentrer?
– Il va rentrer d'Écosse mardi matin.
– Mardi matin, c'est ça?
– Oui, c'est ça.

3 – Et Alice, quand est-ce qu'elle va rentrer?
– Alice va rentrer d'Allemagne vendredi soir.
– Vendredi soir? C'est bientôt!

4 – Et les Simon, est-ce qu'ils vont bientôt rentrer?
– Ils vont rentrer du pays de Galles mercredi après-midi.
– Ah bon – mercredi après-midi.

5 – Luc, il va rentrer de Suisse samedi prochain, non?
– C'est ça. Il va rentrer samedi prochain avec ses grands-parents.

6 – Et Magali, elle va rentrer plus tard, je suppose?
– Oui, elle va rentrer du Maroc la semaine prochaine.
– La semaine prochaine, c'est ça.

7 – Et Daniel va rentrer quand?
– Il va rentrer des États-Unis dimanche prochain.

8 – Sophie et Claire, quand est-ce qu'elles vont rentrer?
– Elles vont rentrer demain matin.
– Demain? Super!

3️⃣ Les transports au Canada

Students listen to a description of travel in Canada and complete the text.

Solution: **1** Canada, **2** métro, **3** bus, **4** train, **5** métro, **6** vélo, **7** vélo, **8** métro, **9** collège, **10** bus, **11** bus, **12** train, **13** car, **14** train, **15** ouest, **16** avion

🎧 Les transports au Canada

Salut! Je m'appelle Martin et j'habite à Montréal au Canada.
Comme transports en commun à Montréal, nous avons le métro, le bus et le train.
Beaucoup de personnes prennent le métro, surtout en hiver, quand il fait très froid et qu'il neige.

Moi, j'ai un vélo, alors j'aime bien prendre mon vélo en été.
C'est bien, parce qu'il y a beaucoup de pistes cyclables ici. Pendant certaines périodes, on peut aussi transporter son vélo dans le métro. Je ne prends pas mon vélo pour aller au collège – c'est trop loin. Je prends le bus. C'est pratique et beaucoup de mes amis prennent le bus aussi.
Quand je vais chez mes grands-parents dans le nord du Québec, je prends le train ou le car.
Il faut environ trois heures pour faire le voyage. J'aime bien prendre le train, parce qu'on peut se déplacer pendant le voyage. On peut lire ou on peut regarder par la fenêtre.
Cet été, nous allons à Vancouver dans l'ouest du Canada et je vais prendre l'avion pour la première fois.

SB 31, CM 2/12
Sommaire

A summary of the main vocabulary and structures of this unit. Students fill in gaps on the copymaster. They should check their answers against the Students' Book page.

CM 2/13
Rappel 2

REVISION

This copymaster can be used at any point in the course for revision and consolidation. It provides revision of numbers, school and computer vocabulary.

The reading and writing tasks are self-instructional and can be used by students working individually for homework or during cover lessons.

Solution:

1 C'est quel numéro?
1 60, **2** 7, **3** 12, **4** 24,
5 26, **6** 1000, **7** 18, **8** 11

2 Et ensuite?
4, 8, 11, 16, 20, 26, 42, 57, 84, 100

3 Un ordinateur
Students label a picture of a computer. They could consult SB 148 for help or to check their work.

4 Un message
~~cinq~~ ~~dix~~ rendez-vous ~~neuf~~ ~~seize~~ ~~à~~ ~~trente-trois~~ la ~~quarante-deux~~ cantine ~~quatre-vingt-deux~~ ~~à~~ ~~cent~~ ~~cinquante-neuf~~ la ~~vingt~~ récré

5 Mots croisés (au collège)

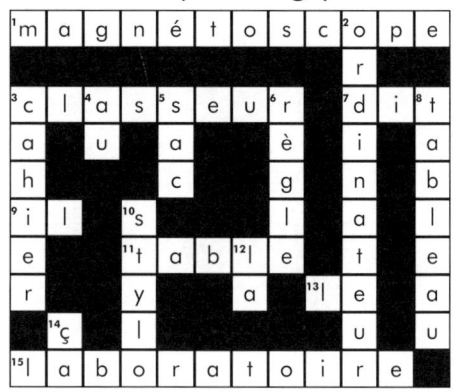

¹m	a	g	n	é	t	o	s	c	²o	p	e
									r		
³c	l	⁴a	s	⁵s	e	u	⁶r		⁷d	i	⁸t
a		u		a			è		i		a
h				c			g		n		b
⁹i	l		¹⁰s				l		a		l
e			¹¹t	a	b	¹²l	e		t		e
r			y			a		¹³l	e		a
		¹⁴ç		l					u		u
¹⁵l	a	b	o	r	a	t	o	i	r	e	

66

Épreuve – Unité 2

These worksheets can be used for an informal test of listening, speaking, reading and writing or for extra practice, as required. For general notes on administering the *Épreuves*, see TB 16.

CM 2/14, 🎧 1/28–31 **LISTENING**

Épreuve: Écouter

A Les moyens de transport (NC 1)

Solution: 1a, 2e, 3d, 4f, 5g, 6b, 7c

(mark /6: 5+ shows the ability to understand short statements)

🎧 **Les moyens de transport**

1 Demain, je vais au cinéma à pied.
2 Mon père va à Paris en métro.
3 Nous allons en Angleterre en bateau.
4 Normalement, mon père va en Allemagne en avion.
5 En Belgique, nous allons voyager en car.
6 Nous allons à la campagne. On va faire des excursions en voiture.
7 Mon oncle a des chevaux. On va voir la campagne à cheval.

B Nos vacances en France (NC 2)

Solution: 1f, 2e, 3d, 4c, 5b, 6a, 7g

(mark /6: 4+ shows ability to understand a range of familiar statements)

🎧 **Nos vacances en France**

1 Lundi, à Paris, je vais jouer au golf.
2 Mardi, je vais visiter des châteaux.
3 Mercredi, je vais faire du camping.
4 Jeudi, on va faire du vélo.
5 Vendredi, nous allons prendre des photos de la ville.
6 Samedi, mon père va à la pêche.
7 Dimanche, on va organiser un pique-nique.

C C'est quelle ville/quel village? (NC 3)

Solution: 1a, 2c, 3e, 4d, 5f, 6b, 7g

(mark /6: 4+ shows ability to understand and identify the main point of short passages made up of familiar language and spoken at near normal speed.)

🎧 **C'est quelle ville/quel village?**

1 – Où habites-tu?
  – J'habite à Marseille.
  – Marseille, c'est comment?
  – Marseille est une grande ville dans le sud-est de la France. C'est sur la côte.

2 – Et toi. Où habites-tu?
  – J'habite à Lorient.
  – Lorient, c'est comment?
  – Lorient est une ville moyenne dans le nord-ouest de la France. Lorient est sur la côte.

3 – Monique, où habites-tu?
  – J'habite à Perpignan.
  – Perpignan, c'est comment?
  – Perpignan est une grande ville dans le sud, près de l'Espagne.

4 – Jean, où habites-tu?
  – J'habite à Charleville-Mézières. C'est une petite ville dans le nord de la France, à la montagne.

5 – Où habites-tu, Paul?
  – J'habite à Beaugency.
  – Beaugency, c'est comment?
  – Beaugency est une petite ville dans le centre de la France. C'est près de Paris.

6 – Anne, où habites-tu?
  – J'habite à Palavas. C'est un petit village dans le sud de la France. Il se trouve sur la côte.

7 – Où habites-tu, Claude?
  – J'habite à Montflanquin.
  – Montflanquin, c'est comment?
  – Montflanquin est un petit village dans le sud-ouest.

D Un coup de téléphone (NC 4)

Solution: 1c, 2b, 3a, 4c, 5a, 6a, 7c, 8b

(mark /7: 5+ shows ability to understand longer passages spoken at near normal speeds and an ability to note main points and some detail)

🎧 **Un coup de téléphone**

– Salut Annette. Merci pour ta lettre.
– Sylvie! Ça va? Quel temps fait-il chez toi? Ici, il fait chaud.
– Ah bon? Il fait très froid. Mais super, tu vas arriver la semaine prochaine. Je vais ranger et préparer ta chambre ce week-end pour ton arrivée.
– Senez, c'est où en France? C'est comment? On peut aller à la plage?
– Senez, c'est dans le sud-est de la France. C'est un petit village à la montagne et il y a beaucoup de choses à faire. En hiver, on peut faire du ski en montagne, mais on ne peut pas aller à la plage, parce qu'il fait froid.
– On peut faire des excursions?
– On habite près de l'Italie et mon père dit que nous allons passer une journée là-bas. Ça va être chouette! On va prendre la voiture de mon père. Mais on ne va pas aller à Rome, parce que c'est trop loin. Bon, à la semaine prochaine!
– À bientôt, Sylvie.

CM 2/15   **SPEAKING**

Épreuve: Parler

Students should be given the sheet up to a week before the assessment, to give them time to choose whether to do 1 or 2 and to give them time to prepare and practice both conversations – the structured one (A) and the open-ended one (B) – with their partners.

Mark scheme

Section A: mark /12: 3 marks per response
- 1 mark for a response that is clear and conveys all of the information requested, in the form of a complete phrase or sentence, though not necessarily an accurate one. The questions and answers may seem a little disjointed, like separate items rather than parts of a coherent conversation.
- 2 marks for a response that is clear and conveys all of the information requested in the form of a complete phrase or sentence, though not necessarily an accurate one. The language must flow reasonably smoothly and be recognisable as part of a coherent conversation.
- 3 marks for a clear and complete response that flows smoothly as part of a clear and coherent conversation. The language must be in complete sentences or phrases that are reasonably accurate and consistent as far as grammar, pronunciation and intonation are concerned.

Section B: mark /13: 3 marks per response, as above, +1 bonus mark for adding one or two items of extra information.

Summary:
Marks	7–13	14–18	19–25
NC Level	2	3	4

CM 2/16 READING

Épreuve: Lire

A Mes projets en vacances (NC 2)

Solution: 1a, 2f, 3b, 4e, 5d, 6g, 7c

(mark /6: 4+ shows ability to understand short phrases)

B Des questions et des réponses (NC 3)

Solution: 1b, 2a, 3d, 4e, 5f, 6g, 7c

(mark /6: 4+ shows ability to write two or three sentences on familiar topics, using aids)

C On cherche des correspondant(e)s (NC 3)

Solution: 1 Jean, 2 Marie, 3 Sandrine, 4 Marc, 5 Pierre, 6 Christine, 7 Sophie

(mark /6: 4+ shows the ability to understand short texts, identifying main points)

D M. Giroux part en vacances (NC 4)

Solution: 1 prochaine, 2 à, 3 en, 4 bateau, 5 louer, 6 va, 7 vient, 8 vont

(mark /7: 4+ shows the ability to understand short stories and note main points)

CM 2/17 WRITING

Épreuve: Écrire et grammaire

A Les activités (NC 1)

Solution: 1 vais, 2 allons, 3 vont, 4 vient, 5 viens, 6 viennent, 7 peux, 8 pouvez, 9 peuvent

(mark /8: 5+ shows ability to select appropriate words to complete sentences and copy them correctly)

B Le week-end (NC 4)

Mark scheme
- 1 mark for each use of *aller/pouvoir* with an appropriate and correct infinitive. Credit repeated use of *aller/pouvoir* but not repeated infinitives.

Subtotal: 6
Accuracy:
- 2 marks: most words are correct
- 1 mark: about half the words are correct
- 0 marks: fewer than half the words are correct

Subtotal: 2
(mark /8: 5+ shows the ability to write individual paragraphs of about three or four sentences)

C Mes vacances (NC 5)

This is an open-ended task.

Mark scheme

Communication:
- 1 mark for each of the 6 sub-tasks communicated clearly
- 1/2 mark for each sub-task which is partially communicated (or just 1 detail in task 4)

Subtotal: 6 (round up half marks)
Accuracy:
- 3 marks: mostly accurate
- 2 marks: about half correct
- 1 mark: more wrong than right
- 0 marks: little or nothing of merit

Subtotal: 3
(mark /9: 6+ shows ability to produce short pieces of writing in simple sentences; although there may be mistakes the meaning can be understood with little or no difficulty)

SB 32–33, CM 133   **READING EXTENSION**

Presse-Jeunesse 1

These pages provide reading for pleasure. They can be used alone or with the accompanying copymaster.

SB 32, CM 133

Louis Laloupe suit Monique Maligne

Students read the picture story which includes a lot of transport vocabulary. The copymaster task comprises questions in French.

Solution:

A Louis Laloupe suit Monique Maligne

Des questions: 1 *Marc Malheur.* **2** *Non, elle sort d'un café.* **3** *Il prend le bus (monte dans le bus) aussi.* **4** *Monique descend sur la place principale.* **5** *Non, elle continue en voiture.* **6** *Non, il prend un taxi.* **7** *Ils vont à la gare.* **8** *Quand le train arrive, Monique et Louis montent dans le train.* **9** *Louis.* **10** *Monique.*

SB 33, CM 133

La Tour Eiffel

This gives some factual information about the Eiffel Tower. Students could also look at the website (www.tour-eiffel.fr) for more information and an on-line quiz. The copymaster task comprises questions in English.

Solution:

B La Tour Eiffel

Des questions: 1 the French Revolution, **2** metal, iron, **3** three, **4** fifty, **5** seventeen, **6** second, **7** (any three) small museum, restaurant, buffet/bar, souvenir shops, post office, **8** 700, **9** by lift, **10** elephant in 1948

SB 33

C'est bon?

This is a food and drink quiz.

Solution: **1c, 2c, 3a, 4b, 5b, 6c, 7b, 8b, 9a** *le thé noir*, **9b** *le thé vert*, **10** *le lait*

CM 133

The copymaster contains three additional tasks.

Solution:

C D'autres activités

Au contraire: 1d, 2e, 3f, 4a, 5b, 6c

Chasse à l'intrus: 1 *un poisson*, **2** *avril*, **3** *une infirmerie*, **4** *une crêpe*, **5** *un mois*, **6** *le Canada*, **7** *le beurre*, **8** *l'été*

Ça commence avec un 'p': 1 *une pièce*, **2** *un passeport*, **3** *une pizza*, **4** *une pêche*, **5** *le petit déjeuner*, **6** *Paris*

unité 2 On fait des projets   Section 3

Encore Tricolore 2
nouvelle édition

unité 3   Au collège

Areas	Topics	Grammar
1	Finding out about school life in France Describing your school	
2		Using the verbs *dire*, *lire* and *écrire*
3	Discussing the school day and school subjects	
4	Describing travel to school Revision of means of transport	Using the verbs *apprendre* and *comprendre* Revision of *prendre*
5	Discussing morning and evening routine	Introduction to reflexive verbs
6		Using other reflexive verbs
7	Discussing school subjects and using the Internet at school	
8	Saying what you want and don't want to do	Using the verb *vouloir*
9	Further activities and consolidation	

National Curriculum Information

Some students   levels 3–5
Most students   levels 3–4
All students   levels 2–3

Revision

Rappel (CM 3/14) includes revision of the following:
- days of the week, months
- weather
- time

Sounds and writing

- the French alphabet
- pronunciation of *h* and *i*
- the ending *-ie*

See *Écoute et parle* (CM 3/11, TB 87).

ICT opportunities

- making a labelled plan of the classroom or school
- laying out a school timetable
- writing a short description
- organising a survey

Reading strategies

Presse-Jeunesse 2 (SB 48–49, CM 134)

Assessment

- Informal assessment is in *Épreuves* at the end of this unit (TB 89, CM 3/15–3/18)
- Formal assessment (*Unités 1–7*) is in the *Contrôle* (TB 190, CM 139–145).

Students' Book

Unité 3 SB 34–47
Au choix SB 126–129

Flashcards

39–44	school rooms
22, 26–28, 30–31	transport
45–54	reflexive verbs
32–38	leisure

CDs

2/1–18
Student CD 1/13–18, 2/7–10

Additional

Grammar in Action 2, pp 12–16, 27

Copymasters

CM 3/1	*La page des jeux* [vocabulary practice]
CM 3/2	*Deux mots croisés* [grammar]
CM 3/3	*L'interview d'un boulanger* [reading]
CM 3/4	Reflexive verbs [mini-flashcards, grammar]
CM 3/5	*La famille Guille* [grammar]
CM 3/6	*La routine du matin* [grammar]
CM 3/7	*J'aime lire* [reading]
CM 3/8	*vouloir* and *pouvoir* [grammar]
CM 3/9	*devoir* [grammar]
CM 3/10	*C'est utile, le dictionnaire!* [dictionary skills]
CM 3/11	*Écoute et parle* [independent listening]
CM 3/12	*Tu comprends?* [independent listening]
CM 3/13	*Sommaire* [consolidation, reference]
CM 3/14	*Rappel* [revision]
CM 3/15	*Épreuve: Écouter*
CM 3/16	*Épreuve: Parler*
CM 3/17	*Épreuve: Lire*
CM 3/18	*Épreuve: Écrire et grammaire*
CM 134	*Presse-Jeunesse 2* [reading]
CM 147–148	*Chantez! Les matières* [song]

Language content

Describing school (Area 1)
la bibliothèque
la cour
la cantine
un demi-pensionnaire
le gymnase
un laboratoire
la salle de classe
le terrain de sports/de football/de rugby

School clothing (Area 1)
un polo
une cravate
une jupe
un pantalon
un sweat-shirt
un uniforme scolaire
une veste

School day (Area 3)
le cours
l'emploi du temps (m)
la pause-déjeuner
la récréation
les matières (f pl)
l'allemand (m)
l'anglais (m)
la biologie
la chimie
le dessin
l'EPS (l'éducation physique et sportive) (f)
l'espagnol (m)
le français
la géographie
l'histoire (f)
l'informatique (f)
l'instruction civique (f)
l'instruction religieuse (f)
les langues vivantes (f pl)
le latin
les maths
la physique
les sciences (naturelles) (f pl)
la technologie

Daily routine (Area 5)
Le matin, …/Le soir, …
Je me lève à …
Je me lave …
Je porte mon uniforme scolaire/un polo et un pantalon etc.
Pour le petit déjeuner, je prends …
Je quitte la maison à …
Je vais au collège en bus/en train/en voiture etc.
Je rentre vers …
Normalement, je mange quelque chose, par exemple …
J'ai du travail pour … (minutes/heures)
Je me couche vers …

Reflexive verbs (Areas 5 and 6)
se réveiller   se lever
se laver   s'habiller
s'occuper de   s'intéresser à
se dépêcher   se reposer
se baigner   se coucher
s'ennuyer   s'amuser

Opinions (Area 7)
C'est …/Ce n'est pas …
amusant
difficile
facile
fatigant
intéressant
important
utile
nul
Quelle est ta (votre) matière préférée?
Qu'est-ce que tu aimes (vous aimez) comme matières?
Qu'est-ce que tu n'aimes pas?
J'aime beaucoup …
Je n'aime pas …
Est-ce que tu aimes …?
Non, pas beaucoup
Je préfère …

Talking about what you want to do (Area 8)
Qu'est-ce que tu veux faire? Qui veut …?
Je veux …/Je ne veux pas …

Useful websites

Schools and education
http://fr.dir.yahoo.com/Enseignement_et_formation/Enseignement_secondaire/
Using the French Yahoo search engine, you can find links to schools throughout France, national educational events like a poetry competition and school festivals, school magazines and newsletters etc.

www.refer.sn/sngal_ct/edu/mermoz/html/presenta/index.htm – a school in Senegal – le lycée Jean Mermoz, Dakar

Zinedine Zidane
www.zidane.fr – the official website of this famous footballer has information about his life, career, family etc.

Au collège unité 3

> **Area 1**
> **Finding out about school life in France**
> **Describing your school**
> SB 34–35, **1**–**5**, SB 36, **1**
> Au choix SB 126, **1**, SB 127, **1**
> CM 3/1
> CD 2/1–3
> FC 39–44

REVISION

Introduction

Find out what students remember from **Encore Tricolore 1** about school life in France by having a brainstorming session or by asking questions and encouraging students to guess the answers. Suggested answers can be written on the board to be checked later, e.g.
En France, on commence l'école à l'âge de quatre, cinq, six ou sept ans?
Comment s'appelle une école pour les élèves de onze à quatorze ou quinze ans? (Une école primaire? Un collège? Un lycée?)
Est-ce que les élèves français vont à l'école tous les jours de la semaine? Et vous?
Est-ce qu'on porte un uniforme scolaire?

FC 39–44   **PRESENTATION**

Au collège

Use the flashcards to teach and practise the following vocabulary: *la bibliothèque, la salle de technologie, le laboratoire, la cour, le gymnase, la cantine.*

Give additonal explanations if required, e.g.
Une bibliothèque est une salle ou un bâtiment où il y a une grande collection de livres.

SB 34–35, 🎧 **2/1,** 💻   **PRESENTATION**
                                                LISTENING
                                                READING

1 Notre collège

Students listen to the recording and follow the text in their books. Explain any difficult vocabulary, e.g.
Un demi-pensionnaire est un élève qui mange à la cantine à midi.
Qui est demi-pensionnaire ici? … Toi, (nom), tu es demi-pensionnaire? Et toi, (nom)?
Un internat est pour les élèves qui dorment à l'école.

To practise the vocabulary for school rooms (if flashcards are not available), ask students to give the number of the correct photo, e.g.
La bibliothèque, c'est quelle photo?
Le laboratoire de sciences, c'est quelle photo?
Et la salle de technologie?

After some work on the text, ask students to close their books while the recording is played. This encourages them to listen without the support of the printed text.

The teacher could also provide a gapped text for individual work in a language laboratory, for homework or for use on a computer.

🎧 **Notre collège**

Voici Michel Denis et Nicole Gilbert. Ils vont au collège. Un collège, c'est une école pour les élèves de 11 à 14 ou 15 ans.
– Il y a environ 700 élèves dans notre collège. C'est une école mixte.
– On ne porte pas d'uniforme scolaire. D'habitude, je porte un pantalon, une chemise et un pull.
– Et moi, je mets un jean et un sweat-shirt.
– Les cours commencent à huit heures. Il y a un cours de géographie dans cette salle de classe.
– Pour les sciences, on va dans un laboratoire.
– Dans la salle de technologie, il y a des ordinateurs. Moi, j'aime bien la technologie.
– Voici la bibliothèque. Il y a des livres de toutes sortes.
– Quand nous n'avons pas de cours, nous pouvons aller à la bibliothèque.
– Voici la cantine. À midi, je mange ici. Je suis demi-pensionnaire.
– Pendant la récréation, le matin et l'après-midi, nous sortons dans la cour.
– Pour l'EPS, c'est à dire, l'éducation physique et sportive, nous allons dans le gymnase ou au terrain de sports.
– En été, nous allons à la piscine une fois par semaine.
– D'habitude, les cours finissent à cinq heures. Il n'y a pas d'internat au collège, alors tous les élèves rentrent à la maison.

SB 35, 💻   **READING**

2 Qu'est-ce qu'on a dit?

This tests comprehension of the previous item, by matching up two parts of a sentence.

The activity may be used in conjunction with *Fun with Texts, Textsalad.*

Solution: 1d, 2c, 3e, 4a, 5h, 6b, 7f, 8g

SB 35   **READING**

3 Jeu des définitions

This task gives practice of school vocabulary.

Solution: **1** un collège, **2** un uniforme scolaire,
                3 la bibiliothèque, **4** la cantine,
                5 la cour, **6** le terrain de sports,
                7 un laboratoire, **8** le gymnase

💻

School or classroom plan

Use any available software to make a labelled plan of the classroom or school. The easiest program to use is *Microsoft® Word* which has an autoshapes function which allows simple shapes to be created which can then be labelled by the add text function. However, there are many programs with graphics capabilities and, if in doubt, consult the ICT co-ordinator who will know what is available and what the students can use. Once complete, the plans could be used for display or sent as e-mail attachments.

CM 3/1   PRACTICE

La page des jeux

These word puzzles practise a range of school vocabulary and can be used at any appropriate point, e.g. in Areas 1 or 3 or later.

Task 3b practises a wide range of school subjects, which may need to be revised beforehand, if used in Area 1.

Solution:

1 Une règle
  A 1 *informatique*, 2 *français*, 3 *sciences*, 4 *géographie*, 5 *technologie*, 6 *maths*
  B *gymnase*

2 Les mots mêlés

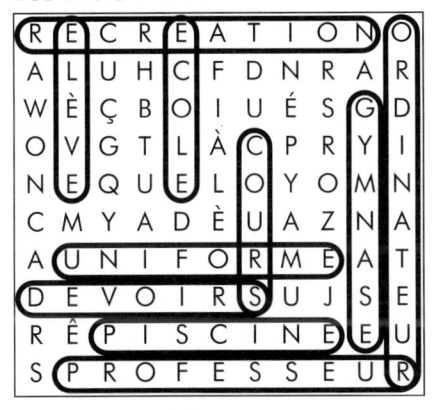

R	E	C	R	É	A	T	I	O	N	O
A	L	U	H	C	F	D	N	R	A	R
W	È	Ç	B	O	I	U	É	S	G	D
O	V	G	T	L	À	C	P	R	Y	I
N	E	Q	U	E	L	O	Y	O	M	N
C	M	Y	A	D	È	U	A	Z	N	A
A	U	N	I	F	O	R	M	E	A	T
D	E	V	O	I	R	S	U	J	S	E
R	Ê	P	I	S	C	I	N	E	E	U
S	P	R	O	F	E	S	S	E	U	R

3 Deux acrostiches

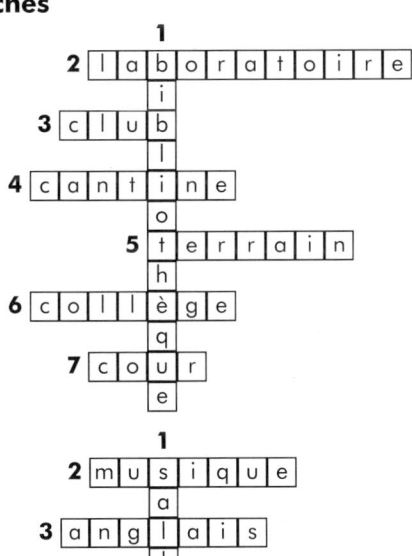

a

2 l a b o r a t o i r e
   i
3 c l u b
   l
4 c a n t i n e
   o
5 t e r r a i n
   h
6 c o l l è g e
   q
7 c o u r
   e

b

2 m u s i q u e
   a
3 a n g l a i s
   l
4 d e s s i n
   d
5 s c i e n c e s
   c
6 a l l e m a n d
   a
7 h i s t o i r e
   s
8 c h i m i e

AU CHOIX SB 127, 2/2   EXTENSION / READING / LISTENING

1 On va à quelle école?

Talk briefly about the different types of schools in France, referring to the diagram (*L'enseignement en France*). A few questions could be asked, e.g.

Quand est-ce qu'on doit aller à l'école en France? À quel âge? À cinq ans? À six ans? À onze ans?

Comment s'appelle la première école, pour les élèves de six à dix ans?

Comment s'appelle l'école pour les élèves de 11 à 14 ou 15 ans?

La première classe au collège s'appelle la sixième? Et ensuite, il y a quelle classe? (La cinquième? La deuxième? etc.)

Pour les trois dernières années, la plupart des élèves vont dans une autre école qui s'appelle un …?

Students should then listen to six French schoolchildren talking about their age, school and year and note down the details.

Solution:

	nom	âge	école (EP/C/L)	classe
1	Luc	11 ans	C	6e
2	Sophie	15 ans	L	2e
3	Marc	16 ans	L	1e
4	Marie	10 ans	EP	–
5	Jean	13 ans	C	4e
6	Anne	12 ans	C	5e

On va à quelle école?

1 Je m'appelle Luc. J'ai onze ans. Je vais au collège et je suis en sixième.

2 Et moi, je m'appelle Sophie. J'ai quinze ans. Je vais au lycée et je suis en seconde.

3 Moi, je m'appelle Marc. J'ai seize ans. Je vais au lycée et je suis en première.

4 Je m'appelle Marie. J'ai dix ans et je vais à l'école primaire.

5 Et moi, je m'appelle Jean. J'ai treize ans. Je vais au collège et je suis en quatrième.

6 Moi, je m'appelle Anne. J'ai douze ans. Je vais au collège et je suis en cinquième.

AU CHOIX SB 126   SUPPORT / WRITING

1 Des photos

Students write the correct caption for each photo.

Solution: 1 *la piscine*, 2 *le laboratoire des sciences*, 3 *la cantine*, 4 *la bibliothèque*, 5 *le terrain de sports*, 6 *la salle de technologie*

unité 3 Au collège — Section 3

SB 35, 🎧 2/3   LISTENING

4   Des clubs et des activités

Talk about after school and lunchtime clubs and write details of any clubs that students go to on the board. List also the clubs needed for the listening task: *un club de gymnastique, un club de théâtre, un club d'informatique*. Students listen to the recording and complete the answers.

Solution:
1 Il y a un club de gymnastique, un club de théâtre et un club d'informatique.
2 Il va au club d'informatique.
3 C'est mardi, après les cours.
4 Elle va au club de théâtre.
5 C'est vendredi, à midi.

🎧   Des clubs et des activités

1   – C'est l'heure du déjeuner. Beaucoup d'élèves sont dans la cour.
    Comment t'appelles-tu?
   – Je m'appelle Claude Legrand.
   – Tu es en quelle classe, Claude?
   – Moi, je suis en cinquième.
   – Est-ce qu'il y a des clubs au collège?
   – Oui, il y a un club de gymnastique, un club de théâtre et un club d'informatique.

2   – Et toi, tu vas à quel club?
   – Moi, je vais au club d'informatique.

3   – C'est quand?
   – C'est mardi, après les cours.

4   – Et toi, tu t'appelles comment?
   – Je m'appelle Louise Bernard.
   – Et tu vas dans un club, Louise?
   – Oui, moi, je vais au club de théâtre. J'aime bien ça.

5   – C'est quand, le club de théâtre?
   – C'est vendredi, à midi.

SB 35   SPEAKING, WRITING

5   Les clubs au collège

Students list clubs at their own school and say which, if any, they go to. This could be done individually, in pairs, or as a class activity.

SB 36, 💻   WRITING

1   Notre collège – un guide

Des renseignements généraux

This is the first of a series of items designed to build up a detailed guide for French-speaking visitors to the school and is an ideal project for students to work on either individually or in groups. The guide is gradually built up as students work through the unit. Students' material could be presented in a loose leaf binder, together with photos, drawings and realia, and items could be extracted for a wall display from time to time. The project could also be done on computer, using word processing or DTP and could be added to the school website.

Work through the example first, asking for information about the fictitious King Henry's school.

Then discuss in class what could be said about your own school and write some notes on the board. Students can then list or record on cassette some of the facts about the school.

If a school plan is available, this could be labelled in French and put on the wall.

Area 2
Using the verbs *dire*, *lire* and *écrire*
SB 36, **2**
Au choix SB 128, **1**–**2**
CM 3/2
CD 2/4
Grammar in Action 2, page 27

SB 36, 🎧 2/4   PRESENTATION
                                                                            LISTENING

2   Dans la cour

Students listen to the conversations and follow the text, noting down the missing words.

The conversations introduce different forms of the verbs *lire*, *dire* and *écrire*.

Solution:
1   **a** *une BD*, **b** *tes amis*, **c** *une histoire*, **d** *une lettre*
2   **a** *souvent*, **b** *j'ai*, **c** *anglais*, **d** *français*
3   **a** *sciences*, **b** *nouveau*, **c** *biologie*, **d** *sévère*

🎧   Dans la cour

1   – Qu'est-ce que tu lis?
   – Je lis une BD. C'est très amusant.
   – Et tes amis, qu'est-ce qu'ils lisent?
   – Hasan lit une histoire de Tintin et Magali lit une lettre de sa correspondante.

2   – Est-ce que tu écris souvent à ta correspondante?
   – Bof! J'écris quand j'ai le temps.
   – Elle écrit en anglais?
   – Oui, et moi, j'écris en français.

3   – On dit qu'il y a un nouveau prof de sciences.
   – Qu'est-ce que tu dis?
   – Il y a un nouveau prof de biologie. On dit qu'il est assez sévère.

SB 36, 💻   GRAMMAR

Dossier-langue
The verbs *dire*, *lire* and *écrire*

Students should refer to the printed text or *Les verbes* (SB 160) to complete the tables. The verbs can then be added to an electronic verb list.

Au choix SB 128 — **GENERAL PRACTICE**

1 Des phrases

Students follow the lines to complete the sentences which can either be written out or read aloud.

Solution:
1 On dit qu'il va faire beau demain.
2 Qu'est-ce que vous dites?
3 Dis bonjour à Pierre de ma part.
4 Écrivez ces mots au tableau.
5 Lisez la conversation à haute voix.
6 Qu'est-ce que tu lis en ce moment?
7 Est-ce que tes amis lisent le journal?
8 À Noël, nous écrivons beaucoup de cartes.
9 Je relis les instructions quand j'ai un problème avec l'ordinateur.
10 Mon correspondant décrit son collège dans sa lettre.

Au choix SB 128, — **GENERAL SPEAKING**

2 À toi!

Students work in pairs to ask and answer questions using the new verbs.

GRAMMAR IN ACTION 2, PAGE 27 GRAMMAR PRACTICE

Using the verbs *dire*, *lire* and *écrire*

This provides further practice of *dire*, *lire* and *écrire*.

CM 3/2 — **PRACTICE**

Deux mots croisés

This contains two crosswords, one practising *dire*, *lire*, *écrire*; one practising *prendre*, *apprendre*, *comprendre*. See Area 4 for details.

Area 3
Discussing the school day and school subjects
SB 36–37, **3**–**7**
Au choix SB 127, **2**, SB 128, **3**
CD 2/5–6

SB 36 — **READING**

3 La journée de Charlotte

Students read the details of Charlotte's school day and then complete the task by matching the clock times to an activity.

Solution: 1d, 2f, 3b, 4a, 5c, 6e

Au choix SB 127, 2/5 — **EXTENSION OPTIONAL LISTENING**

2 On parle de la journée scolaire

This is based on an unscripted recording by a student from a school in Orléans. It is quite demanding but provides good practice in extended listening. Some vocabulary could be explained beforehand, e.g. *plusieurs*, *entrée*, *un plat de résistance*. Students should follow the text in *Au choix* and listen to the recording in order to find out the missing words.

Solution: 1 cinq, 2 dix, 3 des pains, 4 deux, 5 la cantine, 6 fromage, 7 la cour, 8 devoirs, 9 cartes, 10 le quart, 11 récréation, 12 moins

On parle de la journée scolaire

Nous commençons les cours vers huit heures cinq, le matin. Nous avons deux heures de cours et vers dix heures cinq, nous avons une pause récréation de dix minutes où il y a des … où des élèves vendent des pains au chocolat.

De dix heures jusqu'à midi, nous avons encore deux heures de cours. Après, nous avons … euh … nous pouvons aller manger à la cantine ou rentrer chez nous pour manger avec nos parents. Moi, je mange à la cantine. Nous avons plusieurs entrées où nous pouvons des fois en choisir deux. Nous avons un seul plat de résistance. Nous avons des … du fromage, de la salade des fois et plusieurs desserts. Hélas, nous n'avons pas de, de sel, de poivre ni de ketchup. Quand nous avons fini, nous sortons dans la cour où nous révisons nos devoirs ou nous les faisons ou nous jouons aux cartes, cela dépend des personnes. Après, nous retravaillons vers deux heures moins le quart jusqu'à quatre heures moins le quart. Et nous avons une récréation de dix minutes. Et enfin, les cours se terminent à cinq heures moins dix.

School subjects — **PRESENTATION**

If necessary, ask students in advance to bring a selection of their school textbooks to the lesson. These can be used as flashcards to revise the names of school subjects and for vocabulary games and then returned to the students at the end of the lesson, e.g.
Qui a des livres scolaires dans son cartable?
(Student A), *qu'est-ce que tu as comme livres scolaires?*
Est-ce que tu as un livre d'anglais/de géographie/ d'histoire/de sciences/de maths/de technologie etc.?

Pretend to look at them and talk about them briefly.
Voyons, qu'est-ce qu'on a comme livres?
Ça, c'est compliqué – c'est un livre de maths, ça, ou un livre de physique?
Et ça, c'est un livre d'histoire ou un livre de géographie?

Show them to the class, getting them to repeat the names of the subjects, and write the names on the board.

The names of subjects could be written on slips of acetate and used with the OHT for extra practice, e.g. piling them up so part of the word is hidden.

Jeux
LISTENING

For extra practice, play a guessing game. Ask a student to take a book and put it in his/her school bag while you are not looking. Then ask questions to find out which book it is, e.g.

C'est un livre d'anglais? Non? Alors, c'est un livre d'histoire? Non? Voyons, je suis certain(e) que c'est un livre de français ... c'est ça, non?

When the names of the subjects have been adequately revised, students could take over the guessing role.

Other games, such as noughts and crosses (using symbols), dominoes, the Universal board game and a Spelling Bee could be played (see TB 25–29).

SB 37
READING / WRITING

4 L'emploi du temps

Ask some questions and encourage students to guess the answers before studying the timetable, e.g.

À quelle heure environ commencent les cours le matin, en France?

Un cours dure combien de temps?

Est-ce que les élèves français vont à l'école tous les jours de la semaine?

Students should then complete the sentences based on the timetable.

Solution: 1 *anglais*, 2 *français*, 3 *technologie*, 4 *mercredi*, 5 *l'anglais*, 6 *la biologie*, 7 *deux*, 8 *onze heures dix*

SB 37, 🎧 2/6
PRESENTATION / LISTENING

5 C'est quel jour?

Students have to listen and refer to the timetable to identify the day and say whether it is morning or afternoon each time.

Solution:
1 *mardi matin*
2 *lundi après-midi*
3 *samedi matin*
4 *jeudi matin*
5 *mardi après-midi*
6 *vendredi après-midi*

🎧 C'est quel jour?

1 – Qu'est-ce que tu as comme cours maintenant, Marc?
– Alors, physique d'abord, puis maths, et après la récréation ... attends ... ah oui, alors c'est dessin, puis musique. Pas mal, ça!
2 – Et toi, Suzanne, qu'est-ce que tu as comme cours?
– Alors, j'ai français, puis EPS. Je pense qu'on va faire de la gymnastique. C'est tout – je finis à quatre heures.
3 – Qu'est-ce que tu as comme cours maintenant, Paul?
– Alors, instruction civique, puis anglais, et ensuite, c'est la récréation – et après la pause, j'ai français.
4 – Et toi, Anne, qu'est-ce que tu as comme cours?
– Alors, j'ai technologie jusqu'à la récréation et après, on a ... attends ... ah oui, on a anglais. C'est bien, ça.
5 – Qu'est-ce que tu as comme cours maintenant, Françoise?
– Alors, on a histoire, puis après la pause, on a géographie.
6 – Et toi, Christophe, qu'est-ce que tu as comme cours?
– Alors, on a français – deux cours de français – et après, on a ... attends ... ah oui, on a biologie.

Jeux
ORAL PRACTICE

For further practice, if required, use some of the following games.

On a quel cours?
Give a day and a time and get students to work out which subject is on Michel's timetable. This can be played as a team game.

Le jeu du pendu (Hangman)
This could be played to practise spelling, limiting the choice of words to school subjects or school vocabulary.

Jeu des définitions
This game could be played using school subjects, e.g. *Quand on apprend cette matière, on parle des autres pays/on fait du calcul/on travaille dans un laboratoire/on parle une langue différente/on est à la piscine* etc.

AU CHOIX SB 128
GENERAL PRACTICE

3 Quelles sont ces matières?

Students have to unjumble the subjects.

Solution: 1 *dessin*, 2 *biologie*, 3 *histoire*, 4 *anglais*, 5 *musique*, 6 *maths*, 7 *géographie*, 8 *allemand*

WRITING

Timetable

Use a table program such as *Microsoft® Word* or *Excel* to lay out a school timetable. Again, these could be displayed or sent as e-mail attachments to penfriends or a partner school.

Mon emploi du temps
WRITING

Students translate their own timetable into French. Give the French for any additional subjects not included here. Discuss ways of representing subjects which are not directly comparable to subjects taught in a French school; this could be an approximation to a French subject, e.g. 'Humanities' – *c'est comme histoire/géo*, or a short description of the content of the subject.

Students could then look up the words in a dictionary and, if necessary, use the initials to represent the subject. Finally, students fill in their own timetables in French.

Jeux

Here are some games which students could base on their own timetable.

1 The teacher says a subject and students have to say on which day they have it (in teams or groups). (receptive practice)
2 The class is divided into four groups. The teacher says a day and a time (or a lesson number) and students have to give the subject they have very quickly. (productive practice)
3 The teacher gives a subject and students have to say one they have before or after it, again in teams or groups (rather like *Avancez et recule*). (productive practice)

SB 37, **SPEAKING**

6 Un emploi du temps idéal

Students can have fun making up an ideal timetable, first for one day, then for several days, within the constraints given. When complete, these could be dictated for other students to copy down, possibly as a pairwork activity.

The idea could be extended by asking students to make up an ideal timetable for a whole week (perhaps in groups). These could then be presented to the class, who could ask questions about each timetable and then vote on the one they liked best.

The 'ideal' timetables could be used for a game of Timetable bingo. The first one to cover all the subjects for a particular day, and then the whole week, wins.

SB 37, **WRITING**

7 Notre collège – un guide

La journée scolaire
Les matières qu'on apprend cette année

Prepare this as a class activity before students go on to work on it individually or in pairs.

Students give details about the school day, then list the subjects they are studying this year, with the number of lessons or hours devoted to each one. See TB 20 for ideas on using desktop publishing for this.

Area 4
Describing travel to school
Revision of means of transport
Using the verbs *apprendre* and *comprendre*
Revision of *prendre*
SB 38, **1**–**5**
Au choix SB 126, **2**, SB 128, **4**–**5**
CM 3/2
CD 2/7
Grammar in Action 2, page 16
FC 22, 26–28, 30–31

FC 22, 26–28, 30–31

Using flashcards, revise *prendre* and the following means of transport: *le bus, le train, la voiture, le métro, le vélo, à pied*.

SB 38, 2/7 **LISTENING**

1 Pour aller au collège

Students listen to the short discussion about travelling to school and note down the type of transport used.

Solution:
1 *Sophie et Charles prennent le bus.*
2 *Paul prend le métro.*
3 *Marc prend son vélo.*
4 *Claire, Nicole et Lucie prennent le train.*

Students should then give their own means of transport. Some students might want to reply using *je vais au collège à pied/en voiture* and these options could be written on the board.

A quick *sondage* could be done by show of hands and the results written on the board.

Pour aller au collège

– Comment allez-vous au collège, le matin? Sophie, est-ce que tu prends le bus?
– Oui, moi je prends le bus. C'est très pratique.
– Et Charles et Paul, comment vont-ils au collège?
– Charles prend le bus et Paul prend le métro.
– Et toi, Marc?
– Moi, je prends mon vélo. Le collège n'est pas très loin, alors ça marche bien.
– Et vous trois, Claire, Nicole et Lucie, est-ce que vous prenez le bus?
– Non, nous prenons le train.
– Alors, trois personnes prennent le train, deux personnes prennent le bus, une personne prend le métro et une personne prend son vélo.

ORAL PRESENTATION

The verb *apprendre*

Ask the class a few questions about subjects taken in school, e.g.

Ici, on apprend beaucoup de matières. Qu'est-ce qu'on apprend ici comme langues vivantes/sciences/sports?

Et toi, (Student A), tu apprends le basket/la chimie/le latin etc.?

Make sure that the class understands that *apprendre* means 'to learn', and write the infinitive on the board.

ORAL PRACTICE

Jeu
Moi, j'apprends ...

Play a cumulative oral game with school subjects (later this can also be played with sports and musical instruments), e.g.

Moi, j'apprends la biologie. Et toi, qu'est-ce que tu apprends?

Moi, j'apprends la biologie et le français.

This could also be adapted to practise the plural form, e.g. *Nous apprenons ... et vous?*

unité 3 Au collège — *Section 3*

Quelle heure est-il?   PRACTICE

Refer to the *emploi du temps* (SB 37) or put a different *emploi du temps* on an OHT and ask questions using *apprendre*, e.g.

C'est lundi. Michel apprend l'anglais. Quelle heure est-il? (Il est 9h30.)

This could be played as a team game with each team in turn asking a question and then giving the time of the beginning of the lesson.

SB 38   PRESENTATION
2   Tu comprends?

Introduce *comprendre* by writing the infinitive on the board and asking oral questions, e.g.

(Student A), tu comprends l'italien?

Moi, je comprends le français. Et toi, (Student B), tu comprends le français?

Ah bon, toute la classe comprend le français, n'est-ce pas?

Talk students through this short dialogue which presents *apprendre* and *comprendre*. Make sure that they have understood the meaning of the two verbs, then ask them to do the *vrai ou faux?* task.

Solution: 1 *faux*, 2 *vrai*, 3 *vrai*, 4 *faux*, 5 *faux*, 6 *faux*

SB 38,   GRAMMAR
Dossier-langue
Prendre, apprendre and *comprendre*

Ask students to find examples of *apprendre* and *comprendre* in the earlier tasks.

Help them to work out the similarity to *prendre*. Students should be able to complete the missing parts of each paradigm from the parts that are given on the page.

The paradigm could form the basis of an activity using *Fun with Texts, Clozewrite*.

Au choix SB 126   SUPPORT PRACTICE
2   Au collège

This gives practice in matching the subject to the correct part of the verb.

Solution: 1e, 2a, 3b, 4f, 5c, 6d

SB 38   PRESENTATION PRACTICE
3   L'éducation musicale

Revise the names of musical instruments by asking students which instrument, if any, they are learning to play, e.g.

Est-ce que tu apprends un instrument de musique?
Et toi?
Qui apprend (à jouer d') un instrument de musique?

If several instruments are mentioned, write details on the board, e.g.

4 élèves apprennent le violon.
12 élèves apprennent la flûte à bec.

Check that students recognise the instruments in this task and know their names in French. They can then complete the task, which practises all forms of *apprendre* with musical instruments.

Solution:
1 *Moi, j'apprends le violon.*
2 *Toi, tu apprends le piano.*
3 *Mon frère apprend la trompette.*
4 *Mon amie apprend la clarinette.*
5 *Au collège, nous apprenons la flûte à bec.*
6 *Vous apprenez la flûte.*
7 *Mes sœurs apprennent la guitare.*

Au choix SB 128   GENERAL PRACTICE
4   Des questions et des réponses

This gives further productive practice of *apprendre* and *comprendre*.

Solution:
a 1 *comprennent*, 2 *apprend*, 3 *comprend*, 4 *apprends*, 5 *apprenez*

b a *apprends*, b *comprend*, c *apprenons*, d *comprennent*, e *apprend*

c 1d, 2e, 3b, 4a, 5c

Grammar in Action 2, page 16 grammar practice
Using the verbs *prendre*, *apprendre* and *comprendre*

This provides further practice of *prendre*, *apprendre* and *comprendre*.

SB 38,   SPEAKING WRITING
4   À toi!

Students work in pairs to ask each other questions about school travel, languages and musical instruments. Students then write their own answers.

SB 38,   WRITING
5   Notre collège – un guide

Students add details about subjects and musical instruments to the school guide.

Au choix SB 128   GENERAL READING
5   Les langues vivantes

This optional logic puzzle provides more examples of *apprendre* in use. Able students might be able to make up a similar puzzle with sciences (e.g. *biologie, chimie, physique, géographie*).

Solution: 1 *Karine*, 2 *allemand*, 3 *Sophie*, 4 *Karine*

CM 3/2
Deux mots croisés — WRITING

This contains two crosswords, one practising *dire, lire, écrire*; one practising *prendre, apprendre, comprendre*.

Solution:

1 lire, dire, écrire

2 prendre, apprendre, comprendre

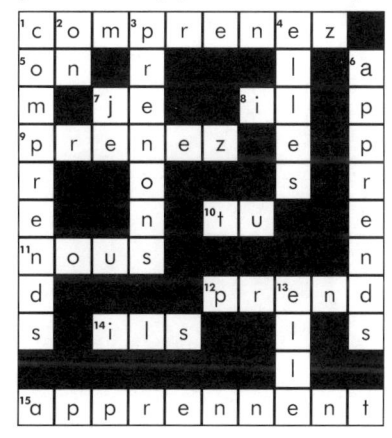

Area 5
Discussing morning and evening routine
Introduction to reflexive verbs
SB 39, **6**–**7**, SB 40, **1**–**2**
Au choix SB 126, **3**–**4**
CM 3/3
CD 2/8–9

SB 39, 2/8 — PRESENTATION / LISTENING

6 Le matin, chez Charlotte

Read through the questions and multiple choice answers first. Students could guess the answers and then listen to the recording to check these.

Solution: 1a, 2c, 3a, 4c, 5b, 6c

Le matin, chez Charlotte

– Charlotte, quand est-ce que tu te lèves, le matin?
– Normalement, les jours de semaine, je me lève à sept heures moins le quart.
– À sept heures moins le quart. Tu portes un uniforme scolaire?
– Ah non. Nous n'avons pas d'uniforme au collège. Alors normalement, je porte un pantalon et un pull.
– Et qui se lève le premier chez vous?
– C'est mon père. Il se lève à six heures, parce qu'il quitte la maison très tôt pour aller au travail.
– Alors, c'est ton père qui se lève le premier. Et qu'est-ce que tu prends pour le petit déjeuner?
– Pour le petit déjeuner, je prends des cérérales et un jus de fruit.
– Alors des céréales et un jus de fruit.
– Oui, c'est ça.
– Quand est-ce que tu quittes la maison, le matin?
– Je quitte la maison vers sept heures et demie.
– Alors, sept heures et demie. Et comment vas-tu au collège?
– Je prends le métro.
– Tu y vas en métro.
– Oui, c'est ça.

La routine du matin — SPEAKING

For extra practice in class, and later in pairs, ask the class the same questions and help them to reply for themselves. There is more practice of this later.

SB 39, 2/9 — PRESENTATION, LISTENING

7 Le soir, chez Michel

This time, students have to guess Michel's replies first, using the clues to help them. Then they listen to the recording to check their answers.

Solution: 1c, 2c, 3c, 4a, 5a

Le soir, chez Michel

– Alors, Michel, à quelle heure est-ce que tu rentres, le soir?
– Alors, après les cours, je parle une demi-heure avec mes copains et mes copines. Puis je rentre chez moi vers six heures.
– Est-ce que tu prends quelque chose à manger pour le goûter?
– Oui, je goûte. Normalement, je prends du pain avec du chocolat. C'est très bon ça. J'adore le chocolat.
– Et qu'est-ce que tu fais ensuite? Tu commences tes devoirs?
– Ah non! Après une journée scolaire, j'ai besoin de me relaxer un peu. Alors je m'amuse – je regarde la télé ou je joue sur l'ordinateur.
– Ah bon. Mais tu as combien d'heures de travail, le soir?
– Ça dépend des jours. Normalement, j'ai du travail pour une heure à peu près. Alors je commence mes devoirs après le dîner.
– Et après, quand tu as fait tes devoirs, à quelle heure est-ce que tu te couches?
– Bon, après mes devoirs, je regarde la télé ou je lis et je me couche vers neuf heures, car je dois me lever à six heures et demie, le matin.

unité 3 Au collège — Section 3

SB 39 — GRAMMAR

Dossier-langue
Reflexive verbs

Go through the explanation and write on the board some examples of reflexive verbs, as suggested by students.

Tu te lèves …? Je me lève … — SPEAKING

Practise these expressions orally with a chain question game, e.g.
- (Student A), *tu te lèves à quelle heure, normalement?*
- *Je me lève avant sept heures.* (Student B), *tu te lèves à quelle heure?* etc.

To answer, they could give an exact, or approximate, time (*avant sept heures, à sept heures et demie environ, après huit heures* etc.).

SB 40 — SPEAKING / WRITING

1 À toi!

Students work in pairs to ask each other questions about morning routine. They then write answers to describe their evening routine. This can be prepared on the board beforehand, or students can do the alternative tasks in *Au choix* support, which give more guidance, instead of or before these tasks.

Au choix SB 126 — SUPPORT / WRITING

3 Le matin
4 Le soir

These two tasks provide more guidance in helping students to describe their daily routine.

Le matin
In task **a**, students match up two halves of a sentence.

Solution: 1e, 2b, 3f, 4a, 5d, 6c

In task **b**, they adapt sentences 1, 4, 5 and 6 to describe their own situation.

Le soir
Students complete sentences to describe their evening routine.

SB 40 — SPEAKING / WRITING

2 Un sondage

Students can then work on a short survey, either in a group or in class.

Different students could ask one question each and note the replies. Students then complete the sentences to summarise the results.

The questions in the *sondage* could be repeated to find out if there are differences during the holidays.

If time is short, the survey could be done quickly with a show of hands and the results summarised on the board.

Une journée scolaire

Use a word processor to write a short description. The students can be provided with a ready made outline as below:

Ma journée scolaire
Je me lève à _____
Je quitte la maison à _____
Je vais au collège _____
En route, je vois _____
J'arrive au collège à _____
À midi, je _____
Les cours finissent à _____
Quand je rentre, je _____

CM 3/3 — READING

L'interview d'un boulanger

This optional reading worksheet gives details about a typical day in the life of a French baker.

Students read the interview and then do the comprehension tasks, based on times, word definitions and finding opposites.

Solution:
1 **À quelle heure?**
   1 à 1h30 du matin
   2 à 2h00 du matin
   3 à 7h30
   4 à 10h00 ou 11h00 ou 12h00
   5 à 20h30
2 **Trouve les mots**
   1 un four, 2 une baguette
3 **Trouve le contraire**
   1 se lever, 2 de bonne heure, 3 un jour de congé, 4 commencer, 5 midi, 6 ouvrir, 7 un peu, 8 chaud

---

Area 6
Using other reflexive verbs
SB 40–41, 3–5
Au choix SB 127, 3, SB 129, 6–7
CM 3/4–3/6
Grammar in Action 2, pages 12–13
FC 45–54

FC 45–54 — PRESENTATION

More reflexive verbs

Use the flashcards to teach and practise a greater range of reflexive verbs, writing each one on the board after it is introduced. Practise the singular forms first.

je me réveille; tu te lèves?; il se lave; elle s'habille; il s'arrête

Then the plural forms:
nous nous reposons; vous vous dépêchez?; ils se baignent; ils s'amusent; elles s'ennuient

SB 40–41 PRESENTATION, READING

3 Qu'est-ce qu'on fait?

Students should now be able to match up the appropriate text with the pictures.

Solution: 1 *je me réveille,* 2 *tu te lèves?,* 3 *il se lave,* 4 *elle s'habille,* 5 *il s'arrête,* 6 *nous nous reposons,* 7 *vous vous dépêchez?,* 8 *ils se baignent,* 9 *elles s'ennuient,* 10 *ils s'amusent*

CM 3/4 PRACTICE

Reflexive verbs

The mini-flashcards can be used for extra practice, individually or in pairs, or to make an OHT (see TB 26).

Solution: 1b, 2a, 3i, 4g, 5e, 6f, 7h, 8d, 9j, 10c

SB 40 WRITING

4 Chez mon oncle

Students supply the correct reflexive pronoun and copy out the subject and verb in full.

Solution: 1a *il s'appelle,* 2a *mon oncle se réveille,* 3c *Il se lève,* 4b *il se lave,* 5a *il s'habille,* 6b *il s'occupe,* 7a *elle ne se lève pas,* 8c *elle s'intéresse,* 9a *je me repose,* 10a *je ne m'intéresse pas,* 11a *je m'ennuie,* 12b *nous nous baignons*

GRAMMAR IN ACTION 2, PAGE 12 GRAMMAR PRACTICE

Using reflexive verbs

This provides further practice of a range of reflexive verbs.

SB 41 GRAMMAR

Dossier-langue

Reflexive verbs in the negative

This explains how to recognise a reflexive verb in the negative. Productive use of this is not required, although for those who wish to practise it a task is given in *Au choix* extension. Able students could learn a few set negative phrases for use in open-ended tasks, if wished.

Students could practise looking up a few reflexive verbs in the glossary to see how they are listed, e.g. *se dépêcher, s'amuser.*

SB 41 PRESENTATION
  READING
  WRITING

5 On s'amuse?

This can be prepared and practised orally first. First draw a smiling face on one side of the board and a sad face on the other side. Read through the questions, then go through each reply and ask the class to allocate it to the appropriate section. When the replies have been categorised, ask similar questions and prompt an appropriate reply with a flashcard of a smiling face or a sad face, e.g.

Tu t'amuses en vacances?
(sad face) *Non, je m'ennuie.*
(smiling face) *Oui, je m'amuse beaucoup ici.*
Tu te couches tard?
Tu te baignes?
Il fait beau?

For consolidation, students read through the sentences again and copy them out as two lists.

Solution:
Je m'amuse – **1, 4, 5, 7, 8**
Je ne m'amuse pas – **2, 3, 6, 9**

CM 3/5 PRACTICE

La famille Guille

1 Benoît et Fabien

This provides practice in understanding and recognising reflexive verbs.

Solution:

1 **F** Il *s'ennuie* à la campagne.
2 **B** Il *se réveille* très tôt et il *se lève* vite, parce qu'il y a beaucoup de travail à la ferme.
3 **F** Il *se lève* tard, parce qu'il est en vacances.
4 **B** Il *s'intéresse* beaucoup à la ferme.
5 **B** Il *se couche* tôt… entre 9h et 9h30.
6 **F** Le soir, il regarde la télé jusqu'à minuit ou plus tard.
7 **F** Il *se couche* tard, souvent après minuit.
8 **B** Le soir, il *se repose* un peu, mais souvent, il répare ses machines.
9 **B** Avant le petit déjeuner, il *s'occupe* des animaux de la ferme.

2 Complète les phrases

In this task, students use the singular forms of common reflexive verbs.

Solution:

A 1 *me réveille,* 2 *me lève, me lave, m'habille,* 3 *me dépêche,* 4 *m'amuse*
B 1 *se lève,* 2 *se lave, s'habille,* 3 *se couche,* 4 *se lève, se couche*

3 Complète le tableau

Students complete the present tense paradigm of the verb *se reposer.*

Solution:

je me repose	*nous nous reposons*
tu te reposes	*vous vous reposez*
il se repose	*ils se reposent*
elle se repose	*elles se reposent*

4 Une liste des verbes

Students complete a reference list of reflexive verbs, with the help of a dictionary, if wished.

Solution:

français	*anglais*
s'amuser	to enjoy oneself
s'appeler	to be called
s'arrêter	to stop
s'ennuyer	to get bored
s'entendre	to get on with someone
se dépêcher	to hurry
se coucher	to go to bed
s'habiller	to get dressed
s'intéresser à	to be interested in
se laver	to get washed
se lever	to get up
s'occuper de	to be busy with something
se promener	to go for a walk
se reposer	to rest
se réveiller	to wake up
se trouver	to be situated

CM 3/6   WRITING

La routine du matin

1 Mélanie

Students read speech bubbles and then write a short caption to the first five pictures, using reflexive verbs.

Solution:
1 Mélanie se réveille.
2 Elle se lève.
3 Elle prend son petit déjeuner.
4 Elle se lave.
5 Elle s'habille.

2 Une journée de travail

This task involves using picture cues to complete a brief account of morning routine.

As follow-up, students could write a few sentences describing their own routine.

Solution:
1 Je me réveille à cinq heures.
2 Je me lève à cinq heures dix.
3 Pour mon petit déjeuner, je prends du chocolat chaud, du jus de fruit et des tartines.
4 Je m'habille. Je mets un pantalon et un pull.
5 Je vais au studio en taxi.
6 Le trajet dure vingt minutes.

Au choix SB 127   EXTENSION PRACTICE

3 Aujourd'hui, c'est différent

This provides practice in using the negative of reflexive verbs for able students.

Solution:
1 Je ne me réveille pas avant sept heures.
2 Je ne me lève pas tout de suite.
3 Je ne m'habille pas très vite.
4 Mon frère ne se lave pas dans la salle de bains.
5 Nous ne nous dépêchons pas.
6 Le bus ne s'arrête pas au coin de la rue.
7 Mes parents ne s'occupent pas de leur travail.
8 On ne se couche pas tôt.

Au choix SB 129   GENERAL PRACTICE

6 Ça commence mal

Students supply the reflexive verb in the third person.

Solution: 1 Claude se lève, 2 Claude se réveille, 3 Il se lève, 4 Il s'habille, 5 le moteur s'arrête, 6 Il se dépêche, 7 le bus ne s'arrête pas

Au choix SB 129   GENERAL

7 Qu'est-ce qu'on fait?

This gives practice in matching captions (with reflexive verbs in the negative) to pictures.

Solution: 1d, 2a, 3c, 4b

Grammar in Action 2, page 13   GRAMMAR PRACTICE

Using reflexive verbs (negative)

This provides further practice of reflexive verbs in the negative.

SB 41   PRACTICE

Describe a holiday

As optional extra practice, students could write a few sentences to describe a holiday, using some of the phrases in *On s'amuse?* (SB 41, task 5).

Area 7
Discussing school subjects and using the Internet at school
SB 42–43, **1**–**6**
Au choix SB 129, **8**
CM 3/7
CD 2/10–11

SB 42, 🎧 **2/10**   PRESENTATION LISTENING

1 Une journée pas idéale

This introduces the topic with some negative opinions about a school day. Students should follow the text and listen to the recording then match up the school subjects with the opinions expressed.

Solution: 1d, 2c, 3a, 4e, 5b

🎧 **Une journée pas idéale**

– Salut, Marc.
– Salut, Pierre. Voici un ami canadien. Il s'appelle Jean Duval.
– Salut, Jean. Tu viens en classe avec nous?
– Oui. Qu'est-ce que vous avez comme cours aujourd'hui?

– On est lundi … alors, d'abord, il y a maths – je déteste ça – puis anglais, ça c'est beaucoup trop difficile. Ensuite, il y a biologie et je n'aime pas ça. Cet après-midi, il y a français. Ce n'est pas intéressant, le français. Et ensuite, il y a éducation physique et ça, c'est fatigant. Tu es sûr que tu veux venir aujourd'hui?

SB 42 SPEAKING / WRITING

2 Une bonne journée?

Work on a description of the school day in class first and build this up on the board. Students could then work in pairs to complete the task orally, or do it individually as a written task.

SB 42, 🎧 2/11 LISTENING

3 Tu aimes quelles matières?

Students listen to the conversations and decide who is speaking each time. Check that students know the names for the different sciences.

Solution: 1 *Magali*, 2 *Marc*, 3 *Fatima*, 4 *Daniel*, 5 *Corinne*

🎧 Tu aimes quelles matières?

1 – Qu'est-ce que tu aimes comme matières?
 – Moi, j'aime beaucoup les sciences, surtout la chimie. Ça, c'est intéressant.
 – Et qu'est-ce que tu n'aimes pas beaucoup?
 – Je n'aime pas beaucoup le dessin. Je suis nulle en dessin. Je trouve ça difficile.

2 – Et toi, est-ce que tu aimes les sciences aussi?
 – Non, je n'aime pas beaucoup les sciences. C'est ennuyeux. Je préfère l'histoire. C'est intéressant et c'est important aussi.

3 – Qu'est-ce que tu aimes comme matières?
 – Moi, j'aime les langues. J'aime beaucoup l'anglais. C'est amusant et c'est utile aussi.
 – Et qu'est-ce que tu n'aimes pas beaucoup?
 – Les maths – je n'aime pas ça. C'est difficile et ce n'est pas intéressant.

4 – Et toi, qu'est-ce que tu aimes comme matières?
 – Moi, j'adore l'EPS, c'est à dire l'éducation physique et sportive. Le sport, c'est fantastique.
 – Est-ce qu'il y a des matières que tu n'aimes pas?
 – Oui, je déteste l'allemand. Ce n'est pas facile.

5 – Et toi, est-ce que tu as une matière préférée?
 – Oui, ma matière préférée est la biologie. Ce n'est pas difficile et c'est intéressant.
 – Et qu'est-ce que tu n'aimes pas?
 – Je n'aime pas la géographie. Ce n'est pas intéressant.

SB 42, READING

4 Mes matières

Read through Charlotte's article and work through the questions, e.g.

Qu'est-ce que Charlotte apprend comme matières?

Est-ce qu'on apprend le latin ici? Qui apprend le latin?
Et l'instruction civique – est-ce qu'on apprend ça?

With able students, additional questions to those in the book could be asked, e.g.

Pourquoi est-ce que Charlotte n'aime pas beaucoup les maths et le latin?
Pourquoi est-ce qu'elle aime l'anglais?

This item could form the basis of an activity using *Fun with Texts*, Copywrite.

Solution: 1 *l'anglais, l'allemand*, 2 *l'anglais*, 3 *les maths et le latin*, 4 *une heure*, 5 *le mercredi*, 6 *la gymnastique*

SB 42, SPEAKING / WRITING

5 À toi!

Go through the questions in class first, getting lots of quick answers. Then students can interview one another in pairs or use the simpler substitution task *Conversations au collège* (*Au choix general*, task 8). If wished, students could write down their partner's answers (without identifying the partner) on a piece of paper and these could be collected in and read out by the teacher (who discreetly corrects any errors in the French!) for the class to identify.

C'est facile/amusant and other opinions are introduced and practised here. The form *c'est* + adjective has been used to avoid the complication of agreement with the subject. If able students query the use of this with feminine or plural subjects, explain that the adjective agrees with *ce* and is invariable.

Au choix SB 129, GENERAL / SPEAKING

8 Conversations au collège

Students read the conversations in pairs and then change the names of subjects to make up different conversations.

Le hit-parade des matières

If wished, the teacher could organise a quick survey on school subjects. Write a list of subjects on the board or on OHT and ask students to put their hands up to vote first for their favourite subject, then their least favourite subject. The results could then be summarised and included in the school guide, e.g. *Voici le hit-parade des matières dans notre classe.* The information could also be entered in a database and displayed pictorially in graphs or charts.

SB 43 READING

6 On surfe sur le Net … Un débat: Internet à l'école, c'est utile?

This is an optional reading item but the topic should appeal to students.

The teacher could read aloud each extract and explain any difficult vocabulary.

a Students read through each extract and find the sentence which corresponds.

Solution: 1a, 2c, 3b, 4f 5g 6d 7e

b Students read the details and note the name of the person to whom they apply.

Solution: 1 *Luc*, 2 *Nathalie*, 3 *Hélène*, 4 *Pierre*

c Finally students should write three advantages of having the Internet in school and one or more disadvantage. This could be done as a class discussion with suitable suggestions written on the board.

CM 3/7 READING

J'aime lire

This worksheet gives practice in reading comprehension and consolidation of school subjects. It includes two short articles and a logic game.

1 Des enfants vraiment 'branchés'
An article about the Internet in a remote village school, followed by a *vrai ou faux?* task.

Solution: 1 F, 2 V, 3 F, 4 V, 5 V

2 Une matière pas comme les autres!
An article about a school specialising in jazz, followed by a sentence completion task.

Solution: 1 *petite ville, sud-ouest,* 2 *cinq, semaine,* 3 *pensionnaires, loin,* 4 *amusant/cool,* 5 *le jazz*

3 C'est lundi – un jeu de logique
Students read the description and complete the timetable grid. They should check this before answering the questions.

Solution:

A	LUNDI
8h40–9h40	français
9h40–10h40	EPS
10h40–10h50	récréation
10h50–11h50	maths
11h50–12h45	maths
12h45–14h15	déjeuner
14h15–15h15	technologie
15h15–16h05	biologie
16h05–16h15	récréation
16h15–17h15	——

B 1 9h40, 2 12h45, 3 *cinq*, 4 15h15, 5 *deux*, 6 *la technologie*

Area 8
Saying what you want and don't want to do (using *vouloir*)
SB 44–45, **1**–**5**
Au choix SB 127, **5**, SB 129, **9**
CM 3/8
CD 2/12
Grammar in Action 2, pages 14–15
FC 32–44 (FC 34–42 ET1)

SB 44, 🎧 **2/12** PRESENTATION
LISTENING

1 Après les cours

This presents different parts of the verb *vouloir* with the infinitive. Students listen to the recording and do the matching activity.

Solution: 1c, 2a, 3g, 4f, 5b, 6e, 7h, 8d

🎧 **Après les cours**

1 – Claire, qu'est-ce que tu veux faire maintenant?
– Je veux aller en ville.

2 – Et toi, Nicole, tu veux aller en ville aussi?
– Non, moi, je veux rentrer à la maison.

3 – Luc, qu'est-ce qu'il veut faire cet après-midi?
– Il veut jouer au tennis.

4 – Et Sophie, qu'est-ce qu'elle veut faire?
– Elle veut faire de l'équitation.

5 – André et Karim, vous voulez jouer aux cartes avec nous?
– Oui, je veux bien.
– Moi aussi.

6 – Qu'est-ce que tu veux faire cet après-midi, Lucie?
– Je ne sais pas.
– On peut aller à la piscine, si tu veux?
– Oui, je veux bien. Alors, allons à la piscine.

7 – Pierre et Daniel, qu'est-ce que vous voulez faire cet après-midi?
– Nous voulons aller au match de football. Tu veux y aller aussi?
– Ah non, merci.

8 – Mélanie et Sika, voulez-vous faire du patin avec nous?
– Ah oui, j'aime beaucoup ça.
– Moi aussi. Alors, vers cinq heures, ça va?
– Oui, d'accord.

FC 32–38, (FC 34–42 ET1), CM 2/4 SPEAKING
PRACTICE

Je veux …

Use the flashcards of activities and places to practise *je veux* + verb, e.g.
aller à la piscine/au parc/au cinéma/à la plage;
jouer au tennis/au volley/au badminton;
faire de l'équitation/de la voile/du vélo.

First hold up two flashcards and ask someone *Qu'est-ce que tu veux faire aujourd'hui?* The student has to choose one of the activities and reply, and then go on to ask someone else a similar question.

Alternatively, let students take a flashcard from a pile and suggest that activity to one or more other people: *Est-ce que tu veux ...?/Est-ce que vous voulez ...?*

They should reply:
Oui, je veux/nous voulons ...

Then ask the rest of the class *Est-ce que (Student A) veut faire ...?* or *Qu'est-ce que (Student B) veut faire ...?* etc.

The OHT could be used effectively for this with a grid of activities (made from CM 2/4). Each activity is blanked out when chosen by one student. When all the activities on the grid have been selected, the whole grid can be shown again and the class asked to recall who chose each activity.

SB 44, 🗣️   **SPEAKING**

2️⃣ Cet après-midi

Students work in pairs to practise the conversation and make up variations on the same model.

SB 44   **GRAMMAR**

Dossier-langue
vouloir (to wish, want)

This presents the full paradigm of *vouloir*.

The use of *je voudrais* as a more polite form than *je veux*, and the fact that *vouloir* is followed by an infinitive are also mentioned at this point.

SB 44   **PRACTICE**

3️⃣ Qu'est-ce qu'ils veulent faire?

This provides practice in using all parts of *vouloir*.

Solution:

1 *Nous voulons regarder le film.*
2 *Tu veux jouer au tennis?*
3 *Moi, je veux jouer au football.*
4 *Elles veulent écouter de la musique.*
5 *Il veut faire du vélo.*
6 *Vous voulez jouer aux cartes?*

FC 32–38, (FC 34–42 ET1) PRESENTATION/PRACTICE

Je ne veux pas ...

Use the flashcards to present and practice *vouloir* in the negative, e.g.
Je ne veux pas aller à la piscine.
Je ne veux pas aller au parc.
Mais je veux aller au cinéma.

SB45   **GRAMMAR**

Dossier-langue
The negative

This explains and illustrates the use of *vouloir* in the negative.

SB 45   **SPEAKING**
                                                                 WRITING

4️⃣ On veut ... on ne veut pas

Students have to say or write one positive and one negative sentence about each picture. This could be prepared orally and written out later.

Solution:

1 *Il veut manger. Il ne veut pas aller dans le jardin.*
2 *Elle veut rester au lit. Elle ne veut pas se lever.*
3 *Il veut jouer au football. Il ne veut pas faire ses devoirs.*
4 *La souris/Elle veut rester à la maison. Elle ne veut pas sortir.*
5 *Ils veulent aller dans un fast-food. Ils ne veulent pas déjeuner à la cantine.*
6 *Elles veulent se reposer au soleil. Elles ne veulent pas travailler dans le jardin.*

SB 45, 🗣️   **SPEAKING**
                                               WRITING

5️⃣ À toi!

Students practise asking and answering questions about plans, then write out some examples.

AU CHOIX SB 129   **GENERAL**
                                               PRACTICE

9️⃣ Des questions et des réponses

This provides practice in completing questions and answers using different parts of *vouloir* and then matching them up.

Solution:

a **1** *vous voulez,* **2** *tu veux,* **3** *Tu veux,* **4** *les autres veulent,* **5** *ta sœur veut,* **6** *ton frère veut*
b **a** *je veux,* **b** *Elle veut,* **c** *Nous voulons,* **d** *Il veut,* **e** *Les adultes veulent, les enfants veulent,* **f** *je veux*
c **1c, 2f, 3a, 4e, 5b, 6d**

GRAMMAR IN ACTION 2, PAGE 14 GRAMMAR PRACTICE

Using the verb *vouloir*

This provides further practice of *vouloir*.

AU CHOIX SB 127, 🗣️   **EXTENSION**
                                               SPEAKING

5️⃣ Inventez des conversations

This task combines *vouloir* + infinitive with *pouvoir* + infinitive and *aller* + infinitive.

A chain game could be played in class first, using flashcards as prompts.

CM 3/8

vouloir et pouvoir

This gives more practice of these two verbs, if required.

unité 3 Au collège

Section 3

85

Au collège unité 3

Section 3

Solution:

1 Le jeu des définitions
1 On peut *faire* de la gymnastique ici. (un gymnase)
2 On va là-bas, si on veut *acheter* un gâteau. (une pâtisserie)
3 Dans cette ville, vous pouvez *voir* la statue de la Liberté. (New York)
4 Si vous voulez *voir* un film, venez ici. (le cinéma)
5 Les touristes peuvent *se baigner* et *se reposer* au soleil ici. (la plage)
6 Les élèves viennent ici s'ils veulent *consulter* ou *lire* des livres. (la bibliothèque)
7 Si vous voulez *acheter* des provisions, nous pouvons *aller* là-bas. (le supermarché)
8 Si nous ne voulons pas *manger* à la cantine, nous pouvons *manger* un sandwich ici. (le café)

2 Des expressions utiles
A Avec pouvoir
1 *Est-ce que je peux regarder la télé?*
  Can I watch TV?
2 *Est-ce que tu peux m'aider?*
  Can you help me?
3 *Pouvez-vous me téléphoner?*
  Can you phone me?
4 *Désolé, mais je ne peux pas venir.*
  Sorry, but I can't come.
5 *Je ne peux pas entendre.*
  I can't hear.
6 *Est-ce qu'on peut aller à Paris en train d'ici?*
  Can you go to Paris by train from here?

B Avec vouloir
1 *Qu'est-ce que vous voulez faire demain?*
  What do you want to do tomorrow?
2 *Qu'est-ce que tu veux faire ce soir?*
  What do you want to do this evening?
3 *Je voudrais voir le nouveau film.*
  I would like to see the new film.
4 *Qui veut aller au cinéma?*
  Who wants to go the cinema?
5 *Moi, je veux bien.*
  I want to. (I'd really like to.)
6 *Les autres ne veulent pas faire ça.*
  The others don't want to do that.

3 Des phrases
Students make up their own sentences based on the starters given.

GRAMMAR IN ACTION 2, PAGE 15 GRAMMAR PRACTICE

Using verbs + infinitive

This provides practice of *vouloir, pouvoir, préférer* and *aller* + the infinitive.

Area 9
Further activities and consolidation
SB 46, **1**–**3**, 47, 48–49
Au choix SB 127, **6**
CM 3/9–3/18, 134, 147–148
CD 2/13–18
Student CD 1/13–18, 2/7–10

SB 46, 2/13 **LISTENING**

1 Le collège Jules Verne

Students listen to the description of the school and complete the résumé.

Solution: 1 *mixte,* 2 *500,* 3 *moderne,* 4 *trois,*
5 *gymnases,* 6 *terrain,* 7 *basket,*
8 *natation,* 9 *piscine,* 10 *technologie*

Le collège Jules Verne

Je vais au collège Jules Verne. C'est dans la rue Jules Verne, au centre-ville. C'est un collège mixte. Il y a à peu près 500 élèves. C'est très sympa. Le collège est bien équipé dans un bâtiment moderne. Il y a trois laboratoires de sciences. Il y a quatre gymnases – ça, c'est bien, parce que j'adore la gymnastique. La cour sert de terrain de sports. Comme sports, nous faisons du handball, du basket et de la natation. Il n'y a pas de piscine au collège, alors nous allons à la piscine municipale toutes les semaines. Pour la technologie, il y a des salles d'ordinateurs.

SB 46 **READING**

2 Une lettre

Students read the letter and correct the errors in the sentences which follow.

The teacher might like to explain about the French school year.

The French school year was restructured some time ago to make it more balanced and to reflect the periods of work and rest which are most beneficial to students. This has resulted in five terms, the first four of seven weeks duration and the last one of eight or nine weeks. School holidays are now fixed for three years at a time.

Solution:
1 Nicolas se lève *avant* sept heures le matin.
2 Il va au collège en *train.*
3 Les cours commencent *après* huit heures.
4 Il va au collège *six* jours par semaine.
5 Le jeudi, il finit à *trois* heures.
6 Comme matières, il aime *l'anglais* et *l'histoire.*
7 La matière qu'il aime le moins c'est la *physique.*
8 Il fait ses devoirs dans *la cuisine.*
9 Il se couche *après* neuf heures.
10 Il va faire *du ski* pendant les vacances d'hiver.

AU CHOIX SB 127 **EXTENSION**
WRITING

6 La journée scolaire

Students write a reply to an e-mail about a typical school day.

SB 46 **SPEAKING**
WRITING

3 Beaucoup de questions

Students can work in pairs asking and answering these questions. Alternatively they can be used for a class chain question game, with one student asking a question and the next student replying, then asking a different question. Finally they could choose eight questions and write down their answers.

SB 46, 2/14, TB 29, CM 147–148   **LISTENING**

Chantez! Les matières

The song could be used at any convenient point in the unit after Area 5. See TB 29 for notes on the use of songs, and CM 147–148 for the music.

🎧 Chantez! Les matières

1 Les maths, je n'aime pas ça,
  L'anglais, c'est pas pour moi,
  C'est difficile, l'informatique,
  Ce que j'aime, c'est la musique.
     J'aime bien mon collège
     Surtout le vendredi,
     Le jour où on fait de la musique
     Tout l'après-midi.

2 Ce que j'aime le moins,
  C'est sûr, c'est le latin.
  C'est fatigant, la gymnastique,
  Ce que j'aime, c'est la musique.
     J'aime bien mon collège
     Surtout le vendredi,
     Le jour où on fait de la musique
     Tout l'après-midi.
        Lundi – l'allemand et la physique,
        Mardi – berck! l'instruction civique,
        Mercredi et jeudi, beaucoup de devoirs,
        Mais vendredi me semble moins noir!

3 Eh oui, les sciences nat.,
  C'est plus facile que les maths,
  Mais c'est loin d'être fantastique,
  Ce que j'aime, c'est la musique.
     J'aime bien mon collège
     Surtout le vendredi,
     Le jour où on fait de la musique
     Tout l'après-midi.

CM 3/9   **GRAMMAR**

devoir

This copymaster contains material on *devoir* for those teachers who wish to teach this verb in this stage. *Devoir* is taught in detail in **Encore Tricolore 3** and many teachers might feel that it is best left until then for most students.

1 Qui va au cinéma?

This presents all persons of the verb. Students read through the text and do the comprehension task.

Solution: **1** *Thomas et Camille,* **2** *Luc et André,*
3 *Claire,* **4** *Nicole,* **5** *Lucie et Sophie,*
6 *Jonathan et Marc*

2 Dossier-langue

Students are encouraged to deduce what they can about the verb *devoir* from the previous text (*Qui va au cinéma?*) and to complete the paradigm.

3 Français–anglais

As the meaning of *devoir* can cause problems, this task involves matching sentences in English and French.

Solution: 1g, 2e, 3c, 4a, 5d, 6b, 7f

4 Au travail

Finally students practise using the different parts of *devoir* to complete sentences about household tasks.

Solution:
1 *Papa doit laver la voiture.*
2 *Maman doit faire la cuisine.*
3 *Moi, je dois ranger ma chambre.*
4 *Mon frère doit passer l'aspirateur.*
5 *Mes sœurs doivent préparer le pique-nique.*
6 *Nous devons travailler dans le jardin.*
7 *Toi, tu dois aider dans la cuisine.*
8 *Et vous, Henri et Claude, vous devez faire la vaisselle.*

CM 3/10   **DICTIONARY SKILLS**

C'est utile, le dictionnaire!

Task 1 gives information and practice on looking up verbs.

In task 2 students have to form the infinitive of regular verbs.

In task 3, students have to find the infinitive of some common irregular verbs. They could consult the verb table in the Students' Book for help.

Solution:

2 Regular verbs

		infinitif	*anglais*
1	je travaille	travailler	to work
2	j'entends	entendre	to hear
3	je choisis	choisir	to choose
4	tu joues	jouer	to play
5	tu vends	vendre	to sell
6	il demande	demander	to ask (for)
7	elle attend	attendre	to wait (for)
8	nous remplissons	remplir	to fill
9	vous parlez	parler	to speak
10	vous finissez	finir	to finish
11	ils choisissent	choisir	to choose
12	elles expliquent	expliquer	to explain

3 Irregular verbs

		infinitif	*anglais*
1	je vais	aller	to go
2	tu prends	prendre	to take
3	il peut	pouvoir	to be able, can
4	elle a	avoir	to have
5	nous sommes	être	to be
6	vous faites	faire	to do
7	ils veulent	vouloir	to want, wish
8	elles lisent	lire	to read

CM 3/11, SCD 1/13–18   **INDEPENDENT LISTENING / SOUNDS AND WRITING**

Écoute et parle

This copymaster provides pronunciation and speaking practice.

1 À la française

🎧 À la française

1 animal   5 maths
2 arrive   6 sciences
3 club   7 site
4 guide   8 théâtre

2 Et après?

Solution: 1c, 2e, 3g, 4k, 5o, 6s, 7w, 8y

🎧 Et après?

1 b, 2 d, 3 f, 4 j, 5 n, 6 r, 7 v, 8 x

3 Des phrases ridicules

🎧 Des phrases ridicules

Henri, le héros heureux, arrive à l'hôpital à huit heures.
En visite ici, Fifi dit mille fois merci.

4 Les terminaisons: -ie

Solution: 1b, 2c, 3a, 4e, 5f, 6d

🎧 Les terminaisons: -ie

1 colonie
2 comédie
3 biologie
4 géographie
5 technologie
6 compagnie

5 Vocabulaire de classe

Solution: 1 *facile*, 2 *prof*, 3 *qui*, 4 *la*, 5 *lettre*, 6 *moi*, 7 *peux*

🎧 Vocabulaire de classe

1 Ce n'est pas facile.
2 On va demander au prof.
3 C'est à qui le tour?
4 Remplis la grille.
5 Note la bonne lettre.
6 Répétez après moi.
7 Est-ce que je peux avoir une feuille, s'il vous plaît?

6 Des conversations

🎧 Des conversations

1 Les matières
– Tu as quels cours aujourd'hui?
(pause)
– Aujourd'hui, on a maths, histoire et technologie.
– Tu aimes la géographie?
(pause)
– Non, je n'aime pas ça.
– Quelle est ta matière préférée?
(pause)
– Ma matière préférée est la chimie.

2 La routine
– Tu arrives au collège à quelle heure, le matin?
(pause)
– J'arrive à huit heures et demie environ.
– Qu'est-ce que tu fais à midi?
(pause)
– A midi, je mange des sandwichs.
– Quand est-ce que tu quittes le collège?
(pause)
– A quatre heures moins le quart.

3 Les vacances
– Tu te lèves à quelle heure pendant les vacances?
(pause)
– Je me lève vers dix heures.
– Tu travailles pendant la journée?
(pause)
– Non, je joue sur l'ordinateur.
– Tu te couches à quelle heure?
(pause)
– Je me couche vers dix heures et demie.

CM 3/12, 🎧 SCD 2/7–10 INDEPENDENT LISTENING

Tu comprends?

Students could do any or all of the four items on this worksheet, now or later as revision.

1 La routine chez nous

Solution: 1 *7h15*, 2 *7h30*, 3 *7h55*, 4 *16h50 (4h50)*, 5 *18h45 (6h45)*, 6 *21h30 (9h30)*, 7 *21h45 (9h45)*

🎧 La routine chez nous

1 Moi, je me lève à sept heures et quart.
2 Mon frère aîné se lève à sept heures et demie.
3 Nous quittons la maison à huit heures moins cinq.
4 L'école finit à cinq heures moins dix.
5 Le soir, nous mangeons à sept heures moins le quart.
6 Je me couche à neuf heures et demie.
7 Mon frère se couche à dix heures moins le quart.

2 Ma journée préférée

Solution: 1 *jeudi*, 2 *anglais*, 3 *technologie*, 4 *maths*, 5 *ennuyeux*, 6 *utile*, 7 *musique*, 8 *flûte*, 9 *ordinateurs*, 10 *travail*

🎧 Ma journée préférée

Ma journée préférée, c'est le jeudi.
Comme matières on a français, anglais, chimie, biologie, histoire et technologie.
On n'a pas maths – c'est bien, parce que je n'aime pas les maths. Je trouve ça difficile et ennuyeux.
J'aime bien les sciences, c'est intéressant.
J'aime l'anglais aussi, parce que c'est utile.
J'aime assez bien la musique. Cette année, j'apprends le violon et mon frère apprend la flûte.
Le jeudi, je vais au club informatique pendant la pause-déjeuner. Nous pouvons utiliser des ordinateurs qui sont connectés à Internet et faire des recherches pour notre travail scolaire.

3 Une journée de vacances

Solution: 1c, 2f, 3a, 4e, 5d, 6h, 7g, 8b

🎧 Une journée de vacances

1 C'est les vacances, c'est super. Je me réveille tard, vers dix heures.

2 Je reste au lit. J'écoute de la musique et je lis mon livre. Je m'amuse.
3 Finalement, je me lève.
4 L'après-midi, je vais à la plage en bus. Le bus s'arrête près d'un café.
5 Je m'installe sur la plage et je me repose au soleil.
6 Puis je me baigne dans la mer. L'eau est bonne.
7 Malheureusement, il commence à pleuvoir. Je m'habille vite.
8 Et je me dépêche de rentrer à la maison.

4 Le week-end
Solution:

		computer	football	tennis	skating	swimming
1	Sophie			X		✔
2	Corinne			✔		X
3	Luc		X			✔
4a	André			✔	X	
4b	Karim			✔	X	
5a	Mélanie	✔		X		
5b	Sika	✔		X		
6a	Pierre	X	✔			
6b	Magali	X				✔

L'activité la plus populaire est la natation.

🎧 Le week-end
1 – Sophie, qu'est-ce que tu veux faire aujourd'hui? Tu veux jouer au tennis?
   – Ah, non, ça ne m'intéresse pas – je ne veux pas jouer au tennis. Mais je veux bien aller à la piscine.
2 – Et Corinne, est-ce qu'elle veut aller à la piscine aussi?
   – Non, elle ne veut pas aller à la piscine, elle veut aller à la patinoire.
3 – Luc, qu'est-ce qu'il veut faire cet après-midi?
   – Il ne veut pas jouer au football. Il préfère aller à la piscine.
4 – André et Karim, vous voulez aller à la patinoire?
   – Non, nous voulons jouer au tennis.
5 – Mélanie et Sika, voulez-vous jouer au tennis?
   – Non, merci. Nous sommes bien ici, nous voulons jouer sur l'ordinateur.
6 – Et vous, Pierre et Magali, qu'est-ce que vous voulez faire cet après-midi?
   – Nous ne voulons pas jouer sur l'ordinateur. Moi, je veux jouer au football, mais Magali, elle veut aller à la piscine.

SB 47, CM 3/13
Sommaire

A summary of the main structures and vocabulary of this unit. Students fill in gaps on the copymaster. They should check their answers against the Students' Book page.

CM 3/14
Rappel 3
REVISION

This copymaster can be used at any point in the course for revision and consolidation. It provides revision of days of the week, months, weather and time. The reading and writing tasks are self-instructional and can be used by students working individually for homework or during cover lessons.

Solution:
1 **Des mots mêlés: Les jours de la semaine**

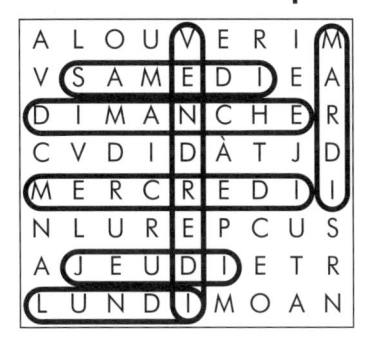

```
A L O U V E R I M
V S A M E D I E A
  D I M A N C H E R
C V D I D A T J D
  M E R C R E D I
N L U R E P C U S
A J E U D I E T R
  L U N D I M O A N
```

2 **Un acrostiche**

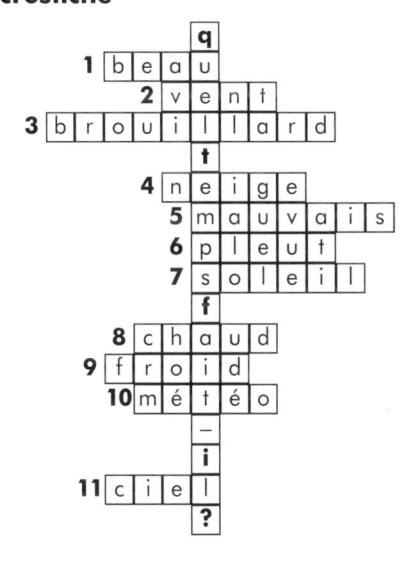

```
              q
         1 b e a u
           2 v e n t
  3 b r o u i l l a r d
              t
         4 n e i g e
         5 m a u v a i s
         6 p l e u t
         7 s o l e i l
              f
         8 c h a u d
      9 f r o i d
     10 m é t é o
              –
              i
        11 c i e l
              ?
```

3 **Les vœux**
A/B **1d** Bonne année! **2f** Joyeuses Pâques! **3b** Bon voyage! **4a** Bon anniversaire! **5e** Bonne fête! **6c** Joyeux Noël! **7h** Bonne nuit! **8g** Au revoir

4 **Les mois de l'année**
1 janvier, **2** décembre, **3** février, **4** avril, **5** mai, **6** août, **7** mars, **8** juin, **9** juillet, **10** septembre, **11** novembre, **12** octobre

Épreuve – Unité 3

These worksheets can be used for an informal test of listening, speaking, reading and writing or for extra practice, as required. For general notes on administering the Épreuves, see TB 16.

Au collège unité 3

Section 3

CM 3/15, 🎧 2/15–18   LISTENING

Épreuve: Écouter

A   Mon emploi du temps (NC 1)

Solution: **1** *chimie,* **2** *allemand,* **3** *physique,* **4** *informatique,* **5** *français,* **6** *géographie,* **7** *technologie*

(mark /6: 4+ shows ability to understand short statements)

🎧 **Mon emploi du temps**

Le lundi à huit heures, j'ai anglais et puis chimie. Après la récré, j'ai allemand et maths, puis c'est le déjeuner. À deux heures, j'ai physique, puis géographie. À quatre heures, j'ai récré et puis informatique.

Le mardi, je commence avec français et anglais. Après la récré, c'est géographie. Puis c'est biologie et après le déjeuner, j'ai technologie. Puis histoire, récré et EPS.

B   La journée de Roselyne (NC 2)

Solution: 1b, 2b, 3a, 4b, 5b, 6c, 7c

(mark /6: 4+ shows ability to understand a range of familiar language that is spoken at near normal speed)

🎧 **La journée de Roselyne**

J'ai douze ans et je suis en cinquième. Le collège est à dix minutes de chez moi et j'y vais à pied. Je commence à huit heures le lundi, le mardi, le jeudi, le vendredi et le samedi. Le mercredi, je reste chez moi. Il y a deux pauses. Le matin, il y a la récréation de dix heures à dix heures quinze. La pause déjeuner est de midi à une heure trente. Je mange à la cantine et j'adore les repas. Les cours finissent à cinq heures.

C   Je déteste le vendredi, mais j'adore le samedi (NC 3)

Solution: 1c, 2a, 3d, 4b, 5f, 6e, 7g

(mark /6: 4+ shows ability to understand short passages made up of familiar language)

🎧 **Je déteste le vendredi, mais j'adore le samedi**

Le vendredi matin, je me lève à six heures. Je m'habille à six heures et demie et à sept heures, je me dépêche … je vais au bureau. Je m'ennuie au bureau. Mais le samedi matin, je m'amuse! À dix heures je vais à la piscine, puis je me repose le reste de la journée.

D   Ma routine (NC 4)

Solution: 1a, 2c, 3a, 4c, 5a, 6b, 7a, 8c

(mark /7: 5+ shows the ability to understand longer passages identifying main points and some detail)

🎧 **Ma routine**

– Daniel, à quelle heure on se lève chez vous?
– Je me lève à sept heures et demie. Ma mère se lève à sept heures et mon père à six heures et demie.
– Et qu'est-ce que tu prends pour le petit déjeuner?
– Je prends un œuf et un verre de lait.
– Et après?
– Après, à huit heures, je quitte la maison.
– Une journée au collège, c'est comment?
– C'est fatigant.
– Qu'est-ce que tu fais après le collège?
– Alors, à cinq heures, je rentre à la maison.
– Tu te reposes?
– Non. À six heures, je fais mes devoirs.
– Tu as beaucoup de devoirs?
– Oui, j'ai toujours beaucoup de devoirs. Je mange à neuf heures et à neuf heures et demie, je me couche.

CM 3/16   SPEAKING

Épreuve: Parler

Students should be given the sheet up to a week before the assessment, to give them time to choose whether to do 1 or 2 and to give them time to prepare and practice both conversations – the structured one (A) and the open-ended one (B) – with their partners.

Mark scheme

Section A: mark /12: 3 marks per response
- 1 mark for a response that is clear and conveys all of the information requested, in the form of a complete phrase or sentence, though not necessarily an accurate one. The questions and answers may seem a little disjointed, like separate items rather than parts of a coherent conversation.
- 2 marks for a response that is clear and conveys all of the information requested in the form of a complete phrase or sentence, though not necessarily an accurate one. The language must flow reasonably smoothly and be recognisable as part of a coherent conversation.
- 3 marks for a clear and complete response that flows smoothly as part of a clear and coherent conversation. The language must be in complete sentences or phrases that are reasonably accurate and consistent as far as grammar, pronunciation and intonation are concerned.

Section B: mark /13: 3 marks per response, as above, +1 bonus mark for adding one or two items of extra information about the week end.

Summary:
Marks	7–13	14–18	19–25
NC Level	2	3	4

CM 3/17   READING

Épreuve: Lire

A   Reflexives (NC 2)

Solution: 1a, 2f, 3c, 4b, 5d, 6e 7g

(mark /6: 4+ shows the ability to understand short phrases presented in a familiar context)

B Mon collège (NC 2)

Solution: 1b, 2f, 3h, 4a, 5c, 6e, 7g, 8d

(mark /7: 5+ shows ability to understand short phrases presented in a familiar context)

C Tous les jours (NC 3)

Solution: 1 lève, 2 quitte, 3 vais, 4 mange, 5 rentre, 6 fais, 7 couche

(mark /6: 4+ shows the ability to understand short texts made up of familiar language)

D Opinions (NC 4)

Solution: 1 André, 2 Dominique, 3 Sophie, 4 Pierre, 5 Bruno, 6 Jeanne, 7 Luc

(mark /6: 4+ shows ability to understand short stories and factual texts and an ability to identify main points and some detail)

CM 3/18   WRITING

Épreuve: Écrire et grammaire

A Mes matières (NC 1)

Solution: 1 maths, 2 français, 3–7 any subjects, 8 EPS, 9 any science

(mark /8: 5+ shows ability to select appropriate words to complete sentences and copy them correctly)

B Les activités (NC 1)

Solution: 1 dis, 2 lit, 3 écrivons, 4 prenez, 5 apprennent, 6 comprennent, 7 me lève, 8 vous couchez, 9 veux

(mark /8: 5+ shows ability to select appropriate words to complete sentences and copy them correctly)

C Le matin (NC 4)

Mark scheme

- 1 mark for each sub-task completed with a correct verb (ignore accents)

Subtotal: 6

Accuracy:
- 3 marks: nearly all words are correct
- 2 marks: most words are correct
- 1 mark: about half the words are correct
- 0 marks: fewer than half the words are correct

Subtotal: 3

(mark /9: 6+ shows the ability to write individual paragraphs of about three or four sentences)

SB 48–49, CM 134   READING EXTENSION

Presse-Jeunesse 2

These pages provide reading for pleasure. They can be used alone or with the accompanying copymaster.

SB 48, CM 134

Zinedine Zidane

This gives information about the French footballer including an account of a typical day. Students could look at the official website (www.zidane.fr) for further information. There are three tasks on copymaster.

Solution:

A Zinedine Zidane

Des questions: 1 Il est footballeur. 2 Il est français. 3 Non, il joue dans l'équipe de France. 4 Il vient de Marseille. 5 Non, (il se lève vers sept heures et demie – huit heures). 6 Il va au parc et au centre-ville. 7 Le Brésil. 8 La France.

Au contraire: 1 grand, 2 marié, 3 sous, 4 un peu, 5 très célèbre, 6 toujours, 7 différent, 8 après

Mots croisés

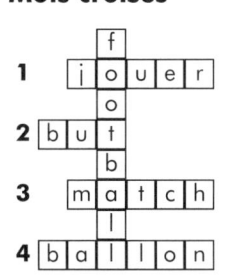

1 jouer
2 but
3 match
4 ballon

(with crossing letters: f, o, o, t, b, a, l, l)

SB 49, CM 134

Les jeunes parlent aux jeunes

This consists of letters to a teenage magazine. A girl describes her problem of blushing easily and a boy describes how he hates getting washed. There are three replies to each letter from other teenagers offering suggestions. There are three tasks on copymaster.

Solution:

B Les jeunes parlent aux jeunes

Des questions: 1 Hélène, 2 la timidité, 3 Luc, 4 Il n'aime pas se laver, 5 Marc, 6 Nicole, 7 (own opinions)

Quel mot?: 1 la salle de bains, 2 un prof (professeur), 3 la timidité, 4 rougir, 5 agréable

C'est presque la même chose: 1 j'ai horreur de / je n'aime pas, 2 favorite, 3 tôt, 4 je rougis

SB 49

Le jeu des nombres

The answers to this quiz are all numbers.

Solution: 1 31, 2 10, 3 0, 4 007, 5 1066, 6 32, 7 7, 8 52, 9 3, 10 32 (2 x 16)

CM 134

This additional task appears on the copymaster.

Solution:

C Une autre activité

Le jeu des pays: 1 Le Canada, 2 La Suisse, 3 Le Maroc, 4 Le Luxembourg, 5 La France, 6 L'Allemagne, 7 L'Italie, 8 Les États-Unis

unité 3 Au collège

Section 3

Encore Tricolore 2
nouvelle édition

unité 4   En famille

Areas	Topics	Grammar
1	Revision of clothing and family vocabulary Introducing people	
2	Staying with a family	Revision of present tense of *avoir*
3	Using expressions of past time	Introduction to the perfect tense Contrasting past and present tenses
4		Perfect tense of regular -er verbs
5	Talking about souvenirs and presents	Using *ce, cet, cette, ces*
6		Perfect tense with *avoir*, regular -ir verbs
7		Perfect tense with *avoir*, regular -re verbs
8	Saying goodbye and thanking people for their hospitality	
9	Further activities and consolidation	

National Curriculum Information

Some students   levels 3–5+
Most students   levels 3–5
All students   levels 2–4

Revision

Rappel (CM 4/12) includes revision of the following:
- household tasks
- sport, music, other leisure activities

Sounds and writing

- numbers
- pronunciation of *g*
- the endings *-ieux, -yeux*

See *Écoute et parle* (CM 4/9, TB 107).

ICT opportunities

- using speech bubbles (call-outs)
- opening an electronic phrase book
- sentence reconstruction

Reading strategies

Presse-Jeunesse 3 (SB 64–65, CM 135)

Assessment

- Informal assessment is in *Épreuves* at the end of this unit (TB 109, CM 4/13–4/16)
- Formal assessment (*Unités 1–7*) is in the *Contrôle* (TB 190, CM 139–145).

Students' Book

Unité 4 SB 50–63
Au choix SB 130–133

Flashcards

55–60   verbs
61–65   souvenirs

CDs

2/19–36
Student CD 1/19–24, 2/11–14

Additional

Grammar in Action 1, p 33
Grammar in Action 2, pp 29–30, 32

Copymasters

CM 4/1	*La famille et les amis* [vocabulary practice]	
CM 4/2	*Chez une famille* [writing, vocabulary practice]	
CM 4/3	*Une lettre* [reading, presentation]	
CM 4/4	*Des activités* [mini-flashcards]	
CM 4/5	*Des souvenirs et des cadeaux* [mini-flashcards]	
CM 4/6	*ce, cet, cette, ces* [grammar]	
CM 4/7	*Des verbes au passé composé* [grammar]	
CM 4/8	*Des mots croisés* [grammar]	
CM 4/9	*Écoute et parle* [independent listening]	
CM 4/10	*Tu comprends?* [independent listening]	
CM 4/11	*Sommaire* [consolidation, reference]	
CM 4/12	*Rappel* [revision]	
CM 4/13	*Épreuve: Écouter*	
CM 4/14	*Épreuve: Parler*	
CM 4/15	*Épreuve: Lire*	
CM 4/16	*Épreuve: Écrire et grammaire*	
CM 135	*Presse-Jeunesse 3* [reading]	

Language content

Introductions (Area 1)

Je te présente mon frère, Marc.
Et voici mes deux sœurs, Laura et Marion.

le beau-père	le fils
le bébé	la grand-mère
la belle-mère	le grand-père
le/la cousin, cousine	le jumeau(x)
le (demi-)frère	la jumelle
la (demi-)sœur	un oncle
un(e) enfant	le parent
la fille	la tante

On peut te tutoyer?
Tu as beaucoup de bagages?
C'est ton premier séjour en France?
Tu as fait bon voyage?

Staying with a family (Area 2)

Est-ce que je peux téléphoner à mes parents?
Où est-ce que je peux mettre mes vêtements?
Il y a de la place dans l'armoire.
Quand est-ce qu'on se lève ici, normalement?
Normalement, on se lève vers 7h30.
Où sont les toilettes et la salle de bains?
Est-ce que tu as une serviette?
À quelle heure est-ce que tu te couches d'habitude?
Tu as bien dormi?

Talking about what you've done (Areas 3–4)

Qu'est-ce que tu as fait ce matin?
Ce matin, j'ai visité la ville.
Dimanche dernier, nous avons passé la journée chez les grands-parents de Nicole.
Hier après-midi, on a joué au tennis.
Hier soir, on a regardé une vidéo.

Expressions of past time (Area 4)

hier
hier après-midi
hier soir
dimanche dernier
samedi matin
la semaine dernière
le week-end dernier

Talking about souvenirs and presents (Area 5)

Nicole a acheté ce livre.
Luc a choisi cet appareil pour son anniversaire.
J'ai choisi cette carte pour Thomas.
Daniel a acheté ces fleurs pour Mme Martin.

Perfect tense of *-ir* verbs (Area 6)

Qu'est-ce que tu as choisi?
J'ai choisi …
Tu as fini?
Il a rempli
Elle a réussi

Perfect tense of *-re* verbs (Area 7)

J'ai perdu …
Tu as entendu quelque chose?
On a vendu …
Vous avez attendu longtemps?
Ils ont répondu
On a rendu

Taking leave (Area 8)

Au revoir.
Merci pour tout.
J'ai passé des vacances merveilleuses.
Bon retour en France/au Canada.

Useful websites

Tourist offices

Rouen – www.mairie-rouen.fr
Montreal – www.tourisme-montreal.org

Shops selling gifts and souvenirs online

www.e-economie.com/annuaire/cadeaux
www.babiole.com (an online shop of Paris souvenirs)

Visits and exchanges

The *CEI Club des 4 Vents* (www.cei4vents.com) offers educational and holiday programmes for foreign students in France. The programmes range from a short holiday stay with a French family to summer camps in France combining sports and French lessons. The club is controlled by the French Ministry of Youth and Sports.

Students can find reports of school exchanges written by students by typing *échange linguistique* using the search engine *Yahoo France*.

En famille unité 4

Area 1
Revision of clothing and family vocabulary
Introducing people

SB 50–51, **1**–**7**
Au choix SB 130, **1**
Au choix SB 131, **1**
Au choix SB 132, **1**
CM 4/1
CD 2/19–21

Appearance — REVISION / PRESENTATION

Revise clothing and colours orally and teach *les cheveux* + hair colour + length. Describe people on flashcards or students (if wearing different clothing) and ask the class to identify them.

SB 50, 🎧 2/19 — READING / LISTENING

1 Bienvenue en France

Students read the descriptions and identify the young people, then check their answers by listening to the recording.

Solution: 1b Hélène, 2c Daniel, 3f Émilie, 4a André, 5d Julie, 6e Christophe

🎧 **Bienvenue en France**

M. Percheron organise la visite des Canadiens en France. Il a une liste des Canadiens et une liste des familles françaises.
– Bonjour, tout le monde. Nous sommes très contents d'être en France. Je voudrais d'abord remercier les familles françaises qui sont ici et qui vont accueillir les membres de notre groupe. Bon, alors, je vais d'abord appeler le jeune Canadien, puis la famille française qui va l'accueillir.
Alors, on commence par la personne à gauche. C'est Hélène Delacroix. Hélène va loger chez la famille Bonnard.
Puis, nous avons Daniel Laforêt. Daniel va loger chez la famille Martin.
Ensuite, il y a Émilie Denis. Émilie va loger chez la famille Duval.
La prochaine personne, c'est André Legrand. André va loger chez la famille Renard.
Ensuite, nous avons Julie Laforêt, c'est la sœur de Daniel. Julie va chez la famille Lebois.
Et à droite, il y a Christophe Laroche. Christophe va chez la famille Dupont.

Bienvenue — SPEAKING / PRACTICE

Some oral practice could be based on the photo, using the language in the captions (clothing, adjectives and descriptions are covered fully in *Unité 7*), e.g.
Qui porte un polo et un jean / un short et un T-shirt?
La veste de Julie est orange? etc.

SB 50 — WRITING

2 C'est moi!

Students write a brief description of themselves, mentioning what they are wearing. This could be done on a piece of paper and collected in. The teacher could read out a few descriptions each lesson (correcting them if necessary) and ask the class to identify the person described.

Au choix SB 130 — SUPPORT / READING

1 As-tu bonne mémoire?

Students have to select the correct words to complete short descriptions of the people on SB 50.

Solution: 1b, 2c, 3c, 4a, 5b, 6a

Au choix SB 131 — EXTENSION / WRITING

1 Une description

Students write a short description of one of the people shown on SB 50.

SB 51, 🎧 2/20 — LISTENING / READING

3 Daniel et la famille Martin

Students listen to the recording and follow the text. This presents the key language for introducing people. After working through the tasks, students could practise reading the conversation in pairs.

🎧 **Daniel et la famille Martin**

Thomas Martin est à la gare avec ses parents. Beaucoup de ses amis sont là aussi avec leurs parents. Il est sept heures du soir et les jeunes Canadiens sont arrivés. Un garçon s'approche de Mme Martin.
– Bonjour, Madame. Je m'appelle Daniel Laforêt.
– Bonjour, Daniel. Bienvenue en France. On peut te tutoyer, non?
– Bien sûr, Madame.
– Je te présente mon mari, Claude Martin.
– Bonjour, Daniel.
– Bonjour, Monsieur.
– Et voici notre fils, Thomas.
– Bonjour, Daniel. Tu as fait bon voyage?
– Oui, merci.
– Bon, allons à la maison, maintenant. Tu as beaucoup de bagages?
– J'ai une valise et un sac à dos.
– Bon, la voiture est dans le parking. Allons-y.
(chez les Martin)
– Entre, Daniel. On va dans le salon.
– Daniel, je te présente mon frère, Marc.
– Bonjour, Daniel.
– Et voici mes deux sœurs, Laura et Marion.
– Bonjour, Daniel. C'est ton premier séjour en France?
– Oui, c'est ça.

SB 51   READING

4   Vrai ou faux?

Students should correct the mistakes in the false sentences.

Solution: **1 F** (*Le groupe arrive à sept heures du soir.*), **2 V**, **3 V**, **4 V**, **5 F** (*Il a une valise et un sac à dos.*), **6 F** (*À la maison, on va dans le salon.*), **7 F** (*Pour Daniel, c'est son premier séjour en France.*)

SB 51   READING

5   Des phrases utiles

Students have to find the correct sentences in the conversation.

Solution:
1 *On peut te tutoyer?*
2 *Je te présente mon mari.*
3 *Je te présente mon frère.*
4 *Voici notre fils.*
5 *Voici mes sœurs.*
6 *Tu as fait bon voyage?*
7 *Tu as beaucoup de bagages?*
8 *C'est ton premier séjour en France?*

La famille   SPEAKING / REVISION

Revise family vocabulary first by asking different students whether they have brothers, sisters, pets, cousins, grandparents etc.

SB 51, 🎧 2/21   LISTENING

6   La famille de Daniel

Students listen to the recording in order to find out the missing details.

Solution: 1 *sœur*, 2 *treize*, 3 *six*, 4 *Julie*, 5 *un chat*, 6 *un lapin*, 7 *deux*, 8 *grands-parents*

🎧 **La famille de Daniel**

– Tu as des frères et des sœurs, Daniel?
– Oui, j'ai une sœur et un demi-frère.
– Ils ont quel âge?
– Ma sœur est ma sœur jumelle, donc elle a treize ans, comme moi. Et mon demi-frère est très jeune. C'est toujours un bébé. Il a six mois seulement.
– Ta sœur, comment s'appelle-t-elle?
– Elle s'appelle Julie et elle est ici en France aussi.
– Ah bon? Elle est à Rouen aussi?
– Oui.
– Et vous avez des animaux à la maison?
– Oui, nous avons un chat et un lapin.
– Tu as des cousins?
– Oui, j'ai deux cousins qui habitent près de chez moi, à Montréal.
– Et des grands-parents?
– Oui, j'ai des grands-parents, mais ils n'habitent pas à Montréal.

Au choix SB 132   GENERAL / READING / WRITING

1   Une grande famille

This extends the work on family vocabulary.

Solution:

cinq mots masculins: *bébé, fils, grand-père, oncle, beau-père*
cinq mots féminins: *grand-mère, demi-sœur, belle-mère, fille, tante*
cinq mots pluriels: *jumeaux, cousins, enfants, parents, frères*

SB 51,   SPEAKING / WRITING

7   À toi!

Students work in pairs to ask and answer questions about their families and then write their own answers to some of the questions.

CM 4/1   PRACTICE

La famille et les amis

These tasks provide further practice of the vocabulary for the extended family and friends.

Solution:

1 Complète les listes

Masculin

le grand-père	grandfather
le père	father
le mari	husband
l'oncle	uncle
le fils	son
le frère (aîné)	(older) brother
le beau-frère	brother-in-law, step-brother
le demi-frère	half-brother
le cousin	cousin
le bébé	baby
un ami	friend
un copain	friend
un camarade	classmate

Féminin

la grand-mère	grandmother
la mère	mother
la femme	wife
la tante	aunt
la fille	daughter
la sœur (aînée)	(older) sister
la belle-sœur	sister-in-law, step-sister
la demi-sœur	half-sister
la cousine	cousin
une amie	friend
une copine	friend
une camarade	classmate

Pluriel

les grands-parents	grandparents
les parents	parents
les enfants	children
les jumeaux	twins (boys or mixed)
les jumelles	girl twins

2 Qui est-ce?
1 *grand-père*, 2 *tante*, 3 *oncle*, 4 *cousine*, 5 *père*, 6 *sœur*

3 Naissances
1 *un*, 2 *deux*, 3 *Nicole*, 4 *le 3 janvier, le 23 janvier*, 5 *Non, elle a un frère*, 6 *Non*

Area 2
Staying with a family
Revision of present tense of avoir

SB 52, **1**–**4**

Au choix SB 132, **2**
CM 4/2
CD 2/22
(FC 13–17 ET1)

(FC 13–17 ET1)   REVISION
                                                               PRESENTATION

Revise rooms in the house, using **Encore Tricolore 1** flashcards or other visuals. Teach or revise basic furniture, e.g. *l'armoire, un placard, une table, un lit, une chaise* etc.

SB 52, 🎧 2/22   LISTENING
                                                                READING

1 Julie et la famille Lebois

Read through the questions first and check that students understand them. They are used in several tasks.

a Students match up the visuals with the questions.

Solution: 1d, 2a, 3c, 4b, 5e, 6f

b Explain that students will hear all the questions in the conversation, but in a different order. Students have to note down the correct order.

Solution: c, e, f, a, b, d

c Students find the correct question for each answer.

Solution: 1c, 2d, 3e, 4f, 5b, 6a

🎧 **Julie et la famille Lebois**

– Viens, Julie, je vais te montrer ta chambre.
– Elle est jolie, la chambre. Alors, où est-ce que je peux mettre mes vêtements?
– Il y a de la place dans l'armoire. Oui, voilà.
– D'accord. Et où sont les toilettes et la salle de bains?
– C'est juste en face.
– Ah oui.
– Est-ce que tu as une serviette?
– Ah non.
– Il y a des serviettes dans ce placard.
– Bon, merci.
– Ça va?
– Est-ce que je peux téléphoner à mes parents?
– Oui, bien sûr. Il y a un téléphone dans la cuisine.
  (après le dîner)
– À quelle heure est-ce que tu te couches d'habitude, Julie?
– Ça dépend. D'habitude, je me couche vers dix heures, mais ce soir, je suis très fatiguée, alors je vais me coucher très tôt.
– Bonne idée!
– Quand est-ce qu'on se lève ici, normalement?

– Mes parents se lèvent assez tôt, vers sept heures, mais pendant les vacances, je me lève assez tard, vers neuf heures et demie, dix heures.

SB 52, 🗣   SPEAKING

2 Invente une conversation

Students work in pairs to practise useful questions and answers when staying with a family in France.

CM 4/2   PRACTICE
                                                                WRITING

Chez une famille

1 Où sont les questions?
This is an optional task which reuses the text of *Julie et la famille Lebois* (SB 52). Students write in the missing questions to complete the text. This can be checked by reference to the Students' Book or by listening to the recording again. Students can then practise reading the conversation in pairs.

2 À la maison
Tasks 2 and 3 practise the vocabulary used in Areas 2 and 3.

Solution:

5 pièces: *la salle à manger, une chambre, la cuisine, une salle de bains, la salle de séjour*
4 meubles: *une chaise, un lit, une armoire, une table*
3 membres: *une grand-mère, un oncle, une tante*
2 appareils: *un téléphone portable, un ordinateur*
1 chose dans la salle de bains: *une serviette*

3 Un acrostiche

Solution: **1** *serviette,* **2** *valise,* **3** *armoire,*
                4 *lit,* **5** *vêtements,* **6** *bagages*

Au choix SB 132   GENERAL
                                                                READING

2 Un jeu des définitions

This gives practice of rooms in a house and some household items.

Solution:

a **1** *la cuisine,* **2** *la chambre,* **3** *la salle à manger,*
       4 *le salon/la salle de séjour,* **5** *la salle de bains*
b **1** *l'armoire/le placard,* **2** *la chaise,* **3** *le lit,*
       4 *la table/la chaise,* **5** *le placard*

SB 52   PRACTICE

3 Des conversations

Revise the present tense of *avoir* orally and write it on the board. Students should then complete the conversations with the correct part of *avoir*. The OHP could be used for this.

Solution: **1** *tu as,* **2** *j'ai,* **3** *je n'ai pas,* **4** *Tu as,*
                5 *j'ai,* **6** *vous avez,* **7** *nous n'avons pas,*
                8 *mes cousins ont,* **9** *Tu as,* **10** *nous avons,* **11** *ma sœur aînée a*

SB 52, SPEAKING / WRITING

4 À la maison

Students work in pairs to ask each other questions and then write a paragraph about their home or room.

PRACTICE / WRITING

Speech bubbles

As there are several dialogues in this area, it would be appropriate to practise using speech bubbles. Speech bubbles can be used for many topics. Depending upon the relative skills of the teacher and students you could work in one or more of the following ways:
- The teacher supplies clip art pictures illustrating the situations and students insert speech bubbles (usually known as call-outs in programs such as Microsoft® Word) with the appropriate text.
- The teacher supplies phrases to be illustrated with images found by students, again using call-outs.
- Students find images and write their own call-outs.

In this unit, you need pictures to illustrate situations such as:
Introducing someone (Area 1)
Saying goodbye (Area 8)
Saying thank you (Area 8)
Can I use the phone? (Area 2)
Where is the toilet? (Area 2)

The final product can be printed out for display on classroom walls or in a class publication.

Area 3
Introduction to the perfect tense
Contrasting past and present tenses
Using expressions of past time
SB 53, 5–7
Au choix SB 130, 2, SB 131, 2, SB 132, 3
CM 4/3
CD 2/23
FC 55–60 (optional)
Grammar in Action 2, page 29

CM 4/3 PRESENTATION

Une lettre

Some teachers like to introduce the perfect tense through the written form, rather than orally. Make an OHT of the letter for this. First read through the letter and fill in the missing words.

1 Complète la lettre

Solution: 1 *ton*, 2 *vacances*, 3 *jour*, 4 *repas*, 5 *poulet*, 6 *minuit*, 7 *matin*, 8 *football*

Then go through the letter again, asking some questions about the content, e.g.

Philippe a passé ses vacances où? À Paris? À la campagne? À la montagne?

Oui, à la montagne. Il a fait du ski, non? Et le dernier jour des vacances, les garçons ont préparé quelque chose. Qu'est-ce que c'est? Un bonhomme de neige? Une grosse boule de neige? Un grand repas? etc.

Next, ask volunteers to come out and underline the verbs. If nobody spots the parts of *avoir*, ask what comes before the past participle and what the past participles have in common. By this process, students should be able to work out for themselves how the perfect tense is formed. If wished, students could refer to the *Dossier-langue* (SB 54) at this point.

The remaining tasks on the copymaster (tasks 2 and 3) could be done at a later stage when students are more familiar with the perfect tense.

2 Un résumé
Students correct the errors in the summary.
Solution:
1 *Philippe a passé de bonnes vacances à la montagne.*
2 *Il a aimé le ski.*
3 *Le dernier jour, les garçons ont préparé le repas.*
4 *Pour commencer, on a mangé du melon, puis du poulet et des frites.*
5 *Comme dessert, on a mangé des glaces.*
6 *Après le repas, on a écouté de la musique.*
7 *On a commencé le voyage du retour à sept heures du matin.*

3 Les verbes au passé composé
Students underline the ten different verbs in the letter which are in the perfect tense.

Solution: *j'ai passé; J'ai aimé; il a neigé; nous avons organisé; Les garçons ont préparé; nous avons mangé (x 2); on a écouté; nous avons commencé; tu as joué; tu as fait*

FC 55–60 (OPTIONAL) PRESENTATION

The perfect tense

Some teachers might prefer to teach examples of the perfect tense using the flashcards, e.g.

Qu'est-ce que j'ai fait hier?
J'ai mangé une pizza.
J'ai téléphoné à mes amis.
J'ai joué de la guitare.
J'ai acheté un CD.
J'ai surfé sur le Net.

These could be written on the board for reference.

Encourage the class to repeat these phrases, then ask individual students and prompt replies with the flashcards, e.g.
Tu as joué de la trompette hier? Non, j'ai … etc.

Gradually add different parts of the verb to the summary on the board and build up the singular, then the plural paradigm.

SB 53 READING

5 Tout va bien

Read the message aloud with students following the text. Then go through the *vrai ou faux?* questions, enlarging on them if necessary, e.g.

1 *Julie est contente en France. Elle trouve la famille Lebois sympa?*

unité 4 En famille

Section 3

97

3 *Julie partage la chambre de Nicole. Est-ce que Nicole et Julie dorment dans la même chambre ou est-ce que Julie a sa propre chambre?*

Some students could correct the false sentences.

Solution: **1 V**, **2 F** *(Ils habitent dans un appartement.)*, **3 F** *(Julie a sa propre chambre.)*, **4 V**, **5 F** *(Elle a acheté des cartes postales.)*, **6 F** *(Ils ont mangé au café.)*, **7 F** *(Ils ont joué au tennis.)*, **8 F** *(Ils ont regardé une vidéo.)*

SB 53 GRAMMAR
Dossier-langue
Present or past?

Go through this with the class, asking them to find more examples of verbs in the present and perfect tenses and writing some on the board. Ask which tense has two verbs. Explain the term 'auxiliary verb', saying that the past participle cannot be used by itself but needs a 'helping' verb to complete it; and also explain 'past participle' (the part of the verb which conveys the meaning).

SB 53, 🎧 2/23 LISTENING
6 Présent ou passé?

Students should listen to each sentence and note down PR (for *présent*) or P (for *passé*).

Solution: **1 PR, 2 PR, 3 P, 4 P, 5 PR, 6 PR, 7 P, 8 PR, 9 P, 10 P**

🎧 **Présent ou passé?**

1 Laura Martin est très sportive.
2 Elle joue au hockey pour l'équipe du collège.
3 En février, Laura a joué un match important.
4 Son équipe a gagné le match.
5 Marc Martin n'aime pas beaucoup le sport.
6 Il aime la musique et il achète souvent des CD.
7 Hier, il a acheté un nouveau CD.
8 Quelquefois, Marc travaille à la maison.
9 Pendant les vacances, il a travaillé dans un magasin de musique.
10 Il a aimé ça.

SB 53 READING
7 Mangetout adore le poisson

In this task, students have to match captions to pictures, which involves identifying which sentence refers to which tense. When read in the order in which they appear, the captions are in pairs, one of each tense, to help to highlight the difference between them.

Solution: **1c, 2d, 3f, 4e, 5h, 6g, 7a, 8b**

Differentiation

Au choix SB 130 SUPPORT
2 Présent ou passé?

Students identify the sentences in the perfect tense.

Solution: **1b, 2a, 3b, 4b, 5a**

Au choix SB 132 GENERAL
3 Un écrivain anglais

This is a similar task with more complex sentences.

Solution: **3, 4, 5, 7, 9**

EXTENSION
The meaning of the perfect tense

More able students could go on to learn more about the English meaning of the perfect tense. The teacher could ask how the verbs in the following sentences would be said in English, aiming to get two or three alternatives for each sentence in French.
- *J'ai téléphoné à la maison*, e.g. *Comment ça se dit en anglais?* (I telephoned home.) *Et aussi? Une autre possibilité?* (I have telephoned home.) etc.
- *Tu as acheté une carte postale, non?*
- *Elle a mangé un sandwich au jambon.*
- *Nous avons organisé une excursion.*
- *Vous avez oublié votre argent?*
- *Ils ont joué au tennis.*

Write suggestions on the board. Explain that, in English, there are three different ways of saying each verb:
- I telephoned/I have telephoned/I did telephone
- You bought?/Have you bought?/Did you buy?
- She ate/She has eaten/She did eat
- We organised/We have organised/We did organise
- You forgot?/Have you forgotten?/Did you forget?
- They played tennis/They have played tennis/They did play tennis.

Follow this with oral practice – the teacher says an assortment of these English alternatives in quick succession, causing students to keep giving the same answers. They soon see that the single French expressions have several alternatives in English.

Au choix SB 131 EXTENSION
GRAMMAR
Dossier-langue
Three translations in English

This explains the different ways of translating the perfect tense into English.

Au choix SB 131 EXTENSION
2 En français

Students have to work out the correct French translation for each sentence in English. This task reinforces the point that the perfect tense can be translated in several different ways in English.

Solution: **1f, 2f, 3c, 4g, 5a, 6b, 7g, 8d, 9e, 10h**

Grammar in Action 2, page 29 GRAMMAR PRACTICE
Identifying present and past tenses

This provides further practice of contrasting the present and the past.

Area 4
Perfect tense of regular -er verbs
SB 54–55, **1**–**6**
Au choix SB 130, **3**, SB 131, **3**
CM 4/4
CD 2/24–25
FC 55–60
Grammar in Action 2, page 30

FC 55–60 — PRACTICE
The perfect tense
Quickly revise some examples of the perfect tense previously learnt, using flashcards as prompts, e.g. *Tu as joué sur l'ordinateur hier? Oui/Non, j'ai joué de la guitare* etc. Practise different verbs and persons of the verbs using flashcard games (TB 26).

SB 54, 2/24 — LISTENING
1 Un coup de téléphone
a Students listen to the conversation and put the pictures in order. They could listen again to check their answers.

Solution: 6, 2, 3, 4, 7, 1, 5, 8

b Students read through the sentences and choose the correct reply.

Solution: 1b, 2a, 3b, 4c, 5a, 6b, 7c

The completed sentences could then be matched with seven of the eight visuals. The eighth is in the present tense so has been omitted.

Un coup de téléphone
– Allô?
– Bonjour, Madame. Est-ce que je peux parler avec Daniel, s'il vous plaît?
– Oui, un instant.
– Bonjour.
– Salut, Daniel, c'est Christophe.
– Bonjour, Christophe. Ça va?
– Oui, ça va bien et toi?
– Oui, ça va bien.
– Qu'est-ce que tu as fait aujourd'hui? Tu as passé une bonne journée?
– Oui. Alors, ce matin, j'ai visité la ville avec Thomas. Nous avons regardé les magasins.
– Tu as acheté quelque chose?
– Oui, j'ai acheté un T-shirt et une carte d'anniversaire pour Thomas.
– Ah bon? C'est bientôt l'anniversaire de Thomas?
– Oui, c'est son anniversaire samedi. Alors, Thomas a décidé d'acheter un CD pour sa fête.
– Et à midi, vous avez déjeuné en ville?
– Oui, à midi, nous avons mangé dans un fast-food.
– Et l'après-midi, qu'est-ce que vous avez fait?
– Eh bien, l'après-midi, nous avons écouté le nouveau CD. C'est de Saint-Germain.
– Tu as aimé ça?
– Oui, c'est super. Puis nous avons joué sur l'ordinateur. Moi, j'ai regardé mes e-mails. J'ai des messages de ma famille. Et maintenant, nous regardons le film à la télé.
– Ah bon? Il y a un bon film? Moi, je vais regarder ça aussi. Au revoir, Daniel.
– À bientôt, Christophe.

SB 54 — GRAMMAR
Dossier-langue
The perfect tense
If not done earlier, go through this section on the past participle of -er verbs.

Write a few infinitives on the board, perhaps of different, but easily recognised verbs (e.g. *terrifier, accepter, refuser, irriter, inspirer*) and ask volunteers to work out the past participle.

SB 54 — READING
2 Samedi après-midi
Read out the captions. Then students match the correct caption to each picture.

Solution: 1h, 2f, 3c, 4d, 5b, 6a, 7g, 8e

CM 4/4 — PRACTICE
Des activités
The mini-flashcards could be used to make an OHT for further practice of the perfect tense of -er verbs or for practice in pairs.

SB 55 — PRACTICE / READING
3 La fête de Thomas
a This task provides practice in forming the past participle from the infinitive. When checking, read out the full sentence from the Students' Book.

Solution: 1 *porté*, 2 *porté*, 3 *invité*, 4 *commencé*, 5 *écouté*, 6 *mangé*, 7 *dansé*, 8 *parlé*

b This task provides practice in adding the correct part of *avoir* to complete the perfect tense.

Solution: 1 *Thomas a invité*, 2 *Nous avons cherché*, 3 *nous avons trouvé*, 4 *Thomas a aimé*, 5 *Les filles ont dansé*, 6 *tu as refusé*, 7 *j'ai rencontré*, 8 *La fête a duré*

GRAMMAR IN ACTION 2, PAGE 30 GRAMMAR PRACTICE
The perfect tense with *avoir* – regular -er verbs
This provides further practice of using the perfect tense of regular -er verbs with *avoir*.

Differentiation
AU CHOIX SB 130 — SUPPORT / WRITING
3 Un après-midi en ville
This gives practice in copying sentences in the perfect tense.

Solution: 1c, 2e, 3a, 4d, 5f, 6h, 7b, 8i, 9j, 10g

99

Au choix SB 131 — EXTENSION
3 Hier

This gives practice in forming sentences in the perfect tense (1st and 2nd person singular only).

Students could read this in pairs before writing it out.

Solution: 1 *j'ai aidé*, 2 *tu as écouté*, 3 *j'ai rangé*, 4 *tu as joué*, 5 *j'ai passé*, 6 *tu as regardé*, 7 *j'ai lavé*, 8 *as téléphoné*, 9 *j'ai travaillé*, 10 *tu as passé*

SB 55, 2/25 — LISTENING
4 Quand exactement?

This presents and practises expressions of past time.

a Students first match the French and English expressions.

Solution: 1f, 2c, 3e, 4g, 5a, 6d, 7b

b They then listen to hear the expressions in use and note the order.

Solution: 1f, 2d, 3b, 4g, 5e, 6c, 7a

Quand exactement?

1 – Qu'est-ce que vous avez fait la semaine dernière?
 – La semaine dernière, nous avons visité Rouen. C'était bien.
2 – Tu as regardé le film à la télévision vendredi dernier?
 – Non, vendredi dernier, je n'ai pas regardé la télé – j'ai joué un match de basket.
3 – Tu as téléphoné à tes parents?
 – Oui, j'ai téléphoné à ma mère hier soir.
4 – Qu'est-ce que tu as fait le week-end dernier?
 – Le week-end dernier, on a tous travaillé à la maison. Moi, j'ai rangé ma chambre et j'ai passé l'aspirateur.
5 – Tu as joué au football dimanche après-midi?
 – Oui, dimanche après-midi, nous avons joué un match et nous avons gagné.
6 – Quand est-ce que tu as lavé la voiture?
 – Hier matin, oui, hier matin, j'ai lavé la voiture.
7 – Qu'est-ce que vous avez fait hier?
 – Hier, nous avons visité Paris. C'était super.

SB 55 — PRACTICE SPEAKING/WRITING
5 Des phrases bizarres

This could be done as a speaking task in pairs or as a written task. Students throw a dice or choose random numbers and then read out the sentence which corresponds.

SB 55 — WRITING
6 L'autre jour

Students write a few sentences in the perfect tense, referring to the table for help, if required. For support, this can be practised orally first. Teachers might prefer to specify how many sentences should be written. This could be done as a group competition to see how many sentences can be written in a given time – only correct sentences will be counted!

PRACTICE
avoir

Teachers could create a sentence reconstruction task to practise the perfect and parts of *avoir*. Use *Word Sequencing* or *Hot Potatoes* and simply type in the eight sentences below (see TB 20).

- J'ai mangé des céréales, mais Alex a mangé un croissant.
- J'ai écouté la radio anglaise, mais Alex a écouté la radio française.
- J'ai porté des baskets, mais Alex a porté des bottes.
- J'ai regardé un film à la télévision, mais Alex a regardé un jeu.
- J'ai parlé anglais, mais Alex a parlé français.
- J'ai porté mon uniforme scolaire, mais Alex a porté un jean et un T-shirt.
- J'ai acheté un souvenir, mais Alex a acheté une BD.
- J'ai cherché une carte postale, mais Alex a cherché un CD.

Area 5
Talking about souvenirs and presents
Using *ce, cet, cette, ces*

SB 56–57, **1**–**8**
Au choix SB 132, **4**
CM 4/5–4/6
CD 2/26–27
FC 61–65
Grammar in Action 1, page 33

SB 56, 2/26 — PRESENTATION, LISTENING
1 Aux magasins

Explain *un appareil-photo jetable* – *un appareil qu'on utilise une fois et qu'on jette à la poubelle après*.

Students listen to the conversations and note down the missing words. They could then practise reading the dialogues in pairs.

Solution: a *maison*, b *cher*, c *prix*, d *cousine*, e *chats*, f *acheter*, g *Canada*, h *copain*, i *intéressant*, j *l'informatique*

Aux magasins

1 Christophe a oublié son appareil à la maison, alors il va acheter un appareil-photo jetable.
 – Cet appareil rouge n'est pas cher.
 – C'est vrai, mais je vais acheter cet appareil bleu. C'est le même prix et je préfère la couleur.

2 Nicole veut acheter des chaussettes pour sa petite cousine.
– Regarde, il y a des chaussettes pour enfants là-bas.
– Ah oui, j'aime bien ces chaussettes avec les petits chats. Elles sont mignonnes.
– Oui, et ces chaussettes avec les fleurs sont jolies aussi.
– Oui, c'est vrai, mais ma cousine aime bien les chats, alors je vais acheter ces chaussettes avec les chats.

3 Daniel cherche des cartes postales.
– Je cherche des cartes postales pour mes copains au Canada.
– Regarde ces cartes postales des sports. Elles sont amusantes, non?
– Ah oui, j'aime bien cette carte postale d'un footballeur. Je vais l'acheter pour un copain qui aime le foot.

4 Hélène regarde les magazines.
– Avez-vous des magazines pour les jeunes?
– Oui, il y a un grand choix de magazines là-bas.
– Regarde ce magazine – c'est intéressant. Il y a des photos et des articles sur la mode.
– Oui, mais moi, je préfère l'informatique. Dans ce magazine, il y a des articles intéressants sur Internet et il y a un CD-ROM gratuit. Je vais acheter ça.

SB 56 — WRITING

2 Qu'est-ce qu'on a acheté?

Students select the items chosen by each person. This presents the different forms of *ce*.

Solution: 1A, 2C, 3F, 4H

SB 56 — GRAMMAR

Dossier-langue
This and that

Ask students to look for different words that mean 'this' and write these on the board under the headings m, f, pl. Then ask students to work out why there are two different words used with masculine nouns.

SB 56 — PRACTICE / READING

3 Ça commence avec c

This gives further examples of *ce, cet, cette, ces* in use.

Solution: 1 *un chat,* 2 *une calculette,* 3 *le café,* 4 *une carotte,* 5 *une casquette/un chapeau,* 6 *un crayon*

SB 56 — PRACTICE

4 La publicité

This provides practice in using correctly, *ce* or *cet*, then *cette* or *ces*.

Solution: 1 *ce,* 2 *ce,* 3 *Cet,* 4 *cet,* 5 *cet,* 6 *ces,* 7 *cette,* 8 *ces,* 9 *ces,* 10 *cette,*

FC 61–65 — PRESENTATION

Souvenirs

Use the flashcards of souvenirs to present and practise: *une affiche/un poster, un porte-clés, un T-shirt, une boîte de chocolats, une BD, un pot de confiture*

SB 57 — PRESENTATION

5 Idées souvenirs

Revise the vocabulary illustrated and teach any new words, e.g. *un porte-clés, un pot de confiture, un drapeau, une affiche.* Students could study the list of items for a few minutes, then close their books and see how many they can remember.

CM 4/5 — PRACTICE

Des souvenirs et des cadeaux

An OHT could be made of these mini-flashcards of souvenirs for oral work. Some pictures could be obscured and students have to guess what they are. Students, in turn, could 'buy' an item. When all the items have been 'purchased', the class have to guess who bought what, e.g.
– (Student A), *qu'est-ce que tu as acheté?*
– *J'ai acheté une BD.*
– *Et toi, (Student B)?*
– *J'ai acheté un porte-clés.*
…
– *Qui a acheté la BD?*

Solution: (matching task) **1j, 2b, 3l, 4d, 5a, 6k, 7f, 8h, 9e, 10g, 11i, 12c**

SB 57, 🎧 2/27 — LISTENING

6 On achète des souvenirs

Students listen to the conversations and note the letter of the item bought by each person.

Solution: **1f, 2b, 3j, 4h, 5a, 6g, 7i, 8c**

🎧 **On achète des souvenirs**

1 – On peut vous aider?
– Oui, je cherche un cadeau pour ma mère.
– Nous avons des petits gâteaux en boîte ou bien un pot de confiture.
– Ah oui. Je voudrais un pot de confiture aux fraises. Elle aime bien ça.
– Voilà un pot de confiture.

2 – Je ne sais pas quoi acheter pour mon père.
– Un porte-clés, c'est toujours utile.
– Oui, c'est vrai. Je voudrais ce porte-clés, s'il vous plaît.

3 – Tu aimes cette affiche?
– Ah oui, elle est très jolie.
– Alors, je vais l'acheter pour ma sœur. Elle aime bien les affiches.

4 – Alors, mon petit frère. Qu'est-ce que je peux lui acheter?
– Ça y est. Je vais lui acheter ce drapeau tricolore. Il a une collection de drapeaux des différents pays.

unité 4 En famille

Section 3

En famille unité 4 · Section 3

5 – Je cherche quelque chose pour une amie.
– Est-ce qu'elle aime les peluches?
– Oui, regardons les peluches. Ah, regarde ça! J'adore ce petit animal. Comme il est mignon. Je vais acheter cet animal en peluche pour Sophie.

6 – Je cherche un livre pour mon grand-père.
– Il y a des livres sur la France et la Normandie là-bas.
– Ah oui. Je vais acheter ce livre sur la Normandie.

7 – Ma grand-mère aime bien la musique. Est-ce qu'il y a un CD de chansons françaises?
– On va demander.
– Est-ce que vous avez un CD de chansons françaises?
– Oui, nous avons ce CD qui est excellent.
– Bon, je vais prendre ça.

8 – J'aime bien ces bandes dessinées. Toi aussi?
– Oui, c'est toujours amusant à lire.
– Bon, je vais acheter cette BD pour moi. Ça fait un beau souvenir.

SB 57, SPEAKING

7 Des cadeaux

Students work in pairs to practise buying presents and souvenirs, using the suggestions given or varying the dialogue with ideas of their own.

SB 57 READING PRACTICE

8 Qu'est-ce qu'on a oublié?

This practises the perfect tense of *acheter* and *oublier*. If wished, the teacher could demonstrate the idea by writing a list of, say, four items on the board and then taking three of the items out of a bag and asking which has been forgotten. This would work well with funny items, e.g. strange hats, odd souvenirs etc. Volunteers could also act this out if suitable props are available.

Solution:

a *Elles ont acheté une peluche, un drapeau et un porte-clés. Elles ont oublié un pot de confiture.*

b *Il a acheté un dictionnaire, une gomme et un cahier. Il a oublié une règle.*

Au choix SB 132, GENERAL SPEAKING

4 Aux magasins

Students read and then invent different conversations about items purchased and forgotten.

CM 4/6 PRACTICE

ce, cet, cette, ces

This provides further practice of *ce, cet, cette, ces* + nouns.

1 Le jeu des définitions

Students have to complete the definitions and then work out the answers.

Solution:

A 1 *Cet animal, Cet animal*
2 *Cette personne, Cet homme, cette femme*
3 *cette machine, Cet appareil*
4 *ce fruit, ce fruit*
5 *ces légumes, ces légumes*

B 1 *un chat,* 2 *un professeur,* 3 *un ordinateur,*
4 *une pêche,* 5 *des carottes*

2 Qui parle?

Solution:

1 *ces chaussettes; C'est Jean-Marc.*
2 *ce T-shirt; C'est Anne-Marie.*
3 *Ces cartes postales; C'est Sophie.*
4 *Cet anorak; C'est Christophe.*
5 *Cette ceinture; C'est Olivier.*
6 *ces baskets, ces sandales; C'est Richard.*

GRAMMAR IN ACTION 1, PAGE 33 GRAMMAR PRACTICE

Using ce, cet, cette, ces

This provides further practice of *ce, cet, cette, ces*, if required.

**Area 6
Perfect tense with *avoir*, regular *-ir* verbs**
SB 58, **1**–**4**
Au choix SB 131, **4**
Au choix SB 133, **5**–**6**
CD 2/28

SB58 PRESENTATION

1 As-tu bonne mémoire?

This links back to *Aux magasins* (SB 56) and introduces the perfect tense of *choisir*.

Solution: 1a, 2b, 3b, 4b

On a choisi … PRACTICE

Use pairs of props or flashcards (e.g. of fruit) and ask a student to choose one of the two items. Then ask the rest of the class which one was chosen, e.g.
– *Voici des fruits – il y a une pomme et une orange. Qu'est-ce que tu choisis?*
– *Une orange.*
– *Qu'est-ce qu'il/elle a choisi?*
– *Une orange.*

Then check with the original student.
– *Tu as choisi une orange, c'est vrai?*

Help the student to say *Oui, j'ai choisi une orange.*

Write the singular paradigm on the board for reference.

SB 58 READING

2 Quelle bulle?

This task contrasts the present and perfect tenses of two more *-ir* verbs, *finir* and *remplir*.

Solution: 1c, 2a, 3d, 4b

SB 58   **GRAMMAR**

Dossier-langue
Perfect tense of *-ir* verbs

When students have read through the explanation, write a few more verbs on the board, e.g. *réussir, abolir, démolir, blanchir, rougir, grossir, maigrir, saisir, punir*. Ask students to guess or look up the meaning and then work out the past participle.

SB 58, 🎧 2/28   **LISTENING**

3   Activités au choix

Students listen to find out which activities have been chosen by each person or group.

Solution:
Le matin: 1d, 2b, 3c, 4a
L'après-midi: 5g, 6f, 7h, 8e

🎧   **Activités au choix**

1 – Qu'est-ce que tu as choisi comme activité, le matin, Julie?
– Moi, j'ai choisi le volley. Tu as choisi ça aussi, Hélène?
– Oui, moi aussi, j'ai choisi le volley.

2 – Et toi, André, qu'est-ce que tu as choisi comme sport?
– J'ai choisi le judo.
– Ah bon, tu as déjà fait du judo?
– Non, mais je veux bien essayer ça.

3 – Daniel et Christophe, vous avez choisi une activité sportive?
– Oui, nous avons choisi le tennis de table.

4 – Et toi, Émilie, qu'est-ce que tu as choisi?
– Moi, j'ai choisi le badminton. Je joue souvent au badminton et j'adore ça.

5 – Puis l'après-midi, qu'est-ce que tu as choisi, Émilie?
– J'ai choisi la visite de la vieille ville. Ça a l'air intéressant.

6 – Et vous deux, Julie et Hélène. Vous avez choisi la même activité?
– Non, moi, j'ai choisi la visite du musée. C'est un musée de beaux arts avec beaucoup de peintures et j'aime bien ça, mais Hélène n'aime pas les musées.

7 – Non, et je n'aime pas beaucoup la peinture, alors j'ai choisi la visite de la cathédrale.

8 – Et vous, les garçons, qu'est-ce que vous avez choisi?
– Nous avons tous choisi l'excursion en bateau.

SB 58,   **SPEAKING**

4   Tu as choisi ça?

Working in pairs, students each choose a morning and afternoon activity and note down their choices. In turn, students ask questions to try to discover the other person's choice. The one who asks the fewest questions wins.

Au choix SB 133   **GENERAL PRACTICE**

5   Des questions et des réponses

This gives practice in supplying the past participle, then the correct part of *avoir* to form the perfect tense of *-ir* verbs, *finir* and *choisir*.

Solution:
a 1 *Tu as fini,* 2 *Elles ont fini,* 3 *Il a choisi,* 4 *Vous avez fini,* 5 *tu as choisi,* 6 *Le match a fini*
b **a** *Il a fini,* **b** *il a choisi,* **c** *je n'ai pas encore fini,* **d** *elles ont fini,* **e** *nous avons fini,* **f** *J'ai choisi*
c 1c, 2d, 3b, 4e, 5f, 6a

Au choix SB 131   **EXTENSION PRACTICE**

4   Une bonne soirée

This gives practice in forming the past participle of a mixture of *-ir* and *-er* verbs.

Solution: 1 *nous avons décidé,* 2 *Nous avons réussi,* 3 *J'ai trouvé,* 4 *Le film a fini,* 5 *nous avons dîné,* 6 *J'ai choisi,* 7 *Émilie … a commandé,* 8 *nous avons rencontré,* 9 *On a passé*

Au choix SB 133   **GENERAL WRITING**

6   Un e-mail

This gives practice in writing sentences which contain the perfect tense of *-ir* and *-er* verbs.

Area 7
Perfect tense with *avoir*, regular *-ir* verbs

SB 59, **5**, SB 60–61, **1**–**5**
Au choix SB 130, **4**–**5**, SB 131, **5**–**6**
Au choix SB 133, **7**
CM 4/7–4/8
CD 2/29–31
Grammar in Action 2, page 32

SB 59, 🎧 2/29   **PRESENTATION LISTENING READING**

5   Une journée difficile

This presents some *-re* verbs in the perfect tense, together with *-er* and *-ir* verbs. The text is in three sections. Students follow the pictures while listening to the recording. The recording can be paused after each section to check comprehension.

a Students match the appropriate text to the first four pictures.

Solution: 1d, 2c, 3a, 4b

b Students complete the text by supplying the missing verbs to the next four captions.

Solution: 5e *manger,* 6f *continué,* 7g *rempli,* 8h *refusé*

unité 4 En famille   Section 3

103

En famille unité 4

Section 3

c Students match the appropriate text to the last four pictures.

Solution: 9j, 10i, 11l, 12k

🎧 Une journée difficile

Le matin
Samedi dernier, tante Marie a demandé à Sophie et à Mélanie de garder son fils, Robert, pour la journée.
Le matin, elles ont trouvé ça facile. Robert a dormi jusqu'à midi.
Sophie et Mélanie ont joué sur l'ordinateur.
Après une heure, elles ont fini leur jeu.
Puis elles ont réussi à préparer le déjeuner dans le four à micro-ondes.

Le déjeuner
Robert a refusé de manger. Puis, il a perdu sa petite voiture et il a pleuré.
Sophie a rendu la voiture à Robert, mais il a continué à pleurer.
Mélanie a rempli une bouteille avec du lait.
Mais Robert a refusé de boire.

L'après-midi
Sophie a téléphoné à tante Marie sur son téléphone portable, mais elle n'a pas répondu.
Les deux filles ont attendu leur tante avec impatience.
Soudain, Robert a entendu un bruit – le chat du voisin a sauté par la fenêtre.
Robert a cessé de pleurer et il a commencé à rire.

SB 60   **GRAMMAR**

Dossier-langue
Perfect tense of -re verbs

As before, write some other examples of -re verbs on the board so students can apply the rule,
e.g. *battre, interrompre, dépendre*.

SB 60   **PRACTICE**

1 Des conversations

Students have to follow the lines to complete the questions (task **a**), then the answers (task **b**) and finally match them up (task **c**).

Solution:

a   **1** *Tu as entendu un bruit?*
      2 *Est-ce que Julie a rendu le CD?*
      3 *Vous avez perdu quelque chose?*
      4 *Est-ce qu'on a vendu des glaces au parc?*
      5 *Vous avez attendu longtemps au café?*
b   **a** *Oui, j'ai perdu mon billet.*
      b *Oui, nous avons attendu les autres pendant une heure.*
      c *Non, mais on a vendu des boissons dans le kiosque.*
      d *Oui, elle a rendu le CD hier matin.*
      e *J'ai entendu le téléphone, mais c'est tout.*
c   **1e, 2d, 3a, 4c, 5b**

SB 60, 🎧 2/30   **LISTENING**

2 Perdu et retrouvé

Students listen to the dialogues to find the answers.

Solution: **1** *baskets, cuisine,* **2** *stylo, table,* **3** *peluche, salle de bains,* **4** *baladeur, lit,* **5** *CD-ROM, l'ordinateur,* **6** *lunettes de soleil, salle à manger*

🎧 Perdu et retrouvé

1 – Maman, j'ai perdu mes baskets.
– Tu as cherché dans la cuisine?
– Non, pas encore … ah oui, elles sont là, mes baskets sont dans la cuisine.

2 – Ça va, Luc?
– Non, j'ai perdu mon stylo.
– Mais, regarde Luc, il y a un stylo sur la table. C'est ton stylo, non?
– Ah oui, voilà mon stylo.

3 – J'ai perdu ma peluche, ma petite chatte blanche.
– Ta peluche? Mais elle est dans la salle de bains, Sophie.
– C'est vrai? Ah oui, voici ma peluche.

4 – Ça ne va pas, je ne trouve pas mon baladeur.
– Qu'est-ce qu'il y a Charles?
– J'ai perdu mon baladeur.
– Ton baladeur? Mais qu'est-ce qu'il y a sous ton lit? C'est ton baladeur, non?

5 – Maman, nous avons perdu notre nouveau CD-ROM.
– Il n'est pas dans votre chambre?
– Non, il n'est pas là.
– Vous avez regardé dans l'ordinateur?
– Ah, bonne idée … oui, le nouveau CD-ROM est là, merci, maman.

6 – Ça va, les filles?
– Non, nous avons perdu nos lunettes de soleil et regarde, il y a du soleil aujourd'hui.
– Vous avez cherché dans la salle à manger?
– Ah oui, voici nos lunettes de soleil.

SB 60   **READING**

3 C'est la vie

Students have to choose the correct past participle to complete the cartoon captions.

Solution: **1** *Ce Parisien a vendu,* **2** *J'ai perdu, je n'ai pas perdu,* **3** *Le zoo a perdu,* **4** *Le gendarme a attendu,* **5** *Tu as entendu*

GRAMMAR IN ACTION 2, PAGE 32 GRAMMAR PRACTICE

The perfect tense with *avoir* – regular -ir and -re verbs

This provides further practice of using the perfect tense of regular -ir and -re verbs with *avoir*.

SB 61   GRAMMAR

Dossier-langue
Summary of regular verbs (perfect tense)

This summarises what has been learnt so far about the perfect tense.

Au choix SB 130   SUPPORT
                                                     READING

4 En classe

Students match classroom instructions in the perfect tense to the English translation. The past participles *fait* and *compris* could be explained, if wished, but they are covered with other irregular past participles in the next unit.

Solution: 1c, 2d, 3b, 4h, 5a, 6e, 7f, 8g

Au choix SB 130   SUPPORT
                                                     READING

5 Un chat perdu

Students have to choose the correct past participle.

Solution: **1b** *nous avons perdu,* **2c** *On a cherché,* **3a** *J'ai crié,* **4b** *Ma mère a entendu,* **5a** *Mon frère et ma sœur ont aidé,* **6c** *Mon frère a imaginé,* **7b** *Ma sœur a trouvé,* **8c** *mes parents ont pensé,* **9c** *nous avons trouvé*

SB 61   PRACTICE

4 Une visite à Paris

This gives practice in forming the perfect tense with all three types of regular verbs.

For support, the task could be prepared orally and the correct verbs written in random order on the board.

Some teachers might like to prepare an OHT based on this.

Solutions: **1** *le groupe a passé,* **2** *Nous avons voyagé,* **3** *nous avons visité,* **4** *On a regardé,* **5** *j'ai acheté,* **6** *on a mangé,* **7** *j'ai choisi,* **8** *Les autres ont choisi,* **9** *nous avons décidé,* **10** *Nous avons attendu,* **11** *Daniel a perdu,* **12** *Julie a retrouvé*

Au choix SB 133   GENERAL

7 Une journée récente

a Students have to supply the missing past participles.

Solution: **1** *j'ai quitté,* **2** *J'ai attendu,* **3** *les cours ont commencé,* **4** *Nous avons bien travaillé,* **5** *on a vendu,* **6** *J'ai retrouvé*

b Students supply the complete perfect tense.

Solution: **1** *j'ai mangé,* **2** *J'ai choisi,* **3** *les cours ont fini,* **4** *j'ai travaillé,* **5** *j'ai regardé,* **6** *nous avons dîné*

                                                       PRESENTATION

Qu'est-ce que tu as fait/vous avez fait?

Teach this question, using flashcards to prompt answers, as it is needed in the following task.

Attention could be drawn to the past participle of *faire* which is also covered with other irregular past participles in the next unit.

SB 61,   SPEAKING

5 Inventez des conversations

Working in pairs, students read and invent different conversations using different time expressions and different verbs in the perfect tense.

Au choix SB 131, 2/31   EXTENSION
                                                   LISTENING

5 À Giverny

This is a more demanding listening task for able students. They listen to the conversation, then complete the *résumé*. Alternatively, they could make a reasonable guess at the missing words and then listen to check their answers.

Solution: **1** *la maison,* **2** *le jardin,* **3** *magasin,* **4** *acheté,* **5** *parents,* **6** *café,* **7** *sandwichs,* **8** *campagne,* **9** *appareil,* **10** *cherché*

À Giverny

– Qu'est-ce que tu as fait hier, Hélène?
– Moi, j'ai passé une belle journée. Nous avons quitté la maison de bonne heure pour aller à Giverny.
– Giverny, qu'est-ce que c'est?
– C'est un petit village où on peut voir la maison et le jardin du peintre Claude Monet.
– Monet, c'est un peintre célèbre?
– Oui, il est très célèbre. Alors, le matin, nous avons visité sa maison et son jardin.
– C'est joli, le jardin?
– Oui, le jardin est très joli avec beaucoup de fleurs. Marc a pris beaucoup de photos. Il y a aussi un magasin de souvenirs.
– Tu as acheté quelque chose?
– Oui, j'ai acheté un livre sur Monet pour mes parents. Ils s'intéressent beaucoup à la peinture. Et j'ai acheté un T-shirt pour moi.
– Et ensuite, qu'est-ce que vous avez fait?
– Eh bien, nous avons trouvé un petit café dans le village pour déjeuner.
– Et qu'est-ce que tu as mangé?
– Moi, j'ai mangé une omelette et les autres ont choisi des sandwichs.
– Et l'après-midi?
– Quand nous avons fini de manger, nous avons décidé de faire une promenade à la campagne. Mais à la campagne, Marc a découvert qu'il n'avait pas son appareil.
– Il a perdu son appareil?

unité 4 En famille   *Section 3*

105

– Oui, alors nous avons cherché partout.
– Et vous l'avez trouvé?
– Finalement, oui. On est retourné au café et on a trouvé l'appareil au café.

Au choix SB 131,

EXTENSION
SPEAKING
WRITING

6 Lundi dernier

Students ask and answer questions, then write a few sentences about a recent day.

CM 4/7 PRACTICE

Des verbes au passé composé

All students could complete this summary sheet which practises forming the perfect tense of regular -er, -ir and -re verbs.

Solution:

A Regular -er verbs
1 J'ai joué, 2 Tu as joué, 3 Il a lavé, 4 Nous avons dansé, 5 Vous avez travaillé, 6 Ils ont regardé

B Regular -ir verbs
1 J'ai rempli, 2 Tu as choisi?, 3 Il a rougi, 4 Nous avons réussi, 5 Vous avez fini?, 6 Ils ont pâli

C Regular -re verbs
1 J'ai rendu, 2 Tu as répondu, 3 Elle a perdu, 4 Nous avons vendu, 5 Vous avez entendu, 6 Elles ont attendu

CM 4/8 PRACTICE

Des mots croisés

These two crosswords give further practice of -er, -ir and -re verbs.

Solution:

1 Des verbes au passé composé (-er)

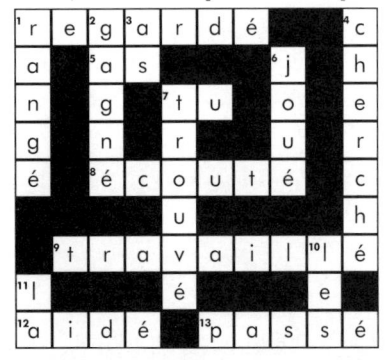

2 Des verbes au passé composé (-ir, -re)

Area 8
Saying goodbye and thanking people for their hospitality
SB 62, **1**–**4**
Au choix SB 133, **8**
CD 2/32

SB 62 READING

1 En famille

This task brings together useful questions and answers when staying with a family in France.
Explain the question *Tu as bien dormi?*

Solution: 1b, 2d, 3e, 4f, 5c, 6a

SB 62, 2/32 LISTENING

2 Bon retour

This provides a useful model for a 'farewell' conversation after a visit to a family. Students should listen and choose the correct word from the options given.

Solution: 1 dernier, 2 des chocolats, 3 les chocolats, 4 en France, 5 au Canada

Bon retour

C'est le dernier jour des vacances. Hier, Daniel a acheté des chocolats pour Mme Martin.
– Merci bien pour les chocolats, Daniel. J'espère que tu as passé de bonnes vacances ici en France.
– Ah oui, Madame, j'ai passé des vacances merveilleuses.
– Alors, au revoir et bon retour au Canada.
– Au revoir, Madame, et merci pour tout.

SB 62 READING

3 La lettre de Julie

Students read through the letter and answer three short questions.

Solution:
1 Elle a passé ses vacances en France.
2 Elle a surtout aimé la visite au jardin de Monet.
3 Ses parents ont aimé les cadeaux.

Au choix SB 133 GENERAL WRITING

8 Une lettre

a Students complete a short thank you letter, selecting from words given. Not all words listed are used.

Solution: 1 Cher, 2 passé, 3 super, 4 beaucoup, 5 la montagne, 6 sœur, 7 musique, 8 voyage, 9 attendu, 10 dormi, 11 Merci

b Students make up a sentence with the remaining words from the box.

Solution: *Les légumes sont bons pour la santé.*

SB 62
WRITING
4 À toi!

Students then practise writing a similar letter with minor variations.

Area 9
Further activities and consolidation
SB 63, 64–65
CM 4/9–4/16, 135
CD 2/33–36
Student CD 1/19–24, 2/11–14

CM 4/9, SCD 1/19–24 INDEPENDENT LISTENING
SOUNDS AND WRITING

Écoute et parle

This copymaster provides pronunciation and speaking practice.

1 À la française

À la française

1 cousin   5 parent
2 garage   6 radio
3 instrument   7 restaurant
4 judo   8 six

2 Et après?

Solution: 2 – 6 – 8 – 11 – 16 – 33 – 45 – 67

Et après?

1 – 5 – 7 – 10 – 15 – 32 – 44 – 66

3 Des phrases ridicules

Des phrases ridicules

Le gentil général fait de la gymnastique dans le gîte. C'est génial!

Le garçon du guichet à la gare gagne un gâteau pour le goûter.

4 Les terminaisons: -ieux et -yeux

Solution: 1f, 2b, 3c, 4e, 5a, 6d

Les terminaisons: -ieux et -yeux

1 furieux   4 ennuyeux
2 anxieux   5 ambitieux
3 curieux   6 délicieux

5 Vocabulaire de classe

Solution: 1 *ça*, 2 *comprends*, 3 *livre*, 4 *ou*, 5 *anglais*, 6 *sais*, 7 *stylo*

Vocabulaire de classe

1 Comment ça s'écrit?
2 Je ne comprends pas.
3 Je voudrais un livre, s'il vous plaît.
4 C'est masculin ou féminin?
5 Qu'est-ce que c'est en anglais?
6 Je ne sais pas.
7 Je n'ai pas de stylo.

6 Des conversations

Des conversations

1 **On arrive**
   – Tu as fait bon voyage?
   (pause)
   – Oui, merci.
   – Tu as beaucoup de bagages?
   (pause)
   – J'ai une grande valise seulement.
   – C'est ton premier séjour en France?
   (pause)
   – Oui, c'est ma première visite.

2 **À la maison**
   – Voici ta chambre.
   (pause)
   – Où est-ce que je peux mettre mes vêtements?
   – Il y a de la place dans l'armoire.
   (pause)
   – Quand est-ce qu'on se lève ici, normalement?
   – Normalement, on se lève vers sept heures, sept heures et demie.
   (pause)
   – Est-ce que je peux téléphoner à la maison?
   – Bien sûr. Il y a un téléphone dans la cuisine.

3 **Hier**
   – Qu'est-ce que tu as fait hier?
   (pause)
   – Le matin, j'ai joué au tennis.
   – Et l'après-midi?
   (pause)
   – L'après-midi, j'ai regardé les magasins.
   – Tu as acheté quelque chose?
   (pause)
   – J'ai acheté un porte-clés pour mon père.

CM 4/10, SCD 2/11–14 INDEPENDENT LISTENING

Tu comprends?

Students could do any or all of the four items on this worksheet, now or later as revision.

1 Aurélie arrive en France

Solution: 1c, 2 *Nanaimo*, 3b, 4a, 5b

Aurélie arrive en France

– Mamie, je te présente Aurélie, une amie canadienne. Aurélie, je te présente ma grand-mère.
– Bonjour, Madame.
– Bonjour, Aurélie. Je peux te tutoyer?
– Mais bien sûr, Madame.
– Tu as fait bon voyage?
– Oui, merci.
– Tu habites où au Canada?
– J'habite à Nanaimo.
– Nanaimo? Comment ça s'écrit?
– N – A – N – A – I – M – O.
– Et tu as des frères et sœurs?
– Non, je suis fille unique.
– Ah, voilà Médor, notre labrador. J'espère que tu aimes les chiens. Vous avez des animaux à la maison?
– Oui, nous avons un grand chien noir. Il s'appelle César et il est adorable.
– Et tu vas passer combien de temps en France?
– Je vais passer dix jours ici en tout.

2 Hier matin

Solution: 1d, 2g, 3e, 4a, 5f, 6h, 7c, 8b

Hier matin

1 Alain et Henri ont travaillé dans le jardin.
2 Amandine et Suzanne ont joué sur l'ordinateur.
3 Pierre était très fatigué, alors il a dormi jusqu'à midi.
4 Hélène a téléphoné à ses amis.
5 Luc a perdu une chaussette à la piscine.
6 Nous avons attendu le bus pendant une heure.
7 Marc a fini son livre.
8 Nous avons choisi des cartes postales.

3 Un écrivain anglais

Solution: 1 *habite*, 2 *est*, 3 *est*, 4 *aime*, 5 *a travaillé*, 6 *a commencé*, 7 *a gagné*, 8 *apprend*, 9 *a tourné*, 10 *s'appelle*, 11 *ai*, 12 *aimé*

Un écrivain anglais

Dick King-Smith habite dans une ferme.
Il est fermier et il est aussi écrivain.
Il aime beaucoup les animaux, surtout les cochons.
Il a travaillé dans une école primaire pendant sept ans.
Il a commencé à écrire des livres à l'âge de 54 ans.
En 1984, il a gagné un prix pour le livre 'Le cochon devenu berger' (Sheep Pig).
Dans cette histoire, un cochon apprend à garder les moutons.
On a tourné un film de cette histoire.
Le film s'appelle 'Babe'.
Moi, j'ai bien aimé ce film.

4 Des cadeaux

Solution:

1	mon grand-père	c	il aime les cravates
2	ma grand-mère	h	elle adore lire
3	mon oncle	a	il aime bien la musique classique
4	ma tante	b	elle adore le chocolat
5	Jonathan	e	il aime les lions
6	Nathalie	d	elle aime les choses un peu différentes
7	le bébé	g	il est mignon
8	moi	f	c'est excellent

Des cadeaux

– Tu as acheté des cadeaux?
– Oui, j'ai acheté beaucoup de cadeaux.
– Qu'est-ce que tu as acheté pour ton grand-père?
– Mon grand-père aime bien porter une cravate. Alors je lui ai acheté cette belle cravate grise.
– Et pour ta grand-mère?
– Ma grand-mère adore lire. Alors pour elle, j'ai acheté ce livre.
– Tu as acheté quelque chose pour ton oncle?
– Oui. Pour oncle Pierre, j'ai acheté ce CD. Il aime bien la musique classique.
– Et pour ta tante?
– Pour ma tante, j'ai acheté cette boîte de chocolats. Elle adore le chocolat.
– Et pour tes cousins?
– Pour mon cousin Jonathan, qui a dix ans, j'ai acheté cette affiche. Il aime les lions.
– Et pour ma cousine, Nathalie, j'ai acheté ces lunettes de soleil fantaisie. Elle aime les choses un peu différentes.
– Tu as acheté quelque chose pour le bébé aussi?
– Mais bien sûr. Pour le bébé, j'ai acheté cette peluche. C'est un petit lapin. Il est mignon, non?
– Oui, il est très chouette … Et toi, tu t'es achetée quelque chose pour toi aussi?
– Mais oui. Je me suis acheté ce nouveau jeu électronique. J'ai déjà joué avec Nicolas et c'est excellent.

SB 63, CM 4/11

Sommaire

A summary of the main structures and vocabulary of this unit. Students fill in gaps on the copymaster. They should check their answers against the Students' Book page.

CM 4/12 — Rappel 4
REVISION

This copymaster can be used at any point in the course for revision and consolidation. It provides revision of household tasks, sport, music and other leisure activities. The reading and writing tasks are self-instructional and can be used by students working individually for homework or during cover lessons.

Solution:

1 Des mots mêlés
sports: voile, ski, équitation, badminton
lieux: patinoire, stade, piscine, gymnase
instruments: guitare, violon, flûte, batterie

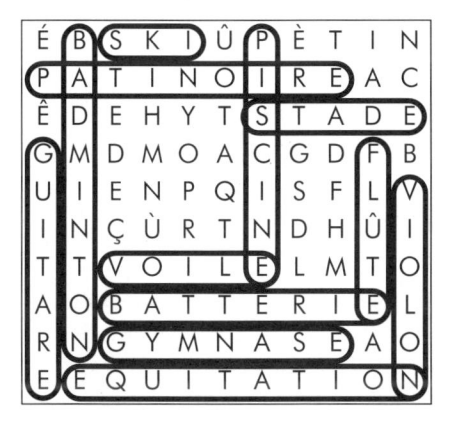

2 5-4-3-2-1
5 distractions: une fête foraine, un feu d'artifice, un concert, une discothèque, une exposition
4 adjectifs: ennuyeux, facile, utile, intéressant
3 sports: l'athlétisme, le VTT, la planche à voile
2 activités artistiques: le dessin, la peinture
1 instrument: le piano

3 Mots croisés (le travail à la maison)

Épreuve – Unité 4

These worksheets can be used for an informal test of listening, speaking, reading and writing or for extra practice, as required. For general notes on administering the *Épreuves*, see TB 16.

CM 4/13, 2/33–36
LISTENING

Épreuve: Écouter

A Du travail (NC 1)

Solution: a1, b6, c3, d4, e7, f5, g2

(mark /6: 4+ shows the ability to understand short statements)

Du travail
1 Maman a préparé un gâteau.
2 Les filles ont décoré la maison.
3 Sophie a rangé le salon.
4 Pierre a aidé dans la cuisine.
5 Marc a organisé la musique.
6 Les garçons ont acheté des chips et du coca.
7 Papa a passé l'aspirateur.

B C'est qui? (NC 2)

Solution: 1 Stefan, 2 Bruno, 3 Carole, 4 Marielle, 5 Véronique, 6 Félix

(mark /5: 3+ shows understanding of a range of familiar statements and questions)

C'est qui?
– Je m'appelle Stefan. J'ai les cheveux longs et je porte des lunettes.
– Je m'appelle Félix et j'ai les cheveux foncés. Je suis très grand.
– Je m'appelle Carole. Je suis petite et j'ai les cheveux longs.
– Je m'appelle Véronique et je suis grande avec les cheveux blonds.
– Je m'appelle Bruno. J'ai une grande valise.
– Je m'appelle Marielle. Je porte toujours une casquette et j'ai une petite valise.

C La journée de Julie (NC 3)

Solution: 1 en ville, 2 des cadeaux, 3 acheté, 4 mère, 5 bibliothèque, 6 rencontré, 7 mangé

(mark /6: 4+ shows ability to understand short passages made up of familiar language)

La journée de Julie
Hier, Julie a décidé d'aller en ville.
Elle a acheté des cadeaux pour sa famille.
Elle a acheté un CD-ROM pour son frère et un magazine pour sa mère.
Puis elle a visité la bibliothèque.
En ville, elle a rencontré Thomas et ils ont mangé dans un fast-food.
Thomas a invité Julie au cinéma.

unité 4 En famille

Section 3

109

D Les activités d'aujourd'hui et les activités d'hier (NC 5)

Pupils need to be told beforehand that the exercise requires them to differentiate between past and present.

Solution: 1c, 2a, 3e, 4d, 5f, 6g, 7b, 8h, 9j, 10i

(mark /8: 5+ shows the ability to understand extracts of spoken language made up of familiar material, including past and present events)

Les activités d'aujourd'hui et les activités d'hier

Hier soir, j'ai joué au tennis, mais aujourd'hui, je joue aux cartes.
Maintenant, je mange une glace, mais hier, j'ai mangé un sandwich au jambon.
Hier matin, j'ai invité Pierre à la maison, mais aujourd'hui, j'invite Nicole.
Maintenant, je regarde un film, mais hier, j'ai regardé un match de football.
Hier, j'ai téléphoné à mes grands-parents. Aujourd'hui, je téléphone à mon ami en Angleterre.

CM 4/14 SPEAKING
Épreuve: Parler

Students should be given the sheet up to a week before the assessment, to give them time to choose whether to do 1 or 2 and to give them time to prepare and practise both conversations – the structured one (A) and the open-ended one (B) – with their partners.

Mark scheme

Section A: mark /12: 3 marks per response
- 1 mark for an utterance/response that is clear and conveys all of the information requested, in the form of a complete phrase or sentence, though not necessarily an accurate one. The questions and answers may seem a little disjointed, like separate items rather than parts of a coherent conversation.
- 2 marks for an utterance/response that is clear and conveys all of the information requested in the form of a complete phrase or sentence, though not necessarily an accurate one. The language must flow reasonably smoothly and be recognisable as part of a coherent conversation.
- 3 marks for a clear and complete utterance/response that flows smoothly as part of a clear and coherent conversation. The language must be in complete sentences or phrases that are reasonably accurate and consistent as far as grammar, pronunciation and intonation are concerned.

Section B: mark /13: 3 marks per response, as above, +1 bonus mark for adding one or two items using the perfect tense. 19–25 shows the ability to take part in short conversations, referring to recent experiences.

Summary:
Marks	7–13	14–18	19–25
NC Level	3	4	5

CM 4/15 READING
Épreuve: Lire

A Jean achète des cadeaux (NC 1)
Solution: 1d, 2e, 3f, 4g, 5c, 6a, 7b

(mark /6: 4+ shows the ability to understand single words)

B L'arrivée en France (NC 2)
Solution: 1f, 2g, 3b, 4e, 5a, 6d, 7c

(mark /6: 4+ shows the ability to understand short phrases)

C Un e-mail (NC 4)

Pupils need to be told that if the questions are in English they must answer in English; otherwise they are awarded no marks.

Solution: 1 no hot water, 2 the flat is not modern, 3 she does not have her own room, 4 there is no room in the wardrobe, 5 they have not got the Internet, 6 the food is bad, 7 the dog is dangerous

(mark /6: 4+ shows ability to understand short texts and to note main points)

D La lettre d'Annette (NC 5)
Solution: 1b, 2c, 3a, 4a, 5a, 6b, 7b, 8c

(mark /7: 4+ shows the ability to understand texts covering present, past and future events)

CM 4/16 WRITING
Épreuve: Écrire et grammaire

A Des cadeaux (NC 1)
Solution: 1 *un CD-ROM*, 2–5 any presents

(mark /4: 3+ shows the ability to select appropriate words to complete sentences and copy them correctly)

B Une visite chez mon correspondant (NC 1)
Solution: 1 *cherché*, 2 *trouvé*, 3 *fini*, 4 *choisi*, 5 *attendu*

(mark /4: 3+ shows ability to select appropriate words to complete sentences and copy them correctly)

C Chez toi (NC 4)

Mark scheme
- 1 mark for each sub-task completed with a correct verb.

Subtotal: 6
Accuracy:
- 2 marks: most words are correct
- 1 mark: about half the words are correct
- 0 marks: fewer than half the words are correct

Subtotal: 2
(mark /8: 5+ shows ability to write individual paragraphs of about three or four sentences)

D Raconte ta journée d'hier (NC 5)

This is an open-ended task.

Mark scheme

Communication:
- 1 mark for each accurate perfect tense
- 1/2 mark for a perfect tense which is incorrect but which communicates

Subtotal: 6 (round up half marks)
Accuracy:
- 3 marks: mostly accurate
- 2 marks: about half correct
- 1 mark: more wrong than right
- 0 marks: little or nothing of merit

Subtotal: 3
(mark /9: 6+ shows ability to produce short pieces of writing in simple sentences, referring to recent experiences. Although there may be mistakes the meaning can be understood with little or no difficulty)

SB64–65, CM 135 READING EXTENSION

Presse-Jeunesse 3

These pages provide reading for pleasure. They can be used alone or with the accompanying copymaster.

SB 64, CM 135

La vente

Students read the picture story and do the two copymaster tasks.

Solution:

A La vente

Des questions: 1c, 2c, 3a, 4b, 5c, 6c

Encore des questions (These questions in English test more detailed understanding of the text. There are various ways of answering, but these facts should be mentioned:)
1. Penfriend coming to stay.
2. Room has been tidied. / He has given things to younger brother and sister.
3. Twins don't want old toys etc. thrown out by their brother.
4. His treasures.
5. They can sell their brother's things at the sale.
6. Michel buys a toy robot for Robert (his own).

SB 65, CM 135

La vie scolaire en Europe

This article gives comparable facts about schools and education in four European countries. Students read the statements on the copymaster and identify the countries.

Solution:

B La vie scolaire en Europe

C'est dans quel pays?: 1 *en France,* 2 *en Allemagne,* 3 *au Danemark,* 4 *en Suède,* 5 *en France*

SB 65, CM 135

Ça nous a changé la vie!

Students read the short articles about inventions and then match them up with their definitions on the copymaster.

Solution:

C Ça nous a changé la vie!

Un jeu de définitions: 1 *le trombone,* 2 *l'aspirateur,* 3 *l'hélicoptère,* 4 *l'escalier roulant,* 5 *le frigo (réfrigérateur)*

CM 135

The copymaster includes a short 'odd one out' activity, using mainly words from SB 64–65.

Solution:

D Une autre activité

Chasse à l'intrus: 1 *un professeur,* 2 *une église,* 3 *La Rochelle,* 4 *un hélicoptère,* 5 *les cadeaux,* 6 *un violon*

Encore Tricolore 2
nouvelle édition

unité 5 Bon appétit!

Areas	Topics	Grammar
1	Finding out about French cafés, drinks and snacks	Using the verb *boire* (present tense) Using *pour* + infinitive (optional)
2	Buying drinks and snacks in a café (including ice-creams)	Revision of perfect tense with regular verbs Practice in distinguishing between present and past tenses
3	Describing food and recent meals	Using irregular past participles
4		Asking and answering questions in the perfect tense Further practice of irregular past participles
5		The perfect tense in the negative Answering questions in the appropriate tense
6	Discussing the menu Expressing likes and dislikes	
7	Ordering meals in a restaurant	Further practice of the perfect tense
8	Further activities and consolidation	

National Curriculum Information

Some students   levels 4–5+
Most students   levels 4–5
All students   levels 3–4

Revision

Rappel (CM 5/12) includes revision of the following:
- colours
- festivals and greetings
- expressions of time (past, present, future)

Sounds and writing

- the letter *r*
- the endings *-u*, *-ue*

See *Écoute et parle* (CM 5/9, TB 129).

ICT opportunities

- text reconstruction
- finding French restaurant menus on the web
- making an illustrated menu

Reading strategies

Presse-Jeunesse 4 (SB 80–81, CM 136)

Assessment

- Informal assessment is in *Épreuves* at the end of this unit (TB 131, CM 5/13–5/16)
- Formal assessment (*Unités 1–7*) is in the *Contrôle* (TB 190, CM 139–145).

Students' Book

Unité 5 SB 66–79
Au choix SB 134–137

Flashcards

66–71 snacks and drinks
7–20 food and drink

CDs

3/1–21
Student CD 1/25–30, 2/15–17

Additional

Grammar in Action 2, p 34
Encore Tricolore 1 FC 56, 62, 78, 81–89

Copymasters

CM 5/1	*Au café* [mini-flashcards]	
CM 5/2	*On prend quelque chose?* [role play]	
CM 5/3	*Un repas en famille* [grammar]	
CM 5/4	*Des mots croisés* [grammar]	
CM 5/5	*Présent ou passé?* [grammar]	
CM 5/6	*Voici le menu* [mini-flashcards]	
CM 5/7	*Comprends-tu le menu?* [dictionary skills]	
CM 5/8	*Au restaurant* [listening]	
CM 5/9	*Écoute et parle* [independent listening]	
CM 5/10	*Tu comprends?* [independent listening]	
CM 5/11	*Sommaire* [consolidation, reference]	
CM 5/12	*Rappel* [revision]	
CM 5/13	*Épreuve: Écouter*	
CM 5/14	*Épreuve: Parler*	
CM 5/15	*Épreuve: Lire*	
CM 5/16	*Épreuve: Écrire et grammaire*	
CM 136	*Presse-Jeunesse 4* [reading]	
CM 149–150	*Chantez! Que désirez-vous?* [song]	

Language content

Buying drinks and snacks in a café (Area 2)

Qu'est-ce que tu prends?
Pour moi, …
Je voudrais …
une bière
une boisson (non-)alcoolisée
une boisson (non-)gazeuse
un cidre
un citron pressé
une menthe à l'eau
un Orangina
un thé (au lait/au citron)
un verre de lait
un sandwich au jambon/au pâté
un sandwich au fromage/au saucisson
une crêpe
un croque-monsieur
une portion de frites
un hot-dog
une pizza
Où sont les toilettes?
Avez-vous le téléphone?
L'addition, s'il vous plaît.
Qu'est-ce que vous avez comme sandwichs?

Buying ice-creams (Area 2)

Je voudrais une glace, s'il vous plaît.
Quel parfum?
une glace à la fraise/au citron/…

Using the perfect tense (Areas 4–5)

Qu'est-ce que tu as bu?
As-tu écrit la lettre?
Qu'est-ce que tu as fait hier?
Où as-tu mangé hier soir?
Je n'ai pas vu le film hier.
Nous n'avons pas mangé à la cantine.

Expressing likes and dislikes (Area 6)

Tu aimes le melon?
Oui, j'aime ça.
Non, je n'aime pas beaucoup ça.

Discussing the menu and ordering meals (Areas 6–7)

comme hors-d'œuvre   *une assiette de charcuterie*
comme plat principal   *fruits de saison*
comme légumes   *garni*
comme dessert   *le plat du jour*
comme boisson   *pâté/gâteau maison*
des crevettes
du saumon
du thon
Avez-vous choisi?
Pour commencer, je vais prendre …
Comme plat principal, je voudrais …
Comme dessert, je vais prendre …

Useful websites

Shopping for food

To find food shops click on *Shopping* from the *Yahoo France* opening page and then select the category *alimentation et boissons*.

Some French supermarkets

Auchan – www.auchan.fr
Carrefour – www.carrefour.fr
F.Leclerc – www.leclerc-cannes.com/

Fast food

www.mcdonalds-cotedamour.fr – this site from one of the branches of the McDonald's chain has information on prices, menus etc.

Restaurant listings

www.restos-pas-chers.fr/ – this lists inexpensive restaurants in Paris and elsewhere.

Restaurant menus

www.adx.fr/l-assiette-lyonnaise/assiett1.html – this is the site for a French restaurant where you can view the menu.

Food, recipes etc.

www.cuisineaz.com – this site gives recipes, tips about food etc.

Books and reading

www.hachette.net/junior – the French publishers Hachette publish a range of books for children and teenagers.
www.harrypotter.gallimard-jeunesse.fr/Pages/Menu.html – the Harry Potter books are published by Gallimard in France.
www.tintin.be – information about Tintin can be found on this site.
www.fnac.fr – see TB 31
www.amazon.fr – see TB 31

Discussion about books

www.momes.net/forum/forum.html – this site has discussion groups on a range of subjects, including Harry Potter, with reviews by children.

Bon appétit! unité 5

**Area 1
Finding out about French cafés, drinks and snacks
Using the verb *boire* (present tense)
Using *pour* + infinitive (optional)**
SB 66–67, **1**–**4**
Au choix SB 134, **1**–**2**, SB 135, **1**
Au choix SB 136, **1**
CD 3/1–2
CM 5/1
FC 66–71, (FC 56, 62, 78, 81–89 ET1)

Section 3

(FC 56, 62, 78, 81–89 ET1) PRESENTATION

Les cafés

Ask questions to find out what students know about cafés in France, e.g.

Est-ce qu'il y a beaucoup de cafés en France?
Est-ce que les cafés sont ouverts toute la journée en France?
Qu'est-ce qu'on peut acheter comme boissons au café? Est-ce qu'on peut aussi acheter des choses à manger?

Suggest some drinks and snacks using flashcards to revise some relevant vocabulary previously met, e.g.

drinks: *un café(-crème), un chocolat chaud, un coca, un jus de fruit, une limonade, un thé* (teach *au lait/au citron*), *du lait* (teach *un verre de lait*), *du vin*

snacks: *du jambon, du fromage, une portion de frites*

SB 66–67, 🎧 3/1, FC 66–71 LISTENING
READING
PRESENTATION

1 Les cafés en France

Use photos and flashcards to introduce and practise new vocabulary for drinks and snacks, e.g.

– *Voici des boissons qu'on peut prendre au café – ça, c'est un Orangina et ça, c'est une bière. Voici une autre boisson, c'est une menthe à l'eau – c'est fait avec du sirop de menthe et de l'eau etc.*
– *(Student A), tu voudrais boire quelque chose?*
– *Oui, je voudrais un cidre* etc.

Students should now be ready to listen to the recording and follow the printed text, perhaps with some further oral work to check comprehension.

🎧 **Les cafés en France**

En France, il y a beaucoup de cafés. Ils sont ouverts toute la journée et souvent jusqu'à minuit.
Voici un café en France.
Le garçon de café sert des boissons aux clients. Dans un café en France, il y a un grand choix de boissons. Par exemple, on boit des boissons froides, comme l'Orangina, le jus de fruit et la limonade …
… et il y a aussi des boissons alcoolisées, par exemple le vin, la bière et le cidre.

Les Français boivent beaucoup d'eau minérale – on peut choisir entre l'eau gazeuse et non-gazeuse.
Beaucoup de clients prennent des boissons chaudes, comme un café-crème, un thé au lait, un thé au citron ou un chocolat chaud.
Voici deux autres boissons, très populaires.
– Moi, je bois une menthe à l'eau. C'est fait avec du sirop de menthe et de l'eau. C'est délicieux!
– Comme il fait très chaud, nous buvons du citron pressé. Il y a du jus de citron, du sucre et de l'eau. C'est très rafraîchissant, mais un peu cher!
On peut souvent acheter des choses à manger dans un café, par exemple des sandwichs ou des hot-dogs …
… ou quelquefois des frites ou des glaces.
Et voici un croque-monsieur, fait avec du jambon, du fromage et du pain.
Les Français vont au café pour boire ou pour manger, mais aussi pour rencontrer des amis et pour regarder les gens qui passent.
Quelquefois, ils regardent un match à la télé ou ils jouent aux cartes. Enfin, on va au café pour s'amuser.

CM 5/1 SPEAKING
WRITING

Au café

This copymaster consists of twelve mini-flashcards including items of food and drink to cover all the main categories (*une boisson chaude/froide/(non-)alcoolisée/(non-)gazeuse, un snack, une glace*). It could be used here, to help with the teaching of new vocabulary, or later for revision or consolidation.
It can be used for pairwork practice (see TB 26) or it could be made into an OHT for oral practice.
For written practice, students can write the name of the food or drink in the actual square or as a list.

Solution: 1c, 2f, 3a, 4b, 5h, 6g, 7l, 8k, 9e, 10d, 11j, 12i

Follow-up

This idea could be used now or later for consolidation.
Write on the board some headings, e.g.
des boissons froides   des boissons chaudes
des boissons alcoolisées des boissons non-alcoolisées
des boissons gazeuses   des boissons non-gazeuses
and add examples underneath to clarify the meaning, e.g. *la limonade, le thé, le vin* etc. Ask students to add further examples in turn.

Perhaps practise the vocabulary for drinks and different types of drinks by a Spelling Bee or by playing *Effacez!*, e.g. *Efface le nom d'une boisson alcoolisée* etc.

SB 67, 🎧 **3/2** LISTENING

2 Qu'est-ce qu'on prend?

Students match up the orders for drinks with the photos of drinks in *Les cafés en France*, noting the numbers of the photos.

Solution: 1 photo 10, 2 photo 15, 3 photo 6,
4 photo 13, 5 photo 3, 6 photo 11,
7 photo 5, 8 photo 7, 9 photo 14,
10 photo 2

🎧 **Qu'est-ce qu'on prend?**

1 Je voudrais un café-crème, s'il vous plaît.
2 Pour moi, un citron pressé, s'il vous plaît.
3 Je voudrais une bière, s'il vous plaît.
4 Je prends un chocolat chaud.
5 Et pour moi, un jus de fruit, s'il vous plaît – un jus de pomme.
6 Je voudrais un thé, s'il vous plaît – un thé au lait.
7 Pour nous, une bouteille de vin rouge, s'il vous plaît.
8 Je prends un cidre, s'il vous plaît.
9 Une menthe à l'eau, s'il vous plaît.
10 Et pour moi, un Orangina.

SB 67 READING

3 Vrai ou faux?

This serves as a check that students have understood the main points about cafés in France. More able students could be asked to correct the untrue statements (see suggestions in the solution below).

Solution:
1 **F** (*Les cafés sont ouverts l'après-midi.*)
2 **F** (*On peut boire des boissons chaudes au café.*)
3 **V**
4 **V**
5 **F** (*Un citron pressé est fait avec du citron, du sucre et de l'eau.*)
6 **V**
7 **F** (*Un croque-monsieur est fait avec du jambon, du fromage et du pain.*)
8 **V**

Differentiation

For further practice of the new vocabulary, students could do the following tasks from *Au choix*.

AU CHOIX SB 134 SUPPORT
WRITING
VOCABULARY PRACTICE

1 Des boissons par catégories

Students refer back to SB 66–67 to find examples of each type of drink. Check that they understand the meaning of the categories by referring to appropriate drinks, e.g.
La limonade et la bière sont des boissons gazeuses, mais la limonade est non-alcoolisée et la bière est une boisson alcoolisée etc.

Solution:
Various solutions are possible, e.g.
1 *des boissons chaudes: le café, le thé, le chocolat chaud*
2 *des boissons froides et non-alcoolisées: le jus de fruit, l'eau, la menthe à l'eau*
3 *des boissons alcoolisées: le vin, la bière, le cidre*
4 *des boissons gazeuses: la limonade, l'Orangina, l'eau minérale gazeuse*

AU CHOIX SB 135 EXTENSION
VOCABULARY PRACTICE

1 Chasse à l'intrus

Students spot the odd one out and explain their choice.

Solution:
1 *un citron pressé (les autres sont des choses à manger*
2 *le coca (les autres sont des boissons chaudes)*
3 *un jus de fruit (les autres sont des boissons alcoolisées)*
4 *du vin blanc (les autres sont des boissons non-alcoolisées)*
5 *la limonade (les autres sont des boissons non-gazeuses)*
(Other explanations are possible and discussion could be encouraged!)

OPTIONAL EXTENSION
SPEAKING

Pour + infinitive

No specific tasks are included for this construction, but there are several examples of it in the captions about cafés. Teachers can draw attention to it and work on it in class, as they wish.

You could ask questions such as
Pourquoi est-ce qu'on va au café?

… and prompt answers with *pour*, e.g.
Pour boire/manger/regarder des matchs à la télé? etc.
Et pour quelles autres raisons? (*Pour rencontrer des amis.*)
Où vas-tu pour rencontrer tes amis?
(*Je vais … pour …*)
More able students could be given beginnings of sentences and asked to make up suitable endings, e.g.
Pour rencontrer mes amis, je …
Pour faire un citron pressé, on …
Pour venir au collège, je/nous …
Pour acheter une boisson, je/on …
Pour visiter la Tour Eiffel, les touristes … etc.

SB 67, 💻 GRAMMAR

Dossier-langue
boire (to drink)

Several parts of this verb occur in the text on SB 66–67 and students should easily spot these. After practising the verb orally, they should add it to their own verb tables (electronic or otherwise).

unité 5 Bon appétit!

Section 3

115

Bon appétit! unité 5

SB 67　　　　　　　　　　　　　　　WRITING
4　Les boissons

Students complete this short conversation about drinks with the correct parts of the verb *boire*. They could then practise the conversation in pairs and more able students could adapt it to include some of their own preferences.

Solution:　1 *boire*, 2 *je bois*, 3 *tu bois*, 4 *je bois*, 5 *nous buvons*, 6 *vous buvez*, 7 *On boit*

Differentiation

For further practice of *boire*, use one of the following activities.

Au choix SB 134　　　　　　　　　SUPPORT
　　　　　　　　　　　　　　　　　　GRAMMAR
2　Qu'est-ce qu'on boit?

This is a matching task (subject + verb).

Solution:　1b, 2a, 3e, 4c, 5g, 6d, 7f

SB 136,　　　　　　　　　　　　　GENERAL
　　　　　　　　　　　　　　　　　　SPEAKING
1　Conversations au choix

Students read aloud the model dialogue and look at the alternatives in boxes A and B. They then throw the dice in turn to make up alternative conversations.

Follow-up

For further practice of *boire* and of the names of drinks, play a chain vocabulary game, e.g.

- easy version:
- Je bois un coca.
- Je bois un coca et une menthe à l'eau etc.
- harder version, using all persons of the verb:
- Je bois un coca.
- Tu bois un coca et une menthe à l'eau.
- Il boit etc.

Area 2
Buying drinks and snacks in a café
(including ice-creams)
Revision of perfect tense with
regular verbs
Practice in distinguishing between
present and past tenses
SB 68–69, **1**–**5**
Au choix SB 134, **3**, SB 135, **2**, SB 136, **2**
CD 3/3–5
FC 66–71
CM 5/1–5/2, 149–150

SB 68, 🎧 3/3　　　　　　　　　　LISTENING
1　On va au café?

Students read through the introductory paragraph, then listen to the recording and do the task which follows, jotting down the initials, then giving the answers in full for practice.

116

Solution:
1 *Claire a commandé un jus d'orange.*
2 *Élise a commandé un coca.*
3 *Tiffaine a choisi un chocolat chaud.*
4 *Paul a choisi un café-crème.*
5 *Marc a demandé un Orangina.*
6 *Jean-Pierre a commandé une limonade.*

🎧　**On va au café?**

– Salut, Paul. Bon anniversaire! C'est bien aujourd'hui, non?
– Bien sûr. Merci, Jean-Pierre. Tu viens au café? Et vous aussi, Marc et Élise? On va au café de la Poste. J'ai déjà invité Tiffaine et son amie Claire. On y va?
(*Les copains arrivent au café.*)
– Bon. Qu'est-ce que tu prends, Claire?
– Un jus de fruit, s'il te plaît, Paul, à l'orange.
– Très bien. Et pour toi, Élise?
– Pour moi un coca. J'ai soif aujourd'hui.
– Alors, un jus d'orange, un coca et toi, Tiffaine, qu'est-ce que tu prends?
– Un chocolat chaud, je crois.
– Bien … et pour toi, Jean-Pierre?
– Pour moi, une limonade, s'il te plaît.
– Bon! Une limonade … et un café-crème pour moi, et c'est tout?
– Et moi?
– Oh, pardon, Marc. Qu'est-ce que tu veux?
– Un Orangina, s'il te plaît.
– Alors … un jus d'orange, un coca, un chocolat chaud, une limonade, un café-crème et un Orangina, c'est ça?
– Oui, merci, c'est ça.

Au choix SB 136　　　　　　　　　GENERAL
　　　　　　　　　　　　　　　　　　PRACTICE
2　Jeu de mémoire

This is a follow-up activity for all. Students study the answers to the previous task (or listen to the tape again), then see if they can remember who ordered which drink. More able students could answer in complete sentences for extra practice of the perfect tense, but they should be reminded that this will involve changing the person of the auxiliary verb.

Solution:
1 *Marc (a commandé un Orangina.)*
2 *Paul (a choisi un café-crème.)*
3 *Claire (a demandé un jus d'orange.)*
4 *Jean-Pierre (a commandé une limonade.)*
5 *Tiffaine (a commandé un chocolat chaud.)*
6 *Élise (a choisi un coca.)*

SB 68,　　　　　　　　　　　　　SPEAKING
2　Qu'est-ce que vous prenez?

In this open-ended pairwork activity, students practise ordering drinks. One student orders a drink for five different people, pausing after each order for the waiter to repeat it. The other acts as the waiter and repeats the order, adding on the new order each time. They then change roles.

This could also be used as a class chain game, where an additional order is added each time, e.g.
Pour mon professeur, un grand café … et pour mon père, une bière etc.

SB 68, 3/4　　　　　　　　　　　　　　LISTENING
3　On vend des glaces

Students should look at the list of ice cream flavours available and see how many of them they can understand or work out. They might need help with *cassis, noisette, pistache* and *pépites de chocolat* (chocolate chip).

Practise pronunciation by asking a few students to order ice-creams, e.g.
- Qu'est-ce que vous voulez?
- Une glace à la vanille, s'il vous plaît.
- Et pour toi, Anna?
- Une glace à la fraise.
- Et pour toi, Richard? etc.

Then play a memory game, with students trying to remember who ordered what:
Anna a commandé une glace à la fraise etc.

Students then listen to the tape and work out which flavour is most popular. It will probably be a good idea to decide in advance on an abbreviation for each one to be mentioned, e.g. vanille (v), abricot (a), café (c), chocolat (ch), citron (ci), fraise (f), fruits de la passion (fp), pépites de chocolat (pc), pistache (p).

Solution: 1 *trois personnes* (f), 2 *deux personnes* (v), 3 *une personne* (a), 4 *fraise*

On vend des glaces
- Bonjour, Monsieur, une glace à la vanille, s'il vous plaît.
- Pour moi, une glace à la fraise, deux boules!
- Je voudrais une glace au café, s'il vous plaît.
- Pour moi, une glace à la vanille, c'est toujours bon!
- Je voudrais une glace avec une boule au chocolat et l'autre au café, s'il vous plaît.
- Bonjour, Monsieur, une glace à la fraise, s'il vous plaît.
- Et moi, je prends une glace à la pistache.
- Je voudrais une glace au citron, s'il vous plaît.
- Pour moi, une glace à trois boules – à la fraise, s'il vous plaît.
- Je voudrais une glace, s'il vous plaît … aux fruits de la passion, c'est mon parfum favori.
- Bonjour, Monsieur. Une glace à l'abricot, s'il vous plaît.
- Mmm! Les pépites de chocolat – trois boules de ça, s'il vous plaît!

SB 68,　　　　　　　　　　　　　　　SPEAKING
4　Tu veux une glace?

Students practise this short dialogue in pairs, changing the ice cream flavours each time.

SB 69　　　　　　　　　　　　　　　GRAMMAR
Dossier-langue
The perfect tense – a reminder

Students read this through, then pick out other examples of the perfect tense in earlier items and add these to a list on the board.

The final list could be used for a game of *Effacez!*.

Students should now watch out for further examples of the perfect tense in action, for example in the memory games in *Au choix*, and in the song (SB 69, see below).

SB 69, FC 66–71, CM 5/1,　　　　　　SPEAKING
　　　　　　　　　　　　　　　　　　　READING
5　Vous êtes au café

First teach and practise asking where the toilets and the telephone are, e.g. *au fond, à droite, au sous-sol* etc.

Service charge: there is no reference to the service charge in this dialogue, since it is now a legal requirement in France to include this in the bill. Teachers could explain this to the class and tell them that it is still common to leave a little extra loose change as a tip if the service has been good.

When students have read the dialogue, ask questions to check comprehension, e.g.
Qu'est-ce qu'on a commandé comme boisson?
Qu'est-ce qu'il y a au fond?

The flashcards could be used to prompt replies to the question *Qu'est-ce que tu as commandé?*

Then students can practise the dialogue in pairs, varying the drinks and the questions as indicated.

CM 5/1 (mini-flashcards) could be used for this and other similar activities (see also notes on flashcard games, TB 26).

Differentiation

The following *Au choix* activities can be used as support and extension.

Au choix SB 134　　　　　　　　　　　SUPPORT
　　　　　　　　　　　　　　　　　　　PRACTICE
3　Qu'est-ce qu'ils ont commandé?

This simple maze puzzle gives further practice of regular perfect tenses and of café vocabulary. The answers could be given in full for extra practice.

Solution:
1 *Marc a commandé une glace au chocolat.*
2 *Claire a commandé une crêpe.*
3 *Jean-Pierre a mangé une glace à la fraise.*
4 *Tiffaine a choisi une portion de frites.*
5 *Paul a mangé un hot-dog.*
6 *Élise a choisi un sandwich au jambon.*

Au choix SB 135

EXTENSION
READING

2 On a mangé cela

This is a slightly harder item on a similar theme which involves a bit more deduction, but again the answers could be given in full for extra practice. At the end, students are asked to make a choice of their own and state what they have ordered.

Solution:
1 *Marc a commandé une omelette aux champignons.*
2 *Claire a commandé un hot-dog.*
3 *Élise a commandé un croque-monsieur.*
4 *Jean-Pierre a commandé une crêpe.*
5 *Paul a commandé un sandwich au pâté.*
6 (open-ended answer: *Moi, j'ai commandé …*)

Follow-up

The following optional activities could be done at this point or later for revision or consolidation.

CM 5/2, **SPEAKING**

On prend quelque chose?

This copymaster begins with a role-play (buying ice-creams) and then has a dice dialogue for buying drinks and snacks.

Au café, j'ai commandé … **SPEAKING**

For this chain game, one student begins by saying: *Au café, j'ai commandé* (+ name of drink). Then a second student is chosen and is asked: *Qu'est-ce que tu as commandé?*

The student repeats the first student's answer and adds a different item.

The game proceeds with the next student adding something else to the list. Students who forget an item or who get the order wrong are out.

Saynètes au café

SPEAKING
EXTENSION

Some able students could work in groups making up very simple café sketches in which one acts as a waiter and three or four order drinks and snacks. These scenes are then acted and the rest of the group or class has to remember what each person ordered. After the sketch, ask questions, e.g.

– *Qu'est-ce que (Student A) a commandé?*
– *Il a commandé un coca.*
– *Et (Student B), qu'est-ce qu'elle a commandé?* etc.

At the beginning, each customer could order one item only, but more items can be added in later scenes to make the game more complicated.

Finally one group could try to re-enact another group's *saynète*.

SB 69, CM 149–150, TB 29, 🎧 3/5 **LISTENING**
SPEAKING

Chantez! Que désirez-vous?

This would be a good time to introduce the song, which includes much of the café vocabulary and also examples of the perfect tense. See TB 29 for notes on using the songs and CM 149–150 for the music.

🎧 **Chantez! Que désirez-vous?**

1 Bien, Messieurs, Mesdemoiselles,
Que désirez-vous?
Mon frère va prendre une menthe à l'eau,
Et pour moi un chocolat chaud.
Mais Monsieur, je suis désolée,
Paul et Marc et Anne et Claire
N'ont pas encore décidé.

2 Bien, Messieurs, Mesdemoiselles,
Que désirez-vous?
Paul désire un verre de lait,
Mon frère va prendre une menthe à l'eau,
Et pour moi un chocolat chaud.
Mais Monsieur, je suis désolée,
• •   Marc et Anne et Claire
N'ont pas encore décidé.

3 Bien, Messieurs, Mesdemoiselles,
Que désirez-vous?
Marc voudrait un Orangina,
Paul désire un verre de lait,
Mon frère va prendre une menthe à l'eau,
Et pour moi un chocolat chaud.
Mais Monsieur, je suis désolée,
• • • •   Anne et Claire
N'ont pas encore décidé.

4 Bien, Messieurs, Mesdemoiselles,
Que désirez-vous?
Anne prend un citron pressé,
Marc voudrait un Orangina,
Paul désire un verre de lait,
Mon frère va prendre une menthe à l'eau,
Et pour moi un chocolat chaud.
Mais Monsieur, je suis désolée,
• • • • • •   Claire
N'a pas encore décidé.

5 Bien, Messieurs, Mesdemoiselles,
Que désirez-vous?
Claire a choisi un coca,
Anne prend un citron pressé,
Marc voudrait un Orangina,
Paul désire un verre de lait,
Mon frère va prendre une menthe à l'eau,
Et pour moi un chocolat chaud.
• • • • • • •
Tout le monde a décidé!

6 Bien, Messieurs, Mesdemoiselles,
Vous mangez quelque chose?
Mon frère prend une portion de frites,
Et pour moi une tranche de quiche.
Mais Monsieur, je suis désolée …
Ne dites rien, déjà j'ai deviné.
Paul et Marc et Anne et Claire
N'ont pas encore décidé.

> **Area 3**
> **Describing food and recent meals**
> **Using irregular past participles**
> SB 70–71, **1**–**5**
> Au choix SB 134, **4**, SB 136, **3**
> CM 5/3–5/4
> CD 3/6–7
> Grammar in Action 2, page 34

SB 70 READING

Racontez-nous!

Before students begin work on this item, mention that some verbs have irregular past participles, give a few examples and suggest that students watch out for more of these in the letters which follow.

After a brief introduction to the article *Des repas intéressants*, students could work alone or in pairs on these letters from young people about interesting meals they have had.

Read some of the letters aloud and ask questions to check on comprehension, as necessary. More able students could perhaps make up some *vrai ou faux?* statements about the letters to set to others.

SB 70 READING

1 Racontez-nous!

This pair-matching activity tests comprehension of the previous article and includes verbs in the perfect tense. Answers could be written or read out in full sentences, to give more practice of the perfect tense in use.

Solution: 1b, 2d, 3g, 4e, 5h, 6a, 7c, 8f

SB 70 GRAMMAR

Dossier-langue
The perfect tense with irregular participles

This gives a recap of how to form the perfect tense and then explains irregular past participles. In the task, students find from the text the past participles for the verbs listed. Most are listed in groups according to the endings of their past participles.

Solution: 1 *eu*, 2 *bu*, 3 *lu*, 4 *pu*, 5 *vu*, 6 *dit*, 7 *écrit*, 8 *mis*, 9 *pris*, 10 *été*, 11 *fait*, 12 *découvert*

SB 70 GRAMMAR
WRITING

2 D'autres verbes utiles

a The aim of the first part of this short task is to add some more common irregular past participles of verbs not included in the article. Students could see which past participles match a group from the list in the *Dossier-langue*.

Solution: 1 *appris*, 2 *compris*, 3 *offert*, 4 *ouvert*, 5 *reçu*, 6 *voulu*

b In this task, students write three sentences, each including a different one of these verbs in the perfect tense.

CM 5/3, SPEAKING
WRITING

Un repas en famille

This copymaster, set in the context of a family meal (for revision), gives further practice of the perfect tense with irregular past participles.

1 Conversations au choix
Students could use dice for practice conversations in pairs.

2 Après chaque conversation
After each conversation there is an optional 'recap' activity in which students ask questions about the choices they have just made. The first set of questions practises the first and second persons of the verb and the second set practises the third person. (This part of the copymaster is suitable for more able students.)

SB 71, 3/6 LISTENING
SPEAKING

3 Dans la rue

Note: this item could be used here or in Area 4 (asking questions referring to the past). It gives practice in listening to questions and answers in the perfect tense and includes some irregular past participles.

Students read the introductory sentence, then listen to the recording. Before starting to listen, they should draw two columns, headed *Oui* and *Non* and enter ticks in these as they listen.

Make sure students are quite clear what is being discussed and what they have to do.

Begin with some oral practice of the key vocabulary, e.g.

Est-ce que tu aimes le déjeuner de dimanche? Qui a mangé un déjeuner traditionnel, dimanche dernier? Qu'est-ce que tu as mangé hier, pour ton déjeuner? etc.

Then play the first bit of the recording (one or two interviews only) and check what was said and what students should have noted down.

Then start again and play the whole item.

Solution: Oui – 4; Non – 4

Follow this by asking the class similar questions about Sunday dinner in their own families, e.g.

Et toi, tu as mangé le déjeuner de dimanche hier? Où as-tu déjeuné hier? Qu'est-ce qu'on a mangé? etc.

Dans la rue

– Excusez-moi, Madame. Est-ce que vous avez pris un déjeuner traditionnel hier?
– Bien sûr, nous avons déjeuné à midi, comme d'habitude.
– Et vous, Monsieur, vous avez mangé le déjeuner de dimanche traditionnel, hier?

unité 5 Bon appétit!

Section 3

Bon appétit! unité 5

Section 3

– Alors moi, j'ai travaillé toute la journée hier et j'ai dîné le soir.
– Ah bon. Et vous, les enfants, avez-vous pris le déjeuner de dimanche traditionnel, hier?
– Ah non, hier, on a fait un pique-nique!
– Un pique-nique! C'est bien. Pardon, jeune homme. Hier, c'était dimanche. Avez-vous mangé le déjeuner de dimanche traditionnel?
– Ben, hier, à midi, j'ai pris un verre au café, avec des copains et nous avons mangé un croque-monsieur.
– Merci. Et vous, Mademoiselle. Où avez-vous déjeuné, hier?
– Hier, nous avons déjeuné en famille, chez ma grand-mère. Elle aime le déjeuner de dimanche traditionnel.
– Et vous, Madame. Est-ce que vous avez pris un déjeuner traditionnel hier?
– Moi non. À midi, j'ai pris une salade et un fruit et puis le soir, nous avons dîné en famille.
– Ah bon. Un groupe de jeunes. Dites-moi, mes amis, qui a mangé un déjeuner traditionnel hier?
– Moi. On a déjeuné en famille. On essaie de faire ça une fois par semaine.
– Moi aussi. J'adore le déjeuner de dimanche, puis je dors tout l'après-midi!
– Excellent! Alors, merci tout le monde. On ne mange pas toujours le déjeuner de dimanche, mais ça existe toujours, c'est certain!

Differentiation

The following *Au choix* activities can be used as support and extension.

AU CHOIX SB 134   **SUPPORT**
                                       WRITING

4 Hier, au café

A simple maze puzzle to practise writing simple sentences about what people have eaten and drunk.

Solution:
Marc a mangé un sandwich.
Claire a choisi un croque-monsieur.
Moi, j'ai pris une crêpe.
Jean-Pierre et Paul ont pris des glaces.
Tous les enfants ont bu des boissons froides et gazeuses.

AU CHOIX SB 136   **GENERAL**
                                       SPEAKING/WRITING

3 Fais des phrases

This could be done as a speaking item, perhaps in groups, or used as an individual writing task. Students make up serious or silly sentences, based on the substitution table. It is left to the teacher to state how many sentences are required.

SB 71   **WRITING**

4 À toi!

This substitution table provides a framework on which students can base their own sentences about recent meals. Make it clear that they can introduce other items of food and drink, not just those listed. More able students could try to describe fuller meals in more detail.

SB 71, 🎧 3/7   **LISTENING**
                                       READING

5 Le sandwich surprise

First revise or teach the following food vocabulary: *pain, beurre, oignon, sel, poivre, sucre, confiture, sardines.*

a Students should next read the advert for the competition and then the descriptions of the sandwiches themselves. Before students read the competition entries, the following words may need explanation – *ajoutez, coupez, mélangez.*

A lot of oral practice can be based on the entries, e.g.
Quel sandwich préfères-tu?
Tu aimes le sandwich de Gisèle?
Préfères-tu les sandwichs des garçons ou les sandwichs des filles?
Dans quels sandwichs y a-t-il du jambon/de la mayonnaise? etc.
Qui aime le sandwich de Paul?
Est-ce que Jean-Pierre a mangé beaucoup de ses sandwichs?
Qui a préparé un sandwich avec des champignons/des radis? etc.
À ton avis, qui a gagné?

Students could vote on which sandwich is the best, before listening to the recording and comparing their choice with the recorded results.

If time, or as a French club activity, students could make up their own recipe for a *sandwich surprise*, perhaps working in pairs or groups to do this.

b Students should listen to the recording and find out who won the competition and who else received prizes. On a second hearing they could be asked to find out what the announcer thought of Jean-Pierre's sandwich and Claudette's sandwich, and what his own favourite sandwich consists of.

🎧 **Le sandwich surprise**

Bonjour, bonjour, bonjour et joyeuses Pâques à tout le monde. Aujourd'hui, c'est vraiment une journée joyeuse pour des personnes très importantes – c'est à dire pour les personnes qui ont gagné des disques dans notre grand concours 'le sandwich surprise'.

Beaucoup d'entre vous ont envoyé vos idées. Et moi, j'ai mangé beaucoup, beaucoup de sandwichs cette semaine … mais je n'ai pas mangé tout le sandwich de Jean-Pierre Léon. J'aime bien les sardines et j'aime bien la confiture d'oranges – mais les deux dans un sandwich … ça alors! Non, non et non! Je suis sûr que votre chien est très malade, Jean-Pierre!

Beaucoup de sandwichs sont très bons, mais ce ne sont pas vraiment des surprises. Le sandwich de Claudette Bernard, par exemple, est délicieux, mais c'est un peu comme un croque-monsieur.

Personnellement, j'aime beaucoup les sandwichs au pâté. Mon sandwich favori est un sandwich au pâté avec un peu d'oignon.

Mais finalement … les résultats. Un sandwich vraiment délicieux est le sandwich de Paul Dubois. Paul a gagné trois CD. Beaucoup d'autres ont gagné un CD, mais la personne qui a gagné le concours … qui a gagné cinq CD, c'est une fille – Gisèle Leblanc. Félicitations Gisèle. Votre sandwich 'salade de fruits' est vraiment un sandwich surprise!

CM 5/4   **PRACTICE**

Des mots croisés

This copymaster provides further practice. It includes most of the past participles introduced in this area, plus a few new ones which students could look up, e.g. *cru* and *su*.

Solution:

¹d	i	t		²a	³p	p	⁴r	i	s
é					r		⁶i	l	
⁷c	o	⁸m	p	r	i	⁹s		¹⁰f	
o		i			¹¹s	u	r		a
u		s							i
¹²v	¹³u		¹⁴é	t	¹⁵é				t
¹⁶e	n		¹⁷p		¹⁸c	¹⁹e			
²⁰r	e	ç	u		²¹c	r	u		
t			²²j		i			²³	
	²⁴o	u	v	e	r	t		²⁵b	u

GRAMMAR IN ACTION 2, PAGE 34 GRAMMAR PRACTICE

The perfect tense with *avoir* (6)

The activities on this page of *Grammar in Action 2* would be useful here.

Area 4
Asking and answering questions in the perfect tense
Further practice of irregular past participles
SB 72–73, **1**–**5**
Au choix SB 134, **5**, SB 135, **3**
CD 3/8–9

SB 72, 🎧 3/8   **LISTENING / READING**

1 Les sandwichs de M. Corot

a First play the recording with students following the pictures and check that they have understood the gist of the story, by asking questions such as:

Qui a fait des sandwichs?
Qui a mangé des sardines?
Qui était malade?
Est-ce que M. Corot a vraiment mangé de mauvaises sardines?

Then go through the text in detail, playing the recording and stopping it at regular intervals to ask questions in French.

b When students are familiar with the development of the story, they should read the captions and note down the correct order.

c This can be checked by listening to the recording again.

Solution: 1f, 2d, 3e, 4b, 5c, 6g, 7a, 8i, 9h

An alternative way to proceed would be to let students do the reading tasks first, perhaps working in pairs, and match up the captions with the pictures, eventually listening to the recording to check if they have done this correctly.

🎧 Les sandwichs de M. Corot

Lundi soir, M. et Mme Corot ont préparé des sandwichs pour mardi. Elle a mis du jambon dans ses sandwichs, mais il a fait des sandwichs aux sardines et il a donné deux ou trois sardines au chat. Minou adore le poisson et il a mangé les sardines tout de suite.
Mardi matin à 8h15, les Corot ont quitté la maison. Mme Corot a amené son mari à la gare en voiture, puis elle a continué son voyage jusqu'à son bureau.
Le matin, pendant leur absence, l'épicier a apporté des provisions chez les Corot: des boîtes, des paquets, des bouteilles. Il a mis les provisions dans le garage.
À midi et demi, Mme Corot a fini son travail et elle a décidé de rentrer à la maison. À son retour, elle a appelé le chat:
– Minou, Minou, où es-tu? Voilà ton lait. Viens, Minou!
Elle a cherché le chat partout.
Finalement, elle a trouvé Minou dans le garage. Le pauvre chat était très malade. Mme Corot a dit:
– Mais, Minou, qu'est-ce qu'il y a? Tu as mangé quelque chose de mauvais?
– Mon Dieu, a pensé Mme Corot! Les sardines …? Les sardines ont empoisonné le chat!
Mme Corot a téléphoné tout de suite à son mari.
– Chéri, ne mange pas tes sandwichs. Minou a mangé des sardines hier soir, et maintenant, il est très malade.
– Mais … j'ai déjà mangé mes sandwichs – j'ai pris trois sandwichs aux sardines. Qu'est-ce que je vais faire?
– Téléphone immédiatement au médecin.
M. Corot a téléphoné à son médecin. Le médecin a envoyé M. Corot directement à l'hôpital. À l'hôpital, ils ont décidé, par précaution, de garder M. Corot pour une nuit. M. Corot a passé la nuit à l'hôpital. Il a bien dormi.
Mercredi matin, Mme Corot a téléphoné à l'hôpital. On a dit que M. Corot allait très bien, alors il a pu quitter l'hôpital.

À ce moment-là, l'épicier a frappé à la porte.
– Bonjour, Madame. Comment va votre chat aujourd'hui?
– Il va beaucoup mieux, merci. Mais …
– Je suis désolé, Madame, mais hier matin, par erreur, j'ai laissé tomber une grosse bouteille de limonade et la bouteille a frappé votre chat très fort sur la tête.

SB 72   WRITING

2 Un résumé de l'histoire

Students complete the sentences with the correct past participles (from the box) to give a summary of the story.

Solution: 1 *préparé*, 2 *fait*, 3 *mangé*, 4 *quitté*, 5 *apporté*, 6 *vu*, 7 *téléphoné*, 8 *mangé*, 9 *passé*, 10 *frappé*, 11 *expliqué*

Differentiation

The following *Au choix* activities can be used as support and extension.

Au choix SB 134   SUPPORT
                                                           READING

5 M. Corot – un résumé

Students read the seven sentences and note down the order to give a short *résumé* of the story. For extra practice they could write this summary out in the correct order.

Solution: 1b, 2c, 3e, 4a, 5d, 6f, 7g

Au choix SB 135   EXTENSION
                                                           GRAMMAR
                                                           WRITING

3 Huit phrases sur M. Corot

Students have to complete the eight sentences, in this case supplying the correct auxiliary verb and past participle and then put the sentences in the right order to tell the story.

Solution:

3 *Lundi soir, les Corot <u>ont préparé</u> des sandwichs.*
1 *M. Corot <u>a fait</u> des sandwichs aux sardines et il <u>a donné</u> des sardines au chat.*
2 *Mardi matin, M. et Mme Corot <u>ont quitté</u> la maison à 8h15.*
6 *Pendant leur absence, l'épicier <u>a apporté</u> des provisions à la maison.*
4 *À son retour, Mme Corot <u>a trouvé</u> le chat au garage – il était malade et Mme Corot <u>a pensé</u> qu'il avait été empoisonné par les sardines.*
7 *M. Corot <u>a mangé</u> ses sandwichs aux sardines, alors le médecin, par précaution, <u>a envoyé</u> M. Corot à l'hôpital.*
8 *M. Corot <u>a</u> très bien <u>dormi</u> à l'hôpital.*
5 *Mais mercredi matin, l'épicier <u>a</u> tout <u>expliqué</u>.*

SB 73   READING
                                                           WRITING

3 Quelle est la bonne réponse?

This is a multiple choice task. Students could just select the right answer by letter or write out the questions and the correct answers. The question words could be revised first and perhaps written on the board. Various question words have been included and by writing out the answers, students will have practice in asking questions in the perfect tense and in associating different forms of answers with different question words.

When checking the anwers, encourage students to say why the other alternatives are incorrect.

Solution: 1a, 2c, 3b, 4a, 5c, 6c, 7b, 8c

Racontez!   EXTENSION
                                                           SPEAKING

Finally, a really able group could try to tell the story themselves from memory, one starting and the next carrying on when the teacher changes the speaker, each accounting for one or two sentences.

SB 73   GRAMMAR

Dossier-langue
Asking questions in the perfect tense

This explains the different ways in which questions can be asked. The main emphasis should be in understanding questions words and questions likely to be asked and in using a few common forms, e.g. *Qu'est-ce que tu as fait?*

SB 73, 🎧 3/9   LISTENING
                                                           READING

4 Au bureau de M. Corot

This provides more practice in recognising question words and questions and answers, using *tu* and *je* with the perfect tense.

Students read the short introductory paragraph, then listen to the recording and write **a** or **b**, according to which reply is correct.

The answers could be checked with one person asking the questions aloud and others answering.

More able students could note down the question words used or how the question is asked, e.g. turning verb round.

Solution: 1b, 2a, 3a, 4b, 5a, 6a, 7b

🎧 **Au bureau de M. Corot**

1 Est-ce que tu as déjeuné à la cantine hier?
2 Qu'est-ce que tu as fait hier après-midi?
3 Qu'est-ce que le médecin a fait?
4 Où as-tu passé la nuit?
5 As-tu été très malade?
6 As-tu bien dormi à l'hôpital?
7 Le chat, a-t-il mangé de mauvaises sardines?

SB 73, 🗣, 💻

READING
WRITING

5 Quelle est la question?

Before working on this task, the teacher could give individual students or groups a written question which has been cut up into individual words or groups of words. Each student/group has to reassemble the correct question. This could be turned into a game in a race against the clock or each other.

a Students can then put the groups of words in the correct order to form a question in the perfect tense and write it out correctly.

This task could be done on the computer using *Fun with Texts – Scrambler*.

Solution:

1 *As-tu déjeuné au collège aujourd'hui?*
2 *Qu'est-ce que tu as mangé ce matin?*
3 *Qu'est-ce que tu as bu?*
4 *Où avez-vous passé vos vacances cet été?*
5 *Est-ce qu'il a fait beau pendant vos vacances?*
6 *Avez- vous fait tous vos devoirs hier soir?*

b Students now choose questions to ask each other in turns.

c This is a follow-up writing activity, in which students choose some of the questions and write their own replies. These can later be added to their electronic phrase book.

READING
Le jeu des questions
PRACTICE

This follow-up task can be used now or later, for extra practice The teacher could write down a series of questions and a series of corresponding answers and cut them up into individual questions and answers. These could be used for the following activities:

1 The slips of paper are distributed to students, so each student has either a question or an answer. The class could be divided into two teams: *Les questions* and *Les réponses*. One person from the 'questions' team reads out a question and everyone in the 'réponses' team has to check to see whether they have an appropriate answer. If so, they read this out and the person who asked the question has to confirm that this is correct. This game could also be played in groups.

2 Individual students or groups could be given a set of five questions and five answers and see how quickly they can assemble the correct answer to each question.

3 The questions and appropriate answers can be used together with the Universal Board Game (see TB 28).

The same questions that feature in the Students' Book tasks could be used, or others. Here are some possible questions and answers.

– *Qu'est-ce que tu as fait samedi?*
– *Samedi, j'ai joué sur l'ordinateur.*
– *Qu'est-ce que tu as fait hier?*
– *Hier, j'ai travaillé dans le jardin.*
– *Comment as-tu voyagé en France?*
– *J'ai voyagé en bateau et en train.*
– *Qu'est-ce que tu as acheté aux magasins?*
– *J'ai acheté un CD et un magazine.*
– *Qui a gagné le match dimanche dernier?*
– *L'équipe du collège Charles de Gaulle a gagné le match.*
– *Qu'est ce que tu as mangé à midi?*
– *J'ai mangé du poulet et des frites avec du ketchup.*

Area 5
The perfect tense in the negative
Answering questions in the appropriate tense
SB 74–75, **1**-**5**
Au choix SB 134, **6**, SB 135, **4**–**5**
CD 3/10–11
CM 5/5

SB 74, 🎧 3/10, 💻

LISTENING
READING

1 Un désastre pour Emmanuel

Revise some of the basic ICT vocabulary, e.g. *une disquette, sauvegarder, imprimer, l'imprimante, taper, effacer, marcher* (to work). Then students could look through the text first, before listening to the recording and following the text in their books.

The conversation could eventually be used as a playscript, perhaps with some students recording it in pairs.

🎧 **Un désastre pour Emmanuel**

– Allô, c'est toi, Caroline?
– Oui, oui, c'est moi. Mais qu'est-ce qu'il y a, Emmanuel?
– C'est mes devoirs d'informatique, tu sais, les résultats de mon sondage sur les cafés en France – c'est un vrai désastre!
– Mais pourquoi? Tu as trouvé les devoirs trop difficiles?
– Non, non. Ils ont été faciles, les devoirs!
– Alors, ton ordinateur n'a pas marché? C'est ça, le désastre?
– Non, non, ce n'est pas ça. Mon ordinateur a bien marché.
– Alors, c'est la disquette? Tu as perdu la disquette avec les devoirs dessus?
– Non, non, je te dis, je n'ai pas perdu la disquette. J'ai mis la disquette dans la machine, l'ordinateur a bien marché, j'ai fait les devoirs sans problème. Zut, zut et zut!
– Mais tu n'as pas sauvegardé ton travail – c'est ça?
– Si, si, je l'ai sauvegardé. J'étais sur le point de l'imprimer et …
– Ah oui, j'ai deviné! C'est l'imprimante qui n'a pas marché. Tu as tapé les résultats de ton sondage, mais tu n'as pas réussi à les imprimer! Mais apporte-moi ta disquette, je peux l'imprimer ici pour toi.

unité 5 Bon appétit!

Section 3

123

– Non, non, Caroline, ce n'est pas ça. Tu n'as pas compris. Écoute un instant et ne me pose plus de questions!!! ... (*silence*) ... Caroline, tu es là?
– Bien sûr, je suis là – mais tu m'as dit d'écouter, alors j'écoute!
– Bon. Alors voilà l'histoire – j'ai fait le travail, je l'ai sauvegardé, mais je ne l'ai pas transféré sur la disquette. J'étais juste sur le point de l'imprimer, lorsque César, mon chat, a sauté sur l'ordinateur, et il a effacé tout mon travail. Tout a disparu et maintenant, l'ordinateur ne marche plus.
– Ça alors, Emmanuel! Ça, c'est un vrai désastre!

READING

Text reconstruction

The text of the conversation between Emmanuel and Caroline would work very well in *Fun with Texts* using the *Text Salad* option. This option requires students to put the lines in the correct order. In other words, they are pairing up the question with the answer. Using *Fun with Texts* or *Hot Potatoes*, you could make this or other texts into cloze exercises.

Dossier-langue
The perfect tense in the negative

This explains the position of *ne* and *pas* around the auxiliary verb, but does not mention the position of *ne... pas* with an inverted auxiliary verb.

SB 74 **READING, WRITING**

2 C'est un vrai désastre!

To emphasise the standard pattern of the perfect tense in the negative, only the third person singular is used in this task. Students refer back to the telephone conversation and complete the sentences with *a* or *n'a pas*.

Stress that they will not be able just to copy from the text, which uses mainly the first and second persons, but must first understand what happened, then fill in the gaps. The answers could first be checked orally, but it would be good practice for students to write out the complete sentences.

Solution: **1** *n'a pas*, **2** *n'a pas*, **3** *a*, **4** *a*, **5** *a*, **6** *a*, **7** *n'a pas*, **8** *n'a pas*, **9** *a*, **10** *a*, **11** *n'a pas*, **12** *a*

SB 75, 3/11 **LISTENING**

3 Oui ou non?

Students listen to these short conversations which contain examples of negative statements in the perfect tense. They write *Non* if the answer is in the negative.

Soution: **1** *Non*, **3** *Non*, **4** *Non*, **6** *Non*, **7** *Non*

Oui ou non?

1 – Tu as lu ce journal?
– Je n'ai pas lu ce journal. Je ne l'aime pas beaucoup.

2 – Tu as vu ce film?
– Je l'ai vu la semaine dernière. Il est excellent.

3 – Tu as aimé le déjeuner à la cantine?
– Je n'ai pas aimé ça. Je déteste le chou-fleur.

4 – Tu as aimé ce repas?
– Je n'ai pas aimé le dessert – c'était trop sucré.

5 – Est-ce que les enfants ont aimé le pique-nique?
– Bien sûr. Ils l'ont trouvé fantastique.

6 – As-tu mangé au nouveau restaurant?
– Non, je n'ai pas fait ça.

7 – C'était bien, ton nouveau jeu électronique?
– Pas du tout. Ça n'a pas marché.

SB 75 **GRAMMAR**
WRITING

4 Hier

Students have to complete these sentences with an auxiliary verb in the negative. This can be done as a writing task, in which case the whole sentence should be written out. Similarly, if answers are checked orally, students should read out the complete sentence.

Solution: **1, 2, 3** *n'ont pas*; **4, 5, 6, 7** *n'a pas*; **8** *n'avez pas*; **9, 10** *n'avons pas*

SB 75, **SPEAKING**
WRITING

5 À toi!

This is an open-ended productive task to practise both the question form and the negative.

À discuter: Students ask each other some of the suggested questions, to which many of the answers are likely to be in the negative.

À écrire: Students write out some of the questions with their own replies.

Differentiation

The following *Au choix* activities can be used as support and extension.

Au choix SB 134 **SUPPORT**
GRAMMAR PRACTICE

6 En classe

This is a simple matching task (subject and verb), with sentences in the negative of the perfect tense.

Solution: 1d, 2a, 3e, 4b, 5g, 6c, 7f

Au choix SB 135, **EXTENSION**
SPEAKING

4 Réponds sans dire oui ou non

This is quite a demanding task, but more able students often find this kind of thing enjoyable. The student answering the question can make up any grammatically correct answer. It doesn't have to be true as long as it is a feasible answer and shows that they have understood the question.

Au choix SB SB 135, 🗣, 💻 **EXTENSION**
SPEAKING
5 Présent ou passé? **WRITING**

This is an optional task, giving further practice of questions in both present and past tenses.

a Students have to decide whether the questions are in the present or perfect tenses. It will be best to check this part of the activity orally before students go on to do part **b**.

Solution: 1 PR, 2 P, 3 PR, 4 P, 5 PR, 6 P, 7 P, 8 PR, 9 PR, 10 P

b Students ask each other four (or more) of the questions, checking that they are using the correct tense for their answers.

They could then choose to write down one or two of these questions and their own answers, adding these to their electronic phrase books.

CM 5/5 **SPEAKING**
WRITING
Présent ou passé?

For further practice of questions and answers in the perfect tense, students can do these three tasks.

1 En vacances
Having matched up the questions and answers they could read out the conversation in pairs.

Solution: 1D, 2A, 3B, 4H, 5F, 6I, 7G, 8C, 9E, 10J

2 Présent ou passé?
Students read through this conversation in a café and decide whether each sentence is in the present or the past. They could then act it out in groups of three.

Solution: 1 PR, 2 PR, 3 P, 4 P, 5 P, 6 PR, 7 P, 8 P, 9 P, 10 PR

3 Normalement et hier
This is a writing task in which students complete the sentences with a past participle.

Solution: 1 bu, 2 pris, 3 dit, 4 pris, 5 appris, 6 écrit, 7 fait, 8 vu

---

Area 6
Discussing the menu
Expressing likes and dislikes
SB 76–77, 1 – 4
Au choix SB 134, 7 , SB 136–137, 4 – 6
CD 3/12–13
CM 5/1, 5/6
FC 7–20, 66–71

FC 7–20, 66–71, CM 5/1, SB 76 **PRESENTATION**
Revision of meal vocabulary

Use flashcards or mini-flashcards to revise food and drink vocabulary. Some of the flashcard games for practising vocabulary can be played, e.g. *Effacez!*, Guess the flashcard, Flashcard *Loto* (see TB 25).

PRESENTATION
C'est un fruit, c'est un légume

Write the names of some fruit and vegetable items on the board, e.g. a randomly placed selection from the following:

un abricot	une carotte
une banane	des champignons
un citron	un chou
une fraise	un chou-fleur
une framboise	des haricots verts
un melon	une laitue
une orange	un oignon
une pêche	des petits pois
une poire	une pomme de terre
une pomme	des radis
des raisins	une tomate

These can be used for practice as follows:
- a variation on *Effacez!* where students have to rub out the word for a fruit or a vegetable, e.g. *Efface un légume. Efface deux fruits.*
- students have to give an example of a fruit or a vegetable in response to the teacher's command, e.g. *Dis-moi le nom d'un fruit/légume.*
- Hangman, using the words on the board.

SB 76 **PRESENTATION**
READING
SPEAKING
1 Les idées de menus

Check that students understand the terms *hors-d'œuvre, plat principal* etc. These menu suggestions are used in several later items.

Perhaps play some cumulative vocabulary games or even a Spelling Bee to familiarise students with the various dishes and drinks listed.

When they have had enough practice, students can go on to the *Jeu des définitions* which follows. Students could work out the answers individually or in pairs and they could be checked orally, one person reading out the definition and the other giving the answer.

Solution: 1 du melon, 2 des haricots verts, 3 du poulet, 4 des petits pois, 5 de l'eau minérale, 6 une pizza, 7 une omelette, 8 des frites

CM 5/6 **PRESENTATION**
PRACTICE
Voici le menu

This copymaster contains twelve items, some of which occur in this area and others from the next area, so it could be used now or later. The mini flashcards can be cut up for oral practice or flashcard games, or made into an OHT.

There is a vocabulary and picture matching task at the bottom of the sheet.

Solution: 1f, 2i, 3d, 4j, 5c, 6e, 7k, 8g, 9b, 10h, 11a, 12l

Au choix SB 136,   **GENERAL SPEAKING/WRITING**

4 Invente une définition

More able students could use the previous tasks as a source of vocabulary and make up their own *Jeu des définitions*. These could be set just to their partners and done orally, but also, a selection could be written down and set to another group or class.

Au choix SB 136,   **GENERAL SPEAKING/WRITING**

5 J'aime ça!

This provides more, very straightforward practice in saying which foods etc. students like or dislike. It could be done in pairs or groups or, if preferred, the answers could be prepared as a written exercise.

SB 77, 3/12,   **LISTENING SPEAKING**

2 Le menu pour ce soir

This task has the twofold aim of practising the menu items and also expressions of likes and dislikes.

a Go through the introductory paragraph with the class and make sure they know how to complete the grid. Then play the recording, first the conversation between Élise and Tiffaine, then the other between the two boys.

Solution:

Tu aimes ça?	Tiffaine	Jean-Pierre
1 le pâté	✔	✘
2 le melon	✔	✔
3 la viande	✔	✘
4 le poisson	✔	✘
5 les légumes	✔	✔
6 les fruits	✔	✔

b This task is based on the language used in the conversations. Students could be given a short time to think out their answers, perhaps with some class practice, before working in pairs, taking turns to ask and answer the questions about their own preferences.

Le menu pour ce soir

1 Élise parle à Tiffaine

– Dis-moi, Tiffaine, est-ce que tu aimes le pâté?
– Le pâté? Oui, je l'aime beaucoup.
– Très bien, et le melon?
– Oui, j'adore ça.
– Tu manges de la viande et du poisson?
– Bien sûr. J'aime bien les deux.
– Mais c'est fantastique, tu aimes tout! Tu aimes les légumes et les desserts?
– J'aime les légumes, mais pour les desserts, je n'aime pas les desserts trop sucrés. Mais j'aime tous les fruits, surtout les fraises. J'adore les fraises.

2 Marc parle à Jean-Pierre

– Tu aimes le pâté, Jean-Pierre?
– Non, je n'aime pas le pâté.
– Alors, le melon, tu aimes ça?
– Oui, j'aime beaucoup le melon.
– Est-ce que tu manges de la viande et du poisson?
– La viande? Ah non, je ne mange pas de viande. Et le poisson, je regrette, mais je ne mange pas ça – je suis végétarien.
– Qu'est-ce que tu aimes, alors?
– Les légumes, j'aime tous les légumes … euh … sauf le chou-fleur. Je déteste le chou-fleur!
– Et les desserts?
– Oui. J'aime tous les desserts et j'adore la glace et les fruits.

SB 77, 3/13   **LISTENING READING**

3 Qu'est-ce qu'on va manger?

a Students should refer to the lists of likes and dislikes, look at the *Idées de menus* and plan a suitable meal for the two guests. Several alternatives are possible.

b They can then listen to the tape to see whether they have made the same choices as Marc and Élise.

Solution: **1** du melon, **2** une omelette au fromage, **3** des frites et des haricots verts, **4** des fraises avec de la glace

Qu'est-ce qu'on va manger?

– Ben … alors qu'est-ce qu'on mange? Comme hors-d'œuvre … du pâté peut-être, avec une salade.
– Pas possible – Jean-Pierre n'aime pas le pâté.
– C'est vrai. Euh, du melon, ça va. Ils aiment ça, tous les deux.
– Oui, oui – ça, c'est facile … le plat principal maintenant. Zut! Jean-Pierre n'aime pas le poisson et il ne mange pas de viande!
– Alors qu'est-ce qu'on prépare?
– Une omelette? Ils aiment les œufs, non?
– Oui, alors une omelette … à quoi?
– Une omelette au fromage – j'adore ça avec des frites.
– Des frites … oui … et des haricots verts. Tu aimes ça, non?
– Oui, j'aime bien les haricots verts.
– Très bien. Puis … euh … comme dessert, il y a un gâteau au café.
– Non, non! Tiffaine n'aime pas les desserts sucrés, mais elle adore les fraises et Jean-Pierre aime les fruits. Alors, des fraises comme dessert, avec de la glace?
– D'accord. Des fraises avec de la glace. C'est idéal! Allons-y!

SB 77,   **SPEAKING**
                                                  WRITING

4 Les menus au choix

Students now invent their own menus and work in pairs, seeing who is first to guess what the other has chosen.

AU CHOIX SB 134   **SUPPORT**
                                         WRITING

7 Voici le menu

This is an easy task in which students complete the menu by supplying the missing vowels.

Solution: **1** *du potage,* **2** *du melon,* **3** *du poulet,*
               4 *du poisson,* **5** *des petits pois,*
               6 *des frites,* **7** *des glaces,* **8** *des yaourts,*
               9 *de l'Orangina,* **10** *de l'eau minérale*

AU CHOIX SB 137   **GENERAL**
                                         READING

6 On a mangé à la cantine

This logigram is a fun reading item.

Solution:

Marc	de la salade; du café
Claire	du steak haché; de l'orangeade
Élise	du poisson; du coca
Jean-Pierre	de l'omelette; du lait
Tiffaine	du poulet; de la limonade

                                                   PRACTICE

Menus

1 Menus on the web

Many French restaurants have their menus on the web. Find examples with a search engine such as *yahoo.fr, altavista.fr* or *google.com* (set to French). Students can then study the menu and choose the dishes they like best.

2 Make your own menu!

Make a menu for a French restaurant using *Microsoft® Word* or *Publisher*. To add a French cultural note, install a French handwriting font on the computer (see TB 20). Use borders from clip art to make the final product more professional.

Alternatively, make an illustrated *carte des glaces* or *carte des boissons*, again using fonts and clip art. You could have different pupils working on different menus. Colour printing and lamination adds a really nice touch and the completed materials can then be used as realistic props in role plays.

Area 7
Ordering meals in a restaurant
Further practice of the perfect tense

SB 78, 1–5
Au choix SB 137, 7–8
CM 5/7–5/8
CD 3/14–17

This area brings together a lot of the topics and language of the unit: eating out, using the perfect tense, expressing preferences.

SB 78   **DICTIONARY PRACTICE**

1 C'est utile, le dictionnaire

Before beginning work on the menu, students should find out the meanings of these terms, often used on restaurant menus.

CM 5/7   **DICTIONARY PRACTICE**

Comprends-tu le menu?

This copymaster is optional and could be used now or later as a homework activity or for a cover lesson. It provides a fuller range of restaurant and food vocabulary and includes dictionary work and vocabulary games.

Some might like to file the completed sheet for future holidays abroad!

Solutions:

1 Choisis un menu
    1 = B, 2 = A, 3 = B, 4 = B, 5 = B,
    6 = A, 7 = A or B, 8 = B
2 C'est quelle image?
    1a, 2f, 3e, 4d, 5b, 6c
3 Quelle est la différence?
    1aC, 1bA, 2aK, 2bE, 2cH, 3aB, 3bD,
    4aF, 4bI, 5aG, 5bJ

CM 5/8, 3/14   **LISTENING**
                                        WRITING

Au restaurant

This copymaster could be used now, to give students practice in hearing people ordering meals before they read and work on the restaurant tasks in the Student's Book, or it could be used later as revision or consolidation material.

Much of the vocabulary practised on CM 5/7 is re-used in this item.

1 Voici le menu

Before playing the recording, go through the items on the menu, reading them aloud. Students then listen to the recorded dialogues and tick or underline the items chosen from the menu.

Solution:

The following items should be ticked for each person:
1 *pâté, poulet rôti, haricots verts, glaces*
2 *crudités, escalope de veau, pommes de terre sautées, petits pois, yaourt*

Bon appétit! unité 5

Section 3

3 *assiette de charcuterie, omelette nature, pommes frites, champignons, crème caramel*
4 *(M.) escargots, côte de porc, fromage*
4 *(Mme) saumon fumé, steak-frites, haricots verts, tarte maison*

Voici le menu

1 – Je voudrais du pâté, s'il vous plaît, puis du poulet rôti et comme légumes, des haricots verts.
  – Oui, Madame. Voulez-vous un dessert?
  – Oui. Je vais prendre une glace à la vanille, s'il vous plaît.

2 – Pour commencer, je voudrais des crudités, s'il vous plaît.
  – Oui, Madame. Et comme plat principal?
  – Alors, une escalope de veau, s'il vous plaît, avec des pommes de terre sautées et des petits pois.
  – Et comme dessert?
  – Comme dessert, un yaourt, s'il vous plaît.

3 – Bonjour, Monsieur. Vous avez choisi?
  – Oui. Pour commencer, je vais prendre l'assiette de charcuterie et après, une omelette nature avec des frites et des champignons.
  – Vous voulez un dessert, Monsieur?
  – Oui, s'il vous plaît: la crème caramel.

4 – Bonjour, Monsieur, bonjour, Madame. Vous avez choisi?
  – Oui. Des escargots pour moi et du saumon fumé pour Madame.
  – Et comme plat principal?
  – Alors, une côte de porc pour moi et steak-frites pour Madame, avec des haricots verts.
  – Et comme dessert?
  – Du fromage pour moi et de la tarte maison pour Madame.

2 Le menu – un acrostiche
Solution:

```
 ¹p â t é
²m e l o n
  ³s a u m o n   f u m é
⁴o m e l e t t e   n a t u r e
⁵c ô t e   d e   p o r c
    ⁶p o u l e t   r ô t i
      ⁷j u s   d e   p o m m e
      ⁸c h o u - f l e u r
      ⁹y a o u r t
     ¹⁰t a r t e   m a i s o n
```

SB 78   **READING**

2 Le Perroquet Vert

Students first study the menu for a while, with the teacher giving information as needed and asking some oral pronunciation and comprehension questions.

SB 78, 3/15   **LISTENING, WRITING**

3 Mme Dubois

This is an easy task in which students listen to Mme Dubois stating what she ate the previous day. The items are all taken from the menu at the restaurant, so the spelling can be copied from this.

Solution: **1** *du pâté,* **2** *du poulet,* **3** *des carottes,* **4** *la mousse au chocolat,* **5** *du vin blanc*

Mme Dubois

Mme Dubois a dîné au restaurant Le Perroquet Vert.
– Hier soir, j'ai dîné au restaurant.
  C'était très bon.
  Pour commencer, j'ai pris du pâté.
  Comme plat principal, j'ai choisi du poulet.
  Comme légumes, j'ai mangé des carottes.
  Ensuite, comme dessert, j'ai choisi la mousse au chocolat.
  Avec ça, j'ai bu du vin blanc.
  Tout était délicieux.

SB 78, 3/16   **LISTENING WRITING**

4 M. Lemaître

This item is similar to the above, but students have to write the description of the meal in full and the recorded text is more difficult. They can use the same phrases as in the previous task to begin each sentence.

Suggested solution:
1 *Pour commencer, il a commandé l'assiette de charcuterie.*
2 *Comme plat principal, il a choisi le cassoulet.*
3 *Il n'a pas pris de légumes.*
4 *Comme dessert, il a pris la crème caramel.*
5 *Comme boisson, il a choisi du vin rouge.*

M. Lemaître

M. Lemaître a dîné au restaurant Le Perroquet Vert.
– Alors, chéri. Tu as bien mangé hier au Perroquet Vert?
– Oui, oui, très bien.
– Qu'est-ce que tu as pris?
– Alors, pour commencer, j'ai pris l'assiette de charcuterie.
– Ah oui, tu as toujours aimé ça.
– Puis comme plat, c'était plus difficile. Comme tu sais, j'aime bien le steak, mais finalement, j'ai choisi le plat du jour.
– C'était quoi, le plat du jour?
– C'était le cassoulet. C'était vraiment excellent.
– Tu as pris des légumes avec?
– Non, non. Je n'ai pas pris de légumes – le cassoulet était énorme!
– Tu as mangé un dessert?
– Oui, j'ai pris la crème caramel.
– Tu l'as aimée?
– Bien sûr, c'est mon dessert favori.
– Et qu'est-ce que tu as bu?

– Du vin rouge, naturellement, du vin de la région. C'était délicieux.

SB 78, 3/17, LISTENING

5 Vous avez choisi?

a Students read through the conversation in their books, then listen to the recording to find out what was ordered and note down the missing items.

Solution: **1** du pâté, **2** du poisson, **3** des pommes frites, **4** la tarte aux pommes

Vous avez choisi?

– Vous avez choisi?
– Oui. Pour commencer, je voudrais du pâté, s'il vous plaît.
– Oui, du pâté. Et comme plat principal?
– Du poisson.
– Et comme légumes?
– Comme légumes, je vais prendre des pommes frites.
– Alors, du poisson avec des pommes frites.
…
– Vous prenez un dessert?
– Oui. Comme dessert, je voudrais la tarte aux pommes, s'il vous plaît.
…
– L'addition, s'il vous plaît.
– Voilà.
– Merci, Monsieur.

b Students practise the conversation in pairs and go through it several times, changing rôles and changing the items ordered, basing their choices on the restaurant menu.

As they do this, the teacher could circulate and ask different groups some questions, e.g.

Qu'est-ce que tu as commandé?
Tu l'as aimé?
C'était bon, le pâté
As-tu préféré le plat ou le dessert?
Qu'est-ce que tu n'as pas aimé?
Qui a commandé le … etc.

Some conversations could be recorded and given to another pair of students who have to note down what has been ordered. This can then be checked with the original pair, e.g.

Tu as choisi du pâté comme hors-d'œuvre, n'est-ce pas?
Oui, c'est vrai, j'ai choisi du pâté.
Ensuite, du steak avec du chou-fleur et comme dessert, la pêche Melba?
Non, j'ai choisi du steak avec des frites.

Alternatively, students can act a sketch in a restaurant and afterwards a memory game can be played, e.g.

Qu'est-ce que (Student A) a choisi pour commencer?
Et après, qu'est-ce qu'il a choisi?
Et qu'est-ce qu'il a pris, comme boisson?
Qui a commandé une omelette?
(Student A), c'est vrai? Tu as choisi du melon? etc.

AU CHOIX SB 137, GENERAL WRITING SPEAKING

7 Les repas à conséquences

Students work in pairs to compile and write out a menu and then practise ordering it, one acting as the customer and the other as the waiter.

AU CHOIX SB 137 GENERAL READING WRITING

8 Essayez cette recette!

Students complete the recipe for *La pêche Melba* by putting the instructions in the order of the illustrations. Some might like to try out the recipe.

Solution: **1b, 2d, 3a, 4e, 5g, 6f, 7c**

> **Area 8**
> **Further activities and consolidation**
> SB 79, 80–81
> CM 5/9–5/16, 136
> CD 3/18–21
> Student CD 1/25–30, 2/15–17

CM 5/9, SCD 1/25–30 INDEPENDENT LISTENING SOUNDS AND WRITING

Écoute et parle

This copymaster provides pronunciation and speaking practice.

1 À la française

À la française

1	biscuit	5	menu
2	chocolat	6	orange
3	dessert	7	portion
4	melon	8	table

2 Et après?

Solution: **1**d, **2**f, **3**g, **4**i, **5**l, **6**p, **7**r, **8**y

Et après?

1c, 2e, 3f, 4h, 5k, 6o, 7q, 8x

3 Des phrases ridicules

Des phrases ridicules

Thierry prend du thé et parle à la télé de ses théories.

Roland le rat refuse de rendre la rose rouge.

4 Les terminaisons: -u et -ue

Solution: **1b, 2d, 3c, 4f, 5e, 6a**

unité 5 Bon appétit!

Section 3

129

Bon appétit! unité 5

Section 3

🎧 **Les terminaisons: -u et -ue**

1 connu
2 continue
3 contenu
4 voulu
5 répondu
6 barbecue

5 Vocabulaire de classe

Solution: 1 mots, 2 dans, 3 fini, 4 livre, 5 ai, 6 mon, 7 qui

🎧 **Vocabulaire de classe**

1 Changez les mots en couleur.
2 Choisis le bon mot dans la case.
3 J'ai fini.
4 Je n'ai pas mon livre.
5 J'ai gagné.
6 J'ai oublié mon cahier.
7 Trouve l'image qui correspond.

6 Des conversations

🎧 **Des conversations**

1 Au café
– Alors, qu'est-ce que tu prends?
(pause)
– Un jus d'orange, s'il te plaît.
– Tu veux manger quelque chose?
(pause)
– Oui, je voudrais un croque-monsieur.
– Et après, on prend des glaces. Tu prends quel parfum?
(pause)
– Une glace à la fraise et au chocolat pour moi.

2 On commande un repas
– Vous avez choisi?
(pause)
– Oui, pour commencer, je vais prendre du melon.
– Et comme plat principal?
(pause)
– Du poisson, s'il vous plaît, avec des petits pois et des frites.
– Vous voulez un dessert?
(pause)
– Oui. Un yaourt, s'il vous plaît.

3 Hier
– Qu'est-ce que tu as fait hier matin?
(pause)
– J'ai fait mes devoirs et puis j'ai regardé la télé.
– Et l'après-midi, tu as joué au rugby?
(pause)
– Au rugby? Non, mais j'ai joué au football.
– Et le soir, tu as surfé sur le Net?
(pause)
– Oui, un peu. Et ensuite, j'ai lu un livre.

CM 5/10, 🎧 **SCD 2/15–17 INDEPENDENT LISTENING**

Tu comprends?

Students could do any or all of the three items on this worksheet, now or later as revision.

1 Qu'est-ce qu'on commande?

Solution: 1d, 2f, 3e, 4g, 5b, 6a, 7c, 8h

🎧 **Qu'est-ce qu'on commande?**

1 – Je voudrais du coca, s'il vous plaît.
– Du coca. Très bien.
2 – De l'eau minérale? Gazeuse ou non-gazeuse?
– Gazeuse.
3 – Un sandwich, s'il vous plaît.
– Un sandwich à quoi?
– Au jambon, s'il vous plaît.
4 – Je voudrais un verre de vin avec mon repas.
– Rouge ou blanc?
– Rouge. Je préfère le vin rouge avec la viande.
5 – Une limonade s'il vous plaît.
– Une limonade, tout de suite, Mademoiselle.
6 – Qu'est-ce que tu prends?
– Un café au lait, s'il te plaît.
– Alors moi aussi, j'adore le café au lait au petit déjeuner.
7 – Tu prends une glace?
– Oui, une glace à la fraise – c'est mon parfum préféré.
8 – Je voudrais un jus de fruit, s'il vous plaît.
– Orange, pomme, citron?
– Un jus de pommes, s'il vous plaît.

2 Vous avez choisi?

Solution:

	hors-d'œuvre	plat principal	légumes	dessert
1	potage	poulet	frites	glace à la vanille
2	melon	poisson	petits pois / frites	glace au chocolat
3	pâté	omelette aux champignons	haricots verts	fruits

🎧 **Vous avez choisi?**

1 – Pour commencer, je voudrais du potage, puis comme plat, du poulet avec des frites.
– Et comme dessert?
– Comme dessert, une glace, une glace à la vanille.
2 – Moi, je vais prendre du melon, puis du poisson avec des petits pois.
– Du poisson avec des petits pois et des frites. Et comme dessert?
– Comme dessert, une glace pour moi aussi, mais au chocolat, s'il vous plaît.
3 – Comme hors-d'œuvre, je vais prendre du pâté, j'adore le pâté. Puis comme plat, je vais prendre une omelette aux champignons avec des haricots verts. Et comme dessert, des fruits, s'il vous plaît.
– Comme dessert, des fruits. Très bien, Madame.

3 Mercredi dernier

Solution: 1a, 2b, 3c, 4a, 5a, 6c, 7a, 8a, 9b, 10c

Mercredi dernier

1. – Mercredi dernier, c'était ton anniversaire, non?
   – C'est vrai.
   – Qu'est-ce que tu as fait?
   – J'ai fait beaucoup de choses.
2. – Alors le matin, j'ai reçu beaucoup de cartes avant d'aller au collège.
3. – Puis à midi, j'ai mangé un sandwich au café avec mes copains.
4. – J'ai passé l'après-midi avec mes copains et nous avons regardé des vêtements en ville.
5. – Qu'est-ce qu'on t'a offert comme cadeaux?
6. – Ma meilleure amie m'a choisi un joli sac.
7. – Mes grands-parents n'ont pas pu venir à la maison.
8. – Mais ils m'ont envoyé une carte avec de l'argent.
9. – Mes parents m'ont acheté des billets pour le concert hier soir.
10. – Comment as-tu trouvé le concert?
    – J'ai surtout aimé le chanteur.

SB 79, CM 5/11
Sommaire

A summary of the main structures and vocabulary of this unit. Students fill in gaps on the copymaster. They should check their answers against the Students' Book page.

CM 5/12 — REVISION
Rappel 5

This copymaster can be used at any point in the course for revision and consolidation. It provides revision of colours, festivals and greetings and expressions of time (past, present and future). The reading and writing tasks are self-instructional and can be used by students working individually for homework or during cover lessons.

Solution:

1 Les fêtes
A 1 *quand*, 2 *fête*, 3 *dimanche*, 4 *faire*, 5 *aimes*, 6 *dernier*, 7 *as*, 8 *cadeau*
   a *vingt*, b *offert*, c *avons*, d *c'était*, e *aime*, f *va*, g *année*, h *juillet*

B 1a, 2h, 3g, 4f, 5e, 6d, 7c, 8b

2 C'est quand?
jours: samedi, dimanche, lundi
présent: aujourd'hui, maintenant, à présent
passé: hier soir, la semaine dernière, samedi dernier
futur: demain, lundi prochain, bientôt

3 Mots croisés (les couleurs)

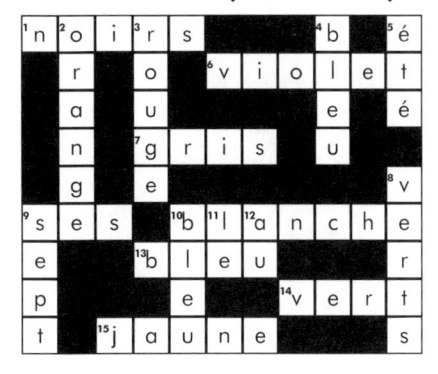

(crossword grid with answers: noirs, orange, roux, violet, bleue, gue, grise, vue, ses, blanche, bleu, vert, jaune)

Épreuve – Unité 5

These worksheets can be used for an informal test of listening, speaking, reading and writing or for extra practice, as required. For general notes on administering the *Épreuves*, see TB 16.

CM 5/13, 3/18–21 — LISTENING
Épreuve: Écouter

A Qu'est-ce qu'on boit? (NC 1)

Solution: 1b, 2f, 3d, 4g, 5c, 6a, 7e

(mark /6: 4+ shows ability to understand short statements)

Qu'est-ce qu'on boit?

1. Je voudrais une bière …
2. Pour moi, un citron pressé …
3. De l'eau minérale, s'il vous plaît …
4. Une limonade, s'il vous plaît …
5. Un café pour moi …
6. Du vin, un grand verre de vin …
7. Une menthe à l'eau, s'il vous plaît …

B Qui parle? (NC 2)

Solution: 1g, 2a, 3d, 4b, 5e, 6f, 7c

(mark /6: 4+ shows the ability to understand a range of familiar statements and questions)

Qui parle?

1. Un croque-monsieur, s'il vous plaît.
2. Vous désirez?
3. L'addition, s'il vous plaît.
4. On peut avoir de l'eau, s'il vous plaît?
5. Une glace au citron, s'il vous plaît.
6. Je n'aime pas ça!!!
7. C'est délicieux!!

C Au restaurant (NC 3)

Solution: 1 *pâté*, 2 *poulet*, 3 *pommes frites*, 4 *petits pois*, 5 *vin rouge*, 6 *eau*, 7 *banane* (both elements of **3–5** needed to score; accept incorrect spelling)

(mark /6: 4+ shows ability to understand dialogues and note main points)

Bon appétit! unité 5

🎧 Au restaurant

– Vous avez choisi?
– Pour commencer, je voudrais du pâté.
– Et comme plat principal?
– Du poulet rôti, s'il vous plaît.
– Et comme légumes?
– Des pommes frites et des petits pois.
– Et à boire?
– Du vin rouge, s'il vous plaît et de l'eau.
– Vous prenez un dessert?
– Une banane, s'il vous plaît.
– Tout de suite.

D Les plats préférés (NC 3)

Solution: 1a, 2g, 3f, 4e, 5b, 6h, 7c, 8d

(mark /7: 4+ shows the ability to understand short passages and note main points)

🎧 Les plats préférés

1 Mon plat préféré? C'est du potage.
2 Je n'aime pas le poisson. Moi, je préfère un steak garni.
3 Pour moi, mon plat préféré est les haricots verts avec du beurre.
4 Moi, je préfère le Yorkshire Pudding.
5 Moi, je préfère les gâteaux au chocolat. J'aime bien les gâteaux aux fruits aussi.
6 Moi, j'adore les omelettes.
7 Les abricots! Ça, c'est la chose que je préfère!
8 Mon plat préféré, c'est le saumon.

CM 5/14 SPEAKING

Épreuve: Parler

Students should be given the sheet up to a week before the assessment, to give them time to choose whether to do 1 or 2 and to give them time to prepare and practice both conversations – the structured one (A) and the open-ended one (B) – with their partners.

Mark scheme

Section A: mark /12: 3 marks per response
- 1 mark for an utterance/response that is clear and conveys all of the information requested, in the form of a complete phrase or sentence, though not necessarily an accurate one. The questions and answers may seem a little disjointed, like separate items rather than parts of a coherent conversation.
- 2 marks for an utterance/response that is clear and conveys all of the information requested in the form of a complete phrase or sentence, though not necessarily an accurate one. The language must flow reasonably smoothly and be recognisable as part of a coherent conversation.
- 3 marks for a clear and complete utterance/response that flows smoothly as part of a clear and coherent conversation. The language must be in complete sentences or phrases that are reasonably accurate and consistent as far as grammar, pronunciation and intonation are concerned.

Section B: mark /13: 3 marks per response, as above, +1 bonus mark for adding one or two items using the perfect tense. 19–25 shows the ability to take part in short conversations, seeking and conveying information and opinions in simple terms.

Summary:
Marks	7–13	14–18	19–25
NC Level	3	4	5

CM 5/15 READING

Épreuve: Lire

A C'est combien? (NC 1)

Solution: **1** 6,00, **2** 5,60, **3** 8,30, **4** 7,90, **5** 4,30, **6** 3,40, **7** 2,70

(mark /6: 4+ shows ability to understand single words with visual clues)

B Trouve les paires (NC 2)

Solution: 1b, 2d, 3f, 4h, 5c, 6a, 7e, 8g

(mark /7: 5+ shows the ability to understand short phrases)

C Le repas d'aujourd'hui et le repas de la semaine dernière (NC 5)

Solution: **1** *haricots verts*, **2** *carottes*, **3** *de l'eau*, **4** *cidre*, **5** *12 euros*, **6** *saumon*, **7** *steak*, **8** *petits pois*, **9** *frites*, **10** *vin*, **11** *coca*, **12** *8 euros*

(mark /12: 8+ shows understanding of a text covering present and past events; they identify main points and specific detail including opinions)

CM 5/16 WRITING

Épreuve: Écrire et grammaire

A Complète les phrases (NC 1)

Solution: **1** *écrit*, **2** *pris*, **3** *bu*, **4** *fait*, **5** *décrit*, **6** *pris*, **7** *vu*, **8** *lu*, **9** *été*

(mark out of 8: 5+ shows the ability to select appropriate words to complete short sentences)

B Ton anniversaire (NC 4)

Mark scheme
- 1 mark for each sub-task completed with a correct verb in the perfect tense

Subtotal: 6
Accuracy:
- 2 marks: most words are correct
- 1 mark: about half the words are correct
- 0 marks: fewer than half the words are correct

Subtotal: 2
(mark /8: 5+ shows the ability to write individual paragraphs of about three or four sentences)

C Une visite au Lion d'Or (NC 5)

This is an open-ended task.

Mark scheme
Communication:
- 1 mark for each accurate perfect tense (exclude the example)
- 1/2 mark for a perfect tense which is incorrect but which communicates

Subtotal: 6 (round up half marks)
Accuracy:
- 3 marks: mostly accurate
- 2 marks: about half correct
- 1 mark: more wrong than right
- 0 marks: little or nothing of merit

Subtotal: 3
(mark /9: 6+ shows ability to produce short pieces of writing in simple sentences, referring to recent experiences and giving opinions; although there may be mistakes the meaning can be understood with little or no difficulty)

SB 80–81, CM 136 **READING EXTENSION**

Presse-Jeunesse 4

These pages provide reading for pleasure. They can be used alone or with the accompanying copymaster. In this case, both the Students' Book pages and the copymaster are mostly about authors and books popular in Britain but also well-known to French children. SB 80 includes two writing activities as well as the usual texts for reading.

SB 80, CM 136

Aimez-vous lire?

Auteurs et personnages internationaux
Students read the introduction, then try to identify the people described in the quiz.

Solution: 1 *Tintin*, 2 *Babe* (the Sheep-pig), 3 *Astérix*, 4 *Charlie* (and the chocolate factory), 5 *Alice* (au Pays des Merveilles / in Wonderland), 6 *Peter Pan*, 7 *Harry Potter*, 8 *Bilbo* (the Hobbit)

Roald Dahl
Students read the article about this author, then do the task which includes the French version of popular books by Roald Dahl, Dick King-Smith and J K Rowling.

Solution:
Complétez les titres
James et la grosse pêche; Le bon gentil géant; L'énorme crocodile; Fantastique Maître Renard Le nez de la reine; Babe, le cochon devenu berger Harry Potter et le prisonnier d'Azkaban; Harry Potter et la coupe de feu

There are two copymaster activities based on this page.
Solution:
A Aimez-vous lire?

5-4-3-2-1
5 personnages littéraires mâles: *Harry Potter, Charlie, James, Babe, Maître Renard*
4 adjectifs: (any four) *célèbre, populaire, international(-aux), roux, intelligent, blanc, petit, rose* etc.
3 animaux: (any three) *un cochon, un mouton, un lapin, un renard*
2 nationalités: (any two) *français, anglais, norvégien*
1 auteur: (any one) *Roald Dahl, Dick King-Smith, J K Rowling*

B Roald Dahl
Des questions: 1 in Wales, 2 pilot, 3 adults, 4 *James and the Giant Peach*, 5 in a hut in the orchard of his house in the country, 6 his children, 7 nature, the countryside, animals, birds, 8 the illustrations

SB 81, CM 136

Harry Potter est arrivé en France!

Students read the introductory article and the letters in the Students' Book and then write the words which complete the sentences on the copymaster. The matching task is based on the last part of SB 81.

Solution:

C Harry Potter est arrivé en France!
Des phrases à compléter: 1 *mercredi 29 novembre 2000*, 2 *quatrième*, 3 *excités*, 4 *juillet*, 5 *lire*, 6 *trois*, 7 *s'appelle*, 8 *de l'humour*
Le saviez-vous?: 1e, 2c, 3f, 4d, 5b, 6a

CM 136
The copymaster also includes an acrostic which revises vocabulary connected with leisure activities.

Solution:
D Une autre activité
Les loisirs

2 vidéo
3 exposition
4 dessin
5 piscine
6 concert
7 fête
8 théâtre
9 frère
10 musique
11 boum
12 jeu

Encore Tricolore 2
nouvelle édition

unité 6   En voyage

Areas	Topics	Grammar
1	Talking about travel plans Revision of time and 24-hour clock Revision of means of transport	Using the verb *partir* (present tense)
2	Introduction to travel by train	Revison of *être* (present tense)
3	Understanding signs at a station Buying a train ticket	
4	Understanding travel information Revision of numbers 0–1000	*Il faut* + infinitive
5		Perfect tense with *être* (masculine singular)
6	Travel by air Revision of countries	Perfect tense with *être* (fem. sing. and plurals)
7	Travel by coach and boat Describing a recent day out	Perfect tense with *être* (all persons)
8		Using the perfect tense with *avoir* and *être*
9	Further activities and consolidation	

National Curriculum Information

Some students   levels 4–5+
Most students   levels 4–5
All students   levels 3–4

Revision

Rappel (CM 6/13) includes revision of the following:
- meals, food, drink
- food shops

Sounds and writing

- numbers
- pronunciation of *u* and *ou*
- the ending *-ment*

See *Écoute et parle* (CM 6/10, TB 149).

ICT opportunities

- making signs using clip art, autoshapes etc.
- planning a journey by train from the SNCF website
- text reconstruction
- using clip art to illustrate a story and using a spell checker

Reading strategies

Presse-Jeunesse 5 (SB 94–95, CM 137)

Assessment

- Informal assessment is in *Épreuves* at the end of this unit (TB 151, CM 6/14–6/17)
- Formal assessment (*Unités 1–7*) is in the *Contrôle* (TB 190, CM 139–145).

Students' Book

Unité 6 SB 82–93
Au choix SB 138–141

Flashcards

72–80 *Max à Paris*.

CDs

3/22–39
Student CD 1/31–36, 2/18–21

Additional

Grammar in Action 2, pp 8, 35–37

Copymasters

CM 6/1	*partir et sortir* [grammar]	
CM 6/2	*À la gare* [reading]	
CM 6/3	*On prend le train* [mini-flashcards]	
CM 6/4	*Max à Paris (1)* [mini-flashcards, grammar]	
CM 6/5	*Max à Paris (2)* [mini-flashcards, grammar]	
CM 6/6	*À la montagne* [grammar]	
CM 6/7	*aller et sortir* [grammar]	
CM 6/8	*Dans le passé* [grammar]	
CM 6/9	*Cartes postales des vacances* [writing]	
CM 6/10	*Écoute et parle* [independent listening]	
CM 6/11	*Tu comprends?* [independent listening]	
CM 6/12	*Sommaire* [consolidation, reference]	
CM 6/13	*Rappel* [revision]	
CM 6/14	*Épreuve: Écouter*	
CM 6/15	*Épreuve: Parler*	
CM 6/16	*Épreuve: Lire*	
CM 6/17	*Épreuve: Écrire et grammaire*	
CM 137	*Presse-Jeunesse 5* [reading]	
CM 151–152	*Chantez! Paris-Genève* [song]	

Language content

Travel plans (Area 1)

Tu pars à quelle heure, le matin?
Moi, le matin, je pars à …

Rail travel (Areas 2–4)

Pardon, Monsieur/Madame, …
Le train pour Paris part à quelle heure?
Le train pour Rouen part de quel quai?
Où est …, s'il vous plaît?
un billet
la salle d'attente
la consigne
le quai
le buffet
le bureau de renseignements
composter votre billet
la gare
le guichet
fumeurs/non-fumeurs
le kiosque
une réservation
les toilettes (f pl)
la voie
trains au départ
arrivées (f pl)
tableau des horaires (m)
un aller simple pour Bordeaux
un aller-retour pour La Rochelle
Cette place est occupée?
Oui, elle est occupée.
Non, c'est libre.

Using *il faut* (Area 4)

Il faut composter son billet avant de monter dans le train.
Il ne faut pas mettre les pieds sur les bancs.

Verbs with *être* (Area 5)

monter
descendre
tomber
rester
venir
aller
sortir
entrer
mourir
naître
arriver
partir
retourner

Other travel expressions (Areas 6–7)

à l'heure
de bonne heure
en retard
l'aéroport
un avion
le vol
l'autoroute
à bord

Useful websites

Travel information

www.sncf.fr – French railways (SNCF) – this site gives details about train journeys, e.g. routes, timetables, fares and special offers.
www.airfrance.fr – this gives details of Air France flights, fares and special offers.

The Channel tunnel

Eurotunnel and le shuttle – **www.eurotunnel.fr**
Eurostar – **www.eurostar.com**

Cross-Channel ferries

Seafrance – **www.seafrance.fr**
P & O Stena – **www.posl.fr** and **www.posl.com**
Brittany Ferries – **www.brittany-ferries.fr**

Eiffel Tower

www.tour-eiffel.fr – this site has a lot of interesting information about the Eiffel Tower including statistics, history, practical information and even an online quiz.

Le Stade de France

www.stadefrance.com – this gives general information and statistics about the stadium.

En voyage unité 6

Area 1
Talking about travel plans
Using the verb *partir* (present tense)
Revision of time and 24 hour clock
Revision of means of transport

SB 82, ■-■
Au choix SB 138, ■, SB 139, ■
CD 3/22–23
CM 6/1
Grammar in Action 2, page 8

SB 82, 🎧 3/22 PRESENTATION / LISTENING / READING

■ On part bientôt

This presents the main characters who feature in this unit. Students should read and listen to the text then answer the questions about each group (task 2). By listening to the recording, students will hear all parts of the verb *partir* (present tense). Remind them that the *-t* at the end of a word is rarely pronounced in French.

🎧 **On part bientôt**

Pierre
– Je pars à Paris pour le week-end avec ma sœur, Sophie, et deux amis, Martin et Émilie. Nous allons prendre le train. À Paris, je veux voir la Tour Eiffel, bien sûr, et ma sœur veut faire une promenade en bateau sur la Seine.
– Vous partez quand?
– Nous partons samedi matin.

Lucie
Lucie part au Canada avec le club de sports. On va prendre l'avion de Paris à Montréal.
– Tu pars quand, Lucie?
– Je pars dimanche après-midi. Le voyage en avion est assez long – six heures – mais je vais prendre un bon livre pour le voyage.

Claire et André
– Mon frère et moi, nous partons en Angleterre avec notre collège. Nous allons à Canterbury dans le Kent. Nous allons prendre le car et le bateau. Nous allons loger chez des familles anglaises. J'espère qu'on va me comprendre.
– Vous partez quand?
– Nous partons lundi prochain, vers sept heures du matin.

SB 82 PRACTICE

■ Où, quand et comment?

This completion task includes parts of the verb *partir* and tests comprehension of the previous item.

Solution:
a **1** à Paris, **2** à Montréal, **3** à Canterbury
b **1** samedi matin, **2** dimanche après-midi, **3** lundi prochain (vers sept heures)
c **1** le train, **2** l'avion, **3** le car et le bateau

SB 82 GRAMMAR

Dossier-langue
partir (to leave)

This presents the present tense of *partir*. The verbs *sortir* and *dormir* could also be mentioned at this point (they are covered in *Unités 7–8*).

Time and 24-hour clock

As times feature extensively in this unit, it would be a good idea to revise the time at various points. Revise some times for morning departure by asking a few students when they leave home in the morning and writing the times on the board, e.g.

Moi, le matin, je pars à sept heures et demie pour aller au collège? Write 7h30 on board.
(Student A), *tu pars avant huit heures du matin? Non?*
À quelle heure pars-tu environ? Vers 8h15, 8h30 etc.?

Use the times for a game of *Effacez!* later.

SB 82, 🎧 3/23 LISTENING

■ Pour aller au collège

Students listen to the conversations and note down times and means of transport.

Solution:

1a 7h30, **b** en bus **2a** 8h15, **b** à pied
3a 7h45, **b** en voiture **4a** 8h00, **b** en train
5a 7h40, **b** à vélo **6a** 7h30, **b** en bus

🎧 **Pour aller au collège**

1 – Tu pars à quelle heure, le matin, pour aller au collège?
– Normalement, je pars à sept heures et demie.
– Et tu pars en voiture?
– Non, je vais au collège en bus.

2 – Et vous deux, vous partez tôt, le matin?
– Non, nous habitons tout près du collège, alors nous partons au dernier moment, vers huit heures et quart.
– Et vous allez au collège à pied, je suppose.
– Oui, c'est ça. Nous y allons à pied.

3 – Et Hasan, quand est-ce qu'il part, le matin?
– Hasan part à huit heures moins le quart.
– Comment va-t-il au collège?
– Il va au collège en voiture avec sa sœur.

4 – Et Dominique et Marc, quand est-ce qu'ils partent, le matin?
– Ils partent vers huit heures.
– Et comment vont-ils au collège?
– Ils vont au collège en train.

5 – Magali, quand est-ce qu'elle part, le matin?
– Normalement, elle part à huit heures moins vingt.
– Est-ce qu'elle prend le train aussi?
– Non, elle va au collège à vélo.

6 – Et Mélanie et Tiffaine, quand est-ce qu'elles partent, le matin?
– Elles partent à sept heures et demie.
– Comment vont-elles au collège?
– Elles vont au collège en bus.

Au choix SB 138 **SUPPORT**
READING/WRITING

1 Tu pars?

Students complete sentences with the correct part of *partir* (the pronoun is always supplied).

Solution: 1 *tu pars*, 2 *Je pars*, 3 *Il part*, 4 *Vous partez*, 5 *Nous partons*, 6 *Ils partent*

Au choix SB 139 **EXTENSION**
READING/WRITING

1 Des questions et des réponses

In this task, students complete questions, then replies and match them up.

Solution: 1 *tu pars*, b *Je pars*; 2 *vous partez*, c *nous partons*; 3 *les garçons partent*, e *Ils partent*; 4 *Le bus part*, d *Le bus part*; 5 *N. et S. partent*, a *Elles partent*

SB 82, **SPEAKING**
WRITING

4 À toi!

Students take it in turns to ask and answer questions about travel. More able students could use some of the questions as part of a class survey, e.g. to find out at what time people leave for school in the mornings, who leaves the first and who the last.

Students then write their own replies to the questions.

CM 6/1 **GRAMMAR PRACTICE**

partir et sortir

Some teachers might like to teach and practise *sortir* briefly at this point, although it is covered more extensively in *Unité 8*. Both *sortir* and *partir* are practised on this copymaster.

1 Les verbes

Students complete verb tables for *partir* and *sortir*. They could check their answer with *Les verbes* (SB 160) before continuing with the other tasks.

2 Le samedi

Students complete the text with the appropriate part of the verb. The initial letter shows which verb is to be used.

Solution: 1 *sors*, 2 *sortons*, 3 *partons*, 4 *sort*, 5 *part*, 6 *partons*, 7 *sors*, 8 *Pars-tu*

3 Les vacances

Solution: 1 *pars*, 2 *partons*, 3 *sors*, 4 *part*, 5 *part*, 6 *sort*, 7 *pars*, 8 *partent*

4 Et toi?

Students write their own sentences.

5 Vrai ou faux?

Students invent four *vrai ou faux?* sentences.

Grammar in Action 2, page 8 **GRAMMAR PRACTICE**

Using the verb *partir*

This provides further practice of the present tense of *partir*.

> **Area 2**
> **Revision of *être* (present tense)**
> **Introduction to travel by train**
> SB 83, 5–7, SB 84, 1–2
> CD 3/24–25

SB 83, 🎧 3/24 **PRESENTATION**
LISTENING
READING

5 À la gare

The three sections can be worked on individually and then students can listen to the complete text.

Explain *en retard*, *guichet*, *aller-retour* and the practice of validating tickets (the machine stamps the date and time on them) before boarding the train.

🎧 **À la gare**

Sous l'horloge

Il est dix heures moins le quart. Pierre et Sophie sont à la gare. Ils attendent Martin et Émilie.

P Où sont-ils, enfin?
S Ah, voilà Émilie.
É Salut. Excusez-moi, je suis un peu en retard. Ça fait longtemps que vous êtes là?
S Non, ça va, mais Martin n'est pas encore là.
P Tiens, il arrive.
M Salut à tous. Excusez-moi, j'ai acheté un magazine au kiosque. Vous attendez depuis longtemps?
P Mais non, tu es un peu en retard, comme toujours, mais ça ne fait rien! Nous sommes tous là maintenant, alors, allons acheter des billets.
É Où est le guichet?
P Il est là-bas.

Au guichet

P Quatre aller-retours pour Paris, s'il vous plaît.
• Voilà, 40 euros.
P Voilà, Monsieur. Merci.
S Le prochain train pour Paris part à quelle heure?
• À 10h15.
S Bon, merci.

Devant le tableau des horaires

M C'est quel quai?
É Je ne sais pas. Il faut regarder le tableau.
M Voilà notre train. C'est quai numéro cinq.
P Il faut composter les billets avant de prendre le train.
S Où est la machine à composter?
P Elle est là-bas.
É C'est bien. Alors, allons sur le quai maintenant.
• Attention, attention. Le train de 10h15 à destination de Paris arrive en gare.

SB 83 READING

6 Ça, c'est faux!

Students correct the false statements. Able students could be encouraged to make up some additional true/false statements for a class or group activity.

Solution:
1 Pierre et <u>Sophie</u> sont à la gare avant les autres.
2 <u>Émilie</u> est un peu en retard.
3 Les amis achètent des billets au <u>guichet</u>.
4 ... part à <u>dix</u> heures quinze.
5 ... c'est quai numéro <u>cinq</u>.
6 ... il faut <u>composter</u> les billets.
7 ... dans une machine à <u>composter</u>.

SB 83

Dossier-langue
Rappel: être (present tense)

Ask some questions or make statements using être and ask students to identify the part of être used and to write it on the board. Build up the complete paradigm of être in this way, e.g.

Qui est votre prof d'anglais?
Vous êtes en quelle salle pour les cours de maths?
(yawning) *Moi, je suis très fatigué(e).*
Tu es fatigué(e), (Student A)?

Students should then copy and complete the paradigm of être.

SB 83, SPEAKING
WRITING

7 Des conversations

This gives practice in using different parts of the present tense of être. Students could write out the missing parts of être, or the full conversations and then practise these in pairs.

Solution: 1 *Tu es,* 2 *je suis,* 3 *es-tu,* 4 *Je suis,*
5 *est-il,* 6 *Il est,* 7 *le train est,* 8 *il est,*
9 *êtes-vous,* 10 *Nous sommes,*
11 *Charlotte et Luc sont,* 12 *ils sont*

SB 84, 🎧 **3/25** LISTENING

1 Au bureau des renseignements

Students listen to the conversations and note down the departure time and platform number for each train.

Solution: 1 *14h50, quai 3,* 2 *12h25, quai 5,*
3 *17h06, quai 9,* 4 *19h28, quai 11,*
5 *14h00, quai 6,* 6 *10h30, quai 1*

🎧 **Au bureau des renseignements**

1 – Oui, Madame?
– Le train pour Lille part à quelle heure, s'il vous plaît?
– Lille? 14h50, Madame.
– Et c'est quel quai?
– Quai numéro 3, Madame.
– Alors, c'est 14h50 du quai 3. Merci, Monsieur.

2 – Monsieur?
– Le prochain train pour Grenoble part à quelle heure, s'il vous plaît?
– Le prochain train part à 12h25, du quai numéro 5.
– Alors, c'est 12h25 du quai 5. Merci.

3 – Mademoiselle?
– Je vais à Calais. Le prochain train part à quelle heure, s'il vous plaît?
– Vous avez un train à 17h06.
– Et le train part de quel quai?
– Quai numéro 9.
– Alors, c'est 17h06 du quai 9. Merci.

4 – Oui?
– Le prochain train pour La Rochelle part à quelle heure, s'il vous plaît?
– Pour La Rochelle? C'est à 19h28.
– Et c'est quel quai?
– Quai numéro 11.
– Bon alors, c'est à 19h28 du quai 11, c'est ça?
– Oui, voilà.

5 – Madame?
– Je vais à Strasbourg. Le prochain train part à quelle heure, s'il vous plaît?
– À 14h00, Madame.
– Est-ce que c'est direct?
– Oui, c'est direct.
– Et le train part de quel quai, s'il vous plaît?
– Quai numéro 6.
– Alors, le train pour Strasbourg part à 14h00 du quai 6. Merci, Monsieur.

6 – Monsieur?
– Le prochain train pour Toulouse part à quelle heure, s'il vous plaît?
– À 10h30.
– Est-ce que c'est direct?
– Oui, c'est direct.
– Et le train part de quel quai, s'il vous plaît?
– Quai numéro 1.
– Alors, pour Toulouse, c'est 10h30 du quai numéro 1.
– Oui, c'est ça.

SB 84, SB 140 SPEAKING

2 Complète l'horaire

This is an information-gap activity in which students ask each other about departure and platform details.

SPEAKING

Class discussion – travelling by train

At some point it would be useful to ask whether anyone in the class has travelled by train in France.

Il y a quelqu'un qui a voyagé en train en France?

Où as-tu pris le train?

Est-ce qu'il y a quelqu'un qui a pris l'Eurostar, de Londres à Paris?

Later in the unit the discussion could be continued with practice of the perfect tense with être, e.g.

Où es-tu allé?

Est-ce que le train est arrivé à l'heure/en retard? etc.

Area 3
Understanding signs at a station
Buying a train ticket
SB 84, **3**-**4**
Au choix SB 138, **2**, SB 139, **2**
CD 3/26
CM 6/2

SB 84, 🖥 **PRESENTATION**

3 Un plan de la gare

Use the station plan to present the names of the different places in a large station, e.g.

Dans une gare principale, il y a un bureau des renseignements, une salle d'attente, un kiosque (pour acheter des journaux et des magazines), une consigne (pour laisser ses bagages), un buffet (pour acheter des boissons et des sandwichs) et un guichet (pour acheter des billets).

Write these words on the board for a game of *Effacez!* at the end of the lesson.

Then read out the name of one of the places shown and ask students to give you the appropriate letter (revising the French alphabet first if necessary), e.g.

Teacher: *Le kiosque.*
Student: *F.*

Later expand this to a question:

Teacher: *Où est le téléphone?*
Student: *D.*

This could also be played as a team game, or form the basis of an ICT activity using *Fun with Texts*.

The places shown are as follows:

A *entrée/sortie*
B *les toilettes pour hommes*
C *les toilettes pour dames*
D *le téléphone*
E *l'horaire/le tableau des horaires*
F *le kiosque*
G *le bureau des renseignements*
H *le guichet*
I *les réservations*
J *la consigne automatique*
K *la consigne (des bagages)*
L *la salle d'attente*
M *le buffet*
N *le restaurant*
O *la machine à composter/le composteur*
P *l'entrée aux quais*

Then ask a few questions, revising *pouvoir*:
Est-ce qu'on peut acheter des billets au kiosque?
Est-ce qu'on peut laisser ses bagages au guichet?
Est-ce qu'on peut acheter un journal au kiosque?
Est-ce qu'on peut manger au buffet?
Où est-ce qu'on peut demander des renseignements?
Où est-ce qu'on peut acheter un sandwich?

Then students can do the task below the plan in which they match the two halves of each sentence and read the answer.

Solution: 1g, 2h, 3d/e, 4e/d, 5b, 6a, 7c, 8f

SB 84, 🎧 **3/26** **LISTENING**

4 Qu'est-ce qu'on cherche?

a Students listen to the recording and match up the place requested with the correct symbol. Check that students understand the symbols on SB 84 and mention that they are not all needed for the listening task. The dialogues include the prepositions *à côté de, en face de, tout près de* and *au fond de*, which could also be revised at this point.

Solution: 1e, 2h, 3a, 4b, 5c, 6f

🎧 **Qu'est-ce qu'on cherche?**

1 – *Où est la salle d'attente, s'il vous plaît?*
  – *La salle d'attente est à côté du buffet, Monsieur.*

2 – *Où est le bureau des renseignements, s'il vous plaît?*
  – *Le bureau des renseignements? En face du guichet, Madame.*

3 – *Où est la consigne, s'il vous plaît, Monsieur?*
  – *C'est derrière le bureau des renseignements, Mademoiselle.*

4 – *Où est le buffet, s'il vous plaît?*
  – *Le buffet est tout près du restaurant.*

5 – *Pardon, Madame, où est le guichet, s'il vous plaît?*
  – *Le guichet est à côté de la salle d'attente.*

6 – *Où sont les toilettes, s'il vous plaît?*
  – *Les toilettes sont au fond du restaurant.*

b This task provides further practice of the vocabulary associated with stations and station signs. Before doing this, you could say each of the following sentences and ask students to imagine what you are going to say next.

1 Je voudrais manger un sandwich.
  (e.g. *Où est le buffet, s'il vous plaît?*)
2 Je voudrais acheter un billet.
3 Je voudrais laisser ma valise.
4 Je voudrais acheter un livre.
5 J'ai encore une demi-heure à attendre.
6 Je voudrais prendre un café.
7 Je voudrais demander des renseignements.
8 Je voudrais acheter un journal.

More able students could practise giving answers by referring to the plan and using *à côté de, près de* etc.

Solution:

a *Où est la consigne, s'il vous plaît?*
b *Où est le buffet, s'il vous plaît?*
c *Où est le guichet, s'il vous plaît?*
d *Où est le kiosque, s'il vous plaît?*
e *Où est la salle d'attente, s'il vous plaît?*
f *Où sont les toilettes, s'il vous plaît?*
g *Où sont les téléphones, s'il vous plaît?*
h *Où est le bureau des renseignements, s'il vous plaît?*

Differentiation

The following *Au choix* activities can be used as support and extension.

AU CHOIX SB 138 — SUPPORT WRITING

2 Une liste de vocabulaire

Students supply the vowels to complete a list of station vocabulary with the English translations.

Solution: 1 la gare, 2 le quai, 3 le guichet, 4 le billet, 5 l'horaire, 6 la consigne, 7 le départ, 8 le kiosque

AU CHOIX SB 139 — EXTENSION READING

2 Suivez le panneau!

This task provides revision of *vouloir* and practice in recognising station signs.

Solution: 1b, 2f, 3d, 4c, 5a, 6e

CM 6/2 — PRACTICE

À la gare

This provides further receptive practice in recognising station signs and can be used here or later for revision. Teach *la voie* (meaning railway track), which is often used instead of *quai*, *une couchette* and *SNCF* (*Société Nationale des Chemins de Fer Français* – the French Railways).

Solution:
1 **Voyager en train**
   1c, 2b, 3a, 4c, 5b, 6b, 7a, 8b
2 **Questions et réponses**
   1d, 2g, 3e, 4c, 5f, 6b, 7a

— PRACTICE

Signs

For further practice with signs, the teacher or students could make signs using clip art, autoshapes and whatever facilities are available in the word-processing or publishing program used, e.g. *Microsoft® Word* or *Publisher*. *PowerPoint* is also quite an effective program for this. Use French handwriting fonts to add cultural authenticity. The signs could be used for matching tasks, for display in the classroom or for props/scenery for role-playing activities.

Area 4
Buying a train ticket
Understanding travel information
***Il faut* + infinitive**
Revision of numbers 0–1000

SB 85, **5**–**8**
Au choix SB 140, **1**
CD 3/27–28
CM 6/3

Note: much of the language taught in this area applies to any form of public transport.

Numbers 0–1000 — REVISION

As numbers (for prices, times etc.) are an important feature of this unit, revise numbers 0–1000, using any suitable number games (see TB 25).

SB 85, 🎧 3/27 — LISTENING

5 Au guichet

Students listen to the recording and match up the correct ticket with each traveller.

Solution: 1d, 2e, 3a, 4c, 5b

4 × 8 × 3

🎧 **Au guichet**

1 – Bonjour, Monsieur. Un aller simple pour Tours, deuxième classe, s'il vous plaît.
 – Voilà, ça fait 25 euros.
 – Merci, Monsieur. C'est quel quai, s'il vous plaît?
 – Voyons. Tours – quai numéro 4.

2 – Bordeaux, s'il vous plaît, Monsieur.
 – Aller simple ou aller-retour?
 – Aller simple, deuxième classe, s'il vous plaît.
 – 50 euros, Monsieur.
 – Merci, Monsieur.

3 – Un aller-retour pour La Rochelle, s'il vous plaît.
 – Deuxième classe?
 – Oui, deuxième classe.
 – 80 euros, Mademoiselle.
 – Merci, Monsieur. Le train part à quelle heure?
 – Le train pour La Rochelle part à huit heures, quai numéro 8.

4 – Un aller-retour pour Avignon, s'il vous plaît.
 – Deuxième classe?
 – Oui.
 – Voilà. 115 euros, Monsieur.
 – Le train part à quelle heure, s'il vous plaît, Monsieur?
 – Avignon – oui, vous avez un train à 8h15.
 – Merci, Monsieur.

5 – Un aller simple pour Grenoble, première classe, s'il vous plaît.
 – 75 euros.
 – Merci, Monsieur. Il y a un train à quelle heure, s'il vous plaît?
 – Vous avez un train à 8h44, quai numéro 3.
 – Merci, Monsieur.

SB 85, — SPEAKING

6 Inventez des conversations

Students read this dialogue at a ticket office, then practise similar conversations.

SB 85, 🎧 3/28 **LISTENING**

7 Dans le train

Students listen to the recording and follow the text, choosing the correct alternative where indicated.

Solution: 1b, 2a, 3b, 4a, 5a

🎧 **Dans le train**
- **S** Il y a du monde, hein?
- **M** Oui, il y a du monde et nous n'avons pas réservé de places.
- **S** Cherchons un compartiment non-fumeurs.
- **M** Voilà. Il y a des places ici, mais il n'y a pas quatre places ensemble.
- **P** Excusez-moi, Madame, cette place est occupée?
- **W** Non, c'est libre.
- **É** Bon, Pierre, nous pouvons nous mettre là. Tu préfères la fenêtre ou le couloir?
- **P** La fenêtre.
- **É** D'accord. Il y a de la place pour nos bagages là-bas.

SB 85

8 Au contraire

This provides practice of more vocabulary for travelling by public transport.

Solution: 1c, 2g, 3f, 4b, 5a, 6h, 7e, 8d

SB 85

Dossier-langue
il faut, il ne faut pas

This explains the use of *il faut* and *il ne faut pas* + infinitive, with the emphasis on understanding rather than active use. Some other examples, relating perhaps to school life, could be given e.g.
Au collège, il faut porter un uniforme scolaire, il faut arriver à …, le matin etc.

Au choix SB 140 **GENERAL READING/WRITING**

1 Qu'est-ce qu'il faut faire?

Students choose *il faut* or *il ne faut pas* to complete sentences about travel.

Solution: 1 *il faut*, 2 *il faut*, 3 *il faut*, 4 *il ne faut pas*, 5 *il faut*, 6 *il faut*, 7a *il ne faut pas*, 7b *il faut*, 8a *il faut*, 8b *il ne faut pas*

PRACTICE

Students could look at the SNCF website (see TB 135) and plan a journey by train from Paris, finding out details of cost, departure and arrival times etc.

CM 6/3, 🗣 **READING WRITING SPEAKING**

On prend le train

This provides further practice of travelling by train, if required.

Solution:
1 **À la gare**
   1e, 2b, 3a, 4c

2 **Les billets**
   1d, 2f, 3g, 4c, 5a

3 **Un lexique à faire**
1 C'est combien?   How much is it?
2 Est-ce qu'il faut payer   Do you have to pay
   un supplément?   a supplement?
3 C'est quel quai?   Which platform is it?
4 Le prochain train   What time is the
   pour Paris part à   next train to Paris?
   quelle heure?
5 C'est direct?   Is it direct?
6 Est-ce qu'il faut   Do you have to change?
   changer?
7 Il arrive à quelle   What time does it arrive?
   heure?
8 Cette place est libre?   Is this seat free/available?

4 **Invente la conversation**
Students invent a conversation in pairs.

Area 5
Perfect tense with *être* (masc. sing.)
SB 86–87, **1**–**5**
Au choix SB 140, **2**
CD 3/29
CM 6/4–6/6
FC 72–80

FC 72–80, SB 86 **PRESENTATION**

Perfect tense with *être*

Use the flashcards to present the sequence of Max at the Eiffel tower. There are only nine flashcards, but ten pictures in the Student's Book. For number 5 in the sequence (*L'ascenseur est monté lentement.*) use the previous flashcard and move it upwards to show *monter*.

1 **(FC 72)** *Max est parti de son hôtel à 9 heures.*
2 **(FC 73)** *Il est allé à la Tour Eiffel en bus.*
3 **(FC 74)** *Il est monté au deuxième étage par l'escalier.*
4 **(FC 75)** *Puis il est entré dans l'ascenseur.*
5   *L'ascenseur est monté lentement.*
6 **(FC 76)** *Enfin, il est arrivé au troisième étage.*
7 **(FC 77)** *Max est resté un bon moment au sommet.*
8 **(FC 78)** *Soudain, son livre est tombé du sommet.*
9 **(FC 79)** *Max est descendu par l'ascenseur.*
10 **(FC 80)** *Il est sorti de l'ascenseur. Voilà son livre.*

Write some of the captions on the board or use an OHT of CM 6/5.

unité 6 En voyage

Section 3

141

Ask students to find the verbs and underline them. Ask which tense they are in. Then ask students what they notice about the auxiliary verb and encourage them to deduce that this time *être* is used rather than *avoir*.

Give plenty of practice of using the *il* form of the verb. Ask them to repeat the sentences which describe Max's trip.

Play some flashcard games, such as Guess the back of the flashcard (see TB 26). For another game, show the first flashcard and say the first sentence, then get one student at a time to come out and select the next card in the sequence, saying what the caption is. If it is correct, they join a line, eventually showing the sequence in order. Students could also play a similar game in which a student comes out and selects (or, for the more able, turns over) any of the cards and says the correct caption for it. If they can't do it, or get it wrong, they must ask someone else. The person who gets it right stands out in front, showing the card, and the game continues until all the cards are being shown, but in random order. Students now put the card-holders in the right order, again by saying the captions in order, one at a time.

For further practice, students could select a card and make any one of the statements about it, with the others saying whether they are *vrai* or *faux*. Eventually a lot of students should be able to re-tell the story, with visual prompts only, as necessary.

CM 6/4–6/5 PRESENTATION
PRACTICE

Max à Paris

These two worksheets can be used to make an OHT of the pictures and/or the captions.

CM 6/4 contains the ten pictures and a small version of the captions in random order. The worksheet can be used as a matching task, where students copy the correct caption under each picture. The pictures can also be cut up without the captions for various practice activities (see TB 26).

CM 6/5 contains the captions in a larger typesize and can be used to make an OHT for various oral activities, e.g. students have to guess the correct sentence when key words are blanked out, sentences put on backwards or upside down etc.

Alternatively, students could work in pairs to cut the sentences into strips, jumble them up, then put them in the correct order etc.

SB 86 READING

1 Max à Paris

Students match the captions to the pictures.

Solution: 1c, 2e, 3g, 4j, 5b, 6f, 7i, 8a, 9h, 10d

SB 86

Dossier-langue
The perfect tense with *être*

This presents the thirteen verbs which use *être* in the perfect tense.

Ask students to look at the past participles and find the three which are irregular (*venu, né, mort*).

From this point on, the teacher could ask different students at odd points in the lesson to say a verb which takes *être* in the perfect and write it on the board.

SB 87 READING

2 Trouve les paires

Read the sentences aloud first and check that students understand *Napoléon est né* and *il est mort*. Students can then match up the pairs of sentences which are opposite in meaning.

Solution: 1b, 2c, 3f, 4e, 5d, 6a

SB 87, READING

3 Un jeu de calcul

a Students complete the sentences then answer the questions.

Solution:

1 *Il est sorti de la maison à 10 heures.*
2 *Il est allé à la gare à vélo.*
3 *Le train est entré en gare.*
4 *Kévin est monté dans le train.*
5 *Le train est parti à 10h40.*
6 *Vingt minutes après, le train est tombé en panne.*
7 *Kévin est resté dans le train pendant trente minutes.*
8 *Une heure plus tard, le train est arrivé à la gare de Saint-Julien.*
9 *Kévin est descendu du train.*
10 *Il est arrivé au stade trente minutes après.*

b Students answer questions in French.

Solution: 1 *Kévin est arrivé au stade à une heure.*
2 *Oui.* 3 *Le voyage a duré trois heures.*

Use a program such as *Fun with Texts* to reconstruct the text of *Un jeu de calcul*.

SB 87, 3/29 LISTENING/READING

4 La vie est facile avec un robot!

Students complete the captions. There are several possibilities, so accept any reasonable choice. Students can then listen to the recording to hear one correct version.

Solution: 1 *est arrivé*, 2 *est sorti, est rentré*,
3 *est allé*, 4 *est monté*, 5 *est descendu*
6 *est tombé*, 7 *est revenu, est entré*,
8 *est parti*

La vie est facile avec un robot!

Quand Dani est arrivé à la maison, vendredi dernier, il a trouvé ses parents très fatigués.

– Nous sommes très fatigués. Peux-tu faire le ménage?

Samedi matin, Dani est sorti très tôt. Après une heure, il est rentré avec un gros paquet. Puis il est allé chez un ami.

– Ce robot va faire tout le ménage pour vous.

Dani a donné le robot à ses parents.

D'abord, le robot est monté dans les chambres pour faire les lits.

Puis il est descendu à la cuisine pour chercher l'aspirateur.

Un livre est tombé par terre. Le robot a passé l'aspirateur partout.

Dani est revenu à six heures et il est entré dans le salon. Quelle horreur!

Lundi matin, Dani est parti très tôt, mais cette fois avec le robot.

SB 87, SPEAKING

5 Trois questions

This is an information gap activity: one student reads the instructions for *Personne A*, chooses a character from those given and replies accordingly; the other asks three questions and then identifies the character who matches the answers.

Au choix SB 140 GENERAL READING

2 Au grand magasin

This task involves putting sentences in the correct order, according to the time and a bit of deduction.

Solution: 1c, 2g, 3d, 4i, 5a, 6e, 7j, 8b, 9h, 10f

CM 6/6 PRACTICE

À la montagne

This practises the perfect tense with *être*.

1 Cédric à la montagne

Students have to write in the correct form of the perfect tense for each caption (**A**), find the corresponding picture (**B**) and finally write an account of the day in the first person (**C**).

Solution:
A 1 *est parti,* **2** *est monté,* **3** *est arrivé,* **4** *est tombé,* **5** *est descendu,* **6** *est entré,* **7** *est sorti,* **8** *est rentré*

B 1e, 2c, 3b, 4d, 5g, 6a, 7h, 8f

2 Les mots mêlés

This is a word search based on the thirteen verbs which take *être*, (*naître* and *mourir* are given in the list). The complete list should be completed with the missing verbs and their past participles.

By now the class should be really familiar with most of these verbs. Stress the need to learn them by heart.

Solution:

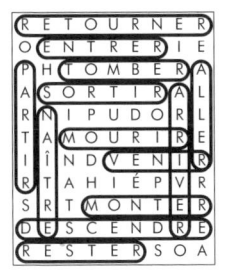

	anglais infinitif	français infinitif	participe passé
	to arrive	arriver	arrivé
	to leave	partir	parti
	to come	venir	venu
	to go	aller	allé
	to enter	entrer	entré
	to go out	sortir	sorti
	to go up	monter	monté
	to do down	descendre	descendu
	to be born	naître	né
	to die	mourir	mort
	to stay	rester	resté
	to fall	tomber	tombé
	to return	retourner	retourné

Area 6
Perfect tense with *être* (fem. sing. and plurals)
Travel by air
Revision of countries
SB 88–89, **1**–**5**
Au choix SB 138, **3**–**4**, SB 139, **3**
Au choix SB 140, **3**
CD 3/30
CM 6/7
Grammar in Action 2, pages 35–37

SB 88, 3/30 LISTENING READING

1 Martin et Émilie

This contrasts the third person masculine and feminine forms. Point out that although the spelling of the past participle is different, it sounds the same.

Solution: Martin: 1a, 2c, 3c, 4c, 5a
Émilie: 1c, 2a, 3a, 4b, 5c

Martin et Émilie
A Martin
– Qu'est-ce que tu as fait, samedi dernier?
– Bon, alors, le matin, j'étais fatigué et je suis resté au lit.
– Mais tu es sorti plus tard, non?
– Oui, je suis sorti à trois heures et demie.
– Où es-tu allé?
– Je suis allé chez un ami qui habite tout près.
– Tu es resté là-bas longtemps?
– Oui, assez longtemps. J'y suis resté trois heures environ.
– Et comment es-tu rentré?
– Je suis rentré à vélo.

B Émilie
– Et toi, Émilie, qu'est-ce que tu as fait?
– Bon, alors, le matin, je suis restée à la maison. J'ai fait mes devoirs.
– Mais tu es sortie plus tard, non?
– Oui, je suis sortie à deux heures.
– Où es-tu allée?
– Je suis allée à la patinoire. J'adore ça.

En voyage unité 6

Section 3

– Tu es restée là-bas longtemps?
– Hmm, non, pas très longtemps. Je suis restée deux heures environ.
– Et comment es-tu rentrée?
– Je suis rentrée en bus.

SB 88   GRAMMAR

Dossier-langue
Past participles

This explains the agreement of the past participle in the feminine singular.

With able students there could be more practice on recognising and using the feminine agreement. The teacher, then students, could write sentences on the board without giving the subject. The class then have to say whether it is a boy or a girl, e.g.
X est allée en ville.
X, c'est un garçon ou une fille?
A est sorti hier soir.
A, c'est un garçon ou une fille? etc.

SB 88   WRITING

2   Deux cartes postales

This provides practice in changing the past participle from masculine to feminine and vice versa. Remind students that the past participle doesn't change with verbs with *avoir*.

SB 88,   SPEAKING / WRITING

3   Le jeu des dés

This is a pairwork activity in which responses are determined by throwing a dice or choosing a sequence of numbers at random.

Students then write out the questions with suitable replies (real or imaginary).

Au choix SB 140   GENERAL / WRITING

3   Hier après-midi

In this task, students complete a description of a journey to an event. In part **a** students just supply the past participle; in part **b** they supply the complete verb.

Solution:
a   **1** *Je suis sorti(e)*, **2** *Je suis allé(e)*, **3** *le bus est arrivé*, **4** *Je suis monté(e)*, **5** *le bus est tombé*,
b   **6** *Je suis resté(e)*, **7** *le bus est reparti*, **8** *il est arrivé*, **9** *Je suis descendu(e)*, **10** *Je suis entré(e)*

SB 89   PRESENTATION / READING

4   À l'aéroport

This introduces some new vocabulary for air travel: *aéroport, vol, porte* etc. Mention that *guichet* is used for the airline desk as well as a ticket office. Students should work out the correct order for the sentences.

Solution: 1d, 2f, 3b, 4e, 5a, 6c

SB 89   READING

Qui est allé au match?

This cartoon gives examples of the agreement of the past participle with the verb *aller* which is then explained in the *Dossier-langue*. Students could just read it for interest.

SB 89   GRAMMAR

Dossier-langue
The past participle of verbs with *être*

This gives a fuller explanation of the agreement of the past participle.

SB 89   READING / PRACTICE

5   Où sont-ils allés?

This task give practice in linking the subject with the correct part of *être* and past participle.

Solution: 1h, 2d, 3c, 4g, 5a, 6e, 7b, 8f

Differentiation

The following *Au choix* activities can be used as support and extension.

Au choix SB 138   SUPPORT / WRITING

3   En ville

Students supply the correct part of *être* and follow the lines to complete the sentences.

Solution:
1   *Je suis allé à la piscine.*
2   *Toi, Sylvie, tu es allée au cinéma.*
3   *Ton ami, Robert, est allé au match de football.*
4   *Suzanne est allée au supermarché.*
5   *Nous sommes allés à la plage.*
6   *Vous êtes allés au parc?*
7   *Mes amis sont allés au musée.*
8   *Les filles sont allées aux magasins.*

Au choix SB 138   SUPPORT / PRACTICE

4   Un long voyage

This gives practice in forming the past participle (third person masculine plural only) of a range of verbs.

Solution: **1** *sortis*, **2** *allés*, **3** *partis*, **4** *arrivés*, **5** *montés*, **6** *descendus*, **7** *allés*, **8** *arrivés*

Au choix SB 139   EXTENSION / WRITING

3   On est allé en ville

Students supply the complete perfect tense of *aller* and follow the lines to complete the sentences.

Solution:
1 *Moi, je suis allé au marché.*
2 *Toi, Pierre, tu es allé au bowling, non?*

3 *Thomas est allé au match de tennis.*
4 *Cécile, elle est allée à la patinoire.*
5 *Hélène et moi, nous sommes allé(e)s à la campagne.*
6 *Paul et Luc, vous êtes allés au théâtre?*
7 *Les garçons sont allés au magasin de sports.*
8 *Anne et Sophie sont allées au café.*

CM 6/7 WRITING

aller et sortir

1 Où sont-ils allés?

Students use all forms of the perfect tense of *aller* with places in a town.

Solution:

1 *Moi, je suis allé(e) au cinéma.*
2 *Et toi, Émilie, tu es allée à la piscine.*
3 *Bruno est allé au centre sportif.*
4 *Sophie est allée au château.*
5 *Nous sommes allés aux magasins.*
6 *Et vous, vous êtes allés au parc.*
7 *Patrice et Jérôme, ils sont allés au cirque.*
8 *Géraldine et Maxime, elles sont allées à la discothèque.*

2 Et toi?

Students write three similar sentences of their own choice.

3 Qui est sorti avec qui?

Students complete the grid of the logic game and work out the answers.

Solution:

1 *Charlotte est sortie avec Bruno.*
2 *Hélène est sortie avec Pierre.*
3 *Nicole est sortie avec Sébastien.*
4 *Sophie est sortie avec Frank.*

GRAMMAR IN ACTION 2, PAGES 35–37

GRAMMAR PRACTICE

The perfect tense with *être*

If required, these pages provide further practice of the perfect tense with *être*.

> **Area 7**
> **Perfect tense with *être* (all persons)**
> **Travel by coach and boat**
> SB 90–91, **1**–**8**
> Au choix SB 140–141, **4**–**5**
> CD 3/31–33
> CM 6/8

SB 90 READING
SPEAKING

1 Un voyage en Angleterre

Students read the itinerary for a trip to England. Some oral work could be based on the travel details, e.g.

Voici l'itinéraire pour un voyage en Angleterre. Quand est-ce qu'on va partir? Comment est-ce qu'on va voyager? Qu'est-ce qu'il faut emporter?

SB 90 READING
WRITING

2 Notre voyage

Students complete the description of the day's journey by supplying the correct past participle in André's diary.

Solution: 1 *Je suis arrivé,* 2 *je suis monté,*
3 *le car est parti,* 4 *nous sommes arrivés,*
5 *nous sommes descendus,*
6 *nous sommes montés,* 7 *nous sommes arrivés,* 8 *nous sommes allés,* 9 *nous sommes restés,* 10 *nous sommes allés,*
11 *je suis rentré,* 12 *je suis monté*

SB 90, 🎧 3/31 LISTENING

3 Une journée en famille

Students listen to the conversations and note down the correct picture for each activity.

Solution: 1f, 2d, 3a, 4h, 5g, 6c, 7b, 8e

🎧 Une journée en famille

1 – *Tu es allé en ville, hier?*
– *Oui, nous sommes allés en ville et nous avons fait du bowling. C'était amusant.*

2 – *Qu'est-ce que tu as fait hier?*
– *Je suis allé à la piscine avec mon correspondant.*

3 – *Tu as fait quelque chose d'intéressant, hier?*
– *Oui, nous sommes allés à la campagne à vélo et nous avons fait un pique-nique.*

4 – *Qu'est-ce que tu as fait hier?*
– *Le matin, nous sommes restés à la maison, puis l'après-midi, nous avons joué au golf dans le parc.*

5 – *Tu as fait quelque chose d'intéressant, hier?*
– *Oui, nous sommes allés en ville. Nous sommes allés aux magasins et à midi, nous avons mangé dans un fast-food.*

6 – *Qu'est-ce que tu as fait hier?*
– *Je suis allé au parc et j'ai joué au tennis avec mon correspondant.*
– *Et qui a gagné?*
– *Mais moi, bien sûr!*

7 – *Tu as passé une bonne journée, hier?*
– *Oui, nous sommes allés à un parc d'attractions.*
– *C'était bien?*
– *Oui, excellent. Nous sommes entrés au parc à neuf heures du matin et nous sommes restés là-bas toute la journée.*

8 – *Qu'est-ce que tu as fait hier?*
– *Le matin, nous sommes restés à la maison. Puis l'après-midi, je suis allée à la patinoire avec ma correspondante.*
– *C'était bien?*
– *Oui, assez bien, mais je suis tombée au moins vingt fois.*

unité 6 En voyage

Section 3

SB 90 — WRITING
4 Un e-mail

This time, students have to complete the text with the correct part of être.

Solution: 1 *Nous sommes partis,* 2 *nous sommes arrivés,* 3 *André est parti,* 4 *je suis rentrée,* 5 *nous sommes sortis,* 6 *les garçons sont venus*

SB 90, 3/32 — LISTENING
5 Un coup de téléphone

Students listen to the telephone conversation then complete the sentences with the missing details.

Solution: 1 *cinéma,* 2 *cousine,* 3 *onze heures,* 4 *voiture*

Un coup de téléphone
– Allô.
– Allô, c'est toi, Bruno? C'est moi, André.
– Salut, André. Ça va? Tu t'amuses bien?
– Oui, oui. Très bien. L'autre soir, nous sommes sortis, Daniel et moi, avec Claire et sa copine, qui s'appelle Katy. Nous sommes allés au cinéma et après, nous sommes allés dans un fast-food.
– Tu as fait autre chose?
– Oui, oui! Hier soir, nous sommes allés à une petite boum chez Katy … et la cousine de Daniel, qui s'appelle Emma, est venue aussi. Elle est très gentille et très jolie. Elle …
– Oui, oui. Je comprends! D'autres filles sont venues aussi, je suppose!
– Ah oui.
– C'était bien, la boum? Ça a duré longtemps?
– Jusqu'à onze heures. Le père de Daniel est venu nous chercher en voiture. Emma passe quelques jours ici. Ce soir, on va tous sortir ensemble.
– Attends, André! C'est très intéressant, mais il faut finir maintenant.
– Pourquoi?
– Parce qu'il y a quelqu'un à la porte. C'est peut-être pour moi.
– Alors, au revoir, Bruno. À bientôt!
– Au revoir, André … et bonne chance!

SB 91 — WRITING
6 Une journée à Londres

Students complete the description by writing out the verbs, using the correct form of the past participle (masculine plural). Remind students that the past participle doesn't agree for verbs which take *avoir* and suggest that they first find the two sentences which take *avoir* (5 and 6). When checking the task, encourage students to read out the complete sentence.

Solution: 1 *nous sommes sortis,* 2 *Nous sommes allés,* 3 *Nous sommes descendus,* 4 *nous sommes allés,* 5 *Nous avons vu,* 6 *nous avons fait,* 7 *nous sommes allés,* 8 *Nous sommes restés,* 9 *nous sommes remontés,* 10 *nous sommes rentrés*

Oral practice — SPEAKING

For extra practice, students could be asked to study the text for a few minutes, then close their books for a memory game. This could be a *vrai ou faux?* task or questions could be asked in English, e.g.
Ils sont allés à Londres en train, vrai ou faux?
Ils ont vu Buckingham Palace, vrai ou faux? etc.
What did they do for lunch?
How did they travel to the Tower of London? etc.

SB 91, 3/33 — LISTENING
7 Une sortie

Students listen to the conversation and choose the correct answer.

Solution: 1b, 2a, 3c, 4b, 5c

Une sortie
– Qu'est-ce que tu as fait pendant ton séjour en Angleterre?
– Un jour, je suis sortie avec ma famille. Nous sommes allés dans un parc d'attractions près de Londres.
– Vous êtes partis très tôt?
– Oui, nous sommes partis à huit heures et demie. Mon frère, André, est venu aussi.
– Et vous êtes restés longtemps au parc? C'était bien?
– Oui, nous sommes restés là-bas toute la journée. Il y avait beaucoup d'attractions. Katy et moi, nous avons essayé le Grand Huit, mais je n'ai pas beaucoup aimé ça. J'ai préféré la Maison Hantée.
– Vous êtes rentrés à quelle heure?
– Nous sommes rentrés assez tard, à sept heures et demie.

SB 91, — SPEAKING
8 Inventez des conversations

Students practise a similar conversation in pairs and then make up variations on the same model.

PRACTICE
Picture story

Students could compose a story about a day out, e.g. in Paris. They could use clip art to illustrate the story and use a spell checker (if available). If students work in pairs, it often boosts the creative dimension and lets them practise the impersonal pronoun *on* or the *nous* form. Microsoft® PowerPoint could also be used.

AU CHOIX SB 140 — GENERAL WRITING
4 À la campagne

This task involves completing captions, mostly using the plural of verbs which take être.

Solution: 1 *nous sommes partis,* 2 *nous sommes arrivés,* 3 *nous sommes montés,* 4 *Nous sommes restés,* 5 *Nous sommes rentrés,* 6 *nous sommes descendus*

unité 6 En voyage

Section 3

AU CHOIX SB 141   GENERAL
                      WRITING

5 Au bord de la mer

This gives practice in completing a conversation using different verbs and parts of the verb.

Solution: 1 *je suis allée*, 2 *Vous êtes partis*, 3 *nous sommes partis*, 4 *vous êtes allés*, 5 *Nous sommes allés*, 6 *nous sommes allés*, 7 *mes parents sont allés*, 8 *Elle est restée*, 9 *vous êtes sortis*, 10 *nous sommes allés*, 11 *vous êtes rentrés*, 12 *nous sommes rentrés*

CM 6/8   PRACTICE
             WRITING

Dans le passé

Further practice of verbs with *être* in the perfect.

Solution:
1 Mots croisés

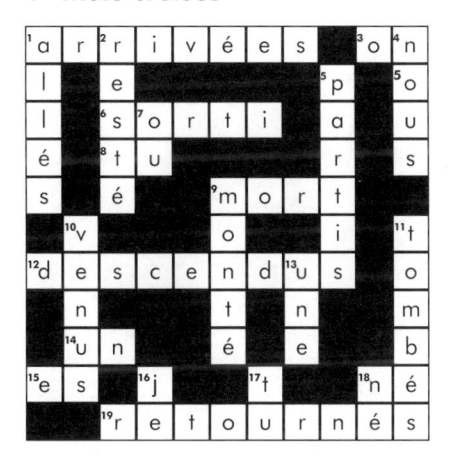

¹a	r	²r	i	v	³é	e	s		³o	⁴n	
l		e						⁵p		⁵o	
l		⁶s	⁷o	r	t	i		a		u	
é		⁸t	u					r		s	
s		é		⁹m	o	r	t				
	¹⁰v			o			¹¹t				
¹²d	e	s	c	e	n	d	¹³u	s			
	n			t		n		m			
	¹⁴u	n		é		e		b			
¹⁵e	s		¹⁶j		¹⁷t		¹⁸n	é			
	¹⁹r	e	t	o	u	r	n	é	s		

2 Où sont-ils allés?
1 Hélène est allée à la piscine.
2 Louis est allé au château.
3 Marc et André sont allés au supermarché.
4 Les filles sont allées au café.
5 Mes parents sont allés à la cathédrale.
6 Notre collège est allé au musée.
7 D. et moi, nous sommes allés au match de football.
8 Et toi, Mélanie, tu es allée au cinéma.

> **Area 8**
> **Perfect tense with *avoir* and *être***
> SB 92, **1**–**2**
> Au choix SB 138, **5**, SB 139, **4**–**5**
> Au choix SB 141, **6**–**8**
> CD 3/34
> CM 6/9

SB 92

1 Des cartes postales

Students read the postcards and answer the questions with the name of the person concerned.

Solution: 1 Martin, 2 Lucie, 3 Mélanie, 4 André, 5 Lucie, 6 Mélanie, 7 André, 8 Mélanie

SB 92   WRITING

2 À toi!

Students write a postcard of their own choice. The teacher could ask for suggestions from the class and some sample postcards could be prepared orally, if wished.

AU CHOIX SB 138   SUPPORT

5 Une carte postale de Londres

This gives practice in selecting the correct word to complete a postcard.

Solution: 1 *passé*, 2 *vu*, 3 *fait*, 4 *allés*, 5 *bateau*, 6 *rentrés*, 7 *car*, 8 *joué*

The following items are all optional and can be omitted if time is short.

CM 6/9   READING
             WRITING

Cartes postales des vacances

1 Dans quel pays sont-ils allés?
Students have to decide which country each person has visited.

Solution:
1 Nicole est allée au Sénégal.
2 Frank est allé en Suisse.
3 Philippe et Martine sont allés au Canada/au Québec.
4 Sophie est allée en Italie.
5 Hélène et Charlotte sont allées en France/à Paris.
6 Laurent est allé au Maroc.

2 Des cartes postales en symboles
Students write a short postcard with four points of inormation based on the details supplied.

Solution: (There may be other acceptable versions.)
1 Nous sommes arrivés ici vendredi. Il neige. Hier, nous sommes allés à la montagne et nous avons fait du ski.
2 Nous sommes arrivés ici samedi. Il pleut. Hier, nous sommes allés à Paris et nous avons visité la Tour Eiffel/nous sommes montés à la Tour Eiffel.
3 Nous sommes arrivés ici mercredi. Il fait beau/Il y a du soleil. Hier, nous sommes allés à Édimbourg et nous avons visité le château.

3 À toi!
Students write a postcard of their own choice.

147

AU CHOIX SB 139

EXTENSION WRITING

4 Une carte postale

This provides further practice, if needed, in writing a postcard in the perfect tense.

GRAMMAR PRACTICE

Perfect tense exercise

A word-sequencing or *Hot Potatoes* activity (see TB 20) could be based on the following text, which practises the correct use of the perfect tense with *avoir* and *être*.

Jean est arrivé à la station de métro.
Il a acheté un billet au guichet.
Il est descendu par l'escalier.
Il est monté dans le train.
À huit heures et demie, il est sorti du train.
Il a rencontré son ami Pierre.
Pierre et Jean sont allés au bureau.
Ils ont beaucoup travaillé.
À midi, Jean a mangé au restaurant.
Jean est retourné au bureau.
Il a écrit des lettres.
Puis il est sorti du bureau.
Il est rentré chez lui.
Il a regardé la télévision.

AU CHOIX SB 141

GENERAL READING

6 Le TGV Duplex

Students have to find the correct missing words to complete the text.

Solution: 1 *train*, 2 *longs*, 3 *introduit*, 4 *passagers*, 5 *fait*, 6 *avion*, 7 *voyage*

AU CHOIX SB 141

GENERAL READING

7 Chasse à l'intrus

This practises some vocabulary taught in the unit.

Solution:
1 la boum – les autres sont des moyens de transport.
2 le mois – on trouve les autres à la gare
3 hier – les autres sont des verbes
4 le jour – les autres concernent un voyage en avion
5 une gare – les autres sont des bagages

AU CHOIX SB 141

GENERAL READING

8 Voyager sans problème

More practice of recognising *il faut* + infinitive.

Solution: 1b, 2a, 3c, 4b, 5c

AU CHOIX SB 139, 3/34

EXTENSION LISTENING

5 Une interview avec Jean-Luc

This is a more demanding listening passage with comprehension questions in English.

Solution:
1 He works at the *gare de Lyon* in Paris.
2 Twelve people are in the team.
3 He's 20.
4 He's there to protect passengers and to help them (with luggage, queries etc.).
5 He wears an orange waistcoat and an official badge.
6 He finds it more difficult to ask teenagers not to smoke or to take their feet off the seats.
7 Generally he likes his work.

Une interview avec Jean-Luc

– Bonjour, Jean-Luc. Tu travailles ici à Paris, à la gare de Lyon, non?
– Oui, c'est ça. Je travaille à la gare comme 'Compagnon de voyage'.
– Tu fais partie d'une équipe?
– Oui, nous sommes une équipe de douze personnes, âgées de 18 à 26 ans.
– Et toi, tu as quel âge?
– Moi, j'ai vingt ans.
– Et qu'est-ce que vous faites exactement? Pourquoi êtes-vous là?
– Nous sommes là surtout pour la protection des voyageurs. Nous les aidons aussi, par exemple avec les bagages ou s'ils ont besoin de renseignements.
– Est-ce que vous portez un uniforme?
– Non, pas exactement un uniforme, mais nous portons un gilet orange et un badge officiel.
– Est-ce qu'il y a des aspects difficiles dans ce travail?
– Oui, quelquefois, il faut demander aux adolescents de ne pas fumer ou de ne pas mettre les pieds sur les bancs. Ça peut être un peu difficile.
– Mais tu es content quand même d'avoir ce travail?
– Oui, en général, j'aime bien ce travail.
– Merci.

Area 9
Further activities and consolidation
SB 92–93, 94–95
CM 6/10–6/17, 137, 151–152
CD 3/35–39
Student CD 1/31–36, 2/18–21

SB 92, CM 151–152, TB 29, 3/35 **LISTENING SPEAKING**

Chantez! Paris–Genève

A song about travelling by train. See TB 29 for notes on using songs and CM 151–152 for the music.

Chantez! Paris-Genève

1 Moi, j'y vais en TGV,
J'ai mon billet, faut le composter.
Départ pour Genève à dix heures trente,
Encore cinq minutes dans la salle d'attente.
(Paris–Genève, Paris–Genève)
J'ai juste le temps d'aller aux toilettes,
On arrive bientôt à Bourg-en-Bresse.

2 Moi, j'y vais en TGV,
J'ai mon billet, faut le composter.
Départ pour Genève à douze heures vingt,
Pardon Monsieur, de quel quai part le train?
(Paris–Genève, Paris–Genève)
Je prends du pain, bois une limonade,
Le train est rapide, voilà Bellegarde!

3 Moi, j'y vais en TGV,
Rendre visite à mon cher Pépé,
À treize heures trente, départ pour la Suisse,
Oh ben, dis donc! Où est ma valise?
(Paris–Genève, Paris–Genève)
J'ai presque fini mon magazine,
La fille en face – c'est une copine!

4 Nous y allons en TGV,
Nos billets, ils sont compostés.
Nous arrivons à Genève en Suisse.
Quelle heure est-il? Quatorze heures six.

CM 6/10, SCD 1/31–36 INDEPENDENT LISTENING
SOUNDS AND WRITING

Écoute et parle

This copymaster provides pronunciation and speaking practice.

1 À la française

À la française

1	arrive	4	destination	7	train
2	attention	5	port	8	transport
3	camp	6	queue		

2 Et après?

Solution: 4 – 9 – 12 – 15 – 20 – 38 – 74 – 97

Et après?

3 – 8 – 11 – 14 – 19 – 37 – 73 – 96

3 Des phrases ridicules

Des phrases ridicules

Dans la rue, Hercule a vu la statue d'une tortue.

En août, tout le groupe joue aux boules sur la pelouse à Toulouse.

4 Les terminaisons: -ment

Solution: 1f, 2c, 3d, 4a, 5b, 6e

Les terminaisons: -ment

1	vraiment	4	absolument
2	lentement	5	évidemment
3	rarement	6	spécialement

5 Vocabulaire de classe

Solution: **1** phrases, **2** vos, **3** pour, **4** ma, **5** fait, **6** 123 (cent vingt-trois), **7** va

Vocabulaire de classe

1 Complète les phrases.
2 Copiez vos devoirs.
3 Écoute pour vérifier les réponses.
4 J'ai oublié ma trousse.
5 Je n'ai pas fait mes devoirs.
6 Une personne regarde cette page, l'autre regarde la page 123.
7 Trouve le mot qui ne va pas avec les autres.

6 Des conversations

Des conversations

1 À la gare
– On peut vous aider?
(pause)
– Un aller simple pour Calais, s'il vous plaît.
– Voilà.
(pause)
– Merci. Le train part à quelle heure?
– À onze heures trente-cinq.
(pause)
– Et c'est quel quai?
– Quai numéro deux.

2 Samedi dernier
– Tu es sorti(e) à quelle heure?
(pause)
– Je suis sorti(e) à deux heures.
– Où es-tu allé(e)?
(pause)
– Je suis allé(e) au centre sportif.
– Tu es rentré(e) comment?
(pause)
– Je suis rentré(e) en bus.

3 Un voyage récent
– Vous êtes partis à quelle heure?
(pause)
– Nous sommes partis à sept heures du matin.
– Quand êtes-vous arrivés à Lille?
(pause)
– Nous sommes arrivés à midi.
– Vous êtes restés combien de temps en France?
(pause)
– Nous sommes restés six jours.

**CM 6/11,
SCD 2/18–21** INDEPENDENT LISTENING

Tu comprends?

Students could do any or all of the four items on this worksheet, now or later as revision.

1 On part en vacances

Solution: 1 d, f, a, 2 b, d, b, 3 a, b, d,
4 e, c, f, 5 c, a, c, 6 f, e, e

On part en vacances

1 – Salut, c'est Hélène à l'appareil.
– Bonjour, Hélène, c'est Marie. Comment ça va?

– Très bien. Écoute, j'ai de bonnes nouvelles – je pars bientôt pour la France! Je vais travailler dans une agence de voyages pendant six mois.
– Oh, tu as de la chance! Tu pars quand exactement?
– Le 27 octobre.
– Et tu prends l'avion?
– Oui, bien sûr.

2 – Élodie, qu'est-ce que tu vas faire pendant les vacances?
– Moi, je vais en Angleterre – je vais passer un mois à Portsmouth. Je pars le deux août et je prends le bateau.

3 – Salut Jean-Pierre. Tu pars bientôt en Allemagne, non? C'est quand exactement?
– Je pars lundi prochain, le 18 juin.
– Et tu prends le train?
– Oui, c'est ça. Je prends le train pour Bonn.

4 – Et Roland, ton frère, il part aussi en vacances?
– Oui, il part le 30 juillet pour l'Italie. Il part en voiture avec des amis. Et toi, est-ce que tu pars en vacances?
– Non, malheureusement, je ne pars pas en vacances cette année. Je reste ici.

5 – Maman, quand est-ce que Michèle et Anne-Marie partent pour l'Espagne?
– Elles partent le vendredi 21 mai.
– Est-ce qu'elles partent en voiture?
– Non, elles partent en car jusqu'à Barcelone.

6 – Salut, Marc. Quand est-ce que tu pars pour la Suisse?
– Je pars le jeudi 19 septembre.
– Et Luc et David, est-ce qu'ils partent jeudi aussi?
– Oui, ils partent jeudi, comme moi. Nous allons voyager ensemble. Nous partons tous à vélo.

2 Les annonces à la gare

Solution:

	Départ	Destination	Notes	Quai
1	10h05	Marseille	–	9
2	11h25	Nice	Retard: 00h20	5
3	12h10	Dijon	changement de quai	8
4	13h20	Lyon	Retard: 00h15	6
5	14h50	Montpellier	–	2
6	15h35	Genève	changement de quai	3

Les annonces à la gare

1 Attention! Attention! Le train de 10 heures 05, quai numéro 9, à destination de Marseille, va partir. En voiture, s'il vous plaît.

2 Le train de 11 heures 25 à destination de Nice, quai numéro 5, a vingt minutes de retard.

3 Attention! Il y a un changement de quai pour le train de midi dix à destination de Dijon. Ce train va maintenant partir du quai numéro 8.

4 Le train de 13 heures 20 à destination de Lyon a quinze minutes de retard.

5 Attention! Le train de 14 heures 50, quai numéro 2, à destination de Montpellier, va partir. En voiture, s'il vous plaît.

6 Attention! Il y a un changement de quai pour le train de 15 heures 35 à destination de Genève. Ce train va maintenant partir du quai numéro 3.

3 Présent ou passé?

Solution: 1 PC, 2 PR, 3 PR, 4 PC, 5 PC, 6 PR, 7 PC, 8 PR

Présent ou passé?

1 – Tu es sorti lundi?
 – Oui, je suis allé au cinéma avec Daniel.

2 – Tu sors beaucoup le soir?
 – Non, je ne sors pas beaucoup en ce moment. J'ai trop de travail.

3 – Tes parents vont en ville tous les samedis?
 – Oui, normalement, ils font des courses en ville le samedi.

4 – Est-ce que Sébastien est allé au match de football, samedi?
 – Oui, il y est allé avec deux amis du collège.

5 – Lucie et Sika sont déjà parties?
 – Oui, elles sont parties à neuf heures ce matin.

6 – Tu descends où quand tu prends le bus en ville?
 – Normalement, je descends place du Marché. C'est tout près des magasins.

7 – Est-ce que Marc est allé au parc avec les autres?
 – Non, il est resté à la maison.

8 – Vous restez combien de temps en France?
 – Nous restons encore cinq jours, jusqu'au vingt mai.

4 Des vacances en Normandie

Solution: 1 Pâques, 2 trois, 3 boulangerie, 4 eau, 5 vaisselle, 6 plage, 7 onze, 8 rentrés, 9 sept

Des vacances en Normandie

Pendant les vacances de Pâques, je suis parti avec un groupe de jeunes en Normandie. Nous avons fait du camping. J'ai partagé une tente avec trois autres garçons.
Chaque jour, on a travaillé par équipe. Une équipe est allée à la boulangerie pour acheter du pain.
Une équipe a cherché de l'eau. Une équipe a préparé les sandwichs pour le pique-nique et une équipe a fait la vaisselle.
Un jour, nous sommes allés à la plage à vélo. Nous sommes partis à neuf heures et nous sommes arrivés à la plage à onze heures. Nous sommes restés là-bas un bon moment.
Mais quand nous sommes rentrés, nous avons pris la mauvaise direction. Finalement, nous sommes arrivés au camping, très fatigués, à sept heures du soir.

SB 93, CM 6/12

Sommaire

A summary of the main structures and vocabulary of this unit. Students fill in gaps on the copymaster. They should check their answers against the Students' Book page.

CM 6/13
Rappel 6
REVISION

This copymaster can be used at any point in the course for revision and consolidation. It provides revision of meals, food, drink and food shops. The reading and writing tasks are self-instructional and can be used by students working individually for homework or during cover lessons.

Solution:

1 Des mots mêlés

Des magasins: *pâtisserie, boulangerie, boucherie, chacuterie, épicerie*

Petit déjeuner: *céréales, œufs, pain, beurre, confiture*

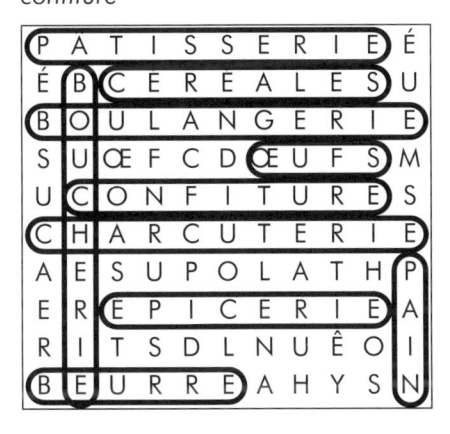

```
P A T I S S E R I E É
É B C E R E A L E S U
B O U L A N G E R I E
S U Œ F C D Œ U F S M
U C O N F I T U R E S
C H A R C U T E R I E
A E S U P O L A T H P
E R E P I C E R I E A
R I T S D L N U Ê O I
B E U R R E A H Y S N
```

2 Des listes

4 fruits: *fraises, pêches, raisins, poires*

4 légumes: *chou, chou-fleur, petits pois, pommes de terre*

4 boissons: *lait, vin, jus d'orange, limonade*

3 Mots croisés (la nourriture)

¹p	o	t	a	g	²e		³c		⁴p
o					a		h		o
m		⁵p		⁶u	n	e			u
⁷m	e	l	o	n		r			l
e		i			⁸f		⁹s		e
		r		¹⁰f	r	u	i	t	
¹¹e	l	¹²l	e	¹³s		i		r	
		a		o		¹⁴t	h	o	n
		¹⁵v	i	a	n	d	e		p
			t			t			s

Épreuve – Unité 6

These worksheets can be used for an informal test of listening, speaking, reading and writing or for extra practice, as required. For general notes on administering the *Épreuves*, see TB 16.

CM 6/14, 🎧 3/36–39 — LISTENING
Épreuve: Écouter

A Dani est à la gare (NC 3)

Solution: 1b, 2a, 3c, 4d, 5f, 6e, 7g

(mark /6: 4+ shows the ability to understand messages and identify main points)

🎧 **Dani est à la gare**

1 Je ne veux pas porter ma valise quand je vais aux magasins.
2 Je veux acheter des journaux.
3 Je voudrais des détails sur les trains.
4 J'ai faim. J'ai très, très faim.
5 Le train est en retard. Il faut attendre encore deux heures.
6 J'ai les mains sales. Je veux me laver les mains.
7 Où va-t-on pour acheter les billets?

B Quatre voyageurs (NC 3)

Solution: 1 *bateau, 11.15;* **2** *train, 12.00;* **3** *voiture, 7.30;* **4** *avion, 9.10*

(mark /6: 4+ shows the ability to understand short passages spoken at near normal speed)

🎧 **Quatre voyageurs**

Voyageur 1
– Vous partez en Angleterre?
– Oui, demain.
– Vous y allez en avion?
– Non, je prends le bateau. Le bateau part à onze heures et quart.

Voyageur 2
– Où allez-vous?
– Je vais à Londres.
– Quand partez-vous?
– L'Eurostar part de la gare du Nord à midi.

Voyageur 3
– Demain, je vais à Lyon.
– A quelle heure partez-vous?
– Je pars à sept heures et demie du matin.
– Comment voyagez-vous?
– Je prends la voiture.

Voyageur 4
– Mercredi, je vais en Angleterre.
– C'est vrai? Vous partez quand?
– J'ai déjà acheté le billet. Je pars de l'aéroport à neuf heures dix.

C Céline et Emmanuel partent en train (NC 4)

Solution: 1a, 2b, 3c, 4c, 5a, 6c, 7a

(mark /6: 4+ shows the ability to understand longer passages, identifying and noting main points)

En voyage unité 6

Section 3

🎧 **Céline et Emmanuel partent en train**

– C'est bon. J'ai acheté des magazines. Céline, tu as acheté les billets?
– Oui, Emmanuel, j'ai pris deux allers simples.
– C'est combien?
– Quatre-vingt-neuf euros.
– Le train est direct?
– Oui, c'est direct, mais ce n'est pas un TGV.
– On part d'où?
– On part du quai numéro 4.
  …
– Voici notre train. On monte?
– Oui.
– Excusez-moi, Monsieur, c'est occupé ici?
– Tout le compartiment est libre.
– Céline, tu préfères la fênetre ou le couloir?
– Le couloir, s'il te plaît.

D François le contrôleur (NC 5)

Solution: **1** French Railways, **2** earlier, **3** check that people have paid/validated their tickets, **4** two, **5** three hours, **6** buffet/to have lunch, **7** likes travel by train/contact with public; dislikes when there are lots of smokers in the train

(mark /7: 5+ shows the ability to understand spoken language including present and past events; they can identify and note main points and identify opinions)

🎧 **François le contrôleur**

– Bonjour François. Vous avez vingt ans et vous travaillez pour la SNCF. C'est bien, ça?
– Oui, je fais la route Paris-Lyon et Lyon-Paris. Je suis contrôleur.
– Vous commencez votre travail à quelle heure, le matin?
– Ça dépend des semaines. En ce moment, je commence à neuf heures et je finis à dix-huit heures, mais la semaine prochaine, je vais commencer à six heures du matin.
– Et qu'est-ce que vous faites exactement?
– Alors, par exemple hier, je suis monté dans le train à Paris et on est parti pour Lyon. J'ai contrôlé les billets. Il faut avoir un billet valable et il faut le composter. Ça, c'est très important. Hier, j'ai trouvé deux voyageurs qui n'avaient pas payé et cinq qui n'avaient pas composté leur billet.
– Et en arrivant à Lyon, qu'est-ce que vous faites normalement?
– Normalement, on part à neuf heures trente et on arrive à midi trente. Alors je vais au buffet pour manger mon déjeuner et je remonte dans le train pour le voyage du retour.
– Vous aimez votre travail?
– Oui, j'aime bien voyager en train et j'aime le contact avec le public, mais je ne l'aime pas beaucoup quand il y a beaucoup de fumeurs à bord du train.

CM 6/15   **SPEAKING**

Épreuve: Parler

Students should be given the sheet up to a week before the assessment, to give them time to choose whether to do 1 or 2 and to give them time to prepare and practice both conversations – the structured one (A) and the open-ended one (B) – with their partners.

Mark scheme

Section A: mark /12: 3 marks per response
- 1 mark for an utterance/response that is clear and conveys all of the information requested, in the form of a complete phrase or sentence, though not necessarily an accurate one. The questions and answers may seem a little disjointed, like separate items rather than parts of a coherent conversation.
- 2 marks for an utterance/response that is clear and conveys all of the information requested in the form of a complete phrase or sentence, though not necessarily an accurate one. The language must flow reasonably smoothly and be recognisable as part of a coherent conversation.
- 3 marks for a clear and complete utterance/response that flows smoothly as part of a clear and coherent conversation. The language must be in complete sentences or phrases that are reasonably accurate and consistent as far as grammar, pronunciation and intonation are concerned.

Section B: mark /13: 3 marks per response, as above, +1 bonus mark for adding one or two items using the perfect tense. 19–25 shows the ability to take part in short conversations, seeking and conveying information and opinions in simple terms.

Summary:
Marks   7–13   14–18   19–25
NC Level   3   4   5

CM 6/16   **READING**

Épreuve: Lire

A Pierre est à la gare (NC 2)

Solution: 1g, 2c, 3a, 4d, 5e, 6b, 7f

(mark /6: 4+ shows ability to understand short phrases)

B Jeanne va en train à Paris (NC 3)

Solution: 1c, 2b, 3a, 4a, 5c, 6a, 7b, 8a

(mark /7: 5+ shows ability to understand short texts)

C Paul va à la Tour Eiffel (NC 3)

Solution: **1** *sorti,* **2** *arrivé,* **3** *monté,* **4** *pu,* **5** *descendu,* **6** *entré,* **7** *allé,* **8** *rentré*

(mark /7: 5+ shows ability to understand short texts)

D Vacaces de neige dans les Pyrénées (NC 6)

Solution: **1** *Marc,* **2** *une jeune fille,* **3** *Pauline,* **4** *Annette,* **5** *Georges,* **6** *Jean,* **7** *Luc*

(mark /6: 4+ shows the ability to understand texts that cover past, present and future events)

CM 6/17   **WRITING**

Épreuve: Écrire et grammaire

A   Jean parle de sa journée (NC 1)

Solution: 1 *resté*, 2 *sorti*, 3 *allé*, 4 *parti*, 5 *arrivé*, 6 *monté*, 7 *descendu*, 8 *entré*, 9 *rentré*

(mark /8: 5+ shows the ability to select appropriate words to complete short sentences)

B   Une visite à Londres (NC 4)

Mark scheme
- 1 mark for each sub-task completed with a correct verb in the perfect tense

Subtotal: 6
Accuracy:
- 2 marks: most words are correct
- 1 mark: about half the words are correct
- 0 marks: fewer than half the words are correct

Subtotal: 2
(mark /8: 5+ shows the ability to write individual paragraphs of about three or four sentences)

C   Un voyage en France (NC 5)

Mark scheme

Communication:
- 1 mark for each accurate perfect tense (exclude the example)
- 1/2 mark for a perfect tense which is incorrect but which communicates

Subtotal: 6 (round up half marks)
Accuracy:
- 3 marks: mostly accurate
- 2 marks: about half correct
- 1 mark: more wrong than right
- 0 marks: little or nothing of merit

Subtotal: 3
(mark /9: 6+ shows ability to produce short pieces of writing in simple sentences, referring to recent experiences and giving opinions; although there may be mistakes the meaning can be understood with little or no difficulty)

SB 94–95, CM 137   **READING EXTENSION**

Presse-Jeunesse 5

These pages provide reading for pleasure. They can be used alone or with the accompanying copymaster.

SB 94, CM 137

Louis Laloupe arrête le voleur

Students read the picture story written in the perfect tense. There are three copymaster tasks.

Solution:

A   Louis Laloupe arrête le voleur
Tu as bien compris?
1 Because he had been burgled.
2 A key.
3 No, he left the town and went into the country.
4 He stopped outside a small house.
5 He approached the house and gently opened the door.
6 He looked for his revolver.
7 He jumped on the thief.
8 Louis picked up the revolver, arrested the thief and then woke up.

Un résumé: e, k, g, a, c, f, h, i

Au contraire: 1 *tôt*, 2 *devant*, 3 *à droite*, 4 *vite*, 5 *il est sorti*, 6 *il s'est couché*

SB 94

Le jeu des couleurs

Students have to choose the correct colour to complete each statement.

Solution: 1 *bleu*, 2 *blanches*, 3 *rouge*, 4 *vert*, 5 *gris*, 6 *noir, bleu, rouge, vert, jaune*

SB 95, CM 137

Le Stade de France

This gives some factual information about the *Stade de France* near Paris which was opened in 1998. For more information, students could consult the official web site (www.stadefrance.com).

Solution:

B   Le Stade de France
Trouve les paires: 1c, 2g, 3e, 4b, 5d, 6a, 7h, 8f

SB 95, CM 137

Les jeux traditionnels

This gives some information about the origins of two traditional games: marbles and a spinning top.

Solution:

C   Les jeux traditionnels

Trouve le mot: 1 *jeux*, 2 *vend/joue*, 3 *noix*, 4 *la toupie*

CM 137

A task based on the vocabulary of all the items.

Solution:

D   Une autre activité

Chasse à l'intrus: 1 *ouvert*, 2 *une clé*, 3 *l'ascenseur*, 4 *des glaces*, 5 *un toit*, 6 *une noix*, 7 *le stade*, 8 *un chou*

Encore Tricolore 2
nouvelle édition

unité 7 Ça va?

Areas	Topics	Grammar
1	Discussing clothes and colours and what to wear	Using the verb *mettre* (present tense, some perfect tense)
2	Describing appearance (mainly facial)	Agreement of adjectives (revision and extension)
3		Using direct object pronouns
4	Talking about parts of the body	
5	Saying how you feel and describing what hurts	*avoir mal* + parts of the body
6		Other expressions with *avoir* (*j'ai chaud/froid/soif/faim/de la fièvre*)
7	At the doctor's Saying how you feel	Using the imperative
8	(This is a short optional area in *Au choix* general only)	Using the verb *dormir*
9	Further activities and consolidation	

National Curriculum Information

Some students	levels 4–5+
Most students	levels 4–5
All students	levels 3–4

Revision

Rappel (CM 7/12) includes revision of the following:
- members of the family
- rooms in a house
- school subjects

Sounds and writing

- nasal vowels: -am, -an, -em, -en; -on
- the ending -ure

See *Écoute et parle* (CM 7/9, TB 169).

ICT opportunities

- phrase generation
- visual presentation of some adjectives using word art, clip art plus text, font sizes etc.
- text reconstruction
- creating a labelled picture using a drawing programme
- finding a French website devoted to animals

Reading strategies

Presse-Jeunesse 6 (SB 109, CM 138)

Assessment

- Informal assessment is in *Épreuves* at the end of this unit (TB 171, CM 7/13–7/16)
- Formal assessment (*Unités 1–7*) is in the *Contrôle* (TB 190, CM 139–145).

Students' Book

Unité 7 SB 96–108
Au choix SB 142–145

Flashcards

81–86 expressions with *avoir*
87–95 clothing

CDs

4/1–16
Student CD 1/37–42, 2/22–25

Additional

Grammar in Action 2, pp 24–25

Copymasters

CM 7/1	*Encore des vêtements* [mini-flashcards]
CM 7/2	*mettre* [grammar]
CM 7/3	*C'est utile, le dictionnaire!* [dictionary skills]
CM 7/4	*Faites des descriptions* [grammar]
CM 7/5	*Les clowns* [writing, vocabulary practice]
CM 7/6	*Ça ne va pas* [listening]
CM 7/7	*Avoir – un verbe utile* [grammar]
CM 7/8	*On est malade* [listening]
CM 7/9	*Écoute et parle* [independent listening]
CM 7/10	*Tu comprends?* [independent listening]
CM 7/11	*Sommaire* [consolidation, reference]
CM 7/12	*Rappel* [revision]
CM 7/13	*Épreuve: Écouter*
CM 7/14	*Épreuve: Parler*
CM 7/15	*Épreuve: Lire*
CM 7/16	*Épreuve: Écrire et grammaire*
CM 138	*Presse-Jeunesse 6* [reading]
CM 153	*Chantez! Alouette* [song]

Language content

Discussing clothes and what to wear (Area 1)

un anorak
des baskets (f pl)
des bottes (f pl)
un casque
une casquette
des chaussettes (f pl)
des chaussures (f pl)
une chemise
une cravate
un imper(méable)
un jean
un jogging
une jupe
un logo
des lunettes de soleil (f pl)
un maillot de bain
la mode
un pantalon
un pull
un pyjama
une robe
des sandales (f pl)
un short
une tenue
un T-shirt
une veste
Je n'ai rien à me mettre.

Describing people/things (Area 2)

carré(e)
content(e)
court(e)
décontracté(e)
fort(e)
grand(e)
gros(se)
haut(e)
jeune
de taille moyenne
long(ue)
lourd(e)
mince
pauvre
petit(e)
riche
triste
vieux (vieille)
les cheveux noirs/gris/blonds/roux/blancs/bruns/châtains/châtain clair/courts/longs/raides/en queue de cheval
les yeux bleus/bruns/gris/verts/marron
la barbe
la moustache
des/pas de lunettes (f pl)

Parts of the body (Area 4)

la bouche
le bras
la cheville
le cou
le cœur
la dent
le doigt
le dos
l'estomac (m)
le genou
la gorge
la jambe
la main
le nez
l'œil (les yeux) (m)
l'oreille (f)
la peau
le pied
la tête
le ventre
le visage

Saying how you feel (Areas 5–7)

Je ne vais pas très bien.
Ça ne va pas très bien/mieux.
Je suis (un peu) malade.
J'ai mal au cœur.
Je suis asthmatique.
Je suis allergique à …
Je ne peux pas dormir.
J'ai mal à la tête/au dos/aux oreilles.
J'ai chaud/froid/de la fièvre.
J'ai faim/soif.

Understanding what the doctor says (Area 7)

Qu'est-ce qui ne va pas?
Qu'est-ce qu'il y a?
Ça vous fait mal là?
Ouvrez la bouche!
Montrez-moi la jambe.
Restez au lit!
Prenez ce médicament.
Prenez votre inhalateur.
Voici une ordonnance.

Useful websites

Mail order companies

www.laredoute.fr – this is the official website for the mail order fashion company, *La Redoute*.
www.3suisses.fr – a similar website for another French mail order company, *3 Suisses*.

Department stores

Galeries Lafayette – www.galerieslafayette.fr
Monoprix – www.monoprix.fr

Animals

www.parcsafari.qc.ca/
http://iquebec.ifrance.com/zoovirtuel/
These two Canadian sites provide photos and facts about different animals and online activities.

Ça va? unité 7

**Area 1
Discussing clothes and colours and what to wear
Using the verb *mettre***

SB 96–97, **1**–**4**
Au choix SB 142, **1**, SB 143, **1**, SB 144, **1**
FC 87–95
CM 7/1–7/2
CD 4/1–2

FC 87–95 PRESENTATION

Revision of clothing vocabulary

Begin with some revision of clothing vocabulary, using actual garments or flashcards and CM 7/1.

CM 7/1 REVISION PRACTICE

Encore des vêtements

Students could use this copymaster for revision and practice of clothing vocabulary and colours. Both this copymaster and **Encore Tricolore 1** CM 5/3 (if available) could be used to make OHTs or for mini-flashcard games (see TB 26).

Solution:

1 1h, 2g, 3e, 4k, 5f, 6b, 7c, 8d, 9i, 10j, 11a, 12l

SB 96, 4/1, LISTENING READING SPEAKING

1 Je n'ai rien à me mettre

This first item is mainly for the revision and practice of clothes vocabulary and colours and the introduction of *mettre* (to put on).

Check that students have worked out the meaning of *mettre* before they spend too long on the text.

a Students first look through the illustrations and the story to get the gist of it, then complete the text with words from the box below.

b They then listen to the recording to check their answers.

Some oral questions could be asked or students could invent *vrai ou faux?* statements to set to each other, e.g. *Le T-shirt de Christine est noir/rouge* etc.

Students could read the sketch aloud and perhaps dramatise it, using any selection of garments and adapting the text accordingly.

The text could also be used for a text re-sequencing activity, e.g. using *Fun with Texts*.

Solution: **1** chemise, **2** jean, **3** jupe, **4** T-shirt, **5** chaussures, **6** pantalon, **7** ceinture, **8** pull, **9** sandales, **10** veste

Je n'ai rien à me mettre

Ce soir, il y a une boum au club des jeunes. Christine regarde ses vêtements.

– Qu'est-ce que je mets? Ma chemise verte avec mon jean bleu? ... Non. Ma jupe noire avec mon T-shirt jaune? ... Oh non, pas ça! Mes chaussures blanches? ... Non. Qu'est-ce que je mets? Je n'ai rien à me mettre.

Christine va chez Véronique.

– Je vais à la boum ce soir et je n'ai rien à me mettre.
– Regardons mes vêtements.

Elles regardent les vêtements de Véronique.

– Tu aimes mon pantalon rouge avec la ceinture noire?
– Oui, il est fantastique. J'adore!
– Voici mon nouveau pull.
– Ah, c'est joli.
– J'ai des sandales noires.
– Chic! Elles sont formidables.
– Voici ma veste grise. Tu veux mettre ça aussi?
– Oui oui. J'aime bien ça!

Véronique donne tous ces vêtements à Christine.

– Véronique, tu vas à la boum ce soir?
– Euh ... non.
– Pourquoi pas?
– Moi, je n'ai rien à me mettre!

Au choix SB 144, GENERAL SPEAKING

1 Qu'est-ce que tu vas mettre?

This is a dice dialogue for practice of clothes and colours. Students might need reminding of the rules of adjectival agreement before doing this task.

They take it in turns to throw the dice and the other person has to describe the corresponding garments.

SB 97, 4/2, READING WRITING LISTENING

2 Mes vêtements favoris

This item includes some new vocabulary: *la mode, un logo, un casque, une tenue, pratique, décontractés, fleuri(es), bottes (f pl), un collier, chic*. This could be introduced orally, using the numbered pictures or mini-flashcards where applicable, and perhaps asking students to guess or look up the meanings.

a Students have to write down the clothes worn by each person, in numbered lists. They should find out the spelling of the new words for themselves, from the speech bubbles. The new vocabulary could later be added to students' own electronic vocabulary lists (see SB 108 for core vocabulary).

Solution:

Alain: 1 *des gants,* **1** *un pantalon noir* **1** *un T-shirt vert,* **1** *un casque*

Caroline: 5 *une veste rouge,* **6** *une chemise noire,* **7** *une jupe blanche,* **8** *des chaussures blanches*

Marc: 9 *des baskets,* **10** *un short,* **11** *un sweat,* **12** *une casquette*

Sandrine: 13 *une robe noire,* **14** *une chemise pourpre,* **15** *un collier orange,* **16** *des bottes pourpres*

b Students should now listen to the recording and identify the speakers, referring to the pictures or their lists. The last four questions include the first and second person singular of the perfect tense of *mettre* which is practised later in the area. These can serve as a model for students' own answers in task 4, À toi!

Solution: 1 *Alain*, 2 *Marc*, 3 *Sandrine*, 4 *Sandrine*, 5 *Caroline*, 6 *Alain*, 7 *Caroline*, 8 *Sandrine*, 9 *Alain*, 10 *Marc*

Mes vêtements favoris

1 Moi, j'adore le skate. Voici le logo de mon club de skate.
2 J'aime les vêtements très décontractés – les baskets, par exemple.
3 Ce soir, je mets ma chemise pourpre – j'adore ça!
4 J'ai des bottes très à la mode … chic, non?
5 Ma jupe est blanche et mes chaussures sont blanches aussi.
6 Tu fais du skate? Alors mets ton casque!
7 – Qu'est-ce que tu as mis hier soir?
  – Hier soir, j'ai mis ma jupe blanche et ma veste rouge.
8 – Qu'est-ce que tu as mis pour la boum, samedi dernier?
  – J'ai mis ma robe noire avec mon collier orange.
9 – Le week-end dernier, qu'est-ce que tu as mis?
  – Ben, j'ai mis mon casque et mon pantalon noir et j'ai fait du skate au club.
10 – Pour la boum, qu'est-ce que tu as mis?
  – Je ne sais pas, mais j'ai mis des vêtements décontractés, ça c'est certain!

PRACTICE

3 Qu'est-ce qu'on met?

This *vrai ou faux?* activity is based on task 2 and brings in the singular and plural third persons of *mettre*.

Solution: 1 *vrai*, 2 *faux*, 3 *vrai*, 4 *vrai*, 5 *faux*, 6 *vrai*

SB 97,   **GRAMMAR**

Dossier-langue
mettre (to put, put on, wear)

Students could be asked to find all the parts of *mettre* in the preceding texts. The different meanings of *mettre* are mentioned and students could try making up some sentences to show these.

Differentiation

The following *Au choix* activities can be used as support and extension.

AU CHOIX, SB 142   **SUPPORT**
                                GRAMMAR PRACTICE

1 Le week-end

This is a straightforward matching task. Students match the subject with the correct part of the verb. When checking, read out the sentences in full.

Solution: 1b, 2e, 3a, 4d, 5c, 6f

AU CHOIX SB 143   **EXTENSION**
                                  WRITING

1 Choisis tes vêtements!

This partly open-ended task involves writing sentences by supplying the correct part of the verb and adding a suitable garment.

In the early sentences more detailed help is given than in the later ones, in which only the beginning of the sentence is supplied.

No mention is made here of the rather tricky point that garments are listed in the singular if each person is wearing only one, e.g. *Tous les garçons mettent un jogging et un sweat pour jouer dehors.*
It is left to the teacher to explain this if necessary.

Solution: (There are several other possibilites.)
1 … on met un T-shirt et un short.
2 … mon frère met un pantalon, un T-shirt et un casque.
3 … nous mettons nos vêtements de fête.
4 … nous mettons un chapeau et des gants.
5 … les enfants mettent un maillot de bain.
6 … on met un imperméable.

SB 97,   **SPEAKING**
                  WRITING

4 À toi!

This provides practice in talking (and writing) about clothing for different occasions, using *mettre* in the present and perfect tenses.

CM 7/2   **PRACTICE**

mettre

This worksheet gives further practice of items of clothing and of *mettre*.

Solution:

1 En vacances

Charlotte:	… je mets un T-shirt et une jupe … qu'est-ce que tu mets …?
Fabien:	… je mets souvent un short et mon casque …
Jean-Marc:	… met des bottes, un jogging et un sweat(-shirt).
Claire et Marie:	… Nous mettons chacune un maillot de bain … je mets toujours un chapeau …
Charlotte:	… Qu'est-ce que tu mets?
Vincent:	… je mets mon imperméable et mes lunettes de soleil.

157

2 Mots croisés

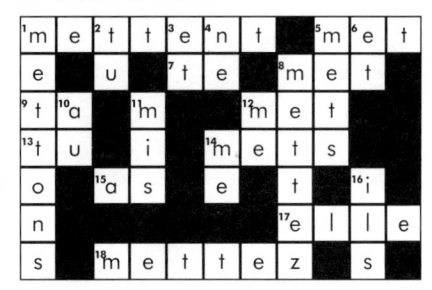

```
 1m e 2t t 3e n t      5m e t
    e    u    7t e    8m e t
 9t 10a    11m       12m e t
13t  u       i    14m e t s
    o 15a  s    e    t    16i
    n             17e  l  l  e
    s 18m  e  t  t  e  z     s
```

On fait des valises   SPEAKING

This game gives further practice of both clothing vocabulary and of the present and perfect tenses of *mettre*. A suitcase full of garments is the essential 'prop'.

First show the garments to the class, one at a time, asking them to say the names of each (and the colours).

Choose an able student to begin. This person shows the class which things they are putting in the suitcase, saying, e.g.

Dans la valise, je mets une chaussette bleue, un jean noir etc.

When the suitcase is closed, ask the class:
Qu'est-ce qu'il (elle) a mis dans la valise?

Students then answer from memory either orally or by first trying to write down the complete list.

This can be adapted as a team or group activity and made harder or easier by varying the number of garments used and by including the colours.

Area 2
Describing appearance (mainly facial)
Agreement of adjectives (revision and extension)
SB 98–99, **1**–**6**
Au choix SB 142, **2**, SB 143, **2**
Au choix SB 144, **2**–**3**
CD 4/3–4
CM 7/3–7/4

Appearance   PRESENTATION/REVISION

This area could be introduced by some revision of nouns, such as *les cheveux, les yeux* and allied vocabulary from earlier units. Adjectives that have been previously met should also be revised, e.g. *petit, grand, jeune, vieux/vieille*. This could be done in a number of ways, e.g. by using flashcards, describing yourself and a few individual students or perhaps making statements for the class to describe as *vrai ou faux*.

To consolidate spelling use a game of *Effacez!* with expressions like *les cheveux blonds/longs, les yeux bleus/bruns* etc. Use *châtain clair* or *bruns* for brown hair and only use *marron* for brown eyes.

SB 98   READING / WRITING
1 Des jeunes

Go through the pictures orally, describing one or two features of several different people first and, by reference to the pictures, teach new expressions, such as *roux, frisés, raides, en queue de cheval*.

Students then allocate the statements to the correct person shown. The answers could first be noted down as **Claire**: c, g, m etc. then checked orally, before the students write down the correct descriptions of the people they have chosen.

Point out to students that the definite article is used with hair, eyes etc. in French, whereas it would not be used in English.

Solution:

Claire: c, g, m
Roxane: d, h
Thomas: e, k, n
Patrick: b, l, n
Mathieu: f, j, n
Lucie: a, i, m

SB 98, 🎧 4/3   LISTENING
2 Qui parle?

This item is based on the previous task. Students look at the pictures and listen and identify the speaker each time.

Solution: 1 *Lucie*, 2 *Claire*, 3 *Patrick*, 4 *Thomas*, 5 *Lucie*, 6 *Claire*, 7 *Mathieu*, 8 *Roxane*

🎧 **Qui parle?**
1 Moi, je suis une fille et j'ai les cheveux roux et frisés.
2 Je suis une fille, j'ai les yeux bleus et les cheveux courts et raides.
3 J'ai les cheveux bruns et longs, en queue de cheval.
4 Moi, je suis un garçon. J'ai les cheveux courts et roux et frisés.
5 Moi, je suis une fille. J'ai les yeux verts et les cheveux frisés.
6 J'ai les yeux bleus et je porte des lunettes.
7 J'ai les yeux bleus et les cheveux blonds, mais je n'ai pas de lunettes.
8 Je suis une fille, j'ai les yeux marron et les cheveux longs et raides. Je ne porte pas de lunettes.

   WRITING
Descriptions

For practice in writing sentences the phrase generation grid on SB 98 (*Pour t'aider*) could be used for work on the computer.

SB 98,   SPEAKING
3 Un jeu d'identité

This activity is based on the same six people as tasks 1 and 2, but involves production of the new language in simple questions. Students work in pairs and could change partners after a few turns.

SB 99 GRAMMAR
Dossier-langue
Les adjectifs (adjectives)

When students have read through this and found some adjectives on earlier pages, these could be written on the board and perhaps used for a game of *Effacez!*, e.g. *Efface un adjectif masculin au singulier.*

SB 99, PRESENTATION/PRACTICE

4 Les mots en images

This is a visual presentation of some adjectives. Students guess or look up the meanings and then design similar sketches for the five other adjectives suggested, perhaps expanding this with ideas of their own.

If equipment is available, students could try out the following suggestion for developing this task.

Les mots en images
This could be done very well on a computer, using features of word or publishing packages, e.g. word art, clip art plus text, font sizes.

Many adjectives could be presented in this way and, if printed, used for display. Adjectives in this unit include:

carré(e)	square-shaped
content(e)	happy
court(e)	short
décontracté(e)	casual (clothes etc.)
fort(e)	strong
grand(e)	tall
gros(se)	fat
haut(e)	high
jeune	young
long(ue)	long
lourd(e)	heavy
mince	slim
petit(e)	small
triste	sad
vieux (vieille)	old
de taille moyenne	medium height

SB 99, READING
WRITING

5 Au voleur!

Students read through this account of a robbery, which contains many adjectives previously introduced. The teacher could ask questions or make up *vrai ou faux?* statements to test comprehension, e.g.

Qu'est-ce qui se passe? Il y a un vol dans un supermarché ou dans une banque?

Il y a combien de voleurs?

Deux hommes, deux femmes ou un homme et une femme?

Est-ce qu'ils sont armés? Est-ce que l'homme a un revolver?

Est-ce que quelqu'un a vu les voleurs?

In the task which follows, students choose the correct adjective to complete the description of each robber. To give extra practice, students could write out their answers in sentences.

Solution: 1 *grand*, 2 *bleus*, 3 *courts*, 4 *carré*, 5 *blanc*, 6 *de taille moyenne*, 7 *gris*, 8 *noire*, 9 *noirs*, 10 *rouges*

PRACTICE

It would also be possible to use the text from *Au voleur!* in a program such as *Fun with Texts* or *Hot Potatoes*. Options which might be used would be a cloze task with adjectives, or *Text Salad* for comprehension.

CM 7/3 DICTIONARY PRACTICE
C'est utile, le dictionnaire!
Looking up adjectives
This would probably be a good time for students to do this dictionary worksheet on adjectives, although it could be used at any time after this, e.g. for homework or for a cover lesson.

Solution:

1 Complète le tableau
  singular
	masculine	feminine
a	grand	grande
b	content	contente
c	long	longue
d	triste	triste
e	blanc	blanche
f	cher	chère
g	délicieux	délicieuse
h	bon	bonne

2 C'est comme l'anglais?
	français	anglais
a	énorme	enormous
b	riche	rich
c	intéressant	interesting
d	possible	possible
e	confortable	comfortable
f	immense	immense, huge
g	parfait	perfect
h	actif	active
i	incurable	incurable

3 Attention aux 'faux amis'
	français	anglais
a	large	wide
b	grand	big, tall
c	joli	pretty
d	mince	slim
e	gentil	kind, nice

AU CHOIX SB 144 GENERAL
PRACTICE

2 Chasse à l'intrus

Students have to identify the word in each group which is not an adjective.

Solution: 1 *magnétoscope (ce n'est pas un adjectif)*, 2 *choisis*, 3 *thé*, 4 *vend*, 5 *yeux*

unité 7 Ça va?

Section 3

159

Ça va? unité 7

AU CHOIX SB 144 GENERAL READING

3 Qui est le voleur?

This activity can be done at two levels, the easier one involving just identifying the thief, by seeing which one matches the description.

Solution: *Daniel Désastre*

The harder, but more interesting task involves speaking in the role of Mlle Maigreton and giving reasons why the others are eliminated, e.g.

Michel Malheur n'a pas de barbe.
Pierre Poison ne porte pas de lunettes.
Claude Cruel a une moustache.
Victor Voleur n'a pas de cheveux etc.

SB 99, WRITING

6 À toi!

Using the table and the one on page 98 to help them, students write a description of a friend or of a member of their family.

They can limit this description to the expressions in the box or can expand it, using other adjectives such as *joli(e), beau/belle, intelligent(e), gentil(le)* – a brainstorming session could be held to produce a suitable range of words, which could be written on the board and either left there for reference or used for a game of *Effacez!*

The finished descriptions could be stored in students' electronic files for future use.

Differentiation

The following *Au choix* activities can be used as support and extension.

AU CHOIX SB 142 SUPPORT READING WRITING

2 Tu vas me reconnaître?

Students look at the three young people and read their description of their appearance. They then correct the descriptions, based on the pictures.

Some students will be able to note down more details than this and could see how much information they can supply.

Solution:

Simon *J'ai les cheveux <u>bruns</u>, courts et <u>frisés</u>. J'ai les yeux <u>bleus</u> et je porte des lunettes. Je porte un pull <u>bleu</u>.*

Magali *J'ai les cheveux <u>noirs</u> et frisés. J'ai les yeux <u>marron</u>. J'ai un T-shirt <u>rouge</u>. (Je ne porte pas de lunettes.)*

Pierre *J'ai les cheveux <u>longs, roux et raides</u> (en queue de cheval) et j'ai les yeux verts. Je porte un sweat <u>noir</u> avec le logo de mon club de VTT.*

AU CHOIX SB 143, 4/4 EXTENSION LISTENING WRITING

2 Vous allez me reconnaître?

Tell students that these French people are going to meet someone for the first time and are describing their appearance and what they will be wearing so that the other person will recognise them.

After students have listened to each description several times, they should complete the descriptions and try to write down as many descriptive features as possible.

Solution:

1 a *blonds,* **b** *courts,* **c** *bleus,* **d** *gris foncé,* **e** *rouge,* **f** *bleu marine*
2 g *verte,* **h** *marron*
3 i *marron,* **j** *frisés,* **k** *marron*

Vous allez me reconnaître?

1 Anne-Marie Lambert
– Allô! Ici le 42-53-09.
– Allô! M. Dupont? C'est Anne-Marie Lambert à l'appareil.
– Bonsoir, Mademoiselle Lambert. Vous arrivez à quelle heure demain?
– J'arrive à la gare de Marseille à sept heures du soir. J'ai les cheveux blonds et courts et les yeux bleus. Je vais mettre un pantalon gris foncé, un pull rouge et un imper bleu marine. Vous allez me reconnaître?
– Ah, oui, certainement. À demain soir.

2 Charlotte
– Allô.
– Écoutez, Madame. J'arrive à la gare d'Orléans à midi et demi. Je porte une robe verte avec une veste marron et un chapeau marron. J'ai les cheveux noirs et les yeux verts. Vous allez me reconnaître?

3 David
– Allô.
– Bonjour, Pierre. C'est ton correspondant David à l'appareil.
– Salut, David. Comment ça va?
– Très bien, merci. Écoute, j'arrive à la gare du Nord à cinq heures de l'après-midi.
– C'est-à-dire, dix-sept heures?
– Oui, c'est ça. Je porte un jean, un T-shirt bleu et un anorak vert. Tu vas me reconnaître? J'ai les cheveux marron et frisés et les yeux marron aussi.
– Très bien, David. Et moi, je porte un jean en velours gris avec une chemise verte et un pull noir.

 WRITING

Description of a friend

Students could use word processing to write a description of a friend. The phrase generators (SB 98–99) could be used to support this. A digital image of the friend could be added. The completed text could become a part of the student's self-description file.

CM 7/4

READING / WRITING

Faites des descriptions

1 Un congrès international

Students look at the pictures and identify each person from the descriptions. They then have to complete the description of one person.

Solution:

A **1** *Karim,* **2** *Magali,* **3** *Lucie,* **4** *Pierre*

B **1** *ans,* **2** *grande,* **3** *cheveux,* **4** *raids,* **5** *yeux,* **6** *porte*

2 Quel type préfères-tu?

They select the correct adjective to complete the opinions in a *sondage*.

Solution: **1** *intelligent,* **2** *gentil,* **3** *grande,* **4** *bleus,* **5** *impossibles,* **6** *polis,* **7** *beaux,* **8** *timide,* **9** *calme,* **10** *sportives*

Area 3
Using direct object pronouns
SB 100–101, 1 – 4
Au choix SB 143, 3
CD 4/5

SB 100

READING PRESENTATION (SPEAKING/WRITING)

1 C'est dans le sac

This item introduces the direct object pronouns and gives further practice of items of clothing.

Students could first look at the garments shown in the carrier bag, and practise them aloud. For further oral or written practice, they could play a short Kim's game, covering the picture and seeing how many of the things they can remember.

They then go on to match up the garments with the descriptions, all of which contain examples of direct object pronouns.

Solution: **1** *un maillot de bain,* **2** *un imper (méable),* **3** *des chaussettes,* **4** *une cravate,* **5** *une casquette,* **6** *des bottes,* **7** *une ceinture,* **8** *des lunettes de soleil*

SB 100

GRAMMAR

Dossier-langue
le, la, l', les

Go through this description with the students, including the four new definitions, checking that they understand the link between the number and gender of the nouns and pronouns.

SB 100

READING / WRITING

2 Le jeu des définitions

Students complete the definitions with *le, la, l'* or *les* and then match them up with the answers.

Solution: **1** *le* – **e**, **2** *le* – **a**, **3** *les* – **b**, **4** *la* – **c**, **5** *le* – **h**, **6** *le* – **d**, **7** *l', le* – **g**, **8** *les* – **f**

SB 101, 4/5

LISTENING SPEAKING/WRITING

3 C'est quelle valise?

This task could just be used for listening or could include simple speaking and writing as well.

Students first look at the five pictures of suitcases and see what each contains. They could just go through these orally or, to help them with the listening task, they could list the things in each case (three things in each, plus one extra in Thomas' case).

They then listen to the recording and work out who owns each case.

There is a deliberate similarity in the contents and each speaker also mentions something that they do not take.

Solution: 1d, 2a, 3b, 4e, 5c

C'est quelle valise?

1 Patrick
– Patrick, tu as fait ta valise?
– Oui, Maman.
– Tu as ton maillot de bain?
– Oui, je l'ai mis dans ma valise.
– Et tes lunettes de soleil et tes sandales?
– Oui oui.
– Tu prends ton pullover?
– Mon pull? Ah non. Je ne le prends pas. Il va faire chaud!

2 Claire
– Voilà! J'ai fait ma valise.
– Tu as pris tes bottes pour marcher, Claire, et un pull?
– Oui, Papa. Je les ai.
– Et ton maillot de bain?
– Non, je ne le prends pas.
– Tu as tes lunettes de soleil?
– Bien sûr, Papa. Je les mets toujours en montagne.

3 Roxane
– J'ai fait ma valise. J'espère que j'ai toutes les choses essentielles. J'ai mon maillot de bain, je l'ai mis dans ma valise. Et j'ai mis mes lunettes de soleil dans ma valise, parce que je ne vais pas les mettre pour le voyage.
– Tu as ton dictionnaire? Ils parlent anglais, là-bas, tu sais!
– Bien sûr. Je l'ai mis dans ma valise aussi. Dis, je ne prends pas de jeans – je vais en acheter pendant les vacances. On dit qu'ils sont beaucoup moins chers qu'ici!

4 Thomas
– Tu as toutes tes affaires,Thomas? Tes lunettes de soleil et tes sandales?
– Ah non, Maman. Je ne les prends pas! Mais j'ai mis mon imperméable dans la valise!
– Tu as le cadeau pour ton correspondant?
– Oui, oui, Maman. Je l'ai. Et j'ai aussi mon dictionnaire français-anglais.
– Ah Thomas, tu n'es pas très optimiste!

unité 7 Ça va?

Section 3

5 Mathieu

– Tu es prêt à partir pour ton stage, Mathieu?
– Oui, Papa. J'ai fait ma valise. J'ai mis mon pull dans la valise, mais je ne prends pas mon imperméable, parce que je vais être dans le collège tout le temps.
– Tu as mis ton jean et tes baskets dans la valise aussi?
– Mon jean, oui, mais je vais porter les baskets pour voyager et j'ai mis mes sandales dans la valise.

SB 101, SPEAKING / WRITING

4 Où sont mes affaires?

Begin by revising common prepositions and using classroom objects to teach the new pattern: *Où est …? Le voilà*, e.g.
– *Où est le livre?* – *Le voilà, sur la table* etc.

Students have to find Dani's belongings and work out the correct reply with the help of a word table. They take it in turns to be Dani and ask the questions.

For further practice of this construction, a student could distribute objects or flashcards, including plural items (e.g. pencils, rubbers, rulers) to other students, then collect them back by asking *Où est le/mon …? Où sont les/mes …?*

The student returning them should say: *Le/La/Les voilà*.

If further practice of garments and prepositions is needed, students could write a description of Dani's room, e.g.

Dans la chambre de Dani, le/son jean et la/sa ceinture sont sous le lit etc.

Au choix SB 143, EXTENSION / SPEAKING

3 Que penses-tu de ça?

Students work in pairs to practise expressing opinions, direct object pronouns and adjectives.

Area 4
Talking about parts of the body
SB 102–103, **1**–**5**
Au choix SB 142, **3**, SB 143, **4**
CD 4/6
CM 7/5, 153

PRESENTATION

Parts of the body

First teach the word *corps*, e.g.
Voici un corps (drawing one on the board, or using an OHT). *En biologie, on étudie le corps.*

Students should also easily link the word with 'corpse'. Then go on to teach or revise the main parts of the body orally, e.g. *la tête, le visage, le cou, les épaules, le bras, la main, le dos, le ventre, la jambe, le genou, le pied.*

Then add in the 'details', e.g. *les cheveux, les yeux, les dents, les oreilles, le nez, la bouche, la gorge, les doigts (de pied).*

La gorge and *les doigts de pied* will need to be explained, but the others are usually learnt easily by acting and repetition.

Any of the following ideas could be used for oral practice:

- Say the words, pointing to yourself. Students repeat, touching their own head etc.
- Stop in mid-list and let students supply the noun, e.g. *la tête, les yeux, les oreilles, le…*
- The first student in the row or group touches his/her head/arm etc. and asks *Qu'est-ce que c'est?* The next person has to say what it is. If the answer is correct, that student does the same to his/her neighbour.
- Game: *Jacques a dit*. Students touch the relevant part of the body if the command is preceded by *Jacques a dit …*

Once students are fairly confident about saying the parts of the body, move on to SB 102, where the written form is introduced.

TB 29, CM 153, 4/6 LISTENING / SPEAKING

Chantez! Alouette

Some teachers might like to use the traditional French action song *Alouette*. You will need to teach *le bec, les ailes, la queue* and *les pattes*. Students can join in with the words of the song, and usually enjoy doing the actions as well. See TB 29 for notes on the use of songs and CM 153 for the music and full words.

Chantez! Alouette

Alouette, gentille alouette,
Alouette, je te plumerai.
Je te plumerai la tête
Je te plumerai la tête
Et la tête, et la tête,
Alouette, Alouette,
Oh …
Je te plumerai le bec …
Je te plumerai le cou …
Je te plumerai le dos …
Je te plumerai les ailes …
Je te plumerai la queue …
Je te plumerai les pattes …

SB 102 PRESENTATION

1 Les parties du corps

Let the class study the words for the parts of the body for a few minutes, before practising them by repetition.

As they get better at this, give them numbers at random and see how quickly they can supply the correct word, e.g. 6 *le genou*, 10 *le nez* etc. This could develop into a team game, each team saying a number in turn. The game could be made increasingly complicated, e.g. by saying masculine and feminine words alternately or by not repeating a number already said.

After students are fairly confident orally, they can practise spelling with a Spelling Bee, or by a team game, as follows: a member of team A says a word, someone in team B has to give instructions to another member of their own team for writing the word on the board.

The words could be left up and used later, either for a game of *Effacez!* or a game in which teams ask each other the meaning of words and rub them off if the answer is correct, e.g. *Une épaule, qu'est-ce que ça veut dire?*

SB 102 SPEAKING/WRITING

2 Qu'est-ce que c'est?

Students complete these sentences with parts of the body. Some students might be able to make up some more similar examples.

Solution: 1 *jambes*, 2 *dents*, 3 *bouche*, 4 *les yeux*, 5 *les oreilles*, 6 *les doigts (les mains)*, 7 *le cou (les épaules)*, 8 *les épaules*

CM 7/5 READING, WRITING

Les clowns

This worksheet provides practice first in recognising, then writing the new vocabulary. Students could do what they can from memory, then check back with SB 102.

Students could do this worksheet now or leave it till later to be used as support when more able students do the dictionary task in *Au choix* (SB 143, task 4).

Solution:
2 Écris le bon texte
1	le cou	neck
2	les épaules	shoulders
3	la tête	head
4	le dos	back
5	le genou	knee
6	le bras	arm
7	le ventre	stomach
8	la jambe	leg
9	la main	hand
10	le doigt	finger
16	le pied	foot
11	l'œil	eye
12	le nez	nose
13	l'oreille	ear
14	la bouche	mouth
15	la gorge	throat

SPEAKING
Chantez!

For extra practice of parts of the body, students could sing a version of the 'Heads and shoulders, knees and toes' song, e.g.

La tête, les épaules, les genoux et les pieds
La tête, les épaules, les genoux et les pieds
Les yeux, les oreilles, la bouche et le nez
La tête, les épaules, les genoux et les pieds

SB 103, READING SPEAKING/WRITING

3 Au zoo 'fantaisie'

Students read the description of the *élé-chat* and complete the descriptions (orally or written) of the other animals. (Some students could be working on the *lap-chien*, while the more able could describe the *pois-souris*.)

They can all then go on to design the *monstre Tricolore*, perhaps working in small groups or using a computer drawing facility.

SB 103, WRITING

4 À toi!

In this pairwork activity, students invent their own animals and write a simple description. They exchange this with another person, who has to draw the animal decribed. A *zoo fantaisie* of the best drawings could be put on display.

Differentiation

The following *Au choix* activities can be used as support and extension.

Au choix SB 142 SUPPORT WRITING

3 Mots et images

This task involves copying the correct words for each picture.

Solution: 1 *le bras*, 2 *l'oreille*, 3 *le pied*, 4 *les épaules*, 5 *le cou*, 6 *les doigts*, 7 *la bouche*, 8 *les dents*

Au choix SB 143 EXTENSION DICTIONARY PRACTICE

4 C'est utile, le dictionnaire

This item should be of interest especially to more able students and presents some common expressions which each include the word for a part of the body.

The teacher could give other expressions to able students and help them to work out the meaning, e.g.
*la **main** dans la main* (hand in hand)
fait à la main (hand-made)
donner un coup de main (to give someone a hand)
*à **bras** ouverts* (with open arms)
croiser les bras (to fold your arms)
*ne tourne pas la **tête*** (don't look round)
j'ai la tête qui tourne (I feel dizzy / my head is spinning)
je vais me laver la tête (I'm going to wash my hair)
avoir la grosse tête (to be big-headed)
*des **pieds** à la tête* (from head to foot)
il a les pieds sur terre (he has his feet (firmly) on the ground)
se lever du pied gauche (to get out of bed the wrong side)
marcher pieds nus (to walk barefoot)

unité 7 Ça va?

Section 3

163

SB 102–103

**READING
WRITING**

5 Tu aimes les animaux?

These two texts are fairly difficult, but it is hoped that students will make a reasonable attempt to guess words they haven't met before, and the amount of help to be supplied is left to the teacher.

Students could read through the section on understanding French in *Tips for language learning* (SB 153). Reference might also be made to the reading strategies taught in **Encore Tricolore 1**.

a À quoi sert le cou de la girafe?
This item is followed by sentences to be completed with words from the article. Students could write their answers out in full for extra practice.

Solution: 1 *long*, 2 *feuilles*, 3 *grande*, 4 *cou*, 5 *impossible (difficile)*, 6 *facile*, 7 *jambes*

b Pourquoi les zèbres sont-ils rayés?
This is slightly more difficult but is followed by comprehension questions in English.

Solution: 1 No. 2 They blur it. 3 When the zebras are in a herd. 4 Not very good (can distinguish contrasts). 5 Each zebra's stripes are different from any others.

**PRACTICE
LISTENING/SPEAKING**

Le corps

Here are some ideas for extra practice of parts of the body.

1 Dessine un corps!
This could be used as a class or group activity. Everyone has a fairly long narrow strip of paper. The first person in the group gives the command *Dessine une tête (et un cou/des épaules)*.

All draw a head (or head and neck/shoulders) and fold it over with the neck or edges of the shoulders showing.

All change papers and the next player says *Dessine les bras, les mains et le ventre (ou le dos)*. The body is drawn leaving the top of the legs showing and then all papers are again passed on.

The next command is *Dessine les jambes et les pieds*. This time after the paper is passed on the resultant masterpieces are opened and sometimes prove very amusing.

For more able students, the finished drawings could be used for extra oral practice. A student could pick up a drawing at random and say as many things about it as possible, e.g.
Il a une grosse tête et un (le) nez très long.

Points could be awarded for correct statements.

2 Une personne extraordinaire
Students may like to draw a picture or stick a photo in their exercise books and label the parts of the body (perhaps with masculine words on one side and feminine on the other or using red and blue for the different genders).

Alternatively, they could create a labelled picture using a computer drawing programme.

Similar but bigger pictures for the classroom wall could be made by groups or pairs using posters of pop stars or fashion pictures from magazines or mail-order catalogues.

As another alternative, students can create their own 'montage monsters' or 'potty people' by combining parts of the body from different magazine or computer-generated illustrations.

PRACTICE

Animals

There are many French websites devoted to animals. Ask pupils to find a site using a search engine in French – *google* is excellent for this. Reports could be compiled which could be presented orally or electronically.

Suggested criteria for reports:
Le site s'appelle …
Il se trouve à …
Il s'agit de …
Il y a des images/sons/textes/liens etc.

**Area 5
Saying how you feel and describing what hurts
avoir mal + parts of the body**
SB 104, **1**–**4**
Au choix SB 144, **4**
CD 4/7
CM 7/6
Grammar in Action 2, page 24

**PRESENTATION
SPEAKING**

J'ai mal à …

Introduce this phrase orally and demonstrate by suitably exaggerated actions saying *j'ai mal à la tête / la main / la jambe / la gorge*, with the class copying you with appropriate mimes.

After a few repetitions, involve students in saying and miming what's wrong with them. Ask *Qu'est-ce qui ne va pas?* After each mime introduce the third person by remarking *Il/Elle a mal …*

Practise with feminine nouns first, then with words beginning with a vowel and gradually add in masculine and plural nouns until the class is familiar with *j'ai mal à* + all suitable nouns. Also, teach and explain *j'ai mal au cœur* (I feel sick).

Games

PRACTICE

For further practice you could play one or more of the following games.

1 J'ai mal ici
Someone says *J'ai mal ici,* touching e.g. their leg. The others have to supply the correct description (involving the second person singular), e.g. *Tu as mal à la jambe* etc.

2 Qu'est-ce qui ne va pas?
Someone decides where they are hurting (and writes it down as a check!) then says *Qu'est-ce qui ne va pas?*

The others guess: *Tu as mal au bras?* etc. and the person who guesses correctly is the next invalid.

3 Tu as mal ici

This is a team or group game. Everyone writes (or draws) on a piece of paper a part of the body for which the name has been taught. These are mixed up and members of the opposing team pick one out in turn, hand it to the teacher or team leader and act and describe the injury correctly.

4 J'ai mal ...

A popular classroom activity to practise this involves the use of a paper hankie, coloured with red ink in the centre. The teacher (and later a student) walks round the room and places it on the head, arm, hand, back etc. of someone, asking *Qu'est-ce qui ne va pas?* for the reply *J'ai mal à ...*

The third person can be introduced as well with the comment *Oui, il/elle a mal à ...*

Practice on similar lines can be done with an OHT, starting with a basic body shape and a sad face with down-turned mouth. The teacher places the 'blood-stained' hanky in different places and students answer in the third person. If an OHP is not available a body can be drawn on the board and the hanky stuck on with Blu-tack.

SB 104 READING

1 Un match amical!

First ask students to look at the pictures of the injured players and ask questions about their injuries, e.g.
Regardez numéro un. Qu'est-ce qui ne va pas? Et voici Mêlée, la petite chienne, la mascotte. (Perhaps explain the meaning of *mêlée* and the choice of the dog's name.)
Où a-t-elle mal? Et ça, c'est l'arbitre. Où a-t-il mal?

Then read aloud the description of the match, with questions and explanations to check comprehension. Students could guess or could look up in a dictionary: *une équipe, le ballon de rugby, l'arbitre, le résultat – match nul.*

Students then try to identify the injured players, e.g.
Numéro 1, c'est Maxime – il a mal à la jambe.

Solution: 1 *Maxime,* 2 *Léonard,* 3 *Marius,* 4 *Didier,* 5 *Auguste,* 6 *Jean-Mathieu,* 7 *Jean-Baptiste,* 8 *Alphonse,* 9 *Clément,* 10 *Mêlée,* 11 *l'arbitre,* 12 *Jean-François*

Note on the team names: these are linked to the names of the two villages. A series of Popes had the name Étienne – nine popes with this name were in office from 254 until 1058. The name Louis has obvious links with the monarchy, featuring many times as the name of kings of France from 778 until 1824. Students could look this information up on the Internet or *le Petit Larousse* and find out more about French place names.

SB 104 GRAMMAR

Dossier-langue
How to say what hurts

This sets out the pattern for *j'ai mal à* + parts of the body.

SB 104 SPEAKING/WRITING

2 Ils sont blessés

Students supply the correct part of *avoir mal*.

Solution: 1 *a mal,* 2 *a mal,* 3 *ont mal,* 4 *ont mal,* 5 *j'ai mal,* 6 *a mal*

SB 104 SPEAKING/WRITING

3 Après le match

Students work out what each of the injured actually says to the doctor. The answers can be given orally or in written form.

Solution: 1 *à l'œil droit,* 2 *à l'oreille gauche,* 3 *J'ai mal au nez,* 4 *J'ai mal au pied,* 5 *J'ai mal au dos,* 6 *J'ai mal à la tête, à la gorge, aux bras, à la main et au ventre*

SB 104, SPEAKING

4 Qui parle?

Students work in pairs, taking turns to pretend to be one of the wounded players and to make an appropriate statement. The other person has to identify the speaker.

CM 7/6, 4/7 LISTENING / WRITING

Ça ne va pas

1 Moi, j'ai mal

The first task on this worksheet is a listening task in which students hear different people saying what hurts and find the matching picture.

Solution: 1e, 2a, 3g, 4b, 5c, 6d, 7h, 8f

Moi, j'ai mal

1 J'ai mal à la tête.
2 J'ai mal au dos.
3 Maman, maman, j'ai mal au genou!
4 Aïe, mon pied!
5 Ça ne va pas ce matin, j'ai mal au ventre.
6 Ça alors! J'ai très mal aux dents.
7 J'ai mal aux oreilles, c'est horrible!
8 J'ai joué au tennis, mais maintenant, j'ai mal au bras.

2 On a mal, mais où?

This is a writing task with practice of the first and third persons of *avoir mal*.

Solution: 1 *J'ai mal à la main,* 2 *Il a mal au pied,* 3 *Elle a mal au bras,* 4 *J'ai mal aux dents,* 5 *Il a mal à la jambe,* 6 *Elle a mal au genou,* 7 *J'ai mal au cou,* 8 *J'ai mal aux oreilles.*

165

Au choix SB 144 — GENERAL PRACTICE

4 Ils sont malades!

Students match the captions to the injuries. When checking, read out the sentence in full, e.g. *Il a mal au ventre*.

Solution: 1h, 2j, 3e, 4a, 5b, 6g, 7c, 8f, 9i, 10d

GRAMMAR IN ACTION 2, PAGE 24 GRAMMAR PRACTICE

Using *avoir mal* + parts of the body

These activities could be used here for extra practice.

Ça ne va pas bien — SPEAKING PRACTICE

For further oral practice, if required, the following dialogue could be written on the board or on an OHT and students could act it in pairs. If an OHP is used, sentences could be written on separate slips and jumbled up, then put in order by students before they begin the pairwork, e.g.
– *Bonjour. Ça va?*
– *Non, ça ne va pas très bien.*
– *Pourquoi?*
– *J'ai mal à …*
– *Et toi?*
– *Oh moi, ça va.*
or
Oh moi, j'ai mal … (Both go off clutching appropriate part of anatomy.)

Area 6
**Other expressions with *avoir*
(*j'ai chaud/froid/soif/faim/de la fièvre*)**
SB 105, 5 – 8
CD 4/8
FC 81–86
CM 7/7
Grammar in Action 2, page 25

FC 81–86 — PRESENTATION

Expressions with *avoir*

Explain that the verb *avoir* is also useful for describing other feelings, e.g. warmth, cold, hunger or thirst.

Present the new expressions first with the flashcards and accompanying exaggerated action. Then speak directly to individual students, e.g.
Moi, j'ai chaud.
(Student A), est-ce que tu as chaud?
Est-ce qu'il/elle a chaud? etc.

For further consolidation, play some flashcard games, e.g. Guess the flashcard, or some mime games, as suggested for *J'ai mal …* above.

SB 105 — READING

5 Quelle description?

This presents the written form of the *avoir* expressions. Students match the captions to the cartoons.

Some students may like to draw their own cartoons, with suitable captions, and there could be a competition based on this.

Solution: 1b, 2f, 3a, 4e, 5c, 6d

SB 105 — GRAMMAR

Dossier-langue
Expressions with *avoir*

When students have read this, ask a few questions or make some statements with suitable mimes, to check that students understand how these expressions are used.

SB 105 — WRITING

6 Qu'est-ce qu'ils disent?

This is a simple maze puzzle to give practice in producing the new expressions.

Solution: 1 *J'ai faim.* 2 *J'ai chaud.* 3 *J'ai soif.*
4 *J'ai faim.* 5 *J'ai froid.*

SB 105, 4/8 — LISTENING

7 C'est quelle image?

Students look at the five pictures for hot, cold etc. then listen to the recording and note down the letter for the correct picture each time. Besides including expressions with *avoir*, most of these short dialogues include a verb in the imperative. Several of the pictures are used more than once.

Solution: 1a, 2d, 3c, 4b, 5e, 6a, 7c, 8d

C'est quelle image?

1 – Moi, j'ai faim. Passe-moi un grand morceau de gâteau, s'il te plaît.

2 – J'ai froid.
– Alors, mets ton anorak et tes gants!

3 – Il fait très chaud aujourd'hui, n'est-ce pas?
– Oui, j'ai trop chaud! Je vais acheter une glace.

4 – Tu as soif, Jean-Pierre?
– Oui oui, j'ai très soif.
– Alors prends ce verre de limonade!
– Oh, merci beaucoup!

5 – Vous avez de la fièvre, Madame?
– Oui, j'ai de la fièvre et j'ai mal à la tête.
– Eh bien, retournez à la maison et prenez de l'aspirine.

6 – Moi, j'ai faim. Tu as quelque chose à manger?
– Tu as faim, Chantal? Voilà, mange cette banane.

7 – Ouvrez la fenêtre, s'il vous plaît.
– Vous avez chaud?
– Oui, il fait très chaud ici.

8 – Entre vite. Tu as froid?
– Oui, il fait très froid en ville.

CM 7/7 PRACTICE

Avoir – un verbe utile

1 Trouve les paires

This is a straightforward matching task to revise the verb *avoir*.

Solution: 1g, 2d, 3b, 4h, 5a, 6f, 7e, 8c

2 Remplis les blancs

Students complete the captions with the correct expression (A) and then match the captions to the pictures (B).

Solution: 1 *chaud,* **f**; 2 *faim,* **b**; 3 *froid,* **d**; 4 *soif,* **c**; 5 *de la fièvre,* **a**; 6 *chaud,* **e**

3 Un petit lexique

Students can use a dictionary to help them complete the list of expressions with *avoir*.

Solution:

avoir chaud	to be hot
avoir de la fièvre	to have a temperature
avoir faim	to be hungry
avoir froid	to be cold
avoir soif	to be thirsty
avoir lieu	to take place
avoir peur	to be afraid
avoir raison	to be right
avoir sommeil	to be sleepy
avoir tort	to be wrong

4 Cinq expressions

Students have to supply the English meaning for some of the expressions from task 3.

1 *Tu as raison* — You are right.
2 *... a lieu* — ... is taking place
3 *J'ai sommeil.* — I'm sleepy.
4 *Vous avez tort.* — You are wrong.
5 *... a peur ... j'ai peur* — is afraid... I'm afraid

GRAMMAR IN ACTION 2, PAGE 25 GRAMMAR PRACTICE

Using expressions with *avoir*

These activities could be used here for extra practice.

SB 105 READING

8 Trouve la réponse!

Students match two statements, practising expressions with *avoir* and commands.

Solution: 1d, 2a, 3f, 4b, 5c, 6e

Area 7
At the doctor's
Saying how you feel
Using the imperative
SB 106–107, **1**–**5**
Au choix SB 145, **5**
CM 7/8
CD 4/9–12

SB 106, 🎧 4/9 LISTENING READING SPEAKING

1 Ça ne va pas!

a This recorded conversation presents the sort of language students might need to use if they were ill in France. Students read through the conversation and listen to the recording. They could then read it in pairs for consolidation.

b Students complete the short *résumé*.

Solution: 1f, 2g, 3b, 4a, 5c, 6e, 7d

🎧 **Ça ne va pas!**

– Bonjour, Charles, ça va?
– Bonjour, Madame. Non, ce matin, je ne vais pas très bien.
– Qu'est-ce qui ne va pas?
– J'ai mal à la tête et j'ai mal à la gorge aussi.
– Quand tu es chez toi, est-ce que tu prends de l'aspirine?
– Oui, Madame.
– Alors, bois ce verre d'eau et prends cette aspirine. Repose-toi un peu et si tu ne vas pas mieux, je vais téléphoner au médecin.
– Merci, Madame.
(Plus tard)
– Ça va mieux, Charles?
– Ah, non. J'ai toujours mal à la tête et maintenant, j'ai mal aux oreilles aussi et je crois que j'ai de la fièvre.
– Alors, je vais demander un rendez-vous chez le médecin.

SB 106, 🎧 4/10 LISTENING WRITING SPEAKING

2 Tout le monde est malade

These three conversations are based closely on the previous one, though they are shorter.

This time students listen and complete the text with the words in the box.

As before, they could practise the completed conversations in pairs.

Solution: 1a, 2g, 3i, 4e, 5c, 6d, 7h, 8j, 9b, 10f

unité 7 Ça va?

Section 3

167

Tout le monde est malade

1 Hélène
- Bonjour, Hélène, ça va?
- Non, Madame, je ne vais pas très bien.
- Qu'est-ce qui ne va pas?
- Je suis asthmatique, vous savez. Je crois que c'est ça.
- Alors, prends ton inhalateur et repose-toi un peu et si tu ne vas pas mieux, je vais téléphoner au médecin.
- Oui, Madame. J'ai soif, aussi, et j'ai chaud.
- Alors, bois ce verre d'eau.

2 Martin
- Alors, Martin. Ça va mieux?
- Non, Monsieur, ça ne va pas mieux.
- Qu'est-ce qui ne va pas?
- J'ai mal au ventre et j'ai mal au cœur.
- Alors, prends ce médicament et reste au lit.

3 Alain
- Ça va, Alain?
- Non, Madame, ça ne va pas très bien.
- Qu'est-ce qu'il y a?
- Je suis allergique au poisson et hier, j'ai mangé des crevettes.
- Alors, bois de l'eau, mais ne mange rien.

SB 106 GRAMMAR

Dossier-langue
Commands (the imperative)

When students have read through this explanation of the imperative (*tu* and *vous* forms), they could look for other examples on SB 105–106.

SB 106 WRITING SPEAKING

3 Il y a un problème?

Students complete these short dialogues with the singular imperative of the verbs, then practise them aloud in pairs. If students find this difficult, the teacher could write the missing words on the board, in random order.

Solution: **1** mange, bois, **2** ouvre, mets, **3** va, reste, va

SB 107, 4/11, LISTENING READING SPEAKING

4 Chez le médecin

After listening to the dialogue, students practise it in pairs, substituting symptoms etc. from the colour-coded sections.

This task contains examples of the plural form of the imperative.

Chez le médecin
- Bonjour! Qu'est-ce qui ne va pas?
- J'ai mal aux oreilles et à la gorge, Docteur, et je ne peux pas dormir.
- Ouvrez la bouche. Ah, oui. Je vois. Ça vous fait mal là?
- Aïe! Oui, un peu!
- Voici une ordonnance. Prenez ce médicament. Et téléphonez, si ça ne va pas mieux.
- Merci, Docteur.

SB 107 READING WRITING

5 Bonne santé

Students complete the poster with the *vous* form of the imperative.

Solution: **1** Mangez, mangez, **2** Buvez, **3** Dormez, **4** N'oubliez pas, écoutez, brossez, **5** marchez, **6** faites, **7** Ne fumez pas, ne commencez pas, **8** restez, ne regardez pas, ne jouez pas, faites

AU CHOIX SB 145 GENERAL READING WRITING

5 Mamie va voir le médecin

Students complete this cartoon story with examples of the imperative.

Solution: **1** Ouvrez, **2** Allez, **3** Prenez, **4** Restez, **5** venez, **6** Demandez

CM7/8, 4/12, LISTENING SPEAKING WRITING

On est malade

For further work about a visit to the doctor, students could do this worksheet.

1 Au téléphone

This item involves taking down messages from phone conversations.

Students read the introduction, asking if there is anything they don't understand. They then listen to the phone conversations and take down the messages.

Solution:
1 M. et Mme Clémenceau ont mal au ventre et le chat a de la fièvre.
2 Annette a mal au cœur et mal à la tête.
3 (La famille Durand) Le bébé a mal à l'œil droit et il ne peut pas dormir.
4 Jeanne a mal au dos, Paul a mal aux oreilles et les deux enfants ont mal à la gorge.

Au téléphone
1
- Allô!
- Bonjour! C'est Mme Clémenceau à l'appareil.
- Bonjour, Madame.
- Est-ce que je peux laisser un message pour Mme Lévy?
- Bien sûr, Madame.
- Alors, mon mari et moi, nous ne pouvons pas venir ce soir, parce que nous avons tous les deux mal au ventre. Et en plus, notre petit chat, Félix, est malade. Il a de la fièvre.
- Ce n'est pas bien, tout ça, Madame! Je vais donner le message à Mme Lévy.

2 – Allô!
– C'est Annette ici. C'est toi, Sara?
– Oui oui, c'est moi.
– Alors, veux-tu dire à Mme Lévy que je ne peux pas venir ce soir, parce que j'ai mal au cœur et j'ai mal à la tête.
– Ah, c'est triste, Annette. Je vais lui dire cela.

3 – Allô!
– Bonjour. Vous êtes la jeune anglaise qui est en visite?
– Oui, Madame. C'est moi.
– Alors, ce soir, nous allons arriver en retard pour la surprise-party. C'est que nous allons chez le médecin, parce que le bébé a mal à l'œil droit et il ne peut pas dormir. Vous allez l'expliquer à Mme Lévy, n'est-ce pas?
– Oui oui, Madame. Je vais lui expliquer.

4 – Allô!
– C'est Sara?
– Oui.
– C'est Jeanne. Tu sais, nous sommes les cousins de Mme Lévy.
– Ah oui. Vous venez ce soir?
– Non, malheureusement, tout le monde est malade. Moi, j'ai mal au dos, Paul a mal aux oreilles et les deux enfants ont mal à la gorge.
– Quel désastre! Je vais expliquer tout ça à Mme Lévy.

2 Chez le médecin

This is a dice dialogue for practice of conversations at the doctors.

3 Tu comprends le médecin?

This is a short writing task to consolidate key language when visiting a doctor.

Solution:

français	*anglais*
Qu'est-ce qui ne va pas?	What is the matter?
J'ai mal à la tête.	My head hurts.
Ça va mieux?	Are you any better?
Ce n'est pas grave.	It's not serious.
Est-ce que vous dormez bien?	Do you sleep well?
Buvez/Bois beaucoup d'eau.	Drink plenty of water.
Avez-vous de la fièvre?	Have you a temperature?
Ne mange(z) pas aujourd'hui.	Don't eat today.
C'est quel nom, s'il vous plaît?	What name is it, please?
Reste(z) au lit	Stay in bed.

Area 8
Using the verb *dormir*
Au choix SB 145, 6

This short optional area has been included for teachers who wish to teach the present and perfect tense of *dormir* more fully. Some teachers might prefer just to ask students to look the verb up in the verb list and add it to their own electronic files. All the students' material is in *Au choix* general (SB 145).

Au choix SB 145   GENERAL READING

6 Tout le monde dort

This short anecdote includes all the parts of the verb *dormir*.

When students have read it, ask some oral questions to check that they understand it all. They can then do the *vrai ou faux?* task (**b**).

Solution: **1** faux, **2** faux, **3** vrai, **4** faux, **5** faux, **6** faux

Au choix SB 145   GRAMMAR

Dossier-langue
***dormir* (to sleep, to be asleep)**

Perhaps begin by revising *sortir* and *partir*, using a verb paradigm game (see TB 27).

Students should read the *Dossier-langue* and then look back at the previous item to find all the parts of *dormir* in the story. They then make up some sentences, each containing parts of the verb.
Tell the class that, if they are staying with a French family, they might be asked *As-tu bien dormi?* and wished a good night with the phrases *Dors/Dormez bien!*

Area 9
Further activities and consolidation
SB 108, 109
CD 4/13–16
Student CD 1/37–42, 2/22–25
CM 7/9–7/16, 138

CM 7/9, 🎧 SCD 1/37–42   INDEPENDENT LISTENING
SOUNDS AND WRITING

Écoute et parle

This copymaster provides pronunciation and speaking practice.

1 À la française

🎧 **À la française**

1	accident	5	pyjama
2	CD	6	sport
3	invitation	7	spécial
4	possible	8	surprise

2 Et après?

Solution: **1** e, **2** j, **3** n, **4** q, **5** t, **6** v, **7** x, **8** z

🎧 **Et après?**

1 d, **2** i, **3** m, **4** p, **5** s, **6** u, **7** w, **8** y

3 Des phrases ridicules

🎧 **Des phrases ridicules**

Cent enfants chantent en même temps.
Le cochon de mon oncle Léon adore le melon.

4 Les terminaisons: -ure

Solution: 1d, 2a, 3e, 4c, 5f, 6b

🎧 Les terminaisons: -ure

1 coiffure
2 aventure
3 confiture
4 ceinture
5 voiture
6 écriture

5 Vocabulaire de classe

Solution: 1 *mot*, 2 *cent deux (102)*, 3 *fini*, 4 *je*, 5 *c*, 6 *livre*, 7 *vos*

🎧 Vocabulaire de classe

1 Écris le mot qui manque.
2 Lisez l'activité 5 à la page cent deux.
3 Qui a fini?
4 Moi, je n'ai pas fini.
5 Trouve un mot qui commence avec c.
6 Tu as oublié ton livre?
7 Vérifiez vos réponses.

6 Des conversations

🎧 Des conversations

1 Une fête chez Alice

– C'est la fête chez Alice demain. Qu'est ce que tu vas mettre?
(pause)
– Je vais mettre un jean avec mon T-shirt noir et blanc.
– Tu vas mettre tes baskets avec ça?
(pause)
– Non, je vais mettre mes sandales.
– Qu'est-ce que tu as acheté comme cadeau pour Alice?
(pause)
– J'ai acheté ces lunettes de soleil.

2 Les photos sont arrivées

– Tu as reçu la photo de ton correspondant?
(pause)
– Oui, mais c'est à la maison.
– Il est comment?
(pause)
– Il a les cheveux courts et frisés et il porte des lunettes.
– Est-ce qu'il est grand ou petit?
(pause)
– Il est grand.

3 Chez le médecin

– Avez-vous un rendez-vous avec le médecin?
(pause)
– Oui, à dix heures vingt.
(pause)
– Alors, qu'est-ce qui ne va pas?
(pause)
– J'ai mal à la tête et aux oreilles.
– Ouvrez la bouche. Avez-vous mal à la gorge?
(pause)
– Oui, Docteur, et je ne peux pas dormir.
– Voici une ordonnance, et téléphonez si ça ne va pas mieux.
(pause)
– Merci, Docteur.

CM 7/10, 🎧 SCD 2/22–25 INDEPENDENT LISTENING

Tu comprends?

Students could do any or all of the four items on this worksheet, now or later as revision.

1 On part en vacances

Solution: 1b, 2j, 3c, 4f, 5e, 6a, 7d

🎧 On part en vacances

– Je prends mon jean – c'est essentiel.
– Oui, et ton maillot de bains. Ça, c'est essentiel aussi.
– Alors, mes baskets, je vais les mettre dans la valise comme ça et puis deux ou trois paires de chaussettes.
– N'oublie pas tes gants – il va peut-être faire froid.
– Oh non, je ne vais pas prendre mes gants, mais ma casquette.
– Et voilà ton T-shirt.
– D'accord, je prends deux ou trois T-shirts et puis mon pull. Et c'est tout.
– Tu ne prends pas ta chemise?
– Ah non. J'ai tous mes T-shirts. Je ne veux pas porter de chemise en vacances.

2 Faites cela, s'il vous plaît

Solution: 1 *mets*, 2 *prends*, 3 *apporte*, 4 *range*, 5 *téléphone*, 6 *demande*, 7 *écrivez*, 8 *cherchez*, 9 *travaillez*, 10 *Jetez*, 11 *cochez*, 12 *N'oubliez pas*

🎧 Faites cela, s'il vous plaît

À la maison
Pouvez-vous m'aider un peu, les enfants? Les visiteurs vont bientôt arriver.
Linda, mets la table, s'il te plaît, et Charles, prends ces assiettes et apporte les serviettes de table.
Ensuite, Linda, range un peu tes affaires et Charles, téléphone à Papa sur son portable et demande-lui à quelle heure il va arriver.

En classe
D'abord, écrivez ces listes de mots dans votre cahier, s'il vous plaît!
Si vous ne comprenez pas tous les mots, cherchez dans le dictionnaire.
Maintenant, travaillez à deux.
Jetez le dé à tour de rôle et cochez les bonnes cases.
N'oubliez pas de corriger les erreurs à la fin.

3 Chez le médecin

Solution: 1V, 2F, 3F, 4V, 5F, 6F, 7V, 8F, 9V, 10F

🎧 Chez le médecin

1 – Bonjour, Madame Dupont. Qu'est-ce qui ne va pas?
– J'ai mal à la tête, Docteur, et je crois que j'ai de la fièvre.
– Attendez! Oui, vous avez de la fièvre – mais ce n'est pas trop grave. Vous avez mal à la gorge et aux oreilles?

– À la gorge, oui, un peu, mais je n'ai pas mal aux oreilles.
– Bon. Voici une ordonnance. Prenez ces pilules, buvez beaucoup d'eau et reposez-vous.
– Merci, Docteur.

2 – Bonjour, Richard.
– Bonjour, Docteur.
– Qu'est-ce qu'il y a?
– Hier, j'ai joué un match de rugby et maintenant, j'ai très mal au genou et au pied gauche.
– Ça te fait mal là?
– Aïe! Oui, très mal, Docteur.
– Ton pied, ça va, mais pour le genou, il faut aller à l'hôpital pour vérifier. Ta mère est avec toi?
– Non, mais mon père est là. Il est dans la voiture.
– Très bien. Je vais tout lui expliquer.
– Merci, Docteur.

4 Voici mes amis

Solution: 1 *Kémi*, 2 *Élise*, 3 *Charles*, 4 *Patrick*, 5 *Lucie*, 6 *Hélène*

🎧 **Voici mes amis**

Ce garçon-ci, c'est Kémi. Il a les cheveux courts et frisés et il porte des lunettes. Il n'est pas très grand.

Mon meilleur ami, c'est Charles. Le voici avec ses cheveux longs en queue de cheval et son pull noir, avec le logo de son équipe de football favorite. Il est grand, non?

Et l'autre garçon, c'est Patrick. Il est aussi grand que Charles, mais il a les cheveux courts et noirs. Regarde, il porte son T-shirt. Il a toujours chaud!

Et les filles sont des amies aussi. Il y a Lucie, avec ses cheveux longs et frisés. Elle est jolie, non? J'aime son sweat-shirt avec les chats dessus.

La fille qui est assez petite et qui a les cheveux courts et raides, c'est Élise, et l'autre fille, plus grande qu'Élise et Lucie, ça c'est Hélène. Sur la photo elle porte ses lunettes de soleil – je ne sais pas pourquoi!

SB 108, CM 7/11
Sommaire

A summary of the main structures and vocabulary of this unit. Students fill in gaps on the copymaster. They should check their answers against the Students' Book page.

CM 7/12   REVISION
Rappel 7

This copymaster can be used at any point in the course for revision and consolidation. It provides revision of members of the family, rooms in a house, school subjects and some general vocabulary, in particular connective words. The reading and writing tasks are self-instructional and can be used by students working individually for homework or during cover lessons.

Solution:
1 Un jeu de définitions
A 1 *enfant unique*, 2 *tante*, 3 *cousins*, 4 *grand-mère*
B 1 *la chambre (à coucher)*, 2 *la cuisine*, 3 *la salle à manger*, 4 *la salle de bains*

2 Des mots utiles
a

	français	*anglais*
1	d'abord	first of all
2	alors	so, then
3	donc	so, then
4	ensuite	next, after that
5	mais	but
6	et	and
7	ou	or
8	puis	next, after that
9	si	if
10	quand	when

b (Suggested answers) **1** d'abord, ensuite, **2** et, **3** Ensuite, **4** mais, **5** donc, **6** Quand, alors

3 Mots croisés (les matières scolaires)

¹a	n	²g	l	³a	i	⁴s			⁵f
l		é		r		c		⁶h	r
l		o		t		i		i	a
e				⁷d	e	s	s	i	n
⁸m	a	t	h	s		n		t	ç
a						c		o	a
n		⁹e	p	¹⁰s		e		¹¹i	c	i
d				u		s		r	s
¹²c	o	u	r	s			¹³n	e

Épreuve – Unité 7

These worksheets can be used for an informal test of listening, speaking, reading and writing or for extra practice, as required. For general notes on administering the *Épreuves*, see TB 16.

CM 7/13, 🎧 4/13–16   LISTENING
Épreuve: Écouter

A Sept personnes vont chez le médecin (NC 2)

Solution: 1d, 2e, 3g, 4a, 5f, 6c, 7b

(mark /6: 4+ shows the ability to understand a range of familiar statements)

🎧 **Sept personnes vont chez le médecin**

1 Docteur, j'ai mal à l'œil.
2 Docteur, j'ai mal à la tête.
3 J'ai mal à la main.
4 Mon bras! J'ai mal au bras.
5 Mon oreille! J'ai mal à l'oreille.
6 Docteur, j'ai mal au pied.
7 J'ai mal à la jambe!

B Au voleur! (NC 3)

Solution: 1g, 2a, 3e, 4f, 5d, 6c, 7b

(mark /6: 4+ shows the ability to understand short passages)

Au voleur!

1. Le voleur? Il a les cheveux longs et noirs. Il est grand, il n'a pas de lunettes et il porte une chemise blanche et un jean blanc.
2. C'est une femme! Elle a les cheveux courts et blonds. Elle est de taille moyenne, elle porte des lunettes. Elle porte aussi une jupe noire et un T-shirt noir.
3. Le voleur? C'est un homme avec les cheveux en queue de cheval.
4. C'est une femme très élégante. Elle est jeune, très mince et elle porte un collier.
5. Le voleur est grand et il est très gros.
6. C'est une femme âgée, très triste, et elle porte des vêtements noirs.
7. C'est un homme très élégant. Il porte une cravate, des lunettes de soleil et il a les cheveux blonds.

C Jeannette est malade (NC 4)

Solution: 1 open her mouth, 2 head ache + stomach ache (2), 3 shrimps, 4 prescription, 5 stay in bed, drink water (2)

(mark /6: 4+ shows the ability to understand longer passages)

Jeannette est malade

– Docteur, je suis malade.
– Qu'est-ce qui ne va pas?
– J'ai mal à la tête et j'ai mal au ventre.
– Ouvre la bouche.
– Ahhh …
– Qu'est-ce que tu as mangé hier soir?
– J'ai mangé des crevettes.
– Ça, c'est le problème!
– Vraiment?
– Oui, voici une ordonnance.
– Je veux aller au collège demain.
– Impossible! Reste au lit pendant deux jours et bois beaucoup d'eau.

D Quels vêtements? (NC 6)

Solution: 1 un imperméable, 2 une cravate, 3 une robe, 4 des bottes, 5 un maillot de bain, 6 un casque, 7 un short, 8 un pyjama

(mark / 5+ shows the ability to understand short extracts which cover various past, present and future events noting main points and specific detail)

Quels vêtements?

1. Regarde! Il pleut! Qu'est-ce que je mets?
2. Au collège de mon correspondant, les élèves portent un uniforme scolaire assez traditionnel. Les garçons portent ça avec une chemise et un pantalon, mais pas les filles.
3. Ma grand-mère met ça quand nous allons au restaurant. Elle n'aime pas les pantalons.
4. Je vais faire des randonnées à la montagne. Je ne veux pas porter mes baskets, alors j'ai acheté quelque chose de plus solide.
5. Me voici au bord de la mer. Deux semaines au soleil! Regarde ce que je vais porter!
6. Je vais faire du vélo pendant les vacances. Regarde ce que j'ai acheté pour me protéger la tête!
7. En été, quand nous faisons du sport au collège, nous portons ça avec un T-shirt.
8. Je suis fatigué. Je vais au lit. Bonne nuit!

CM 7/14 SPEAKING

Épreuve: Parler

Students should be given the sheet up to a week before the assessment, to give them time to choose whether to do 1 or 2 and to give them time to prepare and practise both conversations – the structured one (A) and the open-ended one (B) – with their partners.

Mark scheme

Section A: mark /12: 3 marks per response

- 1 mark for an utterance/response that is clear and conveys all of the information requested, in the form of a complete phrase or sentence, though not necessarily an accurate one. The questions and answers may seem a little disjointed, like separate items rather than parts of a coherent conversation.
- 2 marks for an utterance/response that is clear and conveys all of the information requested in the form of a complete phrase or sentence, though not necessarily an accurate one. The language must flow reasonably smoothly and be recognisable as part of a coherent conversation.
- 3 marks for a clear and complete utterance/response that flows smoothly as part of a clear and coherent conversation. The language must be in complete sentences or phrases that are reasonably accurate and consistent as far as grammar, pronunciation and intonation are concerned.

Section B: mark /13: 3 marks per response, as above, +1 bonus mark for adding an opinion. 19–25 shows the ability to take part in short conversations, seeking and conveying information and opinions in simple terms.

Summary:
Marks	7–13	14–18	19–25
NC Level	3	4	5

CM 7/15 READING

Épreuve: Lire

A C'est quoi? (NC 2)

Solution: 1 des bottes, 2 un imperméable, 3 un pyjama, 4 un maillot de bain, 5 des chaussures, 6 une casquette/ un chapeau, 7 un pull

(mark /6: 3–4+ shows the ability to understand short phrases)

B Qui est-ce? (NC 2)

Solution: 1e, 2b, 3c, 4g, 5a, 6d, 7f

(mark /6: 4+ shows the ability to understand short texts)

C Trouve les paires (NC 2)

Solution: 1b, 2a, 3d, 4e, 5f, 6c, 7g

(mark /6: 4+ shows the ability to understand short texts)

D Un vol (NC 6)

Solution: 1 two, 2 yesterday morning, 3 England, 4 jewellers, 5 cap and sunglasses (both required), 6 shoot, 7 helmet, 8 necklaces

(mark /7: 5+ shows the ability to understand texts that cover past, present and future events)

CM 7/16 — WRITING

Épreuve: Écrire et grammaire

A Dans ma valise, j'ai ... (NC 2)

Solution: 1 *pantalon*, 2 *chaussette*, 3 *chemise*, 4 *short*, 5 *veste*, 6 *baskets/trainers*, 7 *jean*, 8 *casquette*, 9 *pull*

(mark /8: 5+ shows the ability to write items used regularly in class)

B Une carte postale (NC 4)

Mark scheme

- 1 mark for each sub-task completed

Subtotal: 6

Accuracy:
- 2 marks: most words are correct
- 1 mark: about half the words are correct
- 0 marks: fewer than half the words are correct

Subtotal: 2

(mark /8: 5+ shows the ability to write individaul paragraphs of about three or four sentences)

C Une maladie en vacances (NC 5)

This is an open-ended task.

Mark scheme

Communication:
- 1 mark for each accurate statement
- 1/2 mark for a statement which is incorrect but which communicates

Subtotal: 6 (round up half marks)

Accuracy:
- 3 marks: mostly accurate
- 2 marks: about half correct
- 1 mark: more wrong than right
- 0 marks: little or nothing of merit

Subtotal: 3

(mark /9: 6+ shows ability to produce short pieces of writing in simple sentences, referring to recent experiences and giving opinions; although there may be mistakes the meaning can be understood with little or no difficulty)

SB 109, CM 138 — READING EXTENSION

Presse-Jeunesse 6

This page provides reading for pleasure. It can be used alone or with the accompanying copymaster.

SB 109, CM 138

Safari

Students read the answer to the questions in the Students' Book and then do the copymaster tasks.

The Students' Book also includes a short joke. You may wish to explain that *rigolo* means 'funny', from *rigoler* (to laugh).

Solution:

A Safari
Les chiens, ...?: 1V, 2V, 3V, 4F, 5V
Quel animal ...?: 1b, 2a, 3b, 4b, 5b, 6c
À votre avis, ...?: 1 *langue*, 2 *boire*, 3 *dort*, 4 *courir*, 5 *mange*

CM 138

The copymaster also includes two word games loosely connected to SB 109. Students could work in pairs or alone on the wordsearch.

Solution:

B Jeux de mots
Les mots mêlés
5 animaux: girafe, crocodile, hippopotame, chien, antilope
4 adjectifs: dangereux, fantastique, fort, petit
3 parties du corps: cou, bouche, pied
2 prépositions: derrière, devant
1 verbe: mange

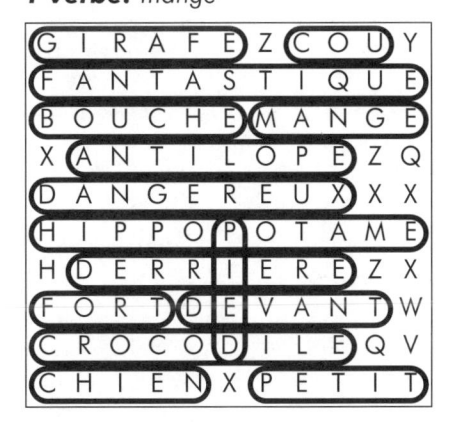

```
G I R A F E Z C O U Y
F A N T A S T I Q U E
B O U C H E M A N G E
X A N T I L O P E Z Q
D A N G E R E U X X X
H I P P O P O T A M E
H D E R R I E R E Z X
F O R T D E V A N T W
C R O C O D I L E Q V
C H I E N X P E T I T
```

Chasse à l'intrus
1 *voir*, 2 *mange*, 3 *la patience*, 4 *mesurer*, 5 *langue*, 6 *un livre*, 7 *carnivore*, 8 *beaucoup*

Encore Tricolore 2
nouvelle édition

unité 8 Rendez-vous!

Areas	Topics	Grammar
1	Revision of the date and time Revision of dates, festivals and 24-hour clock	
2	Finding out what's on	
3		Using the verb *sortir* (present and perfect) Revision of other common verbs, e.g. *faire*, *aller*
4	Asking someone to go out Accepting or refusing invitations	
5	Arranging to meet Buying tickets	
6	Discussing leisure activities and using *si*, *quand*, *mais*	
7	Making comparisons	Using *plus*, *aussi*, *moins*
8	Saying where you went and what you did	Revision and practice of perfect tense *C'était* as a lexical item
9	Further activities and consolidation	

National Curriculum Information

Some students   levels 5–6
Most students   levels 4–5
All students   levels 3–4

Revision

Rappel (CM 8/9) includes revision of the following:
- clothes
- adjectives
- towns and countries

Sounds and writing

- nasal vowels: *-im, -in, -ain; -um, -un*
- the endings *-eau, -aux*

See *Écoute et parle* (CM 8/6, TB 185).

ICT opportunities

- making a virtual trip to a theme park
- developing a matching exercise using authoring software
- making playing cards using clip art
- using a publishing or word processing package to design a party invitation
- organising a survey on going out
- exchanging e-mails

Assessment

- Informal assessment is in *Épreuves* at the end of this unit (TB 187, CM 8/10–8/13)

Students' Book

Unité 8 SB 110–119
Au choix SB 146–147

Flashcards

32–38   leisure
96–100   entertainment

CDs

4/17–31
Student CD 1/43–48, 2/26–29

Additional

Grammar in Action 2, p 9

Copymasters

CM 8/1	*Le calendrier et l'heure* [revision]	
CM 8/2	*Qu'est-ce qu'on fait?* [listening, writing]	
CM 8/3	*On s'amuse* [speaking (pairwork)]	
CM 8/4	*Tu aimes lire?* [reading]	
CM 8/5	*Qu'est-ce qu'on a fait?* [grammar, listening]	
CM 8/6	*Écoute et parle* [independent listening]	
CM 8/7	*Tu comprends?* [independent listening]	
CM 8/8	*Sommaire* [consolidation, reference]	
CM 8/9	*Rappel* [revision]	
CM 8/10	*Épreuve: Écouter*	
CM 8/11	*Épreuve: Parler*	
CM 8/12	*Épreuve: Lire*	
CM 8/13	*Épreuve: Écrire et grammaire*	
CM 154–155	*Chantez! Sabine, ce n'est pas grave ...* [song]	

Language content

Discussing what's on and what to do (Area 2)

Qu'est-ce qu'il y a à faire ce week-end?
Qu'est-ce qu'il y a au cinéma?
C'est à quelle heure, le match?
Qu'est-ce qu'on fait aujourd'hui?
Il y a un match au stade. On y va?
Si on allait au cinéma ce soir?
Tu veux faire ça?

Giving, accepting or refusing invitations (Area 4)

On pourrait peut-être se revoir.
Es-tu libre ce soir?
Oui, je veux bien.
Non, je ne peux pas.

Arranging to meet, buying tickets (Area 5)

Rendez-vous devant la gare à 10 heures.
Je viens te chercher à 2h30.
Deux tickets, s'il vous plaît.
Deux entrées/places, s'il vous plaît.
Il y a un tarif réduit pour étudiants?

Making comparisons (Area 7)

Il est plus grand que moi.
Il est moins grand que moi.
Il est aussi grand que moi.

Note

This is the final unit of **Encore Tricolore 2** and many teachers will not wish to cover it all or will leave it until after school exams. Hence it is fairly light in grammar and contains mainly consolidation material, with quite a lot of speaking, pairwork and listening material.

Useful websites

Paris information

www.pariscope.fr – *Pariscope* gives information about what's on in Paris.

Theme parks

Disneyland Paris – http://2000.disneylandparis.com/
Parc Astérix – www.parcasterix.fr/
Futuroscope – www.futuroscope.fr/

Museums

La Cité des Sciences, la Villette, Paris – www.cite-sciences.fr/
La Cité de l'espace, Toulouse – www.cite-espace.com

Cinema

www.monsieurcinema.com/ – this site gives details and a synopsis of many films.
www.ugc.fr – the *UGC* cinema chain has many cinema complexes in France. This site gives details of current films.

Area 1
Revision of the date and time
Revision of dates, festivals and 24-hour clock

Au choix SB 146, **1**, SB 147, **1**
CD 4/17
CM 8/1

REVISION
PRESENTATION

The date and some festivals

Begin by revising the date with oral questions, e.g. *Quelle est la date aujourd'hui / demain / de ton anniversaire / de Noël / du Jour de l'An / de la fête nationale en France?*

Use some of the following methods:
- dictate some dates to be written down in figures;
- write some dates or names of festivals on the board in figures and play *Effacez!*;
- play *Loto*, e.g. students write three days and three months and tick them off as you say them.

AU CHOIX SB 146 **SUPPORT**

1 Les mois et les jours

A quiz to which the answers are all months and days.

Solution: 1 *juillet*, 2 *janvier*, 3 *décembre*, 4 *août*, 5 *samedi*, 6 *mercredi*, 7 *vendredi*, 8 *février*, 9 *novembre*, 10 *avril*

REVISION
SPEAKING

Time and the 24-hour clock

Revise the time orally, using a clock face if possible and including the 12- and 24-hour clocks.

Practise by dictating times for the class to write down in figures.

AU CHOIX SB 147, 🎧 4/17 **EXTENSION**
LISTENING

1 Quelle heure est-il?

Although this is an extension task, most students could do it. They hear times in the 24-hour clock and match them up to the pictures of clock faces.

Solution   1d, 2c, 3f, 4e, 5a, 6b, 7h, 8g

🎧 **Quelle heure est-il?**
1 Il est neuf heures et quart.
2 Il est cinq heures vingt-cinq.
3 Il est deux heures dix.
4 Il est vingt-trois heures quarante.
5 Il est vingt-deux heures quarante-cinq.
6 Il est quatorze heures dix.
7 Il est sept heures moins dix.
8 Il est seize heures quinze.

CM 8/1 **PRACTICE**

Le calendrier et l'heure

This worksheet could be used for further consolidation of the calendar and time.

Solution:
1 **Où sont les voyelles?**
A **1** octobre, **2** novembre, **3** mardi, **4** avril, **5** hiver, **6** mercredi, **7** automne, **8** printemps, **9** samedi, **10** août, **11** mai, **12** lundi
B **5 mois:** octobre, novembre, avril, août, mai
   4 jours: mardi, mercredi, samedi, lundi
   3 saisons: hiver, automne, printemps
2 **Quelle heure est-il?**
   1d, 2g, 3i, 4h, 5j, 6a, 7b, 8c, 9e, 10f
3 **Mots croisés**

Area 2
Finding out what's on

SB 110–111, **1**–**6**
Au choix SB 146, **2**
CD 4/18–20
CM 8/2
FC 32–38, 96–100

SB 110, 🎧 4/18, FC 32–38, 96–100 **LISTENING**
READING

1 Qu'est-ce qu'on va faire?

Students study the six posters before listening to the recording. Use FC 32–38 and 96–100 to teach and practise relevant vocabulary. Discuss the information further, if necessary, e.g.

Est-ce que la réserve africaine est ouverte le lundi?

Le Bal Populaire et la discothèque, c'est quel jour / quelle date?

Le feu d'artifice commence à quelle heure?

C'est un parc d'attractions où on peut faire de la natation ou jouer aux jeux électroniques. Qu'est-ce que c'est? / C'est quelle affiche?

Students then number from 1–6 and listen to the publicity material, writing down the number of the poster referred to. More able students could write down more details.

Solution: 1D, 2C, 3B, 4A, 5F, 6E

Qu'est-ce qu'on va faire?

– Les vacances sont arrivées. Il faut sortir, il faut s'amuser! Alors, qu'est-ce qu'il y a à faire?

1 – Si vous aimez les sports aquatiques, vous pouvez faire du canoë ou du kayak sur la Dordogne ou du pédalo ou de la planche à voile sur le lac. Visitez Aqua-balade! C'est ouvert tous les jours pendant les vacances!

2 – Vous aimez les animaux? Venez les voir en liberté dans la réserve africaine de Sigean. Vous pouvez circuler dans votre voiture ou à pied. La réserve est ouverte tous les jours de l'année.

3 – S'il pleut, qu'est-ce qu'on peut faire? Passez quelques heures dans le musée des dinosaures. Retournez dans la préhistoire et faites un voyage extraordinaire au pays de ces 'Terribles Lézards'. Visitez Dinosauria – c'est ouvert quand il pleut et quand il fait beau.

4 – Vous aimez les parcs d'attractions? Oui? Allez vite à Planète-vacances. Il y a beaucoup à faire avec ses piscines, ses châteaux gonflables, ses jeux électroniques. Et c'est ouvert à dix heures du matin pendant les vacances.

5 – Vous aimez les spectacles? L'histoire, ça vous intéresse? Ne manquez pas le Mystère de la Cathédrale – un spectacle son et lumière. C'est à neuf heures du soir, tous les dimanches, mardis et mercredis, pendant les vacances. À la cathédrale, bien sûr!

6 – Vous aimez les feux d'artifice? Et la musique, et la danse? Le quatorze juillet, tout ça, c'est gratuit! Passez la soirée sur la place de la Cathédrale. Vous êtes sûr de vous amuser!

Trois conversations

1 Céline et Sophie
– Qu'est-ce qu'on va faire aujourd'hui? On va visiter le musée?
– Ah non, il fait trop chaud. Qu'est-ce qu'il y a d'autre à faire? Regardons les affiches!
– Alors, il y a la réserve africaine. Tu aimes les animaux, toi?
– Non, pas trop. Voyons, si on allait à Aqua-balade. On peut faire du kayak sur la Dordogne.
– Bonne idée!

2 Patrick et Charlotte
Le quatorze juillet, on va danser sur la place, non?
– Bien sûr! Ça commence à quelle heure, le bal?
– Voyons … ah oui, ça commence à vingt-trois heures. Alors, si on allait manger une pizza avant?
– D'accord. Rendez-vous au café vers neuf heures. Plus tard, on va regarder le feu d'artifice!

3 Rachid, Géraldine et Mathieu
– Planète-vacances, c'est quoi?
– C'est un grand parc d'attractions.
– Qu'est-ce qu'il y a à faire?
– Il y a un toboggan aquatique, puis un mini-golf et beaucoup de sports et de jeux.
– On y va?
– Oui, oui, et ce soir, on va voir le spectacle son et lumière à la cathédrale.
– Ah oui. Ça commence à quelle heure?
– À neuf heures. Tu viens, Mathieu?
– Je vais venir à Planète-vacances, mais ce soir, je vais regarder la télé.

SB 110   READING

2 Vrai ou faux?

This true or false quiz is based on the posters.

Solution: **1** vrai, **2** faux, **3** vrai, **4** vrai, **5** faux, **6** vrai, **7** faux, **8** faux, **9** vrai, **10** faux

SB 111, 4/19,   LISTENING / READING / SPEAKING

3 Trois conversations

These conversations include most of the core phrases for discussing what's on and what to do.

Students listen to the recording to complete the text of the three conversations. Note: these answers should be marked before students do task 5 (Où sont-ils allés?).

Students can read the conversations through in groups of two or three.

Solution: **1e, 2h, 3f, 4a, 5d, 6g, 7b, 8i, 9j, 10c**

SB 111   PRACTICE

4 Des phrases utiles

Students match up these key phrases with their meanings. Some students might need help with those which are very similar to each other.

Solution: **1c, 2b, 3e, 4a, 5f, 6d**

AU CHOIX SB 146   SUPPORT / READING

2 Questions et réponses

This matching task could be preceded by revision of dates and the celebrations for the main festivals, e.g. la fête nationale, Pâques, la Saint-Sylvestre.

Solution: **1h, 2b, 3e, 4a, 5f, 6g, 7c, 8d**

SB 111   WRITING

5 Où sont-ils allés?

Students need to refer back to their answers to Trois conversations (task 3) to help them with this task. Draw attention to the past participle agreements with aller

Solution: **1** Aqua-balade, **2** cathédrale, **3** Rachid, **4** n'aime pas, **5** au café, **6** sont allés

unité 8 Rendez-vous!

Section 3

SB 111,

6 Le jeu des questions

SPEAKING

Students use a dice or just choose numbers and make up conversations in pairs.

PRACTICE

Virtual trip to a theme park

For further work on theme parks, students could make a virtual trip to a theme park. Possible sites on-line include *Disneyland Paris, Futuroscope, France Miniature, Parc Astérix* etc. *Yahoo France* has a category on this under *Loisirs*.

Students visit the site and complete a brief report answering questions, e.g.

Comment s'appelle l'attraction?
Où se trouve-t-elle?
Elle est ouverte quand?
Combien coûtent les billets d'entrée?
Qu'est-ce qu'on peut y faire?

A treasure trail could be devised requiring students to collect different pieces of information from a series of such sites. This would be useful as a preparatory (homework) task or as a follow-up task if the students make the trail.

CM 8/2, 4/20

LISTENING
WRITING

Qu'est-ce qu'on fait?

This copymaster gives further practice of finding out what's on and of the perfect tense. There is also some revision of sporting and other leisure activities.

1 Des résumés

Students listen to six conversations about what young people are going to do and indicate what they actually did.

Solution:
1a *12h,* **b** *12h,*
2a *au Roller Rouge,* **b** *18h30,*
3a *au cinéma,* **b** *français,*
4a *à la boum,* **b** *à sept heures et demie,*
5a *à la patinoire,* **b** *l'après-midi,*
6a *à neuf heures,* **b** *en bus*

Qu'est-ce qu'on fait?

1 – Qu'est-ce qu'on fait cet après-midi?
 – Si on allait à l'exposition au musée?
 – Oui, je veux bien. C'est ouvert à partir de quelle heure?
 – À partir de midi.
 – À midi. Bon, on y va à midi alors.

2 – Qu'est-ce qu'on fait ce soir?
 – Tous les autres vont au Roller Rouge.
 – D'accord. On y va. À quelle heure?
 – Rendez-vous à six heures et demie, chez Richard.
 – D'accord. À six heures et demie, chez Richard.

3 – Il y a un bon film au cinéma ce soir. On y va?
 – Qu'est-ce que c'est comme film?
 – C'est 'Jour de fête'.
 – C'est un film américain?
 – Non, c'est un vieux film comique et c'est français.
 – Oui, je veux bien voir ça.

4 – Qu'est-ce qu'on fait demain soir? On va à la fête foraine?
 – Il y a une boum à la maison des jeunes, on y va?
 – Oui, d'accord. Ça commence à quelle heure?
 – Voyons. Euh. À dix-neuf heures trente.
 – À dix-neuf heures trente? C'est un peu tôt!

5 – Si on allait au cirque samedi?
 – Ah non. Moi, je déteste le cirque. Allons au match de rugby.
 – Ah non, pas le rugby.
 – Tiens, regarde cette affiche pour la patinoire Super-Express. Si on allait à la patinoire?
 – D'accord, allons à la patinoire.
 – À trois heures de l'après-midi? Ça va?
 – À trois heures. D'accord.

6 – Il y a un spectacle son et lumière au château de Blois. On y va?
 – Oui, je veux bien. Ça commence à quelle heure?
 – À neuf heures.
 – À neuf heures. Alors, on prend le bus à huit heures et quart ce soir. D'accord?
 – À huit heures et quart. Excellent!

2 Le week-end dernier

Students complete the captions with the correct part of the perfect tense and the right sport.

Solution:
1 *Moi, j'ai fait du vol libre.*
2 *Et toi, tu as fait de l'équitation?*
3 *Louis a fait du cyclisme (vélo/VTT).*
4 *Charlotte a fait du ski nautique.*
5 *Nous avons fait de la voile.*
6 *Vous avez fait du judo?*
7 *Ils ont fait du ski.*
8 *Elles ont fait du patinage.*

3 Sport pour tous

This is a letter about a sports course, to be completed with the correct past participles.

Solution: **1** *passé,* **2** *fait,* **3** *sortis,* **4** *choisi,* **5** *joué,* **6** *allés,* **7** *mangé,* **8** *bu,* **9** *eu,* **10** *retournés,* **11** *fini,* **12** *gagné*

Area 3
Using the verb *sortir* (present and perfect)
Revision of other common verbs, e.g. *faire, aller*
SB 112–113, **1**–**5**
Au choix SB 146, **3**–**4**
Au choix SB 147, **2**
CD 4/21–22
Grammar in Action 2, page 9

SB 112   READING
                                       PRESENTATION

1 Isabelle ne sort jamais

This picture strip story contains all the persons of the present tense of *sortir*. Check that students remember the meaning.

a Begin by introducing the story, e.g.
Voici Isabelle, c'est une nouvelle élève. Est-ce qu'elle sort beaucoup?
Non?
Regardez! Les élèves invitent Isabelle.
Attendez! Voici Jean-Claude. Il invite Isabelle. Ils sortent en groupe etc.

b Students then work on the story, perhaps in pairs, and complete the short *résumé*. This *résumé* lists clearly who Isabelle goes out with on which day and students will find it useful to write out their answers in full and refer to them when doing the listening task which follows.

Solution: **1** *Sophie,* **2** *Guy,* **3** *Magali,* **4** *Alexandre,*
                 5 *Jean-Claude,* **6** *dimanche*

SB 112, 🎧 4/21   LISTENING

2 Qui dit cela?

Students listen to six people speaking and identify them with reference to the list in the box or by looking back to the story or at the *résumé*.

Solution: **1** *la mère d'Isabelle,* **2** *Jean-Claude,*
                 3 *Guy,* **4** *Alexandre,* **5** *le professeur*
                 (d'Isabelle), **6** *Isabelle*

🎧 **Qui dit cela?**

1   Je suis désolée, mais le dimanche, Isabelle ne sort jamais.
2   Samedi, nous sortons en groupe. On va à la nouvelle discothèque.
3   Mercredi, on sort. Nous allons à la campagne.
4   Salut, Isabelle. Est-ce que tu sors vendredi? … Alors, je t'invite à ma fête.
5   Les élèves de cette classe, vous sortez trop!
6   Maintenant, je sors beaucoup! C'est super, mais je suis très fatiguée.

SB 112   GRAMMAR

Dossier-langue
sortir (to go out)

This sets out the present tense of *sortir* for reference.

Differentiation

The following *Au choix* activities can be used as support and extension.

Au choix SB 146   SUPPORT
                                          READING

3 On sort

This task involves matching the subject to the appropriate verb ending.

Solution: 1d, 2e, 3a, 4f, 5b, 6c

                                          PRACTICE

Trouve les paires

For any *Trouve les paires* activity, like the previous task, it is possible to develop a matching exercise using authoring software, e.g. *Hot Potatoes* (TB 20).

Au choix SB 147   EXTENSION
                                          READING

2 Isabelle et sa mère

When students have completed these conversations, they could practise reading them aloud in pairs.

Solution: **1** *je sors,* **2** *Tu sors,* **3** *Tu sors,* **4** *tu sors,*
                 5 *je sors,* **6** *nous sortons,* **7** *Vous sortez,*
                 8 *vous sortez,* **9** *papa et maman sortent*

SB 113, 🎧 4/22   LISTENING
                                       READING

3 Vous sortez souvent?

Check that the class understands *une/deux/trois/… fois par semaine*, e.g.
On a français quatre fois par semaine, n'est-ce pas? Et anglais? etc.

Then students listen to the recording and do the multiple-choice activity. More able students could write down more details if possible.

Solution: 1b, 2c, 3a, 4c, 5a, 6b, 7b, 8c

🎧 **Vous sortez souvent?**

   – Est-ce que tu sors souvent, Sophie?
   – Non, je ne sors pas beaucoup. Je sors peut-être une ou deux fois par semaine.
   – Et qu'est-ce que tu fais d'habitude?
   – Je vais au cinéma ou je vais à la piscine.

   – Et toi, Jean-Claude. Est-ce que tu aimes sortir le soir?
   – Oui, moi, j'aime beaucoup sortir. Je vais à une classe de judo, je joue au football ou au basket. Je fais beaucoup de sport – j'adore ça!
   – Alors, tu sors souvent?
   – Oui, très souvent. Je sors environ cinq fois par semaine.

Rendez-vous! unité 8

– Et vous, Magali et Chantal, est-ce que vous sortez beaucoup le soir?
– Non, pas beaucoup, mais on va à l'orchestre une fois par semaine. On joue du violon, toutes les deux.
– Nous sortons plus souvent pendant les vacances.
– Qu'est-ce que vous faites quand vous sortez pendant les vacances?
– On va en ville et quelquefois, on va à des concerts ou à des festivals de musique.
– Et vous, Guy et Stéphanie, est-ce que vous sortez souvent?
– Oui, nous sortons assez souvent, peut-être trois ou quatre fois par semaine. Quelquefois, nous allons au club d'informatique ou on retrouve des amis au café.

Section 3

SB 113, SPEAKING / WRITING

4 À toi!

These questions can be answered very simply or with fuller answers including expressions such as *en semaine, pendant les vacances* and details of where the speakers go etc.

The questions and answers include other verbs, e.g. *faire, aller, mettre*, which could be revised by referring students to the verb table and by further practice with games (see TB 27).

If time, students could base a classroom *sondage* on one or two of the questions.

SB 113 READING / PRESENTATION

5 Isabelle écrit à sa cousine

In this letter there are several examples of the perfect tense of *sortir* (used in *Unité 6*). When students have read the letter, they can move on to the *Dossier-langue*.

SB 113 GRAMMAR

Dossier-langue
Rappel: *sortir*

This short *Dossier-langue* revises the perfect tense of *sortir*, by a series of questions to be answered from the previous task.

Make sure that everyone understands the answers and perhaps revise the agreement of the past participle, before moving on to the following item.

Solution: perfect tense; auxiliary = *être*; past participle = *sorti*; agreement – add -e for feminine, -s for plural; there are four examples of *sortir* (*je suis sortie, nous sommes sortis, tous mes amis sont sortis, je ne suis pas sortie*) and two examples of *aller* (*nous sommes allés* twice)

AU CHOIX SB 146 SUPPORT / WRITING

4 La semaine dernière

All students could complete the questions with the correct parts of *sortir*.

Solution: 1 *tu es sorti(e)*, 2 *tu es sorti(e)*, 3 *vous êtes sortis*, 4 *tu es sorti(e)*, 5 *sont sortis*

More able students could go on to reply to the questions. They could first be reminded about using the correct past participle agreements and given further help, if necessary, e.g.

Réponses:

1, 2, 4 *Oui, je suis sorti(e) / Non, je ne suis pas sorti(e).*
3   *Oui, nous sommes s...... / Non, nous ne sommes pas s......*
5   *Oui, ils sont .... / Non, ils ne sont pas ....*

GRAMMAR IN ACTION 2, PAGE 9 GRAMMAR PRACTICE

Using the verb *sortir*

For further practice of *sortir*, these activities could be used.

Area 4
Asking someone to go out
Accepting or refusing invitations
SB 114–115, 1 – 4
CD 4/23

SB 114, 🎧 **4/23** PRESENTATION / LISTENING / SPEAKING

1 Es-tu libre ce soir?

The table presents ways of accepting and refusing invitations, and it is hoped that students will find it relevant, useful (and even amusing!).

First go through the expressions to practise pronunciation and perhaps choose students to read out some of the phrases, putting as much expression into them as possible.

Students can then do the listening task, referring to the chart in the Students' Book and writing the letter or drawing the symbol to show which category of reply is given. These conversations are similar, though not identical, to the questions in task 2.

Solution: 1a, 2c, 3d, 4e, 5f, 6e, 7b, 8a

🎧 **Es-tu libre ce soir?**

1 – Est-ce que tu es libre demain? Tu veux aller au concert avec moi?
  – Oh oui, bonne idée!
2 – Qu'est-ce que tu fais ce week-end? On peut sortir ensemble, si tu veux.
  – Euh, ce week-end ... oui, je crois.

180

3 – Tu veux aller à la boum chez Jean, samedi soir?
– Peut-être, je vais voir.

4 – Tu veux aller à la discothèque ce soir?
– C'est très gentil, mais ce soir, ce n'est pas possible.

5 – On va regarder un film vidéo chez moi, ce soir.
– C'est quoi comme film?
– C'est un film sur le football.
– Ah non, merci, ça ne me dit rien.

6 – Si on allait en ville demain matin?
– Désolé, mais demain, je ne suis pas libre.

7 – Il y a un match de rugby demain. On y va?
– Un match de rugby? Oui, pourquoi pas?

8 – Tu es libre ce week-end? Tu veux aller au cinéma?
– Chic alors! Oui, avec plaisir.

SB 114, SPEAKING

Follow-up

For speaking practice using the table on SB 114, students could make playing cards, each with one of the symbols on it, perhaps using clip art.

They practise the words in pairs or groups, e.g. Student A asks *Tu veux sortir ce soir?*

Another turns over one of the symbols and must reply with an expression from that box, trying not to use one said already.

At first, students can refer to the table, but should gradually try to reply without looking.

It is suggested that students should eventually learn at least one expression from each box.

To add an extra element of humour, with suitable classes, teachers could add more refusals to the table of possibilities (e.g. *Non, je vais me laver les cheveux.*).

SB 114, SPEAKING / WRITING

2 Qu'est-ce qu'on dit?

a Students work in pairs one acting as the person in the numbered photo and the other replying to the invitation as if they are Sophie or Bruno, according to the symbols.

This could just be done orally, or the answers could be written for consolidation.

Some students might like to make up short sketches using some of these expressions, e.g. a boy or girl makes up a range of excuses in answer to a variety of invitations out, but is suddenly able to accept when someone really attractive or famous turns up.

b Students now imagine that the invitations made by the people of the opposite sex are addressed to them personally. They should select the two or three they wish to accept and make up their replies to these and their choice of phrases for refusing the others. This can be worked on in pairs, each asking the questions in turn, or the answers could be written first.

SB 115 READING / WRITING

3 Sophie et Bruno sont sortis

Students read the accounts written by Sophie and Bruno about the trips which resulted from their invitations.

a La lettre de Sophie
Students choose the correct five sentences to make up the letter. The incorrect ones are either in the future tense instead of the past, or contain a factual error. It is suggested that students write the letter out in full.

Solution: The correct sentences are **1**, **3**, **6**, **7**, **10**

b La lettre de Bruno
In this case, students write the verbs in the perfect tense to complete Bruno's letter.

Solution: **1** *suis sorti*, **2** *avons passé*, **3** *sommes allés*, **4** *ai pris*, **5** *ai mangé*, **6** *a lu*, **7** *sommes entrés*, **8** *sommes sortis*, **9** *a acheté*, **10** *a répondu*

PRACTICE

Party invitations

For further practice of this area, students could use a publishing or word processing package to design a party invitation. A follow-up task could be to draw invitations out of a hat and then write a reply accepting or declining.

As a second ICT activity, students could match invitations to reasons for their refusal. This could be created using the *Hot Potatoes* suite of programs.

SB 115 WRITING

4 À toi!

In this open-ended task, students imagine they have accepted one of the invitations in task 2 above and write an account of their outing, based on the given outline and using vocabulary and phrases from the previous items.

**Area 5
Arranging to meet
Buying tickets**

SB 115, 5
CM 8/3
CD 4/24

SB 115, 4/24, SPEAKING

5 Rendez-vous

This brings together the language for making arrangements to go out and to meet someone, and for buying tickets.

The core dialogues are recorded to help with pronunciation. Read the dialogues through with the students or play the recording as they follow the conversations. Students then work on the dialogues in pairs.

181

After they have practised for a while, looking at the vocabulary, get them to cover up the options and try to continue just looking at the model conversations, changing parts of them from memory.

When they are fairly confident, give them five or ten minutes to choose what they consider to be their best version of one of the conversations and practise it for a class competition or to be recorded. Give double marks for dialogues done from memory.

🎧 Rendez-vous

– Qu'est-ce qu'on va faire cet après-midi?
– Si on allait à la piscine?
– Ah non! Je ne veux pas faire ça.
– Qu'est-ce qu'il y a d'autre à faire?
– Il y a un concert de rock au stade. On y va?
– Bonne idée! Ça commence à quelle heure?
– À deux heures et demie.
– Alors, rendez-vous devant le stade à deux heures.
– D'accord. À tout à l'heure.

...

– Deux tickets, s'il vous plaît – et est-ce qu'il y a un tarif réduit pour les étudiants?
– Oui. Pour les étudiants, c'est 6 euros. Vous avez vos cartes?
– Oui, voilà.
– Alors deux tickets, tarif réduit – 12 euros, s'il vous plaît.

CM 8/3, **SPEAKING**

On s'amuse

This copymaster could be used here for further practice of leisure activities and arranging to meet, or later, for revision.

1 Conversations au choix

Students practise the conversations in pairs, choosing numbers at random or throwing a dice to change the options.

2 Tu aimes le sport?

This word puzzle introduces some more unusual sports (*l'escrime, le vol libre* etc.). Students could look up any new ones. Explain *un sport à grand frisson*.

Solution:

5 Any five of: *le basket, le football, le hockey, le hockey sur glace, le rugby, le volley*
4 Any four of: *le canoë, la natation, la planche à voile, le ski nautique, la voile*
3 *le hockey sur glace, le patinage, le ski*
2 *l'escrime, le judo*
1 *le vol libre*

3 À ton avis

Finally students are asked to guess the most widely practised sport in France.

Solution: *Le sport le plus pratiqué est la natation.*

Area 6
Discussing leisure activities and using *si, quand, mais*
SB 116, **1**-**2**
Au choix SB 147, **3**

SB 116 **READING**

1 Pour ou contre?

These two pairs of letters present contrasting views on two subjects:
- whether sport should be compulsory in schools;
- whether it's best to be always with a crowd or to spend some leisure time with the family or alone.

Since there is rather a lot of reading, different groups of students could work initially on one letter or pair of letters and compare their findings.

Examples of the conjunctions *si, quand* and *mais* are included in these letters. and students' attention could be drawn to these as a means of writing longer sentences and expressing contrasting views.

SB 116 **READING**

2 Ils ont dit ça

a This is a matching task, divided into two sections to match the two letter topics. The sentences involve the conjunctions *si, quand* or *mais*.

b Students identify the person who holds each opinion.

Solution: **1c** *Clément,* **2b** *Vivienne,* **3a** *Clément,* **4d** *Clément,* **5h** *Alain,* **6g** *Élise,* **7e** *Élise,* **8f** *Alain*

SB 116 **GRAMMAR**

Dossier-langue
si, quand, mais

This highlights the three conjunctions and explains their use. Check that students have understood and ask them to make up similar sentences themselves, if possible.

Au choix SB 147 **EXTENSION SPEAKING/WRITING**

3 À toi!

This task could be done orally before students write their answers. Point out that the expressions in the box all begin with infinitives.

Area 7
Making comparisons
SB 117, **3**–**4**
Au choix SB 147, **4**
CM 8/4
CD 4/25

REVISION
Adjectives

First revise adjectives and agreement, using a range of flashcards or actual objects and perhaps some of the flashcard games outlined on TB 26.

SB 117 **GRAMMAR**
Dossier-langue
Comparing things

This area is linked with the previous one and the *Dossier-langue* uses some examples from the letters to present the words *plus*, *moins* and *aussi* in use.
Go through the explanation with the class and follow it up with some oral question and answer work or games based on the picture of a family.

SB 117 **READING WRITING**
3 On présente ... nos lecteurs

Students compare the age, height and weight of the three young people shown.

First ask some questions, e.g.

Qui est plus grand que Luc/plus jeune que Michel/moins lourd que Luc? etc.

Students read the *vrai ou faux?* sentences, pick the true ones and correct the others.

Solution: **1** *faux – Luc est plus âgé que Nathalie,* **2** *vrai,* **3** *vrai,* **4** *vrai,* **5** *vrai,* **6** *faux – Nathalie est moins lourde que Luc,* **7** *vrai,* **8** *faux – Les deux garçons sont plus lourds que Nathalie,* **9** *vrai,* **10** *vrai*

Au choix SB 147, 4/25 **EXTENSION**
4 On parle des loisirs

This item is an unscripted recording, made by some children in Orléans. Teachers might wish to supply a few words in advance, e.g. *malgré, des fois, s'allonger, presque* and *plutôt*.

Students could listen to the recording several times before doing the multiple choice completion task. This item is ideally suited to work with individual listening equipment.

Solution: **1b, 2c, 3c, 4a, 5c, 6b, 7c, 8a, 9b**

On parle des loisirs
Thomas
La chose que je préfère faire, c'est dormir, bien sûr, mais après, j'aime bien faire du sport. C'est une vraie passion pour moi. J'aime bien lire, mais je trouve ça ennuyeux des fois. Je regarde aussi très souvent la télé, où il y a des belles émissions de variétés. J'aime bien écouter la radio, ça me change les idées.

Vivienne
Quand j'ai du temps libre, je préfère faire du sport, car j'adore ça. Mais, des fois, je n'ai pas de chance – il pleut dehors. Alors, je me mets sur mon lit, ou plutôt je m'allonge, et je lis. Des fois, j'écoute la radio. Enfin, aussi, d'autres fois, j'aime bien dormir.

Max
Malgré tous les devoirs qu'on a à faire, j'arrive à faire de la natation presque tous les soirs. Et le week-end, je fais beaucoup de compétitions. Il m'arrive, des fois, le samedi, de faire du basket avec mes copains. Je lis beaucoup le soir et je regarde des fois la télé, le matin.

PRACTICE
Organising a survey

The class could organise a survey on going out, in conjunction with a partner class in France or another French-speaking country. Each class carries out a survey of where class members go out to and when. This information is then sent to the partner school in France and corresponding information received from them. Comparative charts can then be made.

As a follow-up, individual e-mails could be exchanged with French correspondents asking and answering questions about going out.

SB 117 **WRITING**
4 À toi!

Students now express their own views by writing *plus, moins* or *aussi* in the gaps to complete the sentences about leisure activities and school subjects.

CM 8/4 **READING**
Tu aimes lire?

This is mainly for reading for pleasure and it should be stressed that students need not understand every word. They should be encouraged to guess meaning from cognates (e.g. *estomac* – stomach); or from context, before looking words up in a dictionary. Refer students to *Tips for understanding French* (SB 153).

The copymaster includes a lot of comparatives and some are practised in the tasks which follow the magazine articles.

Solution:

1 Les animaux extraordinaires
1 vrai, 2 vrai, 3 faux, 4 faux, 5 vrai

2 Les Français et leurs loisirs
1 Non, le sport est plus important qu'avant.
2 Non, le tennis est moins populaire qu'avant.
3 Oui, les randonnées sont plus populaires maintenant.
4 Non, la planche à voile est moins populaire que le roller.
5 Oui, on trouve les activités en plein air plus agréables qu'avant.
6 Non, les bandes dessinées sont moins populaires.
7 Non, les films vidéo sont aussi populaires qu'avant.

Area 8
Saying where you went and what you did
SB 118, **1**–**2**
CM 8/5, 154–155
CD 4/26–27

SB 118 READING / WRITING

1 Samedi dernier: un jeu de logique

This task is quite demanding, so students might like to work on it in pairs. With some groups, teachers might prefer to work through this orally in class, noting the results on the board in a grid, e.g.

	Charlotte	Patrick	Géraldine	Mathieu
matin	piscine	piscine	ville	ville
après-midi	ville	maison	cuisine	ordinateur
soir	repas	cinéma	repas	maison

Solution:

Le matin
Mathieu et Géraldine sont allés en ville.
Mathieu a acheté un jeu vidéo.
Charlotte et Patrick sont allés à la piscine.

L'après-midi
Patrick n'est pas sorti, il a dormi.
Charlotte est allée en ville.
Géraldine a fait la cuisine.
Mathieu a joué sur l'ordinateur.

Le soir
Charlotte et Géraldine ont mangé un repas de fête.
Patrick est allé au cinéma.
Mathieu est resté à la maison.

SB 118 GRAMMAR

Dossier-langue
Rappel: the perfect tense

Students could read through this as a reminder of all the main points they have learnt about the perfect tense.

CM 8/5, 4/26 LISTENING / READING / WRITING

Qu'est-ce qu'on a fait?

1 Samedi dernier
This first task is a follow-up from *Samedi dernier: un jeu de logique* (SB 118) but is also a self-contained item. Students read through the *agenda*, then listen to the recording and identify the speakers.

Solution: 1 Géraldine, 2 Charlotte, 3 Patrick, 4 Mathieu, 5 Mathieu, 6 Patrick, 7 Charlotte, 8 Géraldine

Samedi dernier

1 – Qu'est-ce que tu as fait samedi dernier?
  – Alors, samedi dernier, c'était mon anniversaire et on a eu un repas spécial le soir.

2 – Samedi matin, qu'est-ce que tu as fait?
  – Je suis allée à la piscine avec Patrick.

3 – Qu'est-ce que tu as fait samedi après-midi? J'ai téléphoné, mais tu n'as pas répondu!
  – Ah oui, c'était parce que samedi après-midi, j'ai dormi tout l'après-midi!

4 – Tu es allé en ville samedi?
  – Oui, le matin, je suis allé en ville avec Géraldine et j'ai acheté un jeu-vidéo.

5 – Samedi après-midi, qu'est-ce que tu as fait?
  – Samedi après-midi, j'ai joué avec le jeu que j'ai acheté le matin. C'était super!

6 – Es-tu allé à la fête d'anniversaire samedi soir?
  – Non, non. On ne m'a pas invité. Non, samedi soir, je suis allé au cinéma avec ma famille. On a vu un film très amusant, mais j'ai oublié le titre!

7 – Es-tu allée à la fête d'anniversaire samedi soir?
  – Bien sûr. C'était très bien.

8 – Et toi, qu'est-ce que tu as fait samedi après-midi. Tu as dormi?
  – Ah non! Samedi après-midi, j'ai aidé ma mère à préparer le repas.

2 Mots croisés
This crossword includes many examples of the perfect tense.

Solution:

¹a	l	²é	e			³i				⁴m			
r		e			⁵t	é	l	⁶p	h	o	n	é	
⁷r	e	s	t	é		o		s		⁹a	n		
i						m		r		t		⁸g	
⁹v	e	¹⁰n	¹¹u		b		i		é		a		
é		¹²e	n	¹³t	r	é				e		g	
e			o			¹⁴e	¹⁵t		¹⁶e		¹⁷s	o	n
¹⁸s	o	r	t	i			¹⁹s	u	i	s		é	

SB 118, 🎧   SPEAKING
                                                        WRITING

2 À toi!

Students begin by asking each other questions about last weekend and then go on to write a few sentences about their own activities for last Saturday.

SB 119, 🎧 **4/27, CM 154–155,**   LISTENING
TB 29   SPEAKING

Chantez! Sabine, ce n'est pas grave …

This song revises some of the vocabulary from *Unité 7* and brings it together with the theme of going out. See TB 29 for notes on the use of songs and CM 154–155 for the music.

🎧 **Chantez! Sabine, ce n'est pas grave …**

1 Allô, Fabien? C'est Séverine.
   Est-ce que tu veux sortir avec moi?
   Viens à la discothèque à huit heures et quart!
   Il y a de la bonne musique là-bas ce soir.
   Tu ne viens pas?   Je ne peux pas venir
                                  …
   Pourquoi pas?   C'est que je suis
                                  malade …
   Qu'est-ce qui ne va pas? J'ai mal à la gorge.
   Pourquoi est-ce que tu ne téléphones pas?
   Je préfère sortir avec toi, Sabine.

2 Allô, Fabien? Ici Hélène.
   Est-ce que tu veux sortir avec moi?
   Viens au cinéma à sept heures moins le quart!
   Il y a un bon film qui passe ce soir.
   Tu ne viens pas?   Je ne peux pas venir
                                  …
   Pourquoi pas?   C'est que je suis
                                  malade …
   Qu'est-ce qui ne va pas? J'ai mal au ventre.
   Pourquoi est-ce que tu ne téléphones pas?
   Je préfère sortir avec toi, Sabine.

3 Allô, Fabien? Ici Delphine.
   Est-ce que tu veux sortir avec moi?
   Viens au théâtre à huit heures moins le quart!
   Il y a une bonne pièce qui se joue ce soir.
   Tu ne viens pas?   Je ne peux pas venir
                                  …
   Pourquoi pas?   C'est que je suis
                                  malade …
   Qu'est-ce qui ne va pas? J'ai mal aux oreilles.
   Pourquoi est-ce que tu ne téléphones pas?
   Je préfère sortir avec toi, Sabine.

4 Salut, Delphine, Hélène, ça va Séverine?
   Tiens, bonjour, comment vas-tu Sabine?
   Bonjour, Fabien.   Salut, Sabine.
   Est-ce que tu veux sortir avec moi?
   Viens au club des jeunes à sept heures et quart!
   Il y a une surprise-partie là-bas ce soir.
   Tu ne viens pas?   Il ne peut pas venir …
   Pourquoi pas?   C'est qu'il est
                                  malade …
   Qu'est-ce qui ne va pas? Il a mal à la gorge!
   Il a mal au ventre!   Il a mal aux oreilles!
   Comment ça?   Oh, ce n'est pas
                                  grave …

Area 9
Further activities and consolidation
SB 119
CM 8/6–8/13
CD 4/28–31
Student CD 1/43–48, 2/26–29

CM 8/6, 🎧 **SCD 1/43–48**   INDEPENDENT LISTENING
                                 SOUNDS AND WRITING

Écoute et parle

This copymaster provides pronunciation and speaking practice.

1 À la française

🎧 À la française

1 concert   5 place
2 excursion   6 science-fiction
3 international   7 spectacle
4 Internet   8 ticket

2 Et après?

Solution: 1 – 7 – 14 – 17 – 26 – 63 – 89 – 100

🎧 Et après?

   0 – 6 – 13 – 16 – 25 – 62 – 88 – 99

3 Des phrases ridicules

🎧 Des phrases ridicules

   Cinq trains américains apportent du vin au magasin.
   J'adore le parfum brun de Verdun.

4 Les terminaisons: -eau et -aux

Solution: 1c, 2f, 3b, 4e, 5d, 6a

🎧 Les terminaisons: -eau et -aux

1 château   4 drapeau
2 niveau   5 chevaux
3 chapeau   6 animaux

5 Vocabulaire de classe

Solution: **1** *question,* **2** *ton,* **3** *a,* **4** *fini,* **5** *pour,*
              6 *deux,* **7** *et*

🎧 Vocabulaire de classe

1 Pouvez-vous répéter la question, s'il vous plaît?
2 Écris les verbes dans ton cahier.
3 Qui a gagné?
4 Vous avez fini?
5 Puis écoute pour vérifier.
6 Travaillez à deux.
7 Posez des questions et répondez à tour de rôle.

6 Des conversations

🎧 **Des conversations**

1 On va au parc d'attractions
- Le parc d'attractions, ça ouvre à quelle heure?
  (pause)
- À onze heures.
- On prend le bus?
  (pause)
- Oui, on prend le bus à dix heures et demie.
- Est-ce que nous allons faire un pique-nique?
  (pause)
- Non, nous allons manger une pizza au restaurant du parc.

2 Hier
- Où es-tu allé(e) hier?
  (pause)
- Je suis allé(e) au musée des dinosaures.
- Tu es allé(e) avec qui?
  (pause)
- Avec mes parents et ma petite sœur.
- Tu as acheté des souvenirs?
  (pause)
- Oui, un livre sur les dinosaures et des cartes postales.

3 On achète des billets
- Est-ce qu'il y a un tarif réduit pour étudiants?
- Oui, pour les étudiants, c'est cinq euros.
  (pause)
- Trois tickets, s'il vous plaît, tarif réduit.
- Voilà. Quinze euros, s'il vous plaît.
  (pause)
- Le concert finit à quelle heure?
- Vers onze heures et demie – avant minuit en tout cas.

CM 8/7, 🎧 SCD 2/26–29 INDEPENDENT LISTENING
Tu comprends?

Students could do any or all of the four items on this worksheet, now or later as revision.

1 C'est quand?

Solution: 1 23h, 2 10h30, 3 dimanche, 20h15, 4 vendredi, 14h (2h), 5 10 avril 21h (9h), 6 14h25 (2h25), 14h15 (2h15)

🎧 **C'est quand?**

1 – C'est à quelle heure, le feu d'artifice?
- C'est à vingt-trois heures.
- À vingt-trois heures – c'est tard ça!

2 – Ça ouvre à dix heures, le parc d'attractions?
- Non, non. En octobre, ça ouvre à dix heures et demie.

3 – Le spectacle son et lumière au château, c'est samedi prochain?
- Non, non. C'est dimanche, à vingt heures quinze.
- Ah bon. Dimanche, à vingt heures quinze.

4 – Vendredi, on va au musée avec le club de technologie. On prend le car à deux heures de l'après-midi.

5 – Le concert de rock, c'est le dix avril, non?
- Oui, le dix avril, à neuf heures du soir.

6 – Tu viens au cinéma cet après-midi?
- Oui, c'est quand, le film?
- Ça commence à deux heures vingt-cinq.
- Donc, rendez-vous devant le cinéma à deux heures et quart.

2 On sort

Solution: 1b, 2a, 3c, 4c, 5b, 6c, 7a, 8b

🎧 **On sort**

Alice
- Est-ce que tu sors beaucoup dans la semaine, Alice?
- Non, pas beaucoup. Mais je sors assez souvent le week-end.

Mathieu
- Tu vas au marché samedi prochain, Mathieu?
- Bien sûr, le samedi, je sors toujours très tôt pour aller au marché.

Sébastien
- Qu'est-ce que tu fais pendant les vacances, Sébastien?
- Je fais beaucoup de sport avec mes copains. On va quelquefois à la piscine et une fois par semaine, on va à la plage.

Julie
- Tu sors beaucoup en semaine, Julie?
- À mon avis, je ne sors pas beaucoup, mais ma mère dit que je sors beaucoup trop.

3 Où sont-ils allés?

Solution: 1g, 2e, 3a, 4d, 5c, 6f, 7h, 8b

🎧 **Où sont-ils allés?**

Jean-Pierre et Caroline
- Salut, Jean-Pierre!
- Salut, Caroline.
- Tu es allé au match de hockey hier?
- Oui, c'était fantastique. Mais tu n'étais pas là, Caroline.
- Non, je suis allée au cinéma avec Claire.

Aurélie et Nicolas
- C'était bien, le concert samedi dernier, Nicolas?
- Oh salut, Aurélie. Oui, c'était génial. Tu es allée à une boum, non?
- Oui, chez Magali.
- David était là aussi avec son correspondant?
- Non, David et Kémi sont allés à Paris.

La famille Fardeau
- Ah, voici la famille Fardeau. Où êtes-vous allés hier, finalement?
- Marie est allée au stade pour regarder le match de rugby, Vivienne est partie avec des copines faire un pique-nique et les jumeaux ont fait du roller dans le parc.

4 Tu veux sortir?

Solution: 1R, 2A, 3R, 4?, 5?, 6A

🎧 Tu veux sortir?

1 – Tu veux aller au parc d'attractions samedi, Babeth?
 – Samedi – ah non, samedi, je vais chez mes grands-parents.

2 – Demain soir, on va faire du bowling en ville. Tu viens?
 – Génial! Je voudrais bien venir!
 – Alors, rendez-vous devant le bowling, à six heures et demie.

3 – Nous allons faire une randonnée à la campagne ce week-end – ça t'intéresse?
 – Je regrette, mais je n'aime pas beaucoup les randonnées.

4 – Il y a un match de foot ce soir au stade. On y va?
 – Ça dépend. S'il y a un bon film à la télé, je préfère rester à la maison.

5 – Alors, nous sortons ensemble samedi soir, oui ou non?
 – Peut-être. Je vais y réfléchir.

6 – Est-ce qu'on va en ville samedi, comme d'habitude?
 – Pourquoi pas? Il n'y a rien d'autre à faire!

SB 119, CM 8/8
Sommaire

A summary of the main structures and vocabulary of this unit. Students fill in gaps on the copymaster. They should check their answers against the Students' Book page.

CM 8/9 — CONSOLIDATION
Rappel 8

This copymaster can be used at any point in the course for revision and consolidation. It provides revision of clothes, adjectives and the names of some towns and countries. The reading and writing tasks are self-instructional and can be used by students working individually for homework or during cover lessons.

Solution:

1 Chasse à l'intrus
1 *grand (les autres sont des couleurs)*
2 *veste (les autres sont des adjectifs)*
3 *la tenue (les autres sont des parties du corps)*
4 *les cheveux (les autres sont des vêtements / on porte les autres aux pieds)*
5 *un ventre (les autres sont des vêtements)*
6 *les gants (les autres sont des parties du corps)*

2 Au magasin de vêtements
c – (any 6) *les chaussettes, les chaussures, une chemise, une casquette, un casque, une ceinture, une cravate, un chapeau*
b – *les bottes, des baskets*
p – *un pantalon, un pull(over)*

3 Mots croisés (les descriptions)

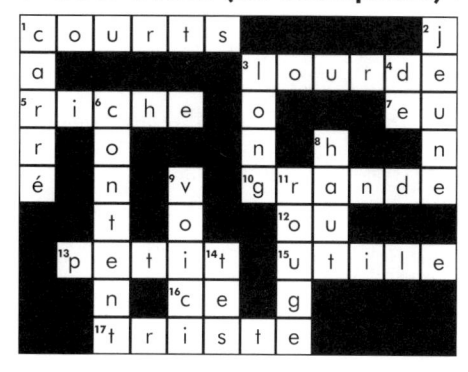

	¹c	o	u	r	t	s			²j	
	a				³l	o	u	⁴r	d	e
⁵r	i	⁶c	h	e		o		⁷e	u
r		o				n	⁸h	n	
é		n		⁹v	¹⁰g	¹¹r	a	n	d	e
		t		o			¹²o	u	
¹³p	e	t	i	¹⁴t		¹⁵u	t	i	l	e
		n		¹⁶c	e		g		
	¹⁷t	r	i	s	t	e			

Épreuve – Unité 8

These worksheets can be used for an informal test of listening, speaking, reading and writing or for extra practice, as required. For general notes on administering the *Épreuves*, see TB 16.

CM 8/10, 🎧 4/28–31 — LISTENING
Épreuve: Écouter

A Quelle heure est-il? (NC 2)

Solution: 1 *1h05*, 2 *5h25*, 3 *7h35*, 4 *13h40*, 5 *20h15*, 6 *22h50*

(mark /5: 3+ shows the ability to understand a range of familiar statements)

🎧 Quelle heure est-il?

1 Il est une heure cinq.
2 Il est cinq heures vingt-cinq.
3 Il est sept heures trente-cinq.
4 Il est treize heures quarante.
5 Il est vingt heures quinze.
6 Il est vingt-deux heures cinquante.

B Réserve Africaine (NC 3)

Solution: 1 25 kilometres from Paris, 2 every day, 3 8 euros, 4 more than 2000, 5 basketball, 6 bouncy castle, 7 free

(mark /6: 4+ shows the ability to understand short passages made up of familiar language)

🎧 Réserve Africaine

Venez visiter la Réserve Africaine! C'est seulement à 25 kilomètres de Paris. Nous sommes ouverts tous les jours et les billets d'entrée coûtent dix euros pour les adultes et huit euros pour les moins de 16 ans. Il y a beaucoup de choses à faire et à voir! Nous avons plus de deux mille animaux, nous organisons des matchs de basket, il y a des châteaux gonflables, et il y a même un spectacle avec des marionnettes qui est gratuit.

unité 8 Rendez-vous!   Section 3

C Samedi dernier (NC 3)

Solution: 1g, 2f, 3a, 4b, 5e, 6c, 7d

(mark /6: 4+ shows the ability to understand short passages made up of familiar language)

🎧 Samedi dernier

1 J'aime nager, alors je suis allée à la piscine.
2 Je suis allée en ville et j'ai acheté des cadeaux pour toute la famille.
3 J'adore faire la cuisine, alors j'ai passé la journée à préparer des plats délicieux.
4 J'ai passé la journée à jouer sur mon ordinateur. J'étais très content de mon nouveau jeu-vidéo.
5 J'étais très fatigué, alors j'ai dormi toute la journée.
6 Je n'aime pas faire du sport, mais j'aime le regarder à la télé. Alors j'ai regardé un match de foot.
7 J'ai beaucoup aimé le dîner chez ma copine. Le gâteau d'anniversaire était délicieux.

D Bruno organise son week-end (NC 5)

Solution: 1 a, A, 2 c, B, 3 e, A, 4 b, C, 5 d, C

(mark /8: 5+ shows the ability to understand extracts including present and future events. They identify main points and opinions.)

🎧 Bruno organise son week-end

– Bonjour Sophie. Je vais au cinéma ce soir. Tu veux venir?
– Bonne idée. On se retrouve où?
…
– Salut, Sylvie. C'est Bruno. Si on allait voir le feu d'artifice vendredi soir?
– Bonjour, Bruno. Le feu d'artifice? Ça ne me dit rien. Je sors avec Paul vendredi soir.
…
– Salut, Françoise. C'est Bruno. Tu veux aller au bal sur la place samedi soir?
– Bonsoir, Bruno. Un bal? Pourquoi pas. Avec plaisir.
…
– Bonjour Yvette. Tu es libre dimanche matin? On peut faire du canoë.
– Bonjour, Bruno. Du canoë? Je vais y réfléchir.
…
– Salut, Charlotte. Cet après-midi, je vais faire une promenade à la campagne. Tu veux venir?
– Salut, Bruno. Peut-être. Je vais voir.

CM 8/11 SPEAKING

Épreuve: Parler

Students should be given the sheet up to a week before the assessment, to give them time to choose whether to do 1 or 2 and to give them time to prepare and practise both conversations – the structured one (A) and the open-ended one (B) – with their partners.

Mark scheme

Section A: mark /12: 3 marks per response
- 1 mark for an utterance/response that is clear and conveys all of the information requested, in the form of a complete phrase or sentence, though not necessarily an accurate one. The questions and answers may seem a little disjointed, like separate items rather than parts of a coherent conversation.
- 2 marks for an utterance/response that is clear and conveys all of the information requested in the form of a complete phrase or sentence, though not necessarily an accurate one. The language must flow reasonably smoothly and be recognisable as part of a coherent conversation.
- 3 marks for a clear and complete utterance/response that flows smoothly as part of a clear and coherent conversation. The language must be in complete sentences or phrases that are reasonably accurate and consistent as far as grammar, pronunciation and intonation are concerned.

Section B: mark /13: 3 marks per response, as above, +1 bonus mark for a clause that starts with *si*, *quand* or *mais*. 19–25 shows the ability to take part in conversations that include past, present and future events, applying their knowledge of grammar in new contexts.

Summary:
Marks	7–13	14–18	19–25
NC Level	4	5	6

CM 8/12 READING

Épreuve: Lire

A Trois parcs d'attractions (NC 3)

Solution: 1 V, 2 V, 3 F, 4 P, 5 F, 6 F, 7 P

(mark /6: 4+ shows the ability to understand short texts)

B Trouve les paires (NC 3)

Solution: 1c, 2e, 3a, 4d, 5b, 6g, 7f

(mark /6: 4+ shows the ability to understand short texts and dialogues)

C Trois élèves (NC 3)

Solution: 1 F, 2 V, 3 P, 4 F, 5 V, 6 V, 7 F, 8 F

(mark /7: 5+ shows the ability to understand short texts and dialogues)

D Un e-mail (NC 6)

Solution:

The following sentences are correct:

3, 4, 5, 7, 8, 10

(mark /6: 4+ shows the ability to understand texts covering present, past and future events)

CM 8/13 **WRITING**

Épreuve: Écrire et grammaire

A Les activités de la famille Levert (NC 2)

Solution: **1** *sors*, **2** *sortent*, **3** *sortons*, **4** *sors*, **5** *fait*, **6** *fais*, **7** *font*, **8** *va*, **9** *vont*, **10** *vais*, **11** *allons*

(mark /8: 5+ shows the ability to write items used regularly in class)

B Un e-mail (NC 4)

Mark scheme
- 1 mark for each sub-task completed with a correct perfect tense
- 1/2 mark for a statement which is incorrect but which communicates

Subtotal: 6 (round up half marks)
Accuracy:
- 2 marks: most words are correct
- 1 mark: about half the words are correct
- 0 marks: fewer than half the words are correct

Subtotal: 2
(mark /8: 5+ shows the ability to write individual paragraphs of about three or four sentences)

C Un concert (NC 6)

This is an open-ended task.

Mark scheme
Communication:
- 1 mark for each accurate statement
- 1/2 mark for a statement which is incorrect but which communicates

Subtotal: 6 (round up half marks)
Accuracy:
- 3 marks: mostly accurate
- 2 marks: about half correct
- 1 mark: more wrong than right
- 0 marks: little or nothing of merit

Subtotal: 3
(mark /9: 6+ shows the ability to use simple descriptive language referring to past, present and future events, applying grammar in new contexts)

Encore Tricolore 2
nouvelle édition

Contrôle

The *Contrôle* provides a block of formal assessment of the vocabulary and structures introduced during the course. It assesses all four National Curriculum Attainment Targets. See TB 16 for the Assessment Introduction.

The National Curriculum Level is indicated in brackets after the title. The tasks test elements of performance at that level.

The Listening and Reading copymasters are designed to be written on, but the Speaking and Writing are re-usable.

Mark scheme:
Do not include a mark for the example. The *Contrôle* has a total of 100 marks (25 for each Attainment Target).

Record sheets:
A record sheet for students is provided on CM 146.

Listening:
All items are repeated on the recording. At all levels, the pause button can be used at any time to give students time for reflection and for writing.

Speaking:
Decide how you wish to conduct this assessment:
- invite students out individually and ask the questions yourself;
- invite them in pairs, listen to the conversation and mark the answers;
- offer your students the option of recording the assessment with a partner, for you to listen to and mark afterwards. It is important, if students record their conversations at home, to obtain some assurance that they are not reading the questions and answers. In practice, this is usually patently obvious when listening to the recording!

The *Contrôle* tests *Unités 1–7*. Teachers wishing to test *Unité 8* should use the separate *Épreuve*, and those not wishing to test *Unités 6–7* could select some items from *Épreuves 1–5* to replace the items indicated as coming from *Unités 6–7*.

CM 139–140, 4/32–36 **LISTENING**

Contrôle: Écouter

A Pierre fait tout ça (NC 2)

This tests material from *Unités 1–5*.

Solution: 1a, 2b, 3c, 4a, 5a, 6b

(mark /5: 3+ shows ability to understand a range of familiar statements)

Pierre fait tout ça

1 Quand je vais en ville, j'aime acheter des chips.
2 Normalement, je vais au collège à pied.
3 Ma matière préférée est la chimie.
4 Dans un café, j'aime boire un coca.
5 Pour aider à la maison, j'aime passer l'aspirateur.
6 Mais je déteste ranger le salon.

B La semaine de Claudine (NC 2)

This tests reflexive verbs and material from *Unités 1–5*.

Solution: lundi et mardi – **b**, mercredi – **a**, jeudi – **d**, vendredi – **f**, samedi – **e**, dimanche – **c**

(mark /5: 3+ shows ability to understand longer passages made up of familiar language)

La semaine de Claudine

Lundi et mardi, elle va au collège, mais elle s'ennuie.
Mercredi après-midi, elle va à la piscine et elle se baigne.
Jeudi, elle est fatiguée! Alors elle se repose!
Vendredi soir, elle veut aller danser. Alors elle se dépêche!
Samedi, elle sort et elle se couche à minuit!
Dimanche, elle invite ses copains et ils s'amusent.

C Tu vas me reconnaître (NC 3)

This task tests clothes and appearance (*Unité 7*).

Solution: 1 Françoise – **c**, 2 Michelle – **a**, 3 Roselyne – **b**, 4 Claire – **d**, 5 Lucie – **e**

(mark /4: 3 + shows ability to understand short passages made up of familiar language)

Tu vas me reconnaître

1 C'est Françoise ici. Tu vas me reconnaître. J'ai les cheveux blonds, je vais porter des lunettes de soleil et un pull blanc avec mon jean.
2 Salut! C'est Michelle. Pour aller à Londres, je vais porter une longue jupe noire et un T-shirt blanc.
3 C'est Roselyne ici. Je vais arriver à midi. Tu vas me reconnaître très facilement. Je vais porter un imperméable blanc, mon pantalon noir et des baskets.
4 C'est moi, Claire. Je vais porter une veste noire avec mon pantalon gris et une casquette avec le logo de mon club de tennis. Tu vas me reconnaître tout de suite.
5 Salut! C'est Lucie. Je vais prendre mon vélo pour aller chez toi. Donc, je vais mettre un T-shirt avec mon short et un casque.

D Paul prend le train (NC 4)

This item tests travelling by train (*Unité 6*) and some elements of clothing and illness (*Unité 7*).

Solution: **1c, 2a, 3c, 4b, 5a, 6b**

(mark /5: 3+ shows ability to understand longer passages, identifying and noting main points and some detail)

🎧 Paul prend le train

Paul va passer la soirée à Paris.
Il se lève et met un jean noir et un T-shirt gris.
Il va à la gare et il entre dans le bureau des renseignements.
Le train va partir à seize heures.
Il achète un aller simple qui coûte cinq euros soixante.
Paul est fatigué et il a mal à la tête, alors il boit beaucoup d'eau.
Il va un peu mieux quand il arrive à Paris.

E Qu'est-ce qu'on va faire? (NC 5)

This item tests food and meals (*Unité 5*) and some elements of transport (*Unité 6*) and leisure (*Unité 2*).

Solution: **1** coffee with milk, **2** toast and jam, **3** horse riding, **4** see Paris, **5** by the river, **6** by bike, **7** good film on TV

(mark /6: 4+ shows ability to identify opinions and understand extracts of spoken language made up of familiar material from several topics, including present, past or future events)

🎧 Qu'est-ce qu'on va faire?

– Simon, qu'est-ce que tu veux pour ton petit déjeuner?
– Un café au lait et des toasts avec de la confiture, s'il te plaît.
– Qu'est-ce qu'on va faire aujourd'hui? Hier, on a fait de l'équitation. Demain, on va voir Paris. Aujourd'hui, je ne sais pas.
– On fait un pique-nique?
– Bonne idée.
– Où va-t-on?
– On va pique-niquer près de la rivière.
– Et comment allons-nous à la rivière?
– À vélo.
– D'accord. On rentre à quelle heure?
– Il faut rentrer avant sept heures, parce qu'il y a un bon film à la télé à sept heures dix.

CM 141–142   SPEAKING

Contrôle: Parler

Students should be given the sheets up to a week before the assessment to give them time to prepare the role play dialogues and to choose their topics for conversation.

The candidate selects two topics and the teacher asks four questions from one of these, including one question referring to the past, one referring to the future, one asking an opinion.

Mark scheme

Section A: mark /12: 3 marks per response
- 1 mark for a response that is clear and conveys all of the information requested in the form of a complete phrase or sentence, though not necessarily an accurate one. The questions and answers may seem a little disjointed, like separate items rather than parts of a coherent conversation.
- 2 marks for a response that is clear and conveys all of the information requested in the form of a complete phrase or sentence, though not necessarily an accurate one. The language must flow reasonably smoothly and be recognisable as part of a coherent conversation.
- 3 marks for a clear and complete response that flows smoothly as part of a clear and coherent conversation. The language must be in complete sentences or phrases that are reasonably accurate and consistent as far as grammar, pronunciation and intonation are concerned.

Section B: mark /13: 3 marks per response as above + 1 bonus mark for adding one or two items of extra information on any of the tasks.

Summary:
Marks	7–13	14–18	19–25
NC Level	3	4	5

CM 143–144   READING

Contrôle: Lire

A Jean parle à son correspondant (NC 2)

This task tests staying with a French family (*Unité 4*).

Solution: **1f, 2a, 3b, 4c, 5d, 6e**

(mark /5: 3+ shows ability to understand short phrases)

B Trois menus (NC 3)

This task tests understanding simple menus (*Unité 5*).

Solution: **1V, 2V, 3F, 4V, 5F**

(mark /4: 3+ shows ability to understand short texts)

C Julie à Paris (NC 4)

This task tests holiday postcards from *Unité 2* and other vocabulary items from *Unités 1–5*.

Solution: **1b, 2a, 3b, 4a, 5c**

(mark /4: 3+ shows ability to understand short texts and identify main points)

D La lettre de Dominique (NC 5)

This task tests information about schools and holidays and includes vocabulary from *Unités 1–5*, especially *Unités 2–3*.

Solution: **1b, 2b, 3c, 4b, 5a, 6c**

(mark /5: 3+ shows ability to understand texts covering past, present and future events and to identify main points)

E Un hold-up à Paris (NC 6)

Solution:
1 March 3rd, 10am
2 three
3 taken by security camera (could allow: his mask fell off)
4 long hair, short moustache
5 cashier in bank
6 was shot in the arm (or was injured/received a bullet in the arm)
7 car number (taken by cashier)
8 ring the police and identify man from photo (on TV and Net)

(mark /7: 5+ shows ability to understand a text that covers past, present and future events)

CM 145   WRITING
Contrôle: Écrire et grammaire

A La famille Dumas   (NC 2)

This task tests knowledge of regular verbs in the present and perfect tenses (*Unités 1–5*).

Solution: 1 *mange*, 2 *prend*, 3 *finissent*, 4 *vend*, 5 *parle*, 6 *a regardé*, 7 *a rendu*, 8 *a choisi*, 9 *ont fini*, 10 *ont joué*

(mark /8: 5+ shows ability to select appropriate words to complete short sentences and to show some understanding of grammar)

B Un e-mail (NC 3)

This is an open-ended task which tests information about self and family and everyday life (*Unités 1–5*).

Mark scheme
- 1 mark for each sub-task.

Subtotal: 6

Accuracy:
- 2 marks: most words are correct
- 1 mark: about half the words are correct
- 0 marks: fewer than half the words are correct

Subtotal: 2

(mark /8: 5+ shows ability to write individual paragraphs of about three or four sentences on a familiar topic expressing personal responses)

C Une fête (NC 6)

This is an open-ended task which tests use of a wide range of vocabulary and of past present and future tenses (*Unités 1–7*).

Mark scheme

Communication:
- 1 mark for each accurate perfect tense
- 1/2 mark for a perfect tense which is incorrect but which communicates.

Subtotal: 6 (round up half marks)

Accuracy:
- 3 marks: mostly accurate
- 2 marks: about half correct
- 1 mark: more wrong than right
- 0 marks: little or nothing of merit

Subtotal: 3

(mark /9: 6+ shows ability to write in paragraphs referring to past, present and future events; although there may be a few mistakes the meaning is usually clear)

CM 146
Record sheet

A record sheet is provided for students to fill in their marks and retain.